PLANNING AREAS AND FACILITIES

for

HEALTH, PHYSICAL EDUCATION, AND RECREATION

by

PARTICIPANTS IN NATIONAL FACILITIES CONFERENCE

REVISED 1965

Price $6.00

THE ATHLETIC INSTITUTE
Merchandise Mart
Chicago, Illinois 60654

and

**AMERICAN ASSOCIATION FOR HEALTH,
PHYSICAL EDUCATION, AND RECREATION**
1201 Sixteenth Street, N.W.
Washington, D. C. 20036

TABLE OF CONTENTS

TABLE OF CONTENTS

FIGURES and TABLES

FIGURES and TABLES

FOREWORD

AT A MEETING of the Board of Directors of the American Association for Health, Physical Education, and Recreation, held in Washington, D.C., in April, 1945, favorable action was taken on a proposal by Caswell M. Miles, AAHPER Vice-President for Recreation, that a grant of money be obtained to finance a national conference on facilities. Subsequently, a request for $10,000 to finance the first facilities workshop was placed before Theodore P. Bank, President of The Athletic Institute. At a later meeting of the Board of Directors of The Athletic Institute, the project was approved and the money appropriated to finance the first workshop.

The National Conference on Facilities for Health, Physical Education, and Recreation was formed for the purpose of organizing and conducting the workshop. The members of the Conference Executive Committee included representatives of the several national organizations co-sponsoring the project.

Almost 20 years have elapsed since the printing of the Guide which resulted from the first workshop, held at Jackson's Mill, West Virginia, in December, 1946. During this interval, there have been 11 printings of the Guide, with a total sale of more than 43,000 copies.

The second workshop was held May 5-12, 1956, at the Kellogg Center for Continuing Education, Michigan State University, East Lansing. The second workshop, as was the first, was financed by The Athletic Institute. The 1956 edition of the Guide, which resulted from the second workshop, has been widely used in the planning and construction of facilities.

During the nine-year interval since the printing of the 1956 edition, there have been many new developments in facility planning and construction. These developments have been due to a number of factors. The population of our country has rapidly expanded, demanding the increasing attention of school administrators, public health personnel, recreation executives, sociologists, architects, engineers, planning consultants, and other community leaders to problems resulting from inadequate facilities for athletics, recreation, and physical and health education. Current emphasis on the need for improving education, recreation, and fitness opportunities for the youth of the nation has been highlighted by the implementation of the reports of the Outdoor Recreation Resources Review Commission resulting in the creation of the Federal Bureau of Outdoor Recreation, by the passage of the Economic Opportunity and the Land and Water Conservation Fund Acts, and by the fine work of the President's Council on Physical Fitness. Much of the research and attention devoted to facility planning and construction during the past twenty years has also been due to the increased leisure time in our society and a growing realization of the concept that recreation is a fundamental human need, essential to the well-being of all people.

In view of the many new needs and developments since the printing of the 1956 edition of the Guide, the National Facilities Conference, comprising representatives of 17 national organizations (see list on page 223), asked the Athletic Institute and the American Association of Health, Physical Education, and Recreation to finance a third workshop for the purpose of bringing the Guide up to date. The respective boards of these two organizations approved this request and appropriated funds to finance the 1965 workshop. Subsequently, the Executive Committee was elected by the Conference and charged with the responsibility of planning and conducting the workshop.

The delegates for the 1965 workshop were carefully selected on the basis of their particular knowledge and contributions. Among those invited were a number of outstanding school, college, and community leaders engaged in conducting programs of athletics, recreation, outdoor education, and physical and health education, In addition, invitations were extended to a number of specialists responsible for planning and constructing facilities for these programs. These specialists included city planners, architects, landscape architects, engineers, and schoolhouse construction consultants.

Early in the planning, chairmen were selected for the various workshop committees. These committees were busily engaged in conducting research and gathering data prior to the third workshop, which was held January 15-24, 1965, at the Biddle Continuing Education Center, Indiana University, Bloomington. A complete list of workshop participants may be found on page 224. A list of those persons who served on a pre-workshop committee but did not actually participate in the workshop appears on page 225.

The workshop participants approached the task of revising the Guide from the standpoint that adequate programs of athletics, recreation, outdoor education, and physical and health education can be provided only through cooperative planning directed toward the most economical and efficient use of the community's total resources. Every effort was made to incorporate in this revision the most recent advances in facility planning and construction. At the same time, an attempt was made to identify in a practical manner new needs and to anticipate future ones.

One significant innovation in the present Guide is that the needs of the disabled and the aging have been considered. A special three-day workshop involving experts in facility planning for the disabled and the aging, including representatives of the American Standards Association, was held well in advance of the 1965 workshop to prepare materials which could be considered in revising the Guide.

Appreciation is extended to all those who contributed their time, effort, and materials to make possible this latest revision of the Guide. It has been a team project, and, therefore, the publication does not necessarily represent the viewpoint of any one individual or the organization he represents. It is a composite of the thinking and effort of the entire group of workshop participants and pre-workshop committee members.

This revised Guide is an answer to a great need throughout this country for concrete information as well as suggestions that can be of material value to all planners of areas and facilities for athletics, recreation, outdoor education, and physical and health education. Not only does it include many diagrams and sketches showing specific measurements, but it provides a check list to prevent the inadvertent omission of an item or a specific that would be difficult to correct later. The fact that it is essentially functional and complete is a credit to those who have prepared this document. It should be in the hands of every school administrator, physical education department head, architect, planning consultant, and all others who may either be interested in planning new areas and facilities or checking the adequacy of those already in use. It should be particularly helpful to boards of education, recreation commissions, and other policy-making groups responsible for approving expenditures for facility planning and construction.

Part One
Basic Concepts

Chapter 1

OBJECTIVES and NEEDS

INTRODUCTION

MAN FUNCTIONS as a total organism. Every experience, every learning leaves its imprint upon his totality. They not only make changes in his mental and physical being, but also in his emotional and social attitudes. Because of this interrelationship and interplay of all the facets of man, it is quite impossible to fractionalize his being. However, for the purpose of clarity, this Guide will categorize some of the needs of this complicated being, knowing full well that whether he is reading, working, visiting, swimming, or fishing, he is functioning as a totality and is being changed accordingly. Changes in man never cease from the cradle to the grave.

Down through the ages, man has adapted himself to his environment very well; otherwise, he would have been extinct like many prehistoric animals. Modern man, however, faces a more rapidly changing environment than his forefathers. Even though much of this change has been brought about by man himself, he has a very difficult time adapting to his new situations. The impact of less physical activity, more leisure, indicting advertisements, confusing propaganda, conflicting ideologies, and everyday threats of disasters and wars has confronted man with myriads of mental, physical, emotional, and social strains in spite of the progress of medicine.

It is apparent that many of the solutions to these problems is proper preparedness through education. For fruitful and purposeful living, man must be an active participant in more phases of educational and recreational endeavors and experiences than those found merely in the classroom during his school years. Thus this Guide is devoted to the needs and desirable facilities for those highly specialized educational fields known as health education, physical education, and recreation. These closely related fields are making great contributions to the physical and mental health and well-being as well as the happiness and longevity of man. These three fields must definitely be given proper consideration in all phases of planning, whether districtwide, countywide, statewide or nationwide.

BASIC OBJECTIVES

Before considering the planning of areas and facilities essential for health education, physical education, and recreation, it is important to understand the basic aims and objectives of these fields.

PHYSICAL EDUCATION[1]

The aim of physical education is to help people of all ages live healthy, satisfying, and energetic lives. Four specific purposes are: to develop and maintain maximum physical efficiency;

[1]This section is adapted from a statement issued by the American Association for Health, Physical Education, and Recreation.

to develop useful knowledge and physical skills; to act in socially useful ways; and to enjoy wholesome physical recreation.

The subject matter of physical education is the science and skill of movement. It uses all types of sports and activities to develop in youth and adults the strength, endurance, coordination, and flexibility essential in both work and play. Through physical education, boys and girls, youth, and adults are taught the physical skills needed for performing daily work; they are trained and conditioned through exercise and sports for the maintenance of mental and physical health; they are taught the skills of those physical activities which form a part of leisure pursuits.

A sound school physical education program includes: required daily teaching and participation in appropriate and diversified activities for all pupils; a wide variety of intramural activities available to all; and, at the senior high school level, a broad program of interscholastic athletics for those of superior athletic ability.

HEALTH AND SAFETY EDUCATION

The aim of health and safety education is the systematic provision of experiences which will favorably influence knowledge, attitudes, habits, and practices related to individual, community, and world health and safety.

Health and safety education seeks to bridge the gap between scientific knowledge of health and safety and its application by people in their daily lives. A school or college health and safety program includes teaching and continuous daily opportunities for pupils to develop health and safety habits and practices which will assist them in effective adaptation to their environment.

RECREATION

The primary function of recreation is the enrichment of living by enabling individuals to find outlets for self-expression and thereby to develop their inherent potential and achieve desired satisfactions. These satisfactions include adventure, fellowship, a sense of accomplishment, the enjoyment of beauty, and the joy of creating, all of which contribute to human happiness. Through recreation programs, people are helped to develop interests and skills which enable them to make constructive use of leisure and which contribute to physical and mental health, safety, good citizenship, confidence, and character development.

Recreation is essentially a kind of experience rather than a set of specific activities. Many types of these experiences have a major place in programs of schools and colleges, as well as recreation agencies. The wide range of recreation activities includes games and sports, music, dance, arts and crafts, drama, social activities, nature and outing activities, hobbies, and service projects. The comprehensive recreation program affords people of all ages, backgrounds, and interests the opportunity to engage in a variety of activities with the help of trained leaders and under conditions which assure maximum enjoyment and benefits. The program includes offerings that appeal to individuals, to families, to clubs, and to informal groups. Activities are offered both indoors and outdoors, near people's homes and at more distant places, and year-round as well as seasonally.

NEED FOR AREAS AND FACILITIES

Increased emphasis on education—not just for making a living, but for living—has accelerated the acceptance of the importance of health and safety, physical education, and recreation.

The evolution of these functions within the school, college, and total community has focused attention on their relationships, their common denominator, their interdependence, and the need for enlightened cooperation and joint planning. Basic in the development of optimum services and opportunities, both for learning and for translating its lessons into practice and full living, are suitable areas and facilities—specialized and general, indoor and outdoor.

INCREASING RECOGNITION OF NEED

Widespread recognition of the growing importance of physical education, health education, and recreation has resulted in unprecedented action by the Federal Government. Examples are the activities of the President's Council on Physical Fitness, the report to the President and to the Congress by the Outdoor Recreation Resources Review Commission, the passage by Congress of the Land and Water Conservation Fund Act, and the establishment of the Bureau of Outdoor Recreation in the U.S. Department of the Interior. These three functions have also received comparable consideration by governmental authorities at the state and local levels, and by private agencies.

The widening impact of public recreation, of physical education, and of a number of major health problems has aroused public consciousness to the importance of more and improved provision for health education, physical education, and recreation programs and services. It has also directed attention unmistakably to the need for additional areas and facilities to meet the growing demand and enable these programs and services to function fully and effectively.

Physical education, as the education of the whole human being, and the drive for fitness to live and function effectively and zestfully in an environment of speed, change, and tension have captured the public consciousness.

Health and safety education is recognized as having a rightful place in the school curriculum, with specialized provisions in the form of instruction, environment, and practice.

Public interest in a wide range of recreation activities has had a phenomenal growth, as reflected, for example, in the demand for facilities required for organized camping, water and winter sports, and the performing arts. Schools and colleges have increasingly accepted the responsibility for teaching skills which contribute to the satisfying use of leisure.

It is obvious that school, college, and municipal authorities share responsibility for providing and operating adequate areas and facilities to serve needed programs and services in health and safety education, physical education, and recreation. It is equally true that these responsibilities can be met effectively and economically only through enlightened and wholehearted cooperation on the part of these groups. A major purpose of this publication is to indicate principles and procedures that have proved useful in achieving such cooperative action.

FACTORS AFFECTING NEED

Among the many factors that have accentuated the demand for facilities and the need to appraise functional planning are:

The population explosion. It is estimated that the number of individuals in the United States requiring areas and facilities will more than double by the year 2000.

The increase in leisure. Children spend more years in school, workday and workweek periods are shorter, vacations are longer, and retirement comes at an earlier age, resulting in a greater number of individuals with much leisure.

Increased incomes. Workers earn more and can, therefore, afford to spend money for recreation for themselves and their families. The public has demonstrated a willingness to spend increasing amounts for recreation, both directly and through tax funds.

Greater mobility. An increasingly large percentage of the population moves from one locality to another, and the federal highway program enables more and more people to use and enjoy recreation areas at a considerable distance from their homes.

Growth of metropolitan areas. The increase in the percentage of the population living in and around metropolitan centers has created a growing need for extensive land areas which afford contact with nature.

Loss of open spaces. Land and water areas suitable and available for recreation are being developed rapidly for other uses, especially in or near centers with high population densities.

Mechanization. The development of machines has not only increased the amount of leisure, but has resulted in a high degree of monotony for the worker, thus accentuating the need for creative activity during leisure.

NEED FOR PLANNING

Functional planning of areas and facilities for health and safety education, physical education, and recreation has become a task of great magnitude. In the acquisition and development of these areas and facilities, the need for sound planning is imperative. Its importance cannot be overemphasized. Wise planning in these fields helps assure successful programs, facilitates the work of the teaching and leadership staff, and enables children, youth, and adults to enjoy full benefits from participation.

In any locality where population growth is evident or where school, college, and recreation facilities require expansion, land should be acquired or set aside for future school sites and recreation areas. The space requirements of such areas need to be determined in the light of projections of population growth as far into the future as can be calculated reasonably, and land should be acquired as early as possible before the needed sites are developed for other uses. Land acquisition which occurs after the need becomes obvious is likely to be too late and the amount too little. Many cities which have failed to acquire suitable areas when they were available and in advance of actual need have been obliged later to settle for inadequate, poorly located sites, and have paid far more for them than if earlier action had been taken. Little time is available for long-range planning in localities with unusual population growth or explosion. Even where the growth is normal, the demand for urgency or expediency often prevents the development of sound plans.

When the need for acquiring areas or developing indoor or outdoor facilities has been recognized by the appropriate governing body, sound planning procedures must be followed. The planning of functional facilities for health and safety education, physical education, and recreation must be geared to meet not only present but future needs, as far ahead as they can reasonably be predicted. Since new structures may well be used for at least fifty years, building plans must be as functional and adaptable as possible to permit changes resulting from varying program needs. Otherwise, desired modifications may be impossible or may create inconvenience, reduction in program, and excessive cost.

BASIC PLANNING FACTORS

A careful determination of the specific needs to be met by the area or facility should be the first step in the planning process. Planning can be effective only if the major purpose of the proposed areas and facilities is clearly defined and interpreted. Since they are provided to facilitate the attainment of specific objectives and to make possible the conduct of definite programs, the objectives and programs must be determined before developing area and facility plans. It cannot be emphasized too strongly that the program should dictate the types of areas and facilities needed.

Among the factors to be considered are the activities to be carried on, the ages and skills of the participants in the program, and the seasons or periods of use. Since both physical education and recreation programs are subject to change and modification, and since they vary in different localities, standardized or stock plans for areas and facilities are rarely practicable. Unless variations in local interests and needs are taken into account in formulating plans, the resulting properties may prove inadequate or unsuited to the effective conduct of the program.

Regardless of the specific program criteria that are established, the following basic planning factors are essential for maximum desired benefits:

- Determination of the type, number, size, and relationship of the areas and facilities.
- Proper balance of environmental factors for the comfort of users in order that they may release the maximum energy for purposeful living. This balance is achieved through the proper control of lighting, heating, and cooling, and desirable acoustical treatment.
- Provision of functional and appropriate furniture, apparatus, and electronic equipment.
- Provision of books, supplies, and other program materials.

In the same manner, all recreation areas for children, youth, and adults need to be designed to facilitate safe, enjoyable, and satisfactory play. In order to assure such conditions, special consideration must be given to such factors as surfacing, grading, drainage, lighting, placement of facilities, landscaping, and circulation.

Long-range planning of all systems, areas, and facilities should precede the involvement of funds. This includes type, size, and location of all desired and essential units. Piecemeal planning results frequently in improvisation, poor substitutes, and false economy in both money and time. It must be realized that no one can predict the future accurately, but provision in terms of expansibility, flexibility, and adaptability can be incorporated into any plan, inside or outside. This requires the use of all available resources for the planning.

The need for intelligent and cooperative planning by all agencies, especially school and municipal authorities, was never greater than at present. Cost of acquisition, construction, development, operation, and maintenance, as well as efficiency in use, will depend heavily upon the degree of cooperative endeavor and farsightedness. Sights must be raised immeasurably if present and future needs are to be met. The time for careful, imaginative long-range planning is now—in fact, it was yesterday!

SELECTED REFERENCES

American Association for Health, Physical Education, and Recreation, **Leisure and the Schools.** Washington, D.C.: AAHPER, 1201 Sixteenth Street, N.W., 1961.

————, **School Recreation.** Washington, D.C.: AAHPER, 1201 Sixteenth Street, N.W., 1960.

————, **Twentieth Century Recreation.** Washington, D.C.: AAHPER, 1201 Sixteenth Street, N.W., 1963.

Butler, George D., **Introduction to Community Recreation.** 3rd ed. New York: McGraw-Hill Book Company, 1959.

California Committee on Planning for Recreation, Park Areas and Facilities, **Guide for Planning for Recreation Parks in California.** Sacramento: California Recreation Commission, 1956.

Joint Committee on Health Problems in Education of the National Education Association and the American Medical Association, **Health Education.** 5th ed. Washington, D.C.: NEA, 1201 Sixteenth Street, N.W., 1961.

National Committee on School Health Policies, **Suggested School Health Policies.** 3rd ed. Washington, D.C.: NEA, 1201 Sixteenth Street, N.W., 1962.

Reports of the Regional Planning Association of New York.

Scott, Harry A., and Westkaemper, Richard B., **From Program to Facilities in Physical Education.** New York: Harper and Brothers, 1958.

Chapter 2

PLANNING PRINCIPLES, PLANNING UNITS, and AREA TYPES

ACCEPTANCE OF the thesis that health, physical education, and recreation programs are necessary to present-day living and of even greater importance to the future well-being and happiness of people makes it logical to state the principles basic to planning areas and facilities for these programs. The term "community" as used in the following statement of guiding principles is not intended to denote the specific planning unit defined later in this chapter but may be applied to any geographic area or political subdivision.

GUIDING PRINCIPLES

- **Every community needs areas and facilities for comprehensive health and physical education, athletic, and recreation programs.** These programs, which are essential to the well-being of the people, cannot be effective unless a wide variety of indoor and outdoor facilities is provided. In addition to their importance to the programs, these facilities help enhance and maintain sound community values.

- **Every community requires a master plan based upon a study of its needs.** Preparation of this plan is the primary responsibility of established planning agencies. Provisions for a system of properties required for physical education and recreation must be included in the master plan. The adoption and enforcement of regulations for zoning, land-use, and subdivision control are essential to the implementation of the plan.

- **The type, location, and size of essential areas and facilities must be related to the total community pattern.** They vary in residential areas of different types and densities and are affected by the location of thoroughfares, business and industrial districts, transportation lines, and other natural barriers.

- **Areas and facilities should be planned in relation to the social and economic characteristics of the community.** The feasibility of providing specific programs in a particular locality is influenced by the interests and financial resources of its total population.

- **Areas and facilities should be planned with due regard for the full potential use of existing and available physical resources.** Plans for land acquisition and development can be justified as economically sound only if made related to an inventory of comparable resources in the community or region. Duplication of facilities and overlapping of services are thereby avoided and a maximum return from expenditures for areas and facilities can be expected.

- **Areas and facilities should make possible programs which serve the interests and needs of all the people.** Consideration should be given to the special needs of persons of all ages and both sexes. Resulting programs should comprise a wide range of activities, including not only sports and athletics, but also arts and crafts, music, drama, dance, camping and outdoor education, social recreation, hobbies, and many other types. In view of the increasing proportion of the population in the older-age group, particularly the retired, special consideration of the needs of senior citizens is desirable. Facilities should also make it possible for disabled citizens, young and old, to participate in most aspects of health, physical education, and recreation programs.[1]

- **Plans for areas and facilities should conform to state and local regulations and, as far as possible, to accepted standards and practice.** Planning groups should become familiar with fire, building, electrical, sanitary, and other pertinent codes and make sure that their plans conform to them. Otherwise, unnecessary expense may be incurred in making changes required in order to secure official approval. Standards developed through research and experience serve as a guide to planning, even though local situations may not permit their application without modification.

- **Close cooperation among all public and private agencies concerned with the location, acquisition, development, and operation of areas and facilities designed for health, physical education, and recreation is of the utmost importance.** Such cooperation involves not only school, park, recreation, and city planning agencies, but also redevelopment authorities and public and private housing agencies, among others. An interagency planning committee can prove an effective means of achieving cooperative action. The legal, fiscal, and administrative powers and responsibilities of each cooperating agency must be defined, understood, and mutually respected.

- **All interested organizations, individuals, and groups should have an opportunity to share in the planning of areas and facilities intended for public use.** Wide participation in the consideration of proposals requiring the expenditure of public funds for areas and facilities gives the people an opportunity to express their desires and needs and helps assure their support of the projects and their use of the areas and facilities when made available.

- **Full use should be made of the knowledge and experience of individuals who are qualified to give expert advice and assistance in planning areas and facilities.** School, park, and recreation department personnel in a wide variety of positions can contribute materially to the determination of the features to be included and can offer valuable suggestions for their design and development. Individuals with professional training and technical competence, such as landscape architects, architects, engineers, and sociologists, can play major roles in overall planning and in the design of areas and facilities.

[1]See Appendixes G and H.

- **Every available source of property or funds should be explored, evaluated, and utilized whenever appropriate.** Tax funds are a primary source, but large numbers of areas and facilities have been acquired, or built entirely or largely, by gifts from individuals or organizations. Localities should take advantage of state and federal funds available for planning and for acquisition and improvement of school and recreation areas. (See Chapter 3 for acquisition methods and sources of funds.)
- **Widespread publicity, sound interpretation, and public discussion facilitate the implementation of area and facility plans.** Appropriate authorities, community groups, and the public-at-large need to be fully informed if acceptance and support are to be achieved.

PLANNING PROCEDURES

No single planning procedure will assure the production and application of a good cooperatively developed plan. However, common-sense practices that have proved useful in the planning process include the following:

- Identify and enlist forces which should be represented in the planning process.
- Enlist the active interest and cooperation of persons representing organized agencies, both governmental and private, that have a concern for planning areas and facilities, so duplication of effort will be avoided.
- Secure the participation of individual citizens from every section and segment of community life whose needs and interests are involved in the planning process and concerned with the results.
- Outline the facility needs in general terms that can be readily understood and accepted; then determine the specific facilities and units needed to accomplish the agreed-upon objectives.
- Secure, whenever desirable, formal agreements from the agencies involved in the planning process, covering such factors as joint financing, property acquisition, development, operation, and use.
- Assign responsibility for specific aspects of the planning process, such as development of the areas and facilities plan, finance, publicity, and implementation, to individuals and groups.
- Recognize the necessity that all agencies and individuals concerned with the planning be kept fully informed as to progress in the development of the plans, thus helping assure their support of the proposals and avoiding possible misunderstandings.
- Make sure that through proper communication and interpretation, proposals for financing, administration, operation, and maintenance of the areas and facilities to be developed will receive general acceptance and approval.

RESPONSIBILITY FOR PLANNING

Soundly conceived plans for areas and facilities are not achieved by chance. They result from the initiative and action of individuals and groups. This statement applies to both comprehensive long-range citywide plans and to plans for specific areas and facilities. Municipal and county authorities, park and recreation departments, and school boards have definite responsibility and authority for planning functions. Many private organizations also have a major concern for the planning of areas and facilities. They study the proposals and arouse support for soundly conceived plans. However, responsibility for the formulation of a master plan for a municipality or larger governmental unit is normally assigned to a legally constituted planning agency.

The planning of areas and facilities for recreation and physical education must be accomplished within the framework of the overall city plan developed by the planning agency. There is no excuse for school and recreational authorities to ignore the city plan when acquiring new areas. Through zoning, subdivision regulation, and programmed public improvements, city authorities exercise a high degree of control over present and future developments. This control affords the basis for total citywide planning, which of necessity includes school and recreation areas. For example, zoning affects school and recreation needs because apartment neighborhoods have different requirements than those composed of single-family dwellings. The location of major thoroughfares affects the development of residential neighborhoods and hence the number, size, and location of needed schools and parks. Districts zoned for business or industry have totally different requirements in the way of open space than residential areas.

Because provision of areas for physical education and recreation is recognized as an essential element in the master plan, it is of the utmost importance that school and recreation authorities make certain that the planning agency is fully informed as to the basic needs and functions of their programs of physical education, athletics, and recreation. In turn, these authorities should be consulted in the development of plans for areas and facilities for which they have a primary concern and should be kept informed of any developments which affect their interests.

Even though the specific authority and responsibility for planning have been officially assigned to various units of government, the variety of service units included in programs of athletics, recreation, and health and physical education necessarily involves many agencies within and without the governmental structure. The governmental agencies have a mandate inherent in their purposes, or specifically assigned by their empowering legislation, to provide facilities and to establish programs, each of which has a place in the mosaic of services serving "fitness" needs. Each of the agencies must plan its facilities and activities within the scope of its responsibility, but in such manner as to complement the facilities and programs of other agencies in the interest of the fullest possible service to all. Obviously, each plan must be conceived, implemented, and adjusted with full knowledge of all other plans, and must become a part of a total comprehensive plan. A team approach is essential to assure optimum results.

The principal agencies involved are: (1) the public school districts, elementary and secondary; (2) the municipal park and recreation department; (3) the counterpart of the municipal park and recreation department in county government; (4) the counterpart in the state government; (5) the federal park and public lands agencies with facilities in the locale; (6) the public housing authority; and (7) the area redevelopment agency. Other agencies that may be involved include the official health agencies, the highway department, and the conservation department.

Concerned with planning for recreation and physical education, although they have no legal responsibility for sharing in the process, are a great variety of community-supported service organizations, such as the YMCA, YWCA, Boys' Clubs, and community centers. The wide range of such agencies, which operate areas and provide services throughout a community, highlights the complexity of the coordinated planning process.

Basic to coordination is communication between the agencies and acquaintance between principals of all agencies involved. Without these two ingredients, coordination is assuredly absent. Other essential conditions must include good will, banishment of jealousies, and common acceptance of clear statements of principles, such as those recommended in this chapter. One writer dramatized the process by calling it "the feet under the table" plan.

Coordinated planning is more readily brought about when some organization is set up to attend to the process. This is often accomplished through a planning council, on which all agencies involved in community recreation, physical education, and health services have representation. It is important that all plans be submitted in their formative stages to the council for review and comment. Unless some such body is created to perform this function, mistakes incapable of future correction are inevitable. There are many examples of properties that have been acquired and improved, which largely duplicate comparable facilities and services of other agencies in the community. Commitments in such situations are most difficult to adjust.

All of the types of agencies mentioned may not be found in any given locality. Some may be expected to be established in the foreseeable future, requiring a modification of the role of existing agencies. In a very small community in which no local agency is ready to accept responsibility for providing recreation areas, facilities, and programs for its people, advice and assistance in establishing recreation service may be secured through an appropriate state or county agency, or the recreation department in a nearby city.

All who are involved in the coordinating process must be aware of developing trends in the fields of health, physical education, and recreation and must view the planning process as a dynamic thing involving numerous facets in which several agencies play a part. Nevertheless, in the final analysis, the attitudes and actions of the public planning, school, and recreation authorities will largely determine the degree to which effective planning will be achieved. Wholehearted cooperation on the part of these agencies assures maximum benefits and services and inevitably fosters the cooperation of all other interested groups.

PLANNING UNITS—TYPES AND FUNCTIONS

Publicly-owned areas and facilities within the scope of this Guide are principally under the jurisdiction of two types of local authorities—school districts and departments of parks and recreation. Other public and quasi-public agencies provide such facilities as libraries and museums. Privately-owned facilities, such as churches, settlement houses, and youth clubs also contribute to the public service. The total effect of these facilities upon health, physical education, and recreation services varies in different cities, but their presence must always be taken into account in planning areas and facilities, and in some localities they play a major role. The real value of the public services hinges largely upon the qualifications of the personnel employed and the nature and quality of the facilities controlled and used by the school and the department of parks and recreation.

Comprehensive programs and services require that indoor and outdoor areas and facilities of many kinds, shapes, and sizes be available throughout the year. Each area and facility has a special function and serves specific uses. These areas and facilities are classified in this Guide according to function, and their sizes are determined by the nature of their services and the number of people to be served. Understanding of this classification is essential to effective planning.

TYPES OF PLANNING UNITS

In planning a system of interrelated areas and facilities, as advocated in this Guide, each type of geographic area—neighborhood, community, city, school district, county, region, state, and nation—must be considered. In some instances, the entire state must be included and, when accessible, areas and facilities provided by the Federal Government must be taken into account.

THE NEIGHBORHOOD

The neighborhood is a residential area with homogeneous characteristics, of a size comparable to that usually served by an elementary school. A typically ideal neighborhood for planning purposes would be an area three-fourths of a mile to a mile square and containing about six to eight thousand people.

Neighborhoods occur in various shapes and sizes. Population densities vary from a few thousand to many thousands per square mile and there is also a wide variation in the numbers of children. Therefore, each neighborhood must be studied carefully. Because most residents live within a short distance of the school or playground, they walk to it and tend to use it frequently, often for shorter periods than in the centers planned for a larger geographic unit.

THE COMMUNITY

The community is a section of a city, primarily a residential area. It usually represents the service area of a high school, contains a large business center, and commonly constitutes a section of the city measuring two or three miles across. It can be thought of as a "community of neighborhoods" because it is usually composed of three to five neighborhoods. Consequently, the population varies, but on the average is three to five times that of a neighborhood, or from twenty thousand to forty thousand people. It may have a less pronounced homogeneity than the neighborhood, but should not be so dissimilar as to make unified planning impossible. If the dissimilarities are pronounced, the community may need to be subdivided for planning.

THE CITY OR SCHOOL DISTRICT

The area designated as the city, town, borough, or village lends itself to the provision of areas and facilities for use by the entire population of the political subdivision. Major parks, golf courses, camps, museums, and botanical gardens, which cannot be provided in each neighborhood and community, are typical citywide areas. In small localities comprising one community and with a single high school, citywide planning is largely comparable with planning for a single community as described above, although some facilities commonly provided in larger citywide areas are included.

School districts vary widely in size and population, but districtwide school planning involves primarily neighborhoods and communities. Some of the large school districts provide districtwide facilities for an outdoor education-recreation complex, interscholastic activities, consolidated educational programs, and some type of post-high school center or community college for day pupils.

LARGER UNITS

The county or the region, which is a geographic area that sometimes includes parts of more than one county, is increasingly used as a unit for recreation planning. Many such planning units are located in close proximity to a metropolitan city and include both the city and the surrounding region. Others are primarily rural in nature and are composed primarily of unincorporated areas. Planning on a regional or district basis lends itself to the provision of extensive properties usable for family outings, winter and water sports, and other activities requiring large land and water areas. Since these properties are distant from dense population centers, people require transportation in order to reach them and, consequently, tend to use them less frequently but for longer periods than is true of the areas in the smaller planning units. The increase in statewide planning makes it important that plans developed for smaller geographic units take into account existing and proposed facilities for statewide use.

UNIT RELATIONSHIPS

Even though area and facility planning is done for various geographic units and political subdivisions and involves a great variety of school and recreational properties, there is a relationship among the resultant plans. The areas and facilities provided in one unit or subdivision often influence the need for them elsewhere. Areas and facilities in the larger units supplement those in the smaller ones and are used by the people living in all these subdivisions. Therefore, cooperation among the agencies involved in planning at different levels is essential in order to achieve coordinated programs.

THE PARK-SCHOOL CONCEPT

Before describing the various types of properties that are commonly included in comprehensive overall plans, the current tendency to provide areas that serve for both education and public recreation deserves special mention.

The park-school as described in this Guide is set forth as the most desirable type of major facility in the neighborhood or community for the day-by-day use for organized programs of recreation and health and physical education. It combines the neighborhood recreation area and the elementary-school site; the community recreation area and the secondary-school site. It is the basic unit which new neighborhoods or communities should provide and, as redevelopment takes place in older areas, it should be considered the most appropriate type of indoor-outdoor unit to replace older and less-adequate properties.

The concept is greater than just a grouping of these facilities on a single site. It is a unit, the wholeness of which is its essential characteristic. It is an outdoor-indoor plant functionally designed to house and make possible an integrated program of education, recreation, and community activities suitable to the geographic area it serves. In addition to the resulting economy in land acquisition and use, construction, operation, and maintenance, it represents a wholeness of environment in which integrated living in education, recreation, and community life takes place. Its application will prevent towns and cities from repeating the mistakes so frequently made in the past when neighborhood schools and recreation sites provided inadequate yet overlapping services in a single neighborhood or community.

The park-school affords an example of cooperative action between school and municipal authorities. It involves a joint agreement as to the location, development, and use of properties to be designed for the school physical education program and for the recreation of both school and community groups. Since the park-school concept is based on the desirability and economy of dual use, it is of the utmost importance that plans be developed jointly by both school boards and municipal authorities responsible for park and recreation services. In order to protect the interests of the cooperating authorities and to assure the most effective application of the park-school plan, a formal agreement should be drawn up and signed by both agencies, specifying their respective responsibility for the purchase, development, operation, maintenance, and use of the park-schools.

Although the park-school concept has won wide acceptance in recent years, separate school sites and municipal recreation areas are still being acquired in many communities. In some cases, this may be due to lack of knowledge of the concept. More frequently, however, it is because the school or municipal authorities fail to recognize the advantages and economy of the plan or are unwilling to subordinate their prerogatives under a cooperative program. Even in cities where the park-school plan has been approved in principle, there are many neighborhoods and communities where suitable land is not available adjoining existing schools and parks, thus preventing the plan from being put into effect. In developing a citywide plan for recreation and physical education, it is therefore necessary to consider not only park-school sites, but also separate school and recreation areas.

The functional concept of the park-school facility is in keeping with the current educational thought which is focused upon developing individuals capable of carrying out their responsibilities as citizens in a democratic society. This concept further recognizes that the day-by-day experiences of children and youth of school age which take place outside the school are also educational. They are as essential in a complete educational program as many of the more formally organized classroom activities. The park-school, therefore, is designed as a facility in which it is possible to integrate both school and community experiences into one overall program.

Possibly the concept of the park-school program, which leads to the designation of the park-school as the basic functional facility, can best be expressed by suggesting that it should be related to the idea of a "community curriculum" of education-recreation. The program is developed and directed through the joint efforts of the agencies and organizations actually concerned with meeting the needs of children, youth, and adults. The park-school presumes the inclusion of the programs of these organizations.

In its design and operation, therefore, the park-school becomes a day-by-day laboratory for training in cooperative democratic citizenship through integration of education and recreation for people of all ages.

The park-school concept also encompasses lands and facilities more remote from densely populated centers, and possibly outside the city or township boundary. Such an outdoor education-recreation complex makes it possible to conduct extended programs in an outdoor environment.

AREA TYPES

The different types of areas which are set forth herein represent a considerable variety of service units which may be used in programs of athletics, recreation, and physical education. Local conditions and needs will dictate to a large extent which types are to be used in any given situation. Hence, different combinations of areas and facilities will emerge as the solution to the problem of meeting the needs of a particular locality. In every situation—neighborhood or larger geographic unit—the facilities are to be selected and designed to meet the needs of the people they are intended to serve. Part Two of this Guide contains a description of the chief characteristics of each type of area as well as the facilities commonly provided therein.

NEIGHBORHOOD AREAS

PLAYLOT

The playlot is a very small area set aside for the play of preschool children. It is not considered as an essential unit in most neighborhoods, but needs to be provided in large-scale housing developments and in congested neighborhoods where back yards are lacking or are unsuitable for the play of young children. The playlot must be easily and safely accessible from the homes of the children. A playlot is commonly included in the neighborhood park-school or playground and is sometimes included in the neighborhood park.

NEIGHBORHOOD PARK-SCHOOL

The ideal neighborhood unit is a combination park playground and elementary-school site. It is designed for frequent periods of ready use and has a service radius of one-fourth to one-half mile, depending primarily upon the density of population of the neighborhood. It should be centrally located and be accessible without crossing thoroughfares bearing heavy traffic. The neighborhood park-school provides for people of all ages, but primarily for children six to fourteen years old. The facilities provided should make possible a year-round program of recreation and outdoor education activities in addition to the more formal school program.

NEIGHBORHOOD PLAYGROUND

In neighborhoods where conditions make it impracticable to combine the elementary school and the recreation center, a neighborhood playground with park characteristics is essential. It has much the same function, service radius, and recreation facilities as the neighborhood park-school. The neighborhood playground needs a recreation clubhouse or shelter building, but requires less acreage than the park-school because it does not include an elementary-school building and related service facilities.

NEIGHBORHOOD PARK

This type of park serves, in a sense, as an outdoor sitting and rest area for the people of a neighborhood. It is primarily a landscape park, requires relatively small acreage, and contains few, if any, facilities for active recreation. As in the case of the elementary school and the playground, a location near the center of the neighborhood is most satisfactory. A neighborhood park is a desirable feature in most neighborhoods and is an essential unit in an apartment area and in congested neighborhoods. It may not be needed, however, where zoning requires large individual home sites.

ELEMENTARY SCHOOL

In situations where a park-school is not practicable because the school was built on a site that cannot readily be enlarged or for another reason, the elementary school occupies a separate site. This should be as near as possible to the center of the

neighborhood and its location should permit access with a minimum of hazards. In addition to the school building and its setting, the site should provide outdoor space adequate for the physical education, recreation, and outdoor education programs of the school.

COMMUNITY AREAS

COMMUNITY PARK-SCHOOL

The community park-school is an area on which are located a junior or senior high school and a variety of recreation and physical education facilities designed for both school and community use. It should be centrally located in the community it is to serve and should provide a park-like environment. If it contains a senior high school, it requires more acreage than a community park-school with a junior high school and its service radius is appreciably more. Many of the people using such centers, especially those with a senior high school, reach them by automobile or public transport. Relatively few live close enough to walk to them. A portion of the area is usually developed as a playground for the children living in the immediate neighborhood, while another portion serves as a landscape park.

The function of this area is similar to that of the neighborhood park-school, although it serves primarily young people and adults rather than children. However, the geographic area served is larger, usually consisting of three or more residential neighborhoods, its space requirements are much greater, and it provides facilities which are not feasible in the neighborhood unit because of the cost and needed space. The community park-school with a senior high school needs more area in order to provide for interschool athletics, spectator space, and extensive parking.

COMMUNITY PARK AND PLAYFIELD

This type of recreation area is required in a community where it is not feasible or possible to acquire and develop a community park-school. The community park and playfield, like the neighborhood playground, is designed primarily to provide facilities for a variety of types of organized recreation activities, but it should also have the characteristics of a landscape park. It usually serves as the playground for the children living in the immediate neighborhood, but its primary service is to a much wider age group. It therefore supplies a greater variety of facilities and a more extensive service than can be justified at the neighborhood playground. The school child, teen-ager, young adult, hobbyist, senior citizen, and family group all find attractive facilities at the well-developed community park and playfield. Because there is no school building at this area, some type of indoor facility is needed. In many cases, a multipurpose recreation building has been provided to meet this need.

SECONDARY SCHOOL

In communities where the park-school plan cannot be put into effect, separate sites are required for the secondary schools—the junior and senior high schools. A smaller site will serve the needs of the school physical education, recreation, and outdoor education programs than if the area were also expected to provide the recreation service for the entire community. The senior high school needs a larger site than the junior high school because the enrollment is usually higher and because of the greater space requirements of the interscholastic athletic program. Even though separate public indoor and outdoor recreation facilities are provided elsewhere in the community, the junior and senior high school plants should be so designed as to facilitate their use for recreation by community groups when not required for school purposes.

CITYWIDE OR DISTRICT AREAS

Citywide recreation properties generally fall into two classifications: the large city park and the special-use facility. Most citywide areas require more space than can be provided in the neighborhood or community, and the services they render can be more economically and efficiently provided at a single center than at a number of smaller, scattered areas.

The large city park usually comprises 100 acres or more and has dominant topographic, scenic, or historic features. Spaciousness and native environment are among its desirable characteristics. It is designed to make possible a variety of recreation activities involving little supervision or organization. Therefore, highly developed recreation programs have comparatively little place in the large city park. Families, organized and unorganized groups, and individuals normally make up the "clientele."

Special-use parks and facilities include golf courses, zoological gardens, arboretums, aquariums, parkways, public libraries, museums, planetariums, stadiums, outdoor theaters, municipal auditoriums, and downtown plazas. Some of these special-use areas and facilities are provided by organizations of a quasi-public nature.

For planning purposes, many large cities are divided into districts, each with a population of 100,000 or more, which have some of the characteristics of a smaller city. They require areas and facilities similar to those provided by citywide properties.

OUTDOOR EDUCATION-RECREATION COMPLEX

A land area or a cluster of acreages suitable for more extensive outdoor education-recreation programs, owned by the school district, city, or township, is an important adjunct of the park-school. Such a complex should be located as near the city as possible, yet should include some of the following: a resident camp; extensive nature trails; primitive areas for outpost camping and exploration; an outdoor skills and sports center; and plots for forestry and wildlife management, pioneer and modern farms, and other uses.

COUNTY AND REGIONAL AREAS

County and regional parks are relatively large land areas which are intensively developed for recreation purposes and which supplement the facilities furnished by the urban parks and recreation areas. Natural surroundings and spaciousness are emphasized to a greater degree than in the large city park, although some county parks in rural counties have characteristics of the community park and playfield. County and regional parks are commonly used for day-long or weekend outings. They supplement the resources of nearby communities and provide, for people of all ages, opportunities to engage in a variety of activities requiring more space than is afforded by most local parks. In some counties, consolidated or centralized schools provide facilities which serve not only children through the twelfth grade, but people of all ages. In some states, the entire public school system is planned and operated on a county basis.

A second type of regional area is the preserve or reservation, which generally consists of extensive land areas with relatively little development for recreation and with major emphasis upon the preservation of their natural, scenic qualities. Conservancy areas, wildlife refuges, flood-control areas, and forest preserves fall in this category and are often accessible for recreation.

STATE AND NATIONAL AREAS

The expansion of outdoor recreational activities and experiences has increased the significance of state and national facilities within reasonable access to urban centers. Interpretive programs to promote understanding and enjoyment of the geologic, historic, biologic, and other park features have been developed in state and national parks and have proved to be very popular. In many cases, they require special facilities to carry out the program. Camp grounds, picnic areas, and, in some instances, sites for summer homes are provided in state and national forests, as well as at some federal reservoirs, T.V.A. areas, and other federal properties. National recreation areas, seashores, and waterways are more recent concepts within the National Parks System. Recreation activities in these areas are broad in scope and geared to mass use. These and similar developments should be considered in any comprehensive and cooperative program.

FACTORS AFFECTING FUTURE PLANNING

The challenging and important task of the facility and program planner is to take the "long look" and project plans and designs that are new, and some of which may be untried—plans and patterns for a decade hence and not the entrenched plans of the past, or even the present. Several trends now discernible that may affect the classification and standards of areas and facilities for athletics, recreation, and health and physical education in the future are:

- **Redevelopment of the central part of cities.** In this process, more open space is bound to result. Some open space will be in public parks, but of what kind? So-called "rest parks," "ornamental parks," "walkways," or parks for occasional exhibition or attraction, such as a skating act, visiting choir, or a famous personality? A new class of park may be spawned. As this redevelopment takes place, there is a tendency for older-age groups to move back to the city and occupy newly-constructed apartments, thus affecting recreation needs.

- **Redevelopment of all or a large part of a city.** This possibility may seem remote, but there are small towns (10,000 to 25,000 population) which are old and obsolete, yet healthy and apparently important enough to qualify under an expanded program of redevelopment. This situation may warrant a reexamination of present area classification and standards.

- **Reorganization of metropolitan government.** As a planning unit, a metropolitan government comprising a central city and surrounding suburban communities may afford a means of developing areas with special-use facilities which are not now included in citywide regional systems.

- **Green belts in future planning.** Some progressive planners have envisaged a locale for living in the midst of parks— parks surrounding the home; parks as ways to and from school, shopping, and church; and parkways to and from work. Such a profusion of parkland could take place only in a few special places and would surely not be in accordance with current standards.

- **Clustering.** This is a modification of normal zoning regulations whereby open space and building space are each planned as a more concentrated area without changing the proportion of each. This procedure provides a larger and more useful park instead of having the open space scattered in small yards. It may also make more park area available through the reduction of streets and alleys.

- **County and state zoning.** It appears logical that with a

continued expansion of urban centers, more attention will be given to county and state zoning. The requirements for recreation areas in less densely populated localities will necessitate a revision of city standards.
- **Large home tracts.** More and more suburban communities are establishing residential zones in which a minimum of from one to five acres is required for a single-family residence. This type of zoning may well require modifications in normal space and facility standards.

- **The effect of private enterprise.** As the people become more affluent and are willing to spend more for recreation, the private entrepreneur is encouraged to provide a growing number and variety of recreation facilities involving large investments. A continuation of this trend will affect current standards for public recreation areas.

The rapid changes taking place in America present the planner with both a challenge and an opportunity.

SELECTED REFERENCES

Butler, George D., **City-School Cooperation in Planning of Recreation Areas and Facilities.** New York: National Recreation Association, 8 West 8th Street, 1953.

California Committee on Planning for Recreation, Park Areas and Facilities, **Guide for Planning for Recreation Parks in California.** Sacramento: California Recreation Commission, 1956.

International City Managers Association, **Local Planning Administration.** 3rd ed. Chicago: The Association, 1958.

National Recreation Association, **Standards for Municipal Recreation Areas.** New York: The Association, 8 West 8th Street.

Reports of the Regional Planning Association of New York.

Rodney, Lynn S., **Administration of Public Recreation.** New York: The Ronald Press Company, 1964.

Part Two
Outdoor Areas
and Facilities

Chapter 3

PLANNING OUTDOOR AREAS and FACILITIES

THE PRESENT population explosion and the growth projections for the next twenty years provide evidence that few, if any, metropolitan areas in America have sufficient open space to meet the demands of the future. It is imperative, then, that planning boards of all types, at all governmental levels, be developing new master plans and reviewing old ones.

As open space becomes less and less available, greater consideration must be given to multiple use of these lands and every measure taken to utilize them in the best possible and most efficient manner. It is highly desirable that municipal and school authorities acquire, plan, and develop areas for joint use. This calls for professional guidance in the fields of planning, designing, and engineering, and the advice and counsel of professionals in the fields of education and recreation.

There is also a need to utilize the thinking and experience of others who, by training and day-by-day assignments, are qualified to contribute to the planning work. The most efficient and successful planning is accomplished when everyone in the organization, particularly those who will be identified with the finished product, have an opportunity to participate in the planning process. Those who are to be served also have a voice in the planning. This can be accomplished by community meetings where those to be served have an opportunity to express their interests and needs.

AREA STANDARDS

A variety of standards relative to the size, location, and development of school and recreation areas and facilities have been proposed over the years. These standards, which have been prepared by committees composed of individuals with long experience in the operation of such areas and facilities, have been widely adopted and used as a basis for planning. The standards have been valid insofar as they have been designed to provide the space and facilities that make possible a program which serves the basic needs of people for physical education and recreation.

Standards are essential in the development of plans for a school or recreation system and they afford a useful guide in the acquisition and improvement of a single area. However, standards can seldom, if ever, be applied completely, or without modification, because a typical or ideal situation is seldom found. Standards are designed to indicate a basis for the intelligent development of local plans. Therefore, the standards relative to areas and facilities should be reviewed and appraised from time to time and modified whenever changing conditions warrant their revision.

The present-day standards for areas and facilities, which were developed with the cooperation of private planning firms, public agencies, and service organizations at the local, state, and national levels, have been widely adopted throughout the United States and have provided the basis for recommendations in scores of long-range plans for school, park, and recreation systems. The proposal that at least one acre of recreation and park space be set aside by urban areas for every 100 of the

present and estimated future population has been more widely accepted than any other space standard. Professional and governmental authorities, including the National Recreation Association and the National Park Service, have pointed out the desirability of providing even more than one acre for every 100 of the population in towns and small cities.

Modification of this general standard has also been suggested for large, densely populated cities. Some municipal planning officials have expressed the opinion that possibly one acre to 200 people is reasonable in cities above 500,000 population, and perhaps one acre to 300 or more in cities above 1,000,000. They have pointed out that the development of large outlying properties would help meet the recognized deficiency in the larger cities. However, since the need for open space is as great, and usually greater, in these cities, this proposal should not be considered as a standard, but as a practicable substitute indicative not of need but of feasibility.

The standard of one acre per 100 population does not include the acreage necessary for schools. The National Council on Schoolhouse Construction has recommended that an elementary school provide a 10-acre site, with an additional acre for every 100 pupils. The junior high school should provide a minimum site of 20 acres, plus an additional acre for each 100 pupils of predicted ultimate enrollment. The Council further recommends that senior high schools provide a minimum of 30 acres, plus an additional acre for each 100 pupils of predicted ultimate maximum enrollment.[1]

It can be assumed that when school areas are to be utilized by the community, additional acreage will be necessary beyond that recommended by the National Council on Schoolhouse Construction. Recommendations for desirable acreage for recreation, park, and school areas will be covered in Chapter 4.

DEVELOPING A MASTER PLAN

Planning is the process of analyzing data and preparing plans to implement a detailed program based on needs.

The master plan should reflect a comprehensive program of conservation and of recreation activities and facilities which will serve the needs and interests of all the people in the community. It must look to the future, and should be based, not on preconceived ideas, but on an analytical, realistic evaluation of the socio-economic potentials in relation to the requirements of conservation and recreation for the community's long-range development.

A master plan for a school or recreation system should be based on the changing physical, economic, and social requirements and capabilities of the community at large. It requires the collection of facts about the community—its history, economy, natural resources, development trends, streets, schools, existing recreation areas, roads, transportation, sanitation, and water supply—as well as facts about the potential recreation areas concerned. These facts must be analyzed and

[1]*Guide for Planning School Plants*, National Council on Schoolhouse Constriction, 1964.

13

translated into a well-coordinated and functional plan which will be an outline in words, charts, and maps to guide public officials and private citizens in all future development.

The task of recreation planners is to create this plan and to insure that each project is not an isolated improvement, but part of a coordinated development program. A master plan will vary in detail and complexity according to the size of the community and its resources. Coordination of the various elements of the plan is perhaps the most important single function which planning performs. This function will insure cohesive effort among the various governmental and nongovernmental agencies to avoid waste resulting from competition for lands and funds.

The sponsoring agency must interpret the thinking of the citizenry in suggesting a schedule of development based on:
- **inventories** of existing physical, social, and economic conditions;
- **projections** of population density and composition, economic base, traffic patterns, land use, leisure, and income;
- **recreation philosophy, principles, and needs;**
- **engineering and design principles** relating to current and future developments in building materials, methods, and equipment.

This should be a long-range schedule of improvements, with an initial phase and a continuing phase spread over 5, 10, or even 20 years. Problems of implementing the recommendations should be considered, including land acquisition, financing, legislation, administration, and maintenance.

The master plan for a school or recreation system will:
- Identify the criteria applicable to the project;
- Establish an overall scheme for the integration of the components of the project;
- Provide basic information from which forecasts of costs may be determined;
- Establish a timetable for the separate design of related elements and a schedule of future construction.

METHODS OF LAND ACQUISITION

The implementation of a master plan requires land and land rights, the acquisition of which may be accomplished by a number of methods.

OUTRIGHT OWNERSHIP

Outright ownership of land is made possible by the right of the municipality or school district to purchase, or otherwise receive or appropriate land in fee simple. Some of the common methods are:
- **Negotiation;**
- **Outright purchase** as well as such techniques as **purchase-leaseback** and **lease with option to purchase;**
- **Condemnation**—Exercise of the municipality's right of eminent domain;
- **Tax sale**—Repossession of tax-liened property;
- **Subdivision regulations**—Requiring developers of tracts of land to sell, or contribute, to the municipality a percentage of that land (usually between 3% and 10% of the total area) for recreational use—in some cases, where regulations require contribution rather than sale, the developer is given the option of contributing an equivalent amount of money which may be used to acquire recreational land elsewhere in the municipality;
- **Donations**—Bequests, gifts, and the establishment of trusts.

LESS THAN OUTRIGHT OWNERSHIP

Use of land not owned outright is possible in many cases through cooperative agreements with various governmental agencies, civic groups, and private owners, and through the municipality's right to use, control, restrict, or otherwise regulate land. A great advantage of using land not owned outright is that the land is often still assessable, though usually at a reduced valuation, for tax purposes.

Some of the methods of using land not owned outright are listed below.
- **Cooperative agreements**—Joint municipal-school use; municipal-college use; municipal-utility company agreements; soil conservation cooperatives; recreation department-park department use; and municipal arrangements with civic groups, voluntary agencies, and private citizens.
- **Lease, license, and letter permits**—Permit use, for recreational purposes, of highway right-of-way, flood-control or watershed areas, and flight clearance paths adjacent to airports.
- **Zoning**—Cluster zoning, flood-plain zoning, and open-space zoning.
- **Restrictive covenants**—Deed restrictions which govern the way land must be used even though the ownership changes.
- **Developmental rights**—Purchase of developmental rights can also insure that an area presently used as recreation or park land will continue to be used for this purpose even if it is sold to another owner.
- **Easements**—Purchase or acquisition of certain rights to a given piece of property for a specific period of time or in perpetuity. These can take such forms as scenic easements along a highway (preventing billboards and other obstructions of the view) or easements that permit such activities as hunting, fishing, hiking, and boat launching on a piece of land.
- **Regulations**—Building codes, health ordinances, etc. requiring that a given amount of space be devoted to recreational use.
- **Negotiated arrangements**—May take the form of a lease or an arrangement whereby recreational use fees must be paid to the property owner.

METHODS OF FINANCING

A wide variety of methods have been used to produce funds for the acquisition and operation of recreation areas. Some of these methods are discussed below.

BOND ISSUE

Most municipalities and school districts have the power to issue bonds for the financing of land acquisition or capital improvements. Such financing must usually be approved by a referendum vote.

CREATION OF A NONPROFIT CORPORATE BODY

Quasi-public, nonprofit corporations, districts, or authorities have been established in certain instances to provide a specific area or facility such as a stadium or marina. Financing is then accomplished by a sale of stock, bonds, or debentures in this corporation to its members or to the public, or by other methods.

TAXATION

Various levels of government have the authority to levy taxes on such items as real property, sales, personal property, and gasoline, for various public purposes that may include recreation. In some instances, legislation has been passed requiring that revenues from a specific tax be used to acquire and develop land for recreational use. An outstanding example of this is the federal tax on motorboat fuel which formerly went into a highway fund. Under legislation enacted in 1964, all revenues from this tax as well as from federal admission fees and surplus property receipts accrue to the Land and Water Conservation Fund described later in this chapter.

SALE OF LICENSES AND PERMITS

The sale of licenses and permits for hunting, fishing, boat ownership, and the use of tennis facilities, beaches, or parks is a commonly-used method of producing revenue. In some states, the revenue from hunting and fishing licenses is used to acquire, and provide access to, additional land for these activities.

LEVY OF FEES AND CHARGES

Entrance, parking, use, and membership fees are also commonly-used sources of revenue that may be used to finance land acquisition.

CONCESSIONS

Concession agreements permitting private operators to provide lodging, food service, rental of equipment, and other services and activities are other commonly-used sources of revenue.

UTILIZATION OF GRANTS, LOANS, AND SERVICES

An increasing number of programs are being established for the purpose of assisting local community agencies in the acquisition of recreation land and open space. Some of these programs are listed below. A more complete listing of federal programs can be found in the booklet **Federal Assistance in Outdoor Recreation.** (See selected references at the end of this chapter.)

FEDERAL PROGRAMS

Open-space Land Program

This program was initiated to assist states and local governments in taking prompt action to preserve open-space land essential to the long-range development of the area. It authorizes grants of up to 30% of the cost of predominantly undeveloped land for the purpose of parks, recreation, conservation, or scenic or historic uses. The program is administered by the Housing and Home Finance Agency of the Urban Renewal Administration.

The Land and Water Conservation Fund Act

This act establishes a special 25-year fund to provide for federal matching grants-in-aid of up to 50% of the cost of state and local planning, land acquisition, and facility development for outdoor recreation projects. This program is administered by the Bureau of Outdoor Recreation through a designated state agency in each state. Another portion of the fund is available to federal agencies for similar purposes.

Surplus Federal Land at Reduced Cost

A federal law administered by the General Services Administration permits state and local agencies to apply for and, if approved, purchase surplus federal land at 50% of its fair market value if it is to be used for park and recreation purposes. If the land is to be used for historic monument purposes, there is no charge.

The Watershed Protection and Flood Prevention Act

This law was enacted to assist state and local governments in acquiring land easements and rights-of-way for reservoirs and other areas to be used for public recreation. It authorizes the Department of Agriculture to share up to 50% of the cost of acquisition for such projects and provides that they may also share the development costs of certain necessary facilities. The program is administered by the Soil Conservation Service of the U. S. Department of Agriculture.

Loans

There are a number of programs under which federal agencies may make loans to facilitate planning and land acquisition for recreation purposes, as well as for the development of recreation facilities. Some of these programs are mentioned below. A more complete listing of federal programs can be found in the booklet **Federal Assistance in Outdoor Recreation.** (See selected references at the end of this chapter.)

Loans for the purpose of planning and land acquisition are available to the local government agency through the Community Facilities Administration of the Housing and Home Finance Agency.

The Farmers Home Administration of the Department of Agriculture is empowered to make loans up to one million dollars to nonprofit associations serving or benefiting farmers and other rural families in making changes in land use, including the development of recreation facilities.

Watershed loans, including funds for developing recreation facilities, may be made by the Farmers Home Administration to finance the local share of costs of improvements in watershed projects which have been approved by the Soil Conservation Service of the U. S. Department of Agriculture.

Technical services are available from the Coast and Geodetic Survey, the Soil Conservation Service, and other agencies. These services may facilitate land acquisition by eliminating or reducing expenses involved.

STATE PROGRAMS

Many states are initiating programs which provide grants to local governmental agencies for recreation and open-space land acquisition. Outstanding examples of this are New Jersey's Green Acres Program, New York's Open-Space Bond-Issue Program, Pennsylvania's Project 70, and California's Park and Recreation Facilities Bond Issue.

DEVELOPING A SITE PLAN

The procedures necessary for the planning of any one site in the education, recreation, and conservation program are:
- Physical examination of the site;
- Assembly and analysis of pertinent facts, such as development conditions, trends, and population needs;
- Assembly of site information, including: site survey information; borings; soil tests; depth of topsoil; erosion; surface water resources (streams, lakes, and ponds); ground water; precipitation; climate; open spaces; vegetation; utilities (electricity, potable water, and sewage); existing buildings and roads; projected approach roads; present and projected nearby residential, commercial, and industrial development; easements; rights-of-way; and zoning restrictions;
- Attendance at meetings with officials, citizens' committees, and other interested groups to determine the specific needs of the program;
- Analysis of recreational, aesthetic, and engineering features;
- Preparation of diagrammatic studies showing comparative functional component uses;

- Following approval of the above, the final features of the site plan should be incorporated and budget material prepared as required.

In designing the site, the following factors should be considered:
- Off-site nuisances;
- Safety factors;
- Proper drainage for turf and hard-surface areas;
- Separation of component areas by fencing and planting;
- Placement of the service building for control and supervision;
- Layout of walkways for safe and efficient circulation;
- Night lighting of fields, courts, and general areas;
- Level and cost of maintenance required;
- Provision for first-aid facilities, equipment, and supplies;
- Anticipated recreation, health education, physical education, and driver and safety education activities;
- Space required to meet peak-load demands for instruction and recreation;
- Advantage should be taken of existing topographic features, trees and other vegetation (if they fit in with intended uses), prevailing winds, and other natural conditions;
- Accessibility and use of the site for the aging and the disabled (see "Site Development" in Appendix H);
- Use of durable and vandal-proof materials and equipment.

THE COMMUNITY PARK-SCHOOL

It is becoming increasingly common for the recreation and park authorities, city council, and school board to acquire acreage jointly for the development of areas and facilities needed for physical education and recreation. In such joint acquisition and development of areas and facilities, tax money is used to the greatest advantage. In the community park-school, the combined school and park site should be planned co-operatively to provide adequate areas and facilities and to insure the greatest return for the amount of money spent for property acquisition and development. Communities which have utilized school sites as a part of a community park have avoided duplicating costly expenditures.

The following additional site planning principles are suggested in developing the park-school site:
- The area should be developed according to the integrated master plan.
- Zones of use should be established for all parts of the combined site.
- Educational and recreational areas and facilities for joint use should be conveniently located.
- Classrooms should be separated from recreation areas by sight and sound barriers.
- Service drives, walks, parking areas, etc. should be located to serve both school and community needs.

FACILITIES AND EQUIPMENT

To meet the health education, physical education, and recreation needs of any community, a wide variety of facilities and equipment is necessary. The variety of interests, local emphasis, different age levels, and many other factors will dictate what is needed. The use of any equipment or facility in a site plan should follow sound principles of planning for outdoor facilities to insure the most orderly and best functional arrangement. The size and number of facilities and pieces of equipment will depend on the needs and type of the area to be served.

EQUIPMENT

Playground equipment includes multipurpose, movable elements as well as the more or less permanently placed equipment designed for physical development and creative play. Playgrounds should contain some equipment which will give opportunities for experimentation in movement and for development of the large muscles. Equipment is also needed which will give opportunities for physical coordination—climbing, hanging, balancing, pushing, and pulling.

Equipment for the young child should be low enough to be safe, versatile enough to meet a short interest span, and geared to his coordination abilities. It is especially important that the equipment area for younger children be located near the school or service building.

The older child requires larger and stronger equipment to test his skill and strength and to challenge him in developing new skills. It is important to point out that all outdoor equipment should be constructed of heavy-duty materials.

It is important to orient and organize equipment areas so as to separate the various age groups. This is necessary from the standpoint of both safety and actual supervision and use. Orientation of game equipment in relation to the sun is also important.

Some of the play equipment should challenge the imagination of the child and should present an element of unpredictability. There is no need for equipment to be dull, drab, and unattractive. The use of gaily-colored equipment is recommended. Sculptured forms of animals and natural objects are recent innovations and are widely used. Materials for play equipment, in addition to conventional use of metals, wood, and concrete, now include plastics, Fiberglas, and bronze. Colors impregnated in plastics and concrete prevent the necessity of frequent painting.

Suggested play equipment for preschool children is listed under PLAYLOT in Chapter 4. Equipment for the elementary-age child is also discussed in Chapter 4 under NEIGHBORHOOD PLAYGROUND.

SURFACING

Surfacing under play equipment should be soft and/or resilient to lessen the chance of injury. A variety of materials is now being utilized. Tanbark adds a rich, attractive coloring and provides some resiliency. Ground wood products are also being used. Both tanbark and other wood products tend to pulverize after considerable traffic. Sand is popular in a number of communities but has some limitations. Other materials being used include interlocking rubber blocks, rubber pellets mixed with a bituminous base, and rubberized or plastic surface normally applied over asphalt construction. Some experts feel there should be further study and experimentation in this field. (For further information, see Chapter 9.)

MULTIPLE-USE PAVED AREA

This area is a paved all-weather space used for games requiring a hard surface, such as softball, kickball, basketball, volleyball, badminton, tennis, paddle tennis, handball, and shuffleboard. It also provides for activities requiring areas of variable size, such as dancing, roller skating, and games of low organization.

Concrete or asphalt surfaces are commonly used. Local conditions will determine the type and particular specifications needed.

Figure 1
Tots' Equipment, Columbian Playground, East Orange, N.J.

MULTIPLE-USE TURF AREA

The multiple-use turf area may be separate or combined with the field-games area. Its size, shape, and treatment will depend on the needs and space available. It should contain open-turf areas, with peripheral planting, benches, and tables. This space is used for active games of low organization, informal class work, storytelling, and creative free play.

FIELD-GAMES AREA

The field-games area should be laid out for large-space games such as field hockey, touch football, football, soccer, speedball, baseball, and softball. Fields, backstops, and goals for the various games should be located in such a way as to permit overlapping use of the area during different seasons. The size of specific sports facilities will depend on the age group served (see Table 1 for recommended dimensions for game areas). Multiple use of field areas can be facilitated if various colors of water-base rubberized paint are used for field markings.

COURT-GAMES AREA

The court-games area may be combined with the multiple-use paved area or it may be a series of separate court areas. The surface of the area should be asphalt or concrete. Basketball, volleyball, badminton, tennis, and shuffleboard are games which can be played on small areas with smooth playing surfaces. Enclosures and backstops will be needed and, in some cases, lighting for night play. If a court game is to be laid out on a multiple-use paved area, removable net posts should be provided and suitable plates or covers supplied for capping the post-holes. (See Table 1 for recommended dimensions for game areas.)

Figure 2
Court-Games Area, Alverthorpe Park, Abington, Pa.

TABLE 1

RECOMMENDED DIMENSIONS FOR GAME AREAS*

Games	Elementary School	Junior High School	High School (Adults)	Area Size (Including Buffer Space)
Basketball	40' x 60'	50' x 84'	50' x 84'	7,200 sq. ft.
Basketball (College)			50' x 94'	8,000 sq. ft.
Volleyball	25' x 50'	25' x 50'	30' x 60'	2,800 sq. ft.
Badminton			20' x 44'	1,800 sq. ft.
Paddle Tennis			20' x 44'	1,800 sq. ft.
Deck Tennis			18' x 40'	1,250 sq. ft.
Tennis		36' x 78'	26' x 78'	6,500 sq. ft.
Ice Hockey			85' x 200'	17,000 sq. ft.
Field Hockey			180' x 300'	64,000 sq. ft.
Horseshoes		10' x 40'	10' x 50'	1,000 sq. ft.
Shuffleboard			6' x 52'	640 sq. ft.
Lawn Bowling			14' x 110'	1,800 sq. ft.
Boccie			15' x 75'	1,950 sq. ft.
Tetherball	10' circle	12' circle	12' circle	400 sq. ft.
Croquet	38' x 60'	38' x 60'	38' x 60'	2,200 sq. ft.
Roque			30' x 60'	2,400 sq. ft.
Handball (Single-wall)	18' x 26'	18' x 26'	20' x 40'	1,200 sq. ft.
Handball (Four-wall)			23' x 46'	1,058 sq. ft.
Baseball	210' x 210'	300' x 300'	400' x 400'	160,000 sq. ft.
Archery		50' x 150'	50' x 300'	20,000 sq. ft.
Softball (12" Ball)**	150' x 150'	200' x 200'	275' x 275'	75,000 sq. ft.
Football			160' x 360'	80,000 sq. ft.
Touch Football		120' x 300'	160' x 360'	80,000 sq. ft.
6-Man Football			120' x 300'	54,000 sq. ft.
Soccer (Men) Minimum			165' x 300'	65,000 sq. ft.
Maximum			240' x 360'	105,000 sq. ft.
Soccer (Women)			120' x 240'	40,000 sq. ft.

*Table covers a single unit; many of above can be combined.

**Dimensions vary with size of ball used.

SELECTED REFERENCES

Bureau of Outdoor Recreation, U.S. Department of the Interior, **Federal Assistance in Outdoor Recreation.** Washington, D.C.: The Bureau, Publication No. 1, 1964.

Butler, George D., Recreation Area Standards, **Recreation,** January, 1963.
          , **Standards for Municipal Recreation Areas.** New York: National Recreation Association, 8 West 8th Street, 1962.

Fourth National Institute in Recreation Administration, **Planning Recreation Facilities.** New York: National Recreation Association, 8 West 8th Street, 1959.

National Council on Schoolhouse Construction, **Guide for Planning School Plants,** East Lansing, Mich.: The Council, c/o Floyd G. Parker, Secretary, Michigan State University, 1964.

Outdoor Recreation Resources Review Commission, **Land Acquisition for Outdoor Recreation—Analysis of Selected Legal Problems.** Washington, D.C.: U. S. Government Printing Office, Study Report No. 16, 1962.

          , **Open Space Action.** Washington, D.C.: U.S. Government Printing Office, Study Report No. 15, 1962.

          , **Outdoor Recreation for America.** Washington, D.C.: U.S. Government Printing Office, 1962.

          , **Paying for Recreation Facilities.** Washington, D.C.: U.S. Government Printing Office, Study Report No. 12, 1962.

Chapter 4

RECREATION, PARK, and SCHOOL AREAS

THE PARK-SCHOOL concept of combining education and recreation facilities on a single site, as described in Chapter 2, has great merit. This combination makes possible a wider variety of opportunities on less acreage and at a lower cost than do separate installations. This approach is discussed here as it applies to areas at the neighborhood, community, and citywide levels.

Separately-located recreation areas are also treated since there may be certain circumstances under which the park-school may not be possible. It must be emphasized, however, that the combined approach is highly recommended.

NEIGHBORHOOD AREAS AND FACILITIES

PLAYLOT

A playlot is a small recreation area designed for the safe play of preschool children.

LOCATION

As an independent unit, the playlot is most frequently utilized in large housing projects or in other densely-populated urban areas with high concentrations of preschool-age children. More often, it is incorporated as a vital feature of a larger recreation area. If a community is able to operate a neighborhood playground within one-quarter mile of every home, playlots should be located at the playground sites. A location near a playground entrance, close to rest rooms, and away from active game areas is desirable.

SIZE

The space devoted to a playlot depends upon the total open space available for development on a particular site. It may vary from 2,500 to 10,000 square feet.

GENERAL FEATURES

The playlot should be enclosed with a low fence or solid plant materials in order to assist mothers or guardians in safeguarding their children. Careful thought should be given to placement of benches, with and without shade, for ease of supervision and comfort for parents and guardians. A drinking fountain with a step for tots will serve both children and adults.

Play equipment geared to the preschool child should combine attractive traditional play apparatus with creative, imaginative equipment. Such proven favorites as chair, bucket, and glider-type swings, six-foot slides, and a small merry-go-round can be used safely. Hours of imaginative play will be enjoyed with such features as a simulated train, boat, airplane, and playhouse, and Fiberglas or concrete animals. A small climbing structure should be included as well as facilities for sand play.

Figure 3
Playlot In Small Park, Gorgas Park, Philadelphia, Pa.

NEIGHBORHOOD PARK-SCHOOL (ELEMENTARY)

The neighborhood park-school is the primary unit in planning for physical education, recreation, and health education. This is a combination of an elementary school, neighborhood park, and playground. It is planned in such a manner that all areas and facilities are used to meet the educational and recreational needs of the people living in a neighborhood. It is essential that areas and facilities be cooperatively planned for the dual purpose of instruction and recreation, and that the school and community recreation programs be coordinated for maximum use of these areas and facilities by the entire neighborhood.

LOCATION

The neighborhood park-school should service an area with a maximum radius of one-half mile and a population of approximately 8,000 people. Any deviation in the population density (larger or smaller communities) may alter the service radius and/or acreage required for this installation.

SIZE

The minimum area recommended for a neighborhood park-school is 20 acres.

GENERAL FEATURES

It is suggested that this area be developed as follows:

	Acres
School building	2.0
Parking	1.0
Playlot and apparatus	1.0
Hard-surface game courts and multiple-use area	2.5
Turf field-games area	5.5
Park area, including space for drama and quiet activities	5.5
Buffer zones and circulation	2.0
Recreation service building	.2
Corner for senior citizens	.3
Total	20.0

The school building should be at the edge of the area to provide for maximum development and utilization of the site, and playground equipment should be located far enough from the building to keep noise from interfering with class instruction.

A separate building containing the recreation leader's headquarters and public rest-room facilities should be provided in close proximity to hard-surface and game areas.

Hard-surface areas should be contiguous to provide a larger area for recreational, recess, physical education, and intramural activities. The field area should be large enough for baseball and softball diamonds to accommodate all age levels, for various field games, and for special events. Paths and walks between areas should be placed so as to avoid traffic over lawns, and the arrangement of facilities and landscaping should make for ease of supervision.

NEIGHBORHOOD PLAYGROUND

Designed primarily to serve children under 14 years of age, the neighborhood playground should have additional features to interest teen-agers and adults. The trend in recent years is for the neighborhood playground to become increasingly the center of activity for the wide variety of needs expressed by all residents. The more diversified interests of today's recreation consumer challenge the facility planner to provide for a broader program, with more attention devoted to multiple use by different age groups.

Modern planning for outdoor recreation at the neighborhood level places heavy emphasis on combining elementary-school needs with those of the community. This type of joint development is treated in the immediately preceding section on the neighborhood park-school.

Where elementary-school facilities are unavailable or inadequate, or joint development is impossible, a separate playground will be needed in each neighborhood.

LOCATION

The neighborhood playground serves the recreation needs of the same population served by the neighborhood elementary school. Its maximum use radius will seldom exceed one-half mile, with most of the attendance originating within a quarter-mile distance. It should be located close to the center of the area to be served and away from heavily-traveled streets and other barriers to easy and safe access.

SIZE

In order to have the desired features, the neighborhood playground would normally require a minimum of eight acres. The particular facilities required will depend on the nature of the neighborhood, with space being allocated according to needs.

GENERAL FEATURES

It is recommended that this area be developed as follows:

	Acres
Turf area for softball, touch football, soccer, speedball, and other field games	3.00
Hard-surface area for court games, such as netball, basketball, volleyball, and handball	.50
Open space for informal play	.50
Corner for senior citizens	.30
Space for quiet games, storytelling, and crafts	.20
Playlot	.20
Children's outdoor theater	.15
Apparatus area for elementary-age children	.25
Service building for rest rooms, storage, and equipment issue, or a small clubhouse with some indoor activity space	.15
Circulation, landscaping, and buffer zones	2.00
Undesignated space	.75
Total	8.00

Depending upon the relationship of the site to school and other recreation facilities in the neighborhood, optional features such as a recreation building, a park, tennis courts, or a swimming pool might be located at the neighborhood playground. If climatic conditions warrant, a spray or wading pool should be provided. The following space for optional features should be added to the standards listed above:

	Acres
Recreation building	.2
Park area (if there is no neighborhood park)	2.0
Swimming pool	.5
Tennis courts	.4
Total	3.1

The addition of optional features may require provision for off-street parking.

EQUIPMENT

The following types of equipment are recommended:
Several pieces of equipment designed as simulated stage-coaches, fire engines, boats, locomotives, etc.

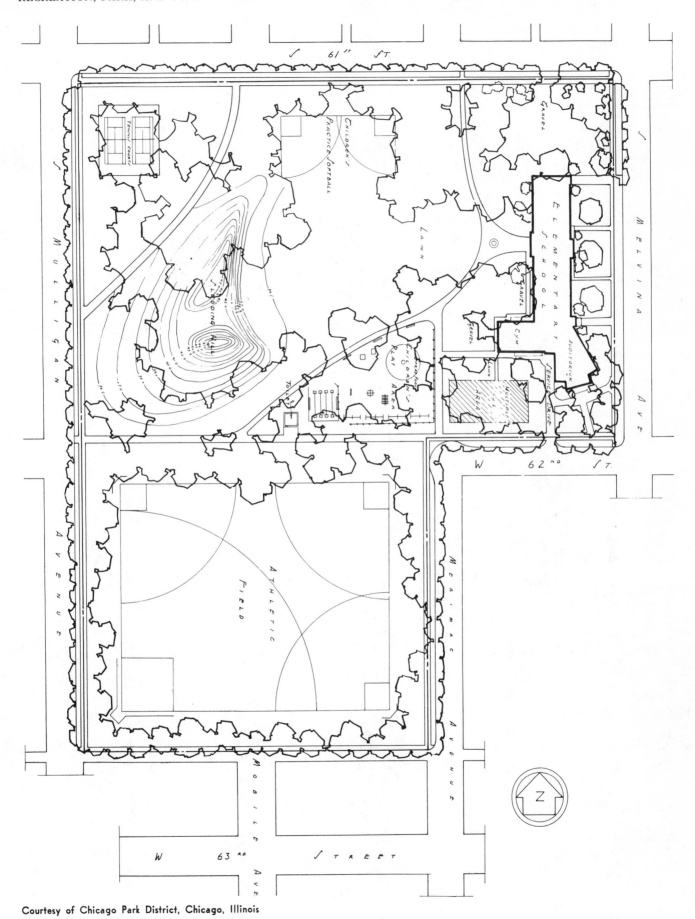

Figure 4
Neighborhood Park-School (Elementary)

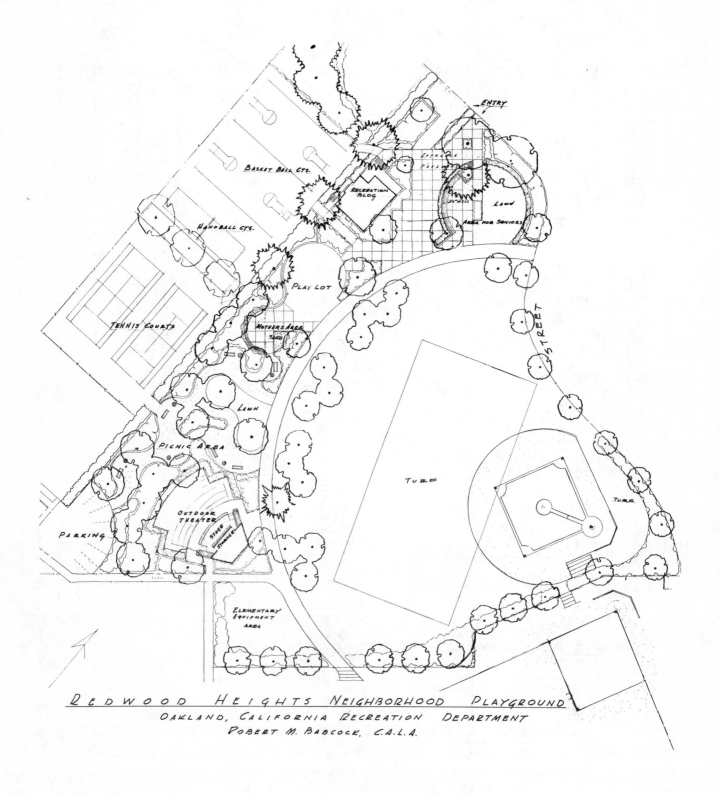

REDWOOD HEIGHTS NEIGHBORHOOD PLAYGROUND
OAKLAND, CALIFORNIA RECREATION DEPARTMENT
ROBERT M. BABCOCK, C.A.L.A.

Figure 5
Neighborhood Playground, Redwood Heights, Oakland, California

Physical-fitness or obstacle-course features, such as a scaling wall, cargo net climber, etc.

Balance beam

Climbing structure, not to exceed 9' high

Horizontal ladder, not to exceed 7' high

Three horizontal bars with fixed heights, of rust-resistant metal

Straight slide 8' high or spiral slide 10' high

Six or more conventional swings, with low protective barriers

Pipe equipment formed into shapes

Sculptured forms

Merry-go-round, safety-type

The various apparatus groupings should be separated by plantings or attractive medium-height fencing.

NEIGHBORHOOD PARK

The neighborhood park is land set aside primarily for passive recreation. Ideally, it gives the impression of being rural, sylvan, or natural in its character. It emphasizes horticultural features, with spacious turf areas bordered by trees, shrubs, and sometimes floral arrangements. It is essential in densely-populated areas, but not required where there is ample yard space attached to individual home sites.

LOCATION

A park should be provided for each neighborhood. In many neighborhoods, it will be incorporated in the park-school site or neighborhood playground. A separate location is required if this combination is not feasible.

SIZE

A separately-located neighborhood park normally requires three to five acres. As a measure of expediency, however, an isolated area as small as one or two acres may be used. Sometimes the neighborhood park function can be satisfactorily included as a portion of a community or citywide park.

GENERAL FEATURES

The neighborhood park plays an important role in setting standards for community aesthetics. Therefore, it should include open lawn areas, plantings, and walks. Sculptured forms, pools, and fountains should also be considered for ornamentation. Creative planning will utilize contouring, contrasting surfaces, masonry, and other modern techniques to provide both eye appeal and utility.

Figure 6
Small Neighborhood Park, Lindberg Park, Philadelphia, Pa.

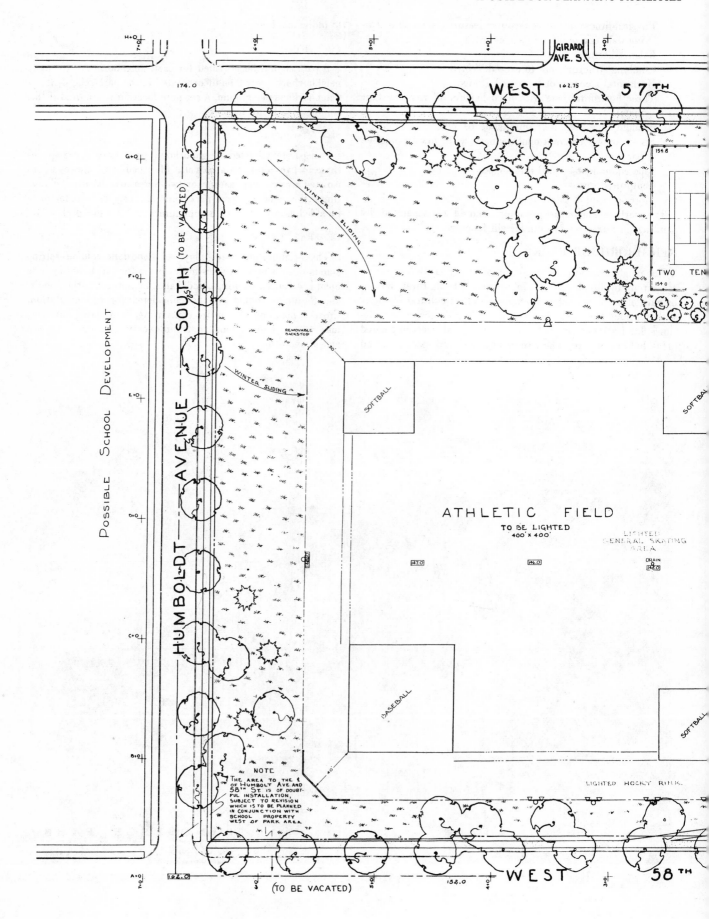

NOTE
THE AREA TO THE E
OF HUMBOLT AVE AND
58TH ST IS OF DOUBT-
FUL INSTALLATION,
SUBJECT TO REVISION
WHICH IS TO BE PLANNED
IN CONJUNCTION WITH
SCHOOL PROPERTY
WEST OF PARK AREA.

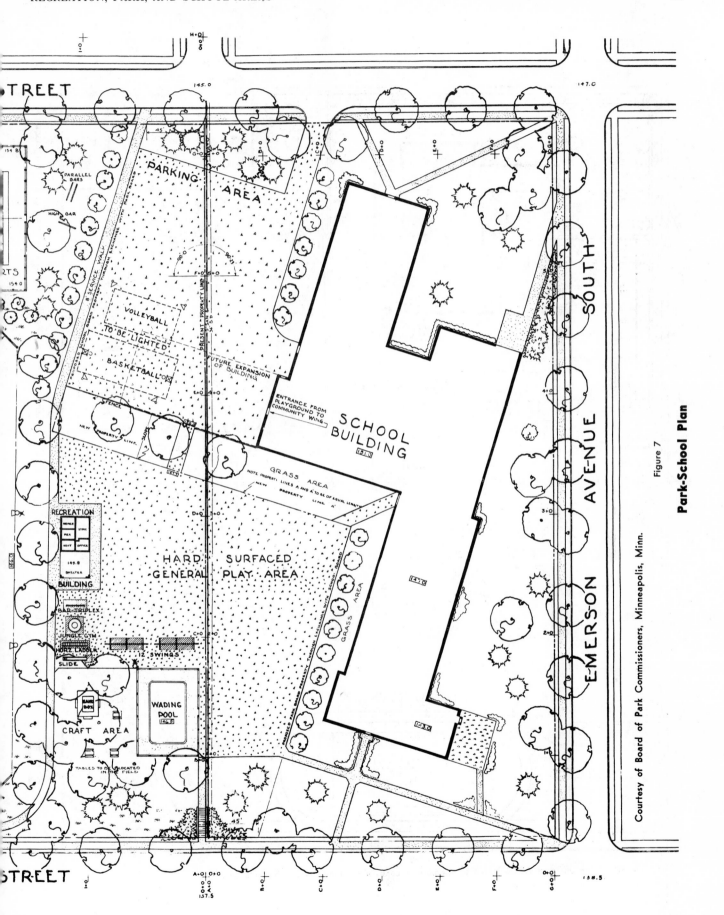

Figure 7

Park-School Plan

Courtesy of Board of Park Commissioners, Minneapolis, Minn.

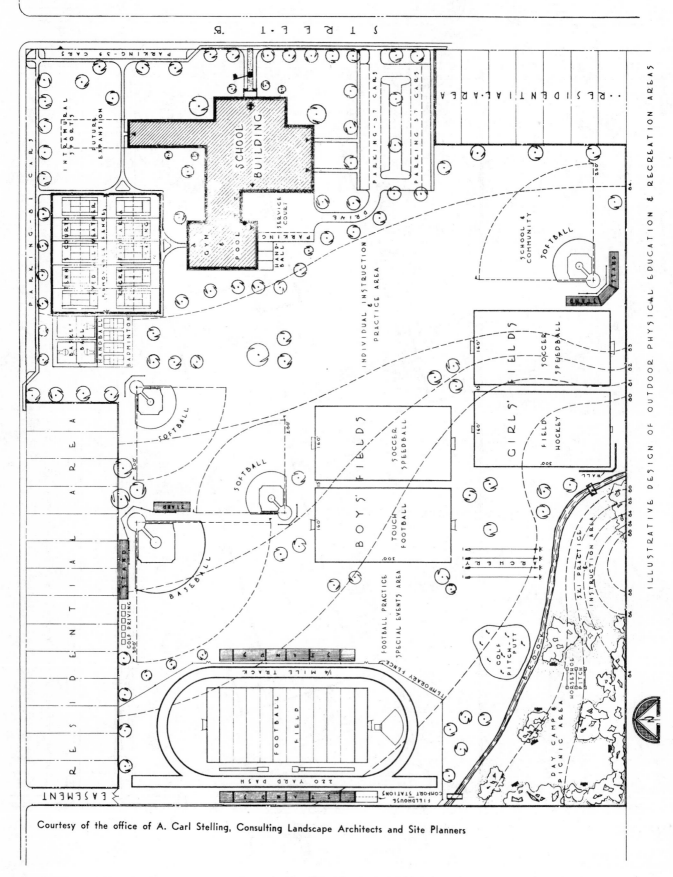

Courtesy of the office of A. Carl Stelling, Consulting Landscape Architects and Site Planners

Figure 8
Community Park-School (Senior High) One-Building Type

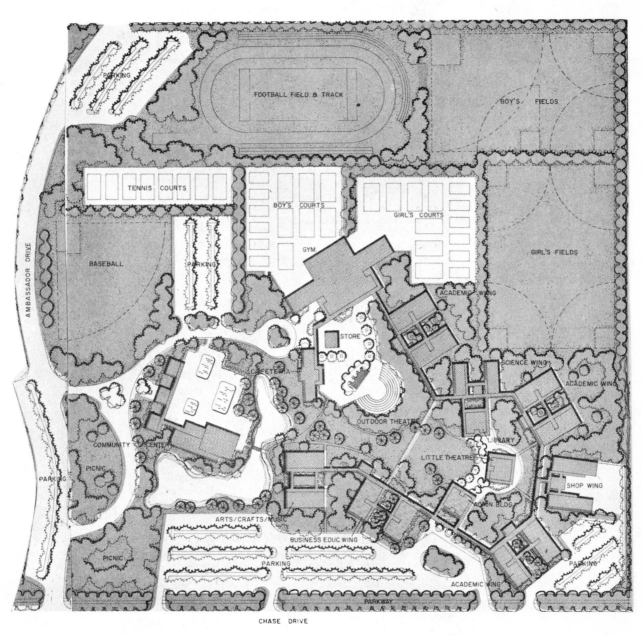

Courtesy of Cordova Recreation and Park District, Sacramento County, California

Figure 9
Community Park (Senior High) Campus Type Cordova Recreation
and Park District, Sacramento County, California

COMMUNITY AREAS AND FACILITIES

COMMUNITY PARK-SCHOOL (JUNIOR HIGH)

The community park-school (junior high), a joint development of school and community, provides an economical and practical approach to a communitywide facility for educational, cultural, social, and recreational programs. This educational and recreational center generally refers to the combination of a junior high school and a community park.

LOCATION

It is suggested that this facility provide service for an area with a radius of 1/2 to 1-1/2 miles. Such an area will normally contain 20,000 to 30,000 people, but population density may modify the size of the area served.

SIZE

Based upon current formulas for establishing junior-high-school and community-park sites, a minimum area of 35 acres is desirable.

GENERAL FEATURES

It is suggested that the area be developed as follows:

	Acres
Buildings (school and community recreation)[1]	5.00
Turf field-games area	8.00
Hard-surface games court and multiple-use area	2.75
Tennis courts	1.00
Football field with 440-yard track (220-yard straightaway)	4.00
Baseball field with hooded backstop	3.00
Playlot and apparatus	1.00
Park and natural areas	5.00
Parking	1.25
Buffer zones and circulation	4.00
Total	35.00

The following may be included as standard or optional features:

Swimming pool (usually related to the building)
Nature study trails and/or center
Day-camping center

There are many optional features which may be included in the community park-school. The inclusion of these is dependent upon the section of the country, available space, topography, community needs, climate, socio-economic composition of the community, and other variables. The following may be included as optional features:

Archery range	Hard-surface area for dancing
Band shell	Horseshoe pits
Boccie courts	Ice-skating or roller-skating rink
Botanical garden	Lake for boating
Croquet courts	Lawn-bowling greens
Golf-driving range	Lighted courts and fields
Golf-putting course	Shuffleboard courts

In designing the community park-school, planners should consider the proper placement of apparatus and areas which serve multiple use, and also bear in mind appropriate safety features in the development of each area or facility.

COMMUNITY PARK-SCHOOL (SENIOR HIGH)

A community park-school (senior high) is planned to provide facilities for youth and adults to meet a wide range of educational and recreational needs and interests on a single site. It generally refers to a combination of a high school and a community park.

It is essential that coordination and cooperation be exercised by school and municipal authorities to insure the maximum development and use of all facilities for instruction and recreation, both during and after school hours.

LOCATION

It is suggested that the population density of the area as well as the total population of the community determine the scope and size of the area to be served by this facility. For example, the higher the population density, the smaller the service radius.

SIZE

Based on current formulas, a minimum area of 50 acres is suggested.

The site size should be based upon program needs, which will include: the physical education instructional program; school-supervised games, sports, and athletics; and school and community recreation activities during out-of-school hours.

GENERAL FEATURES

It is suggested that the area be developed as follows:

	Acres
Buildings (including a gymnasium and an aquatics center)	6.00
Turf field-games area for instruction, intramurals, interscholastic athletics practice, and recreation use	8.00
Hard-surface games court and multiple-use area	3.00
Tennis courts	1.50
Apparatus area for instructional use (optional)	.12
Recreation area	5.00
Hard-surface area (for shuffleboard and outdoor bowling)	
Turf area (for horseshoes and croquet)	
Turf area (for golf and archery)	
Football field with bleachers and 440-yard track (220-yard straightaway)	6.00
Baseball field	3.50
Playlot and apparatus	.50
Park and natural areas	5.00
Recreation building with senior-citizen center	.50
Parking and driver-education range	6.00
Buffer zones and circulation	5.00
Total	50.12

For other features which may be incorporated into this facility, see the sections in this chapter devoted to the community park-school (junior high) and the citywide or district park.

An adequate number of each kind of facility should be provided to permit full participation by the largest group that will be using the facility at any given time.

The total community park-school area should be landscaped to create a park-like setting which enhances and does not interfere with the instructional and recreational areas.

COMMUNITY PARK AND PLAYFIELD

The community park and playfield is designed to provide a variety of active and passive recreational services for all age groups of a community served by a large junior high school (20,000 to 30,000 residents). Primary requisites are outdoor fields for organized sports, indoor space for various activities, special facilities, and horticultural development.

LOCATION

It is highly desirable that this facility be incorporated into the complex of a community park-school (junior high). Where this is not feasible, the community park and playfield should be located within 1/2 to 1-1/2 miles of residents in its service area, depending upon population density and ease of access.

SIZE

A separate community park and playfield requires an area of 15 to 20 acres. At least two-thirds of the area should be developed for active recreation purposes.

GENERAL FEATURES

The following should be provided:
Fields for baseball, football, field hockey, soccer, and softball
Courts for tennis, basketball, boccie, volleyball, handball, horseshoes, shuffleboard, paddle tennis, and other games
Recreation building containing an auditorium, a gymnasium, and special-use rooms for crafts, dramatics, and social activities
Quiet recreation area
Hard-surface area for dodgeball and kickball
May include a neighborhood playground. (See features under Neighborhood Playground)

CITYWIDE OR DISTRICT PARK

The citywide or district park serves a district of a larger city, or a total community of a smaller city. This facility should serve a population of from 50,000 to 100,000. It is designed to provide a wide variety of activities.

LOCATION

This facility should be incorporated with a high school as a park-school development. Where this is not feasible, consideration should be given to placing the park as close as possible to the center of the population to be served. The land available will be a determining factor in site selection. While the service area will vary according to population density, a normal use radius is two to four miles.

SIZE

The citywide or district park may have from 50 to 100 acres.

GENERAL FEATURES

Depending upon available acreage, topography, and natural features, the citywide or district park will contain a large number of different components. These would include, but not be limited to, the following:
A number of fields for baseball, football, soccer, and softball
Tennis center
Winter sports facilities
Day-camp center
Picnic areas (group and family)
Bicycling paths or tracks
Swimming pool
Lake for water sports
Pitch-and-putt golf course
Recreation building
Nature-centered trails
Skating rinks (ice and roller)
Playlot and apparatus
Parking areas
Outdoor theater

The above facilities should be separated by large turf and landscaped areas. Natural areas and perimeter buffers should be provided.

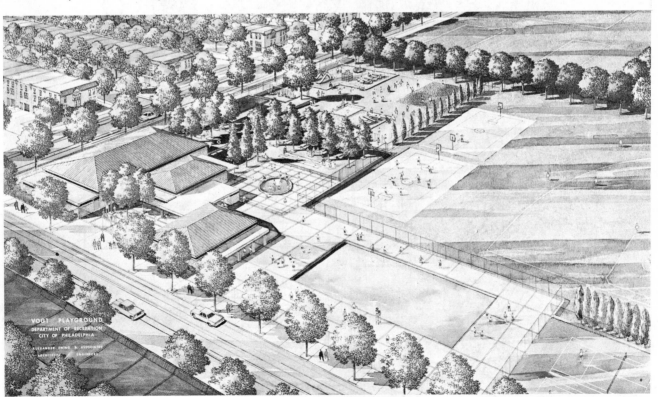

Figure 10
Citywide or District Park

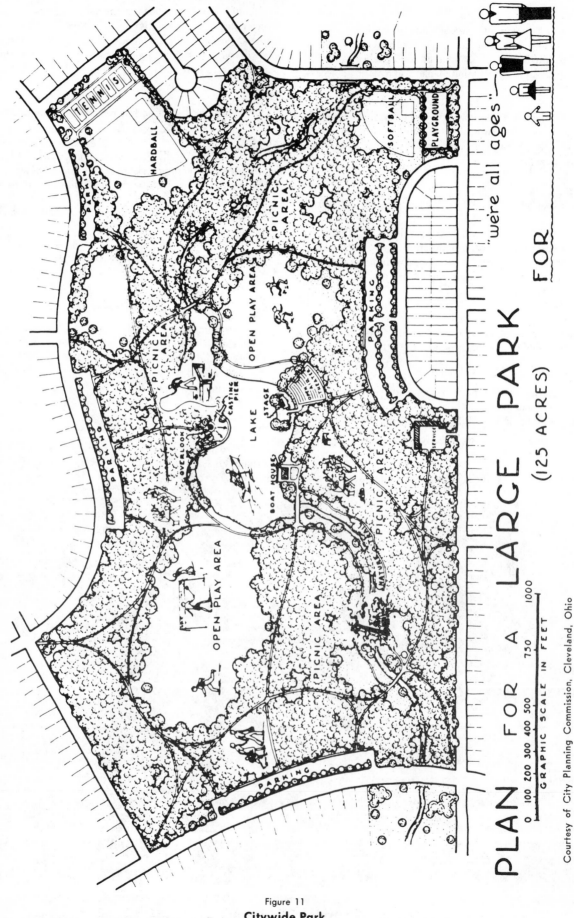

PLAN FOR A LARGE PARK

"were all ages"

FOR

(125 ACRES)

GRAPHIC SCALE IN FEET

0   100 200 300 400 500   750   1000

Courtesy of City Planning Commission, Cleveland, Ohio

Figure 11
Citywide Park

COUNTY AND REGIONAL PARKS, PRESERVES, AND PARKWAYS

PURPOSE, FUNCTIONS, AND OBJECTIVES

County and regional parks and preserves are recreation areas that serve the residents of more than one municipality, and whose size, location, and characteristics make it desirable that their development and operation be undertaken by regional cooperative agencies.

With some exceptions, the preserves generally consist of extensive land areas with relatively little development for recreation. Conservancy areas, wildlife refuges, and flood-control areas fall in this category and are often made accessible for recreation use. County and regional parks are land areas which are usually more intensively developed for recreation purposes and which supplement the facilities and activities furnished by the urban parks and recreation areas.

Many municipalities have difficulty in providing land areas to satisfy the recreation demands of their population. Regional studies should be made to determine existing facilities, future demand, and potential for acquisition and development of new facilities to meet present and future needs. To undertake these studies and to administer park areas that are formed to serve the population of more than one governmental unit, it is desirable that regional cooperative agencies be established.

The following are examples of different types of agencies: counties, such as Essex County, New Jersey, and Westchester County, New York; special-purpose authorities, such as the Huron-Clinton Metropolitan Authority and the Cleveland Metropolitan Park District; regional agencies, such as the East Bay Regional Park District in California; state agencies, such as the Huntington Beach State Park in California and the Jones Beach State Park in New York; or interstate agencies, such as the Palisades Interstate Park Commission in New Jersey and New York. Although the greatest number of park visitors will be from the population centers nearest the county or regional park, the increasing mobility of the population as a whole will permit people from greater distances to use regional facilities.

CRITERIA FOR COUNTY AND REGIONAL PARKS

Certain criteria can be established for the size, location, and types of county park facilities required to meet present and future needs. At the present time, adequate lands are still available and their cost must be evaluated in terms of their present and future value to the welfare of the people. For example, a recreation program appropriate for a regional or county park might require 1,000 acres, with a minimum of 400 to 500 acres recommended.

Although suitable acreage of this size may appear to be difficult to secure, a careful analysis may sometimes reveal land areas designated as submarginal which can be developed for recreation.

TYPES OF ACTIVITIES IN COUNTY AND REGIONAL PARKS

The activities for which facilities are usually developed in county and regional parks fall into the four general classifications described below.

- **Passive Recreation**—This includes driving for pleasure, picnicking, sight-seeing, outdoor events, walking for pleasure, and nature walks.
- **Water**—This includes fishing, boating of all types, water skiing, swimming, underwater recreation, and surfing.
- **Active Programs**—This includes games and sports, horseback riding, and bicycling.
- **Primitive**—This includes camping and hiking.

PARKWAYS

The original concept of parkways as landscaped pleasure drives connecting major park areas is still valid. The basic idea of incorporating a passenger car roadway and a pleasure way for leisurely travel and enjoyment of the scenery is still a predominant characteristic of parkways. In the United States, there are several outstanding examples of such parkways in existence.

With the creation of extensive regional parks outside of the immediate metropolitan area, it will be necessary to construct traffic arteries to facilitate travel from the urban area to these parks. The planning and construction of new roads in accordance with parkway standards, or the expansion and improvement of existing roads by acquisition of scenic easements, should be given every consideration in planning for regional park facilities. An outstanding example of such a parkway is the Palisades Interstate Parkway, leading from the George Washington Bridge in New York City to the Bear Mountain-Harriman State Park, approximately 40 miles north of the City in New York State. This limited-access, landscaped parkway provides a pleasurable approach to this vast recreational area serving the metropolitan population of New York City.

During the past 30 years, a new parkway concept has evolved whose right-of-way incorporates sufficient land areas to constitute, in effect, an elongated park. When this concept is used, consideration should be given to the acquisition of a sufficiently wide right-of-way to provide for equestrian, pedestrian, and cycling paths, and also extended areas for appropriate recreation activities to serve local requirements. These might include picnic areas, rest areas, scenic vistas, and service areas.

The parkway right-of-way, held in fee simple, can be expanded by the acquisition of scenic easements for varying distances parallel to the parkway. These are especially desirable to preserve scenic vistas and to prevent aesthetic blight by prohibiting the erection of billboards and other obtrusive structures. Average right-of-way widths vary from 200 to 1,000 feet, with scenic easements extending varying distances depending on the types of peripheral development.

It is generally desirable that parkways should be designed to provide for divided roadways with landscaped center malls. To keep the pavement width to a minimum, consideration should be given to the use of low curbs and grass shoulders. The design should provide for a flowing horizontal and vertical alignment and the development or preservation of vistas and offscapes.

When designing parkways, it is essential that the distinction between parkways and other major highways such as freeways, throughways, and expressways, be constantly kept in mind.

STATE AND NATIONAL PARKS, FORESTS, AND RECREATION AREAS

STATE PARKS

State parks are relatively spacious areas of scenic or wilderness character, which may also contain historic, archaeological, ecological, geological, or other scientific values. They are preserved as nearly as possible in their original or natural condition, and appropriate types of recreation are permitted where they will not destroy or impair the features and values to be preserved. Commercial exploitation of resources is usually prohibited.

CHARLES LEE TIL

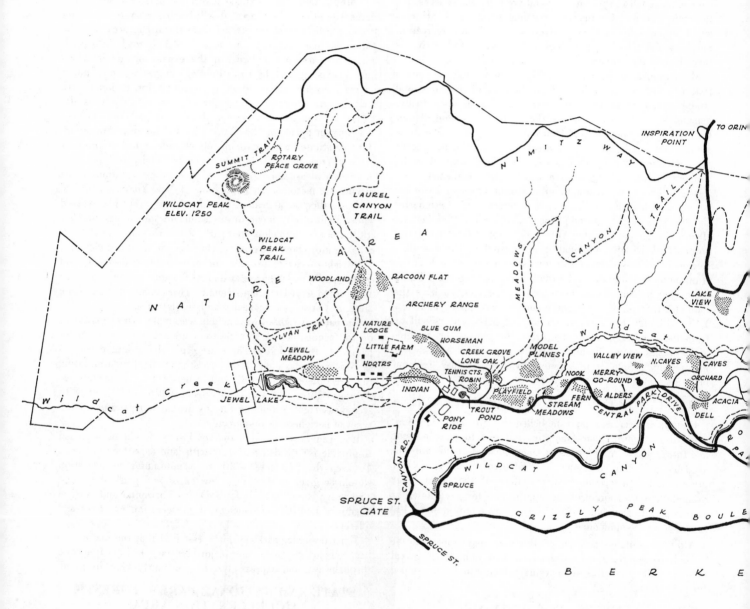

Figure 12

Tilden Regional Park, East Bay Regional Park District, Oakland, Calif.

EN   REGIONAL   PARK

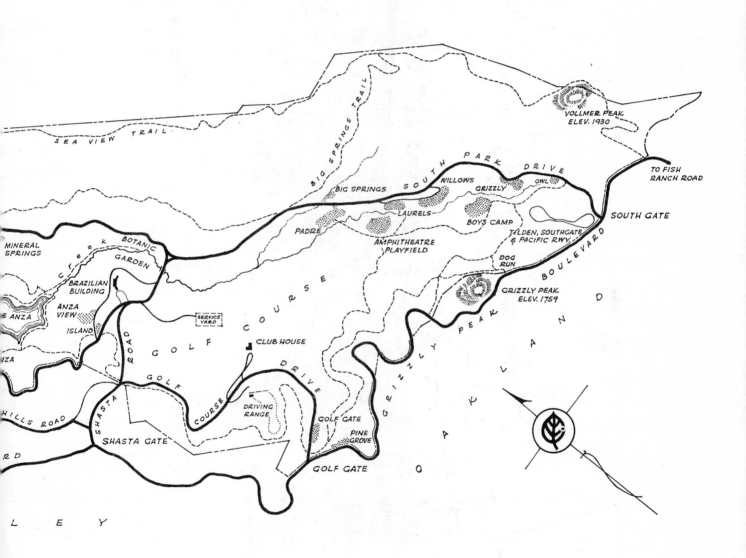

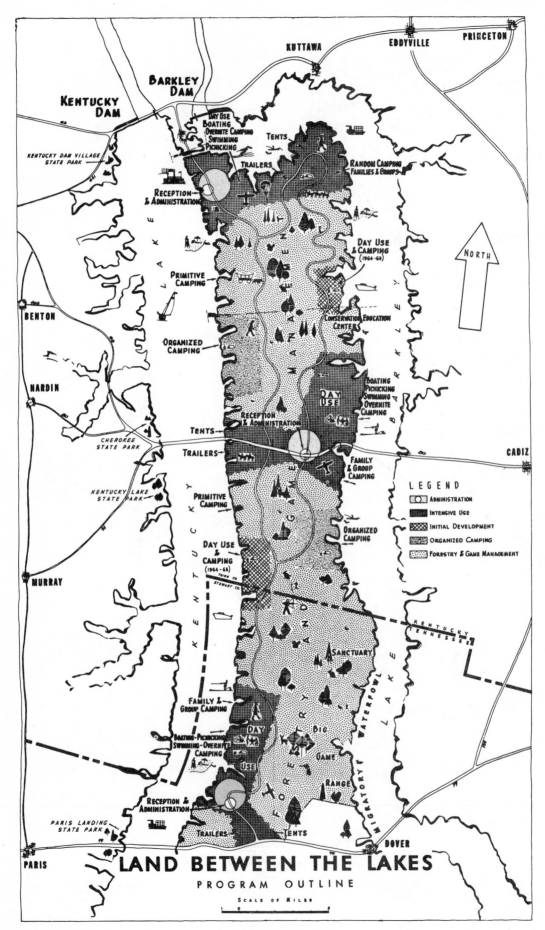

Figure 13

The historic, scientific, inspirational, and wilderness values of state parks are usually of sufficient significance to attract visitors from all sections of the state, and perhaps outside the state. Population pressures have forced many states to reevaluate their criteria in establishing state parks. The time is approaching when any large acreage reasonably close to centers of population must be considered.

State parks vary in size from a relatively few acres preserving a historic building or archaeological site to large wilderness areas containing many thousands of acres. Today, some state parks are intensively developed from a recreation standpoint and provide camping, picnicking, hiking, fishing, horseback riding, golf, winter sports, and all types of water sports. Group camps, resident camps, and nature centers are also included in some states.

STATE FORESTS

State forests are areas established and managed primarily for timber production, watershed protection, and wildlife management. However, with the increasing pressure for additional areas for recreation, this is becoming an increasingly important use where it is compatible with the primary purpose for which the forest was established.

NATIONAL PARKS

Beginning with the creation of Yellowstone National Park in 1872, the United States has established a system of national parks, monuments, historic sites, and other types of areas which include the most inspiring of the nation's scenery as well as sites distinguished for their historic importance or scientific interest. National parks are large land areas, essentially of primitive or wilderness character, which contain scenery or natural wonders so outstanding in quality that they have been designated and set aside by the Federal Government to be preserved unimpaired for the benefit, enjoyment, and inspiration of the people.

Since outstanding natural scenery is where you find it, national parks are located without regard for the relationship they may have to population concentrations. However, with improvements in transportation facilities, many national parks once considered remote are experiencing tremendous increases in visitation, and distance is becoming a less-important factor each year.

Recreation activities in national parks are generally those which can be provided with the least impairment of natural features. They may include any or all of the following: sightseeing, camping, picnicking, hiking, fishing, horseback riding, boating, swimming, natural study, and most types of winter sports.

NATIONAL FORESTS

National forests are federal lands administered under a multiple-use policy for outdoor recreation, timber, range, watershed, and fish and wildlife purposes. They encompass very large acreages although not always in a single block. They may include within their boundaries large areas set aside as primitive wilderness areas where all development is excluded except for trails and primitive camping.

To meet ever-increasing demands, the U. S. Forest Service has, in recent years, greatly accelerated its program for promoting recreational facilities in the national forests, including a tremendous expansion in camp grounds and picnic areas. In addition to fostering hunting, fishing, hiking, horseback riding, water sports, and other outdoor activities, the Forest Service also issues permits to private interests for the construction of lodges with adjoining cabins and extensive winter sports areas.

NATIONAL RECREATION AREAS

National recreation areas are spacious areas developed, managed, and conserved to provide broad public recreation opportunities. National seashores and national waterways also fall into this general category in that broad recreation opportunities are permitted. In general, this type of area is selected on the basis of providing nonurban recreational opportunities accessible to large numbers of people. Therefore, geographical distribution of these areas and their relationship to concentrations of people are paramount considerations. Exceptions are made, however, especially in the case of large artificial water impoundments, where the recreation potential is such as to warrant national status. Many of these large reservoirs are in relatively remote and inaccessible areas.

No specific criteria have been established for national recreation areas, and general policies concerning their management and operation are still being formulated. In general, they should contain a minimum of 20,000 acres. Recreation activities include all those listed under national parks and, in addition, can include hunting, areas for individual and team sports, swimming pools, resident camps and education centers, and, in some cases, golf courses.

SELECTED REFERENCES

Butler, George D., **Recreation Areas—Their Design and Equipment.** New York: Ronald Press Company, 1958.

California Public Outdoor Recreation Plan Committee, **California Public Outdoor Recreation Plan, Part II.** Sacramento: State of California, Documents Section, Printing Division, 1960.

Delamater, James B., **The Design of Outdoor Physical Education Facilities for Colleges and Schools.** New York: Bureau of Publications, Teachers College, Columbia University, 1965.

Gabrielsen, M. A., and Miles, C. M., **Sports and Recreation Facilities for School and Community.** Englewood Cliffs, N.J.: Prentice-Hall, Inc., 1958.

National Park Service, U.S. Department of the Interior, **Parks for America.** Washington, D.C.: U.S. Government Printing Office, 1964.

Taylor, James L., **School Sites—Selection, Development, and Utilization.** Washington, D.C.: U.S. Department of Health, Education, and Welfare, No. 7, 1950.

Tennessee Valley Authority, **Land Between the Lakes** (Revised Concept Statement). Knoxville, Tenn.: TVA, 1964.

Chapter 5

SELECTED OUTDOOR AREAS and FACILITIES

SPORTS AREAS AND FACILITIES

A BASIC PRINCIPLE throughout this Guide is that the program should determine the facilities required. Therefore, the facilities needed for outdoor activities will depend upon the nature of these activities. The activities, in turn, will depend upon program purposes and upon the interests, needs, and capacities of the participants.

The following criteria should be considered in selecting activities and in planning areas and facilities to accommodate these activities: (1) feasibility (capable of being used successfully in the situation); (2) seasonableness (appropriate to the season in the geographic area); (3) progression (a part of the total program and leading on to other skills or activities); and (4) variety.

This section of the chapter is aimed at acquainting the facility planner with the nature, purpose, and requirements of certain individual, dual, and team sports when they are played outdoors. In most instances, the sports listed are competitive in nature. The term "individual sport" refers to a sport in which one participant plays opposite or in competition with one opponent. The term "dual sport" refers to a sport in which two people play opposite or in competition with two opponents. In a "team sport", three or more participants play opposite or in competition with another group of three or more opponents.

AERIAL DARTS OR AERIAL TENNIS

This is a net game involving two or more players who use a shuttlecock and rackets and who follow rules similar to those for volleyball. All individuals over ten years of age may participate in this sport in an organized class in intramurals, or in a recreation program.

Courts should be 20' x 50' for singles and 26' x 50' for doubles. The lining is similar to that for tennis courts, except the serving line is 10 feet from the end line. Courts should be oriented so that play is in a north-and-south direction.

The surface is the same as for tennis or badminton courts. A multipurpose area may be utilized. On such an area, however, lines should be of an identifiable color for the activity.

ARCHERY

This sport has appeal to a sizable group in most communities. It is important to provide sufficient space in order to insure the safety and enjoyment of the participants.

The range should provide shooting distances of 100 yards, 80 yards, 60 yards, 50 yards, 40 yards, and 30 yards. For junior use, target ranges can be from 10 to 50 yards. Targets are 48 inches wide and should be at least 15 feet apart. Generally, the target line is fixed and varying shooting lines are used. The side boundaries should extend 10 yards beyond each end of the range.

In the interest of safety, additional space should be provided beyond the target. This should be free from stones and other substances which might cause the breakage of arrows falling wide of their mark. This space may be protected by an earth bunker or bales of hay and straw piled up to the top of the target.

An archery range should be fairly flat. Orientation should be north and south so that archers will not be facing the sun.

A fence enclosure is desirable but not essential. The public should be controlled in some manner, however, so that they do not walk through the range.

Storage sheds for butts and other equipment are sometimes a part of the archery range. Some storage rooms have been placed within the earth bunker behind the targets.

So that the same facility may be used by the disabled, it is desirable to design other features in an archery course. This should involve a four-foot width, ground-level, hard-surface walk for wheelchair use along the shooting lines. Another walk could extend to the target line (preferably down the center), and perhaps another walkway behind the targets to provide access for extracting arrows. Such walks reduce interference from inclement weather, increase the use of the range, and reduce maintenance costs.

FIELD ARCHERY

Field archery is a simulation of actual shooting conditions in the field. Up to 28 targets are used on the field course. The site selected for such a course should be heavily wooded and have rolling terrain. It should be fairly well isolated or in an area that can be controlled so that the general public will not walk through it.

Targets should be mounted on built-up banks or on the side of a hill. Each target has various pins (shooting positions). The farthest target is 80 yards and the nearest is 30. The targets should simulate either animals or concentric circles. The size is dependent upon the distance from the target. The scoring is similar to that for golf—the score is totaled for each target, the grand total giving the score for the complete round.

CLOUT SHOOTING

Clout shooting requires a variation in target size and arrangement. The target face is marked on the ground with white lines. The size of the target is enlarged so that one inch on a regular 48-inch target would equal 12" on the ground. The center of the bull's-eye must be indicated by a single-color flag. The range for men is 180 yards; 120 yards for women and juniors.

FLIGHT SHOOTING

The field dimensions are approximately 200 yards x 600 yards. The field should be roped off on all sides except that from which the archers shoot. A distance of not less than 10 yards behind the shooting line is reserved for the flight shooting space. Officially, the flight must be from a series of colored or numbered pegs set in the ground, usually about six feet apart.

BADMINTON

Badminton is an individual and dual sport of the net type utilizing a shuttlecock and rackets. The activity may be included in programs for class instruction and intramural and recreation competitions.

Players of all ages and both sexes may participate in the game. It is an excellent coeducational activity. Night lighting affords longer use of the courts.

The court dimensions are 44' x 20' for doubles and 44' x 17' for singles.

Posts should be set 5'1" high in the center of the sidelines. The net should be 5' high at the center. The orientation should be so that play is in a north-and-south direction. A multipurpose space may be utilized for the courts. In such instances, the courts should be in batteries of two or more, with the 1-1/2" painted or taped lines superimposed on other appropriate areas. All measurements are to the outside of lines. It is recommended that additional space of 4 or 5 feet for the sidelines and 8 feet for the ends be provided.

Entrances and exits should be accessible at each end of the court. Fencing should enclose all courts in places accessible to the public.

The surface of the outdoor court should be bituminous or concrete material, although loam or turf is satisfactory. The slope of 1/8" to 1' maximum pitch from side to side will permit quick drainage.

BASEBALL

Baseball is one of the most popular team sports in the United States and has held this distinction for over a century. It currently serves junior, interscholastic, college, and adult groups on a large scale.

The baseball field should be located away from the activities for small children. It should not overlap the football or track areas. The high school or college field requires approximately 3 acres. If an outfield fence is used, it is generally placed approximately 325' to 340' from the home plate down each foul line. The fence in straightaway center field is usually from 385' to 410' from the home plate. The diamond is 90' square.

It is important that there be a large frame backstop, with sturdy wire netting, stationed 60' behind the home plate. This backstop ought to be 20' to 25' high to help keep the ball in the field of play. Attached to each end of the backstop should be a fence at least 4' high, 60' from the nearer foul line, and extending to the outfield fence where it joins it on foul ground 60' from the foul line. Where it is necessary to put the backstop a great deal less than 60' behind the home plate, a hood which slopes 45 degrees toward the field should be installed.

Turf is the ideal surface for the unskinned areas. These areas should be of a mixture of natural earth, sand, clay, or loam. The pitcher's mound should be largely of clay and is, by rule, required to be 15" above the base line level. Fixed hollow posts should be driven beneath the bases to secure them.

A 2% slope from the pitcher's plate to the outfield facilitates drainage. Subsurface drainage in the direction of the slope is considered indispensable to good playing conditions.

Seating should parallel home-to-first and home-to-third base lines.

Junior baseball facilities are similar to baseball, except that the playing area may be reduced, depending upon the age bracket of the participants. The distances between the bases, and from the pitcher's plate to home plate may also be reduced. Some of the national organizations which sponsor junior baseball programs have modified the official baseball rules to fit the needs of the players. For example, the distance between bases is shortened as are the distances from home base to the outfield fences and from home base to the pitcher's plate. For these and other dimensions refer to the court and field dimensions and diagrams in the Appendix.

BASKETBALL

Basketball is a particularly popular, fast-running, goal-type team game which is played on a rectangular court. Ability to shoot the ball through a ring-type basket is the key skill, although a coordinated team effort is generally vital for success.

This sport is commonly played by upper elementary, junior high, and senior high school as well as college-age groups. Boys or girls may play, but with different rules.

Basketball can be played outdoors or indoors, but "varsity" games are generally played indoors. Outdoor league play is increasing, however, in urban areas. A bituminous surface is considered to be the most functional and economical for outdoor courts. Loam surfaces will not withstand the heavy play under the basket and are unusable for long periods in wet weather.

Dimensions vary with the age level: elementary, 60' x 40'; junior and senior high, 84' x 50'; and college, 94' x 50'. For the younger age group, goals 8' high are suggested. Official rules specify goals 10' high. Courts should be oriented so that play is in a north-and-south direction.

Night lighting is desirable. Lines should be permanently painted or taped in a color contrasting to the surface. A 1/8 inch drainage slope from side to side is recommended. Batteries of two or more courts are usually essential, with provision for auxiliary or practice backboards and baskets on the sides. Maximum safety can be attained by using single-pole backboards with 4 or more feet offset. Posts should be located outside of boundary lines. A 10-foot zone of unobstructed space outside the side and end lines is recommended. (See the court diagram in the Appendix.)

BOCCIE

Boccie is an individual or dual court game which is an adaptation of bowling and is especially popular with people of Italian ancestry. Boys and men of all ages play the game in numbers of two or four.

The court dimensions are 75' x 15'. It is generally preferable to play the game in the shade in an area remote from the play areas for younger children. Lighting for night use is desirable. It is recommended that an additional 3 feet at the sides and 9 feet at the ends be provided as minimum buffer areas. The surface should be level and should contain a mixture of sand and clay (loam).

CANOEING, BOATING, AND SAILING

Canoeing, boating, and sailing are activities requiring a water area. They are participated in by people of all ages and both sexes. The number competing depends upon the size of the craft and the type of event. These activities may be conducted on a lake, pond, river, reservoir, bay, or other body of water. They may be of a class, intramural, interschool, intercollegiate, or recreational nature.

The water area should have such accessory facilities as floats, docks, markers, or buoys. Various sizes of water bodies are required for different activities and events. For instance, canoe-racing courses are 100, 200, 440, and 880 yards as well as 1 mile. Sailing requires a wider body of water because the boats usually finish to windward. The different classes of sailboats, such as sunfish and sailfish, require different courses.

CRICKET

Cricket is a team sport utilizing a bat or racket and a core-centered ball. It is participated in by boys and men of all ages. Twenty-two persons participate.

The game can be played on a multipurpose field 500' to 550' in length and 450' to 520' in width. The direction of play should be north and south, perpendicular to the sun's path. The field of close-cropped turf should have good subsurface drainage, with the ground pitching away from a flat area 40' square in the center of the game area.

CROQUET

Croquet is a court game requiring only mild physical effort. Boys and girls and men and women of all ages play the game in numbers of two to eight. The activity may be included in class instruction, intramural, and recreation programs at all levels. It is usually played on turf or loam areas.

The court dimensions are 60' x 30'. Although the most desirable surface is close-cut turf, the game may be played on a multipurpose area. The surface should be level and the area of play should be defined by a boundary cord secured by six staples.

CROSS COUNTRY

Cross country is an individual or team distance-running event generally limited to male athletes. Race courses vary from 1-1/2 to 6 miles, depending upon age and level of competition. The course should not exceed 3 miles for senior-high-school participants.

The running course is usually established in areas such as large community or county parks. Turf fields, hiking trails, and golf courses provide suitable course areas, although relatively unused public areas provide the best conditions. Red, white, and blue flags posted at intersections indicate the course direction for participants.

DANCING

This activity involves hopping, running, shuffling, stepping, or walking movements to music. It may be included in classes, intramurals, and recreation programs at all levels.

Boys and girls and men and women of all ages may enjoy the activity. It is an excellent social mixer.

A sealed, smooth, hard-surface area provides the most desirable surface for dancing. Paved multipurpose areas are most frequently used for this activity.

FENCING

Fencing is an individual sport in which the two opponents use foils, epees, or sabres. It is participated in by persons of both sexes over 14 years of age. Contestants wear masks, jackets, and gloves.

A fencing bout takes place between two persons on a paved or turf strip, or on a mat. The area used can be a multipurpose area. The activity may be included in class, intramural, and recreation programs serving this age level.

The court should be oriented so that play is in a north-and-south direction. It should be well drained with a pitch no less than 1/8" per foot. The length of the court is 40' plus end zones of 6' 6-3/4"; the width is 5' 10-7/8" to 6' 6-3/4". The court should have an adequate safety zone plus space for judges, timers, and other officials. There should also be a fence or hedge around the court to prevent accidents or horseplay.

FIELD HOCKEY

Field hockey is a field-type team game in which the 11 players on each team use hockey sticks (curved-base stick with one flat surface) to propel a small white leather-covered ball. The game is played primarily by girls and women at the high-school and college age levels.

The game may be played on a multipurpose turf or loam field 100 yards long and from 50 to 60 yards wide; 85 yards x 45 yards for younger players. The field is marked with two-inch white lines. On the larger-size field, the lines should divide the length of the field into four equal parts 25 yards apart. Where fields are smaller, the 25-yard lines should be 25 yards from the goal lines, the 5-yard lines 5 yards from the sidelines, and the striking circles should be regulation size. For experienced players, the division lines need only to be extended seven yards from the sideline. For men, the alleys should be 7 yards wide instead of 5. All dimensions are inside the lines. The goal posts should be 2" x 3" and painted white. Goal posts are located on the center of the goal line, 12 feet apart. The posts are joined by a cross bar 7 feet above the ground.

Grading, surfacing, drainage, and orientation are the same as for the football field described in the paragraphs to follow.

FOOTBALL

Football is a highly competitive contact team sport played with an inflated ball on a field 360' x 160' or smaller, depending on the number of players on a team (6, 8, or 11). Each player is uniformed with protective equipment.

The goal posts are 18' 6" apart and 20' high. The crossbar is 10' above the ground.

Lines should be marked with a material which is not injurious to the eyes or skin. No lime or caustic material of any kind may be used. Measurements are from the inside edges of the boundary lines.

Flags with flexible shafts should be installed at each intersection of the sidelines and goal lines, and on the end lines 53' 4" toward the goal posts from the intersections of the sidelines and end lines. The field should be crowned down the center, sloping 1/4" per foot toward the sidelines.

The junior football game is an example of a team game that has been adapted from regulation football for use by young boys between 11 and 16. There are usually 6, 8, or 11 players on a team. The game is usually played on a multipurpose field. Junior football may be included in a class, intramural, or recreation program.

The field should be oriented so that play is in a north-and-south direction. The field should have the same construction features as a regulation football field, including team benches, goal posts, and a scoreboard.

HANDBALL (ONE-WALL)

Handball is a fast physical activity played by persons of both sexes over 14 years of age. The game is played with a hard rubber ball which is stroked against the wall by the palm of a player's hand. It may be played by two or four players on a smooth concrete or bituminous surface 20' x 40' with a wall 20' high.

Courts may be constructed so as to allow for one court on each side of the wall. At least 6' of clear space should be provided beyond the side and end lines. All lines are 1-1/2" wide. The courts may be erected near or between batteries of tennis courts to permit tennis players to use the walls as batter boards.

Courts should be pitched away from the wall with a grade of

1/8″ per foot. The wall is 8″ to 12″ thick and is generally constructed of reinforced concrete.

HORSESHOES

The game is of individual or dual type requiring the skillful tossing of "horseshoes." It may be included in programs for class instruction, intramurals and other competitions, and recreation. Persons of both sexes and nearly all ages may participate in the game, both during the day and in the evening where night lighting is provided.

Horseshoe courts require a space 60′ long and as wide as is necessary to accommodate pitching stations 10′ apart and leave 10′ on each side of the total area. The area should be protected by a fence or low pipe rail. If spectator benches are provided at the ends, a protective fence will be required.

The courts should be level and the pegs placed at the proper angle for championship play. The stakes should be 1″ in diameter and 3′ long, should extend 14″ above the top of the box, and each should incline 3″ toward the other. They should be 40′ apart for men and 30′ for women and for boys under 16 years of age. A surfaced walkway between stakes is desirable. The courts should be oriented so that play is in a north-and-south direction.

LACROSSE

Lacrosse is an increasingly popular team sport requiring agility and skill. It is played on a multipurpose turf or loam field by persons of both sexes.

The inside dimensions of the field for men are 330′ x 210′. There are no definite boundaries, but goals must be placed not less than 270′ nor more than 330′ apart. The minimum width is 150′.

The goals lie on the 15-yard lines at each end of the field. These goals consist of two square posts 6′ apart and joined at the top by a rigid crossbar which is seven feet (6′ for women) above the ground (all inside dimensions). The posts are 2″ x 2″ wood painted white. Netting of not more than 1-1/2″ mesh must be attached to the posts and crossbar and to a point 7′ (6′ for women) behind the center of the goal. The net is firmly pegged to the ground. A line called the goal line is drawn from post to post.

Orientation, surface, and grading are the same as given earlier for football. A 5 or 6-foot barrier fence at least 10′ outside the end and sidelines is recommended.

LAWN BOWLING

Lawn bowling is a popular sport for men and women of all ages. Little physical effort is required, but skill is essential to properly roll a bowl to the target jack.

The game is played on a 120′ x 120′ bent-grass green, or loam surface. The green, which should be located in a quiet section of the recreation area, is divided into eight 14′ x 11′ rinks. Each rink will accommodate two or four players.

The green is surrounded by a depressed ditch or wall with a width of 10″ to 15″ and a depth of 2″ to 4″. A bank at least 18″ high should be constructed around the green. The ditch and bank are necessary to stop overthrow bowls.

Play should be rotated to avoid excess wearing of the turf on any two sides.

OBSTACLE COURSE

The obstacle course contains a series of obstacles designed to test individual skill, strength, and agility. The course may be used by persons of both sexes, with from one to three persons participating.

Since turf would wear and cause excessive maintenance, the course is constructed with an adequately-drained surface of pavement, clay, or sand. The course should be contained on a fenced or buffered area to prevent horseplay and to provide control and safety. It should have two entrances or exits.

The course should include fences, a tunnel, parallel bars, balance beams, and wood, brick, or concrete panel walls. The total course should be located in or adjacent to the apparatus area.

PADDLE TENNIS

Paddle tennis is a fast-moving sport played by two or four players.

The rules and regulations are similar to those for tennis, except that the court is reduced to 44′ x 20′ (doubles) and 44′ x 16′ (singles). It is recommended that an additional 6′ at the sides and 8′ at the ends be provided as buffer areas.

Officially, paddle tennis should be played on a wooden platform, but it is commonly played on a bituminous, concrete, or loam surface in neighborhood park-school or recreation facilities.

The net height is 3′ 1″ at the posts and 2′ 10″ at the center. Net posts may be the same as those used for badminton, volleyball, and deck tennis.

QUOITS

Quoits is an individual or dual game participated in by persons of both sexes over 10 years of age. It is an excellent coeducational activity. Two or four persons throw a quoit (a circular metal ring 4″ in diameter, 2-1/2″ wide, and flat on one side) toward flat-headed pins, set flush with the ground in a ring 4′ in diameter at each end of the court. Calipers are used to measure the distance from quoit to pin.

The game is played outdoors on a paved or turf area. For women and children, the court dimensions are 12′ x 44′ and the pitching distance between pins (stakes) should be 30′. For men, the stakes should be 54′ apart in a court space of 25′ x 80′. The court should be oriented so that play is in a north-and-south direction in order that the players' line of sight is away from the sun's path.

The court should be on a well drained sanded or turf area pitched at least 1/8″ per foot. The circular ring should be of stiff clay at least 6″ deep. Wood foul lines should be perpendicular to the line of play, bisecting the circular ring. The entire court should be fenced or shrubbed in with low border plantings to prevent people from cutting through the court area and for control and supervision purposes. Lighting could be provided for night play.

ROLLER SKATING

This is an individual or group activity on skates. It is informally enjoyed by persons of both sexes and all ages in intramural and recreation programs during the entire year.

Roller skating may be permitted on a multipurpose area, or on sidewalks and streets under proper safety controls. A rink may be built or rented. If a rink is built, it is suggested that the area be 100′ x 200′. A track for speed skating can encircle the figure or leisure-skating area. The track should be banked at the curves and the interior should be slightly pitched for drainage. Boundaries of the track should be defined with flags, wooden blocks, or pylons. Each turn should be marked with pylons. The starting and finish lines should be indicated. The rink should be oriented so that skaters travel in a north-and-south direction.

The surface should be smooth wood (wide) or concrete sprinkled with rosin or a similar substance. If the areas for skating are speed rinks or multipurpose areas, there should be a fence around the area for safety and control.

ROQUE

Roque is a refined mallet-and-ball type of game played by persons of both sexes from teen-agers to older adults. Play is on either a paved or clay court area. Most neighborhood and community park-schools and colleges utilize the activity for class instruction, intramurals, and recreation.

The court should be 60' x 30' in size and should be smooth, flat, and level. The surface should be of sand-clay mixture or asphalt sprinkled with fine sand. It should be pitched toward the corners to a drainage outlet in the border. This border should be of wood or concrete with an iron rim for better re-bound deflection and should be not less than 5" high. A painted or taped boundary line should be 28" inside the curb. Steel arches are set into concrete blocks below the surface.

The facility should be placed in the court games area, and unless specific local conditions demand more, only one should be constructed.

ROWING

Rowing is an individual, dual, or team activity performed on a water course in sculls, kayaks, or shells. The course may be on a lake, river, or bay. Rowing is a class, recreational, and competitive activity found primarily at the community park-school and college levels.

The shells are four and eight-oared and the sculls are single or pair-oared. The course should run as close to a north-south axis as possible to prevent the sun from interfering with the coxswain's or oarsmen's functions. However, this orientation does interfere with spectator viewing.

The lanes are marked with targets at the end of the course, either on shore or in anchored rowboats. The shells are started together from separate anchored stake-boats on the starting line. The limits of the course are marked by log booms or buoys to prevent passing boats from disturbing it.

SHUFFLEBOARD

Shuffleboard is a popular year-round activity for all age groups of both sexes. It is played on a smooth concrete, terrazzo, or sealed asphalt surface.

The game is played by pushing discs with a cue to a point-numbered target. The playing area is 52' x 6'. Authorities recom-mend an additional two feet on each end and six feet at each side. It is most economical to construct the courts in batteries of three, with depressed walkways between courts to facilitate drainage.

Shuffleboard may be played by two or four players. It is desirable to locate the courts in a relatively quiet area with some shade. Enjoyment will be increased with the installation of a canopy-type roof at each end. Night lighting is also feasible.

SMALL GAMES

The small games include such activities as marbles, hopscotch, and circle games. They are conducted for children of both sexes in the age range of 5 to 16. The number competing depends upon the quality of the areas. The entire small-games area can be utilized as a multipurpose area. The small-games space is found primarily at the neighborhood park-school and community park-school levels and may be utilized for both class instruction and recreation programs.

The small-games area should be a minimum of 25' x 25'. It should be adjacent to the crafts-and-apparatus area. The area should be well drained and should be surrounded by a fence or shrubbery barrier for maximum safety and control. The surface should be of sandy loam, asphalt, or concrete pavement.

SOCCER

Soccer is a fast-moving team game in which players utilize the head and feet to propel the ball. It may be played in classes and in interscholastic, intercollegiate, intramural, and other forms of recreational competition.

Persons of both sexes participate from the age of 12. There are 11 players on a team. The object is to kick or "head" the ball through an opponent's goal, which is protected by a "goalie" who may use his hands.

The field dimensions are 360' x 240' for boys and men, 300' x 180' for college women, and 240' x 120' for high-school girls. The field should be oriented so that play is in a north-and-south direction. White side and end lines should be 2" wide. If lime is used, it should be thoroughly slaked. All dimensions are inside the line measurements. The distance between goal posts is 24' inside measurement. The height of the crossbar is 8' measured to its lower edges. Stock posts 4" x 5" or 5" x 5", painted white, are specified for the goal posts.

The surface should be level turf or loam. Lighting for night use is desirable where high interest exists.

SOFTBALL

Softball is a team game played on turf and/or skinned fields. It appeals to both sexes and practically all age groups. An area of 275' x 275' is generally specified.

The game is very similar to baseball, but the field space needed is generally smaller. For men, the distance between bases is 60' and the pitcher's plate is 46' from the apex of the home plate. For girls and women, the distance between bases is 45' and the pitcher's plate is 38' from the back end of the home plate.

The 12-inch ball is larger than a baseball but is equally hard. The pitcher must pitch with an underhand motion. Nine players are on each team. A hooded backstop is commonly installed for recreation and intramural-type league play.

SLOW-PITCH SOFTBALL

Slow-pitch softball is a modified version of softball geared to players with fewer or lost skills. The ball is bigger (16" in circumference for boys, 14" for girls) and the pitcher must hurl the ball in a high arch.

The bases are 50' apart for men and 45' apart for girls and women. The pitching distance is 35'.

SPEEDBALL

Speedball is a vigorous team sport played on an area 160' x 300'. The game combines the skills of soccer and basket-ball. It requires goal posts, end zones, and a soccer ball.

The game is played by persons of both sexes from the age of 12. However, it is not played coeducationally. The game is participated in by 7 or 9 players on a team. This sport is used as a class, intramural, recreational, and competitive activity.

The size of the field should be reduced for young players and for intramural activities. A multipurpose field or soccer field can be adapted to the game. Markings should be laid out on the field with noncaustic powder or tape. It is important that the field be well drained.

TENNIS

Tennis is a very popular sport among most age groups, and most communities either have tennis courts or are considering them for future construction.

SIZE AND SOPE

The minimum size of the area required for constructing a tennis court is 60' x 120'. When a battery of courts is to be developed, a minimum distance of 10' and a maximum of 12' should be allowed between courts. A minimum of 12' and a maximum of 15' should be allowed from the sideline of a court, or battery of courts, to the edge of the court surface. A distance of 21' should be allowed from the base line to the rear of the court surface. When courts are enclosed by a fence, these distances should be allowed between the court lines and the fence. The court surface should then be extended 6" beyond the fence to simplify maintenance. (See diagram in the Appendix for playing-area dimensions.)

SITE SELECTION

Tennis courts should be located in a relatively flat area. They should also be in an area which provides protection from the prevailing breezes. When this is not possible, protection may have to be provided by the use of plant material, tarpaulins, nettings, or other types of wind screens.

ORIENTATION

Courts should be oriented so that play is in a north-and-south direction unless they are to be used strictly for night play.

DRAINAGE

Surface and subsurface drainage are of prime importance in the construction of tennis courts. The various acceptable methods of surface drainage, in order of preference, are as follows:

- Sloping from side to side or diagonally
- Sloping from one end (rear of court) to the other
- Sloping from center line to rear of courts
- Sloping from rear of courts to center (toward net)

Each of these drainage methods has its own advantages and disadvantages, but the main objective is to shed the water and still provide the players with a playable surface.

The percentage of slope of the courts is dependent upon the type of surfacing to be used. The ideal court is level. This can only be accomplished by building the court inside a building, or by using such surfaces as crushed chips or lawn with excellent subsurface drainage. The following are recommended percentages of slope for the various types of tennis-court surfaces:

Type of Surface	Minimum % Slope	Maximum % Slope
Concrete	0.5%	1.0%
Bituminous (various types)	1.0%	1.5%
Clay	0.75%	1.0%
Crushed Materials	0.75%	1.0%
Lawn	0.75%	1.0%

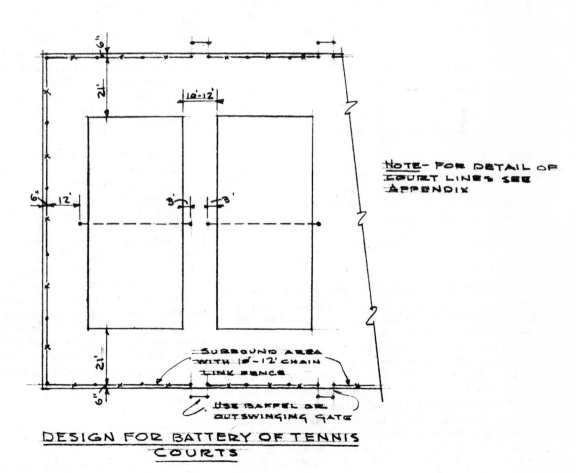

DESIGN FOR BATTERY OF TENNIS COURTS

Figure 14
Design for Battery of Tennis Courts

SURFACING

There are two basic types of surfacing to be considered for tennis courts: porous and nonporous. Many different kinds of materials are available for each of these types of surfacing.

Porous Surfacing

This type of surfacing includes clay, lawn, and crushed materials. No matter which of these surfaces is used, there is a constant maintenance problem throughout the season.

Nonporous Surfacing

This type of surfacing includes concrete and the various bituminous combination surfaces. Most nonporous surfaces provide lower maintenance costs and can usually be colored if desired.

FINANCING

It is more economical to build a battery of tennis courts than an individual court. Some nonporous-surfaced courts may be more costly at the time of construction, but this is counteracted by the low maintenance costs.

FENCING

The most common material used for the fencing of tennis courts is chain-link fabric. This fencing should have a minimum height of 12' along the rear lines of the courts and a minimum height of 10' on the sides.

If possible, the courts should be entirely enclosed by fencing. Where cost is a major factor, the fencing may be placed along the rear of the courts, with a 20-foot wing return on the sides. The fence fabric should be placed on the inside of the fence posts.

SPECIAL CONSTRUCTION FEATURES

The lighting of tennis courts is dependent upon the popularity of the activity within the geographic location. Practice boards (batter boards) may be included in tennis courts for practice and instructional purposes when finances permit.

MULTIPURPOSE

Should it be desirable to adapt tennis courts for multipurpose uses, consideration of the necessary construction changes should be made prior to court construction. Later revisions may be prohibitively high in cost.

TETHERBALL

Tetherball is an individual or dual game utilizing a ball and paddles. It is played separately or coeducationally by boys and girls 8 through 18 years of age. The game is played as a class, intramural, and recreational activity.

The court contains a 10-foot upright wooden pole 7-1/2" in circumference at the ground and tapering to the top. A 2-inch black line is painted on it 6' from the ground. A cord with a covered tennis ball attached hangs from the top of the pole to 2-1/2' from the ground. The pole is placed in the center of an area approximately 25' in diameter. There is no particular orientation of the court. The space should, however, be provided adjacent to other court facilities. The court should be of concrete or macadam pitched at least 1/8" per foot for adequate drainage. The play lines should be painted or taped on the surfacing. The court should be shrubbed or fenced in to provide maximum safety and control.

TOUCH FOOTBALL

Touch football is a game in which the player touches rather than tackles an opponent. The game involves more passing and outside running than football since all players are eligible to receive a pass.

A team consists of six or nine players. Any number of players from 4 to 11 may be used, however, by mutual consent. It is a game played mostly by the male sex in classes, intramurals, and recreation programs on the community park-school and college levels.

The field area is the same as for regular football, but yard stripes are drawn 10 yards apart. The field may be made shorter for class play if space is limited.

TRACK AND FIELD

Track and field activities include events in which an individual has an opportunity to perfect his skills. Athletes of both sexes participate.

Track events are generally conducted on a quarter-mile running track with a minimum straightaway of 140 yards to a maximum of 240 yards. The individual running events include dashes, distance events, and hurdles (low and high). In addition to the individual running events, there are relay events in which there are four runners on a team.

The track, the surface of which is composed of cinders or synthetic material, should be flat. Track rules require that there be a two-inch solid curb constructed around the interior of the track. This curb may be made of wood, concrete, asphalt, or steel. Inclination of the track should be limited to the ratio of 1:100 laterally and 1:1,000 in the running direction (for field events, in the jumping or throwing direction). Most tracks are constructed so that lateral inclination is toward the inside curb, where small scuppers permit the water to drain from the track to the edge of the infield.

The track should contain at least 6 lanes. These lanes should be at least 36" wide, but a width of 42" to 48" is preferred. They should be marked with materials not injurious to the eyes or skin.

Field events which should be considered in planning track and field areas and facilities are: road walk; steeplechase; high, broad, and triple jump events; discus; shot-put; javelin; and pole vault. A raised landing platform covered with huge chunks of foam rubber is generally placed over the pole-vault landing pit so that the competitor does not have so far to fall when landing. In the high-jump pit, this same safety device is sometimes used, with the landing platform being placed closer to the landing pit.

For field events in which the competitors must land in a pit, the landing area must be filled with sawdust or other soft material to protect the participants. The landing pit for the running broad jump and triple jump must have a minimum width of 9' and a minimum length of 15'. The scratch line for the broad jump is approximately 12' from the nearer edge of the landing pit. For the triple jump, the scratch line should be placed at least 36' from the near edge of the landing pit. The high-jump and pole-vault landing pit(s) must be not less than 16' wide and 12' long.

VOLLEYBALL

Volleyball is a team game utilizing the hands to propel the ball over a net. The game may be played in class, intramural, interscholastic, intercollegiate, and recreation competition.

Persons of both sexes over ten years of age may participate.

Twelve people are needed to play a game. It is an excellent coeducational activity.

The court is 60' x 30' in size (outside dimensions) and should be oriented so that play is in a north-and-south direction. It may be located on a multipurpose macadam or clay-loam surfaced area. The surface should be sloped from sideline to sideline, allowing 1/8" per foot for drainage. Two or more courts should be planned according to anticipated needs.

SELECTED REFERENCES

American Association for Health, Physical Education, and Recreation, **Physical Education for High School Students.** Washington, D.C.: The Association, 1201 Sixteenth St., N.W., 1960.

Armbruster, David A.; Irwin, Leslie W.; and Musker, Frank F.; **Basic Skills in Sports for Men and Women.** St. Louis: The C. V. Mosby Co., 1963.

Butler, George D., **Recreation Areas.** New York: Ronald Press Co., 1938.

Construction and Maintenance of Tennis Courts. New York: U.S. Lawn Tennis Association, 120 Broadway.

Division for Girls' and Women's Sports, **Field Hockey—Lacrosse Guide.** Washington, D.C.: American Association for Health, Physical Education, and Recreation, 1201 Sixteenth St., N.W., 1964.

————, **Soccer-Speedball Guide.** Washington, D.C.: AAHPER, 1964.

————, **Tennis-Badminton Guide.** Washington, D.C.: AAHPER, 1964.

————, **Volleyball Guide.** Washington, D.C.: AAHPER, 1963.

Donnelly, Richard J.; Helms, William G.; and Mitchell, Elmer D.; **Active Games and Contests.** New York: Ronald Press Co., 1958.

Gabrielsen, M. Alexander, and Miles, Caswell M., **Sports and Recreation Facilities for School and Community.** Englewood Cliffs, N.J.: Prentice-Hall, Inc., 1958.

National Collegiate Athletic Association, **Soccer Guide.** New York: National Collegiate Athletic Bureau, 1964.

Scott, Harry A., and Westkaemper, Richard B., **From Program to Facilities in Physical Education.** New York: Harper and Brothers, 1958.

The Athletic Institute, **Badminton.** Color-Sound 35mm. Film Kit, Instructor's Guide, and Student Handbook. Chicago, Ill.: The Institute, 805 Merchandise Mart, 1963.

————, **Baseball.** Color-Sound 35mm. Film Kit, Instructor's Guide, and Student Handbook. Chicago, Ill.: The Institute, 1948.

————, **Basketball.** Color-Sound 35mm. Film Kit, Instructor's Guide, and Student Handbook. Chicago, Ill.: The Institute, 1958.

————, **Fencing.** Color-Sound 35mm. Film Kit, Instructor's Guide, and Student Handbook. Chicago, Ill.: The Institute, 1959.

————, **Field Hockey.** Color-Sound 35mm. Film Kit, Instructor's Guide, and Student Handbook. Chicago, Ill.: The Institute, 1964.

————, **Soccer.** Color-Sound 35mm. Film Kit, Instructor's Guide, and Student Handbook. Chicago, Ill.: The Institute, 1960.

————, **Softball.** Color-Sound 35mm. Film Kit, Instructor's Guide, and Student Handbook. Chicago, Ill.: The Institute, 1952.

————, **Tennis.** Color-Sound 35mm. Film Kit, Instructor's Guide, and Student Handbook. Chicago, Ill.: The Institute, 1962.

————, **Track & Field.** Color-Sound 35mm. Film Kit, Instructor's Guide, and Student Handbook. Chicago, Ill.: The Institute, 1958.

————, **Volleyball.** Color-Sound 35mm. Film Kit, Instructor's Guide, and Student Handbook. Chicago, Ill.: The Institute, 1959.

————, **Intramurals For Elementary School Children.** Chicago, Ill.: The Institute, 1964.

————, **Intramurals for the Junior High School.** Chicago, Ill.: The Institute, 1964.

————, **Intramurals for the Senior High School.** Chicago, Ill.: The Institute, 1964.

Tournament Rules of the National Archery Association of the U.S. Chicago: The Association, 23 E. Jackson Blvd.

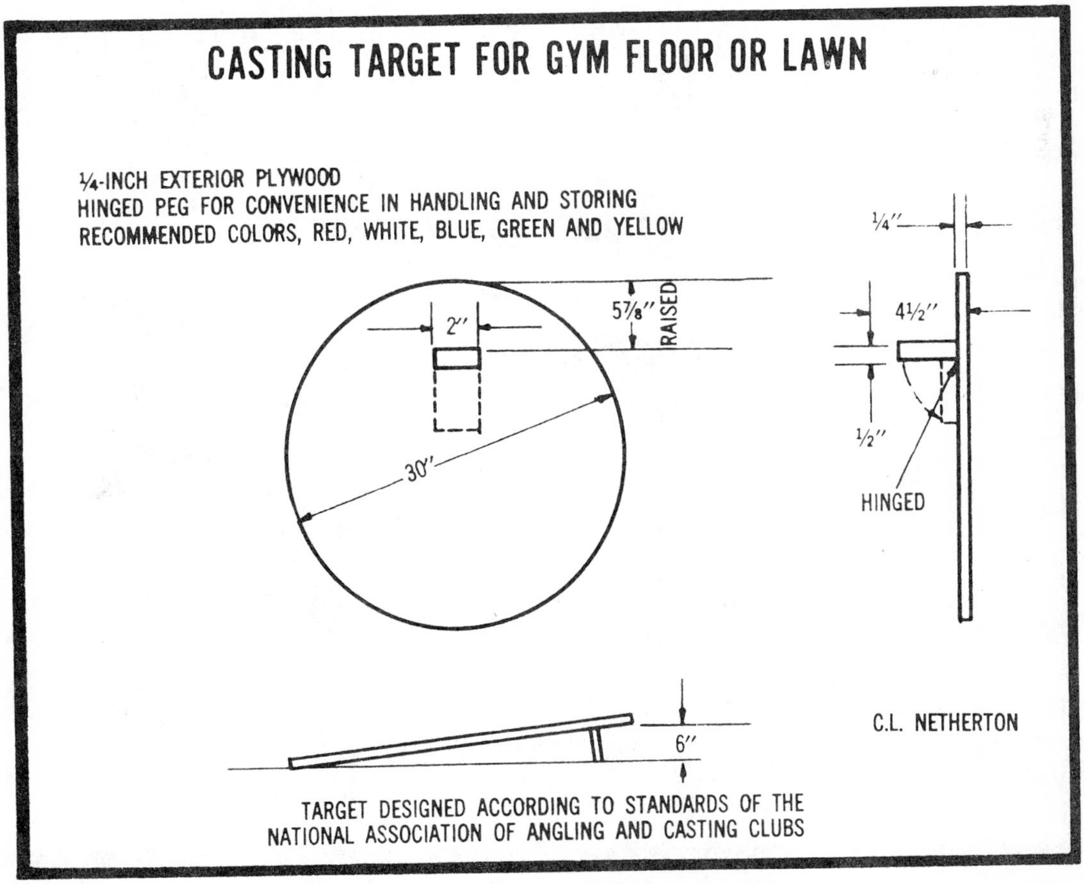

Figure 15
Casting Target for Gym Floor or Lawn

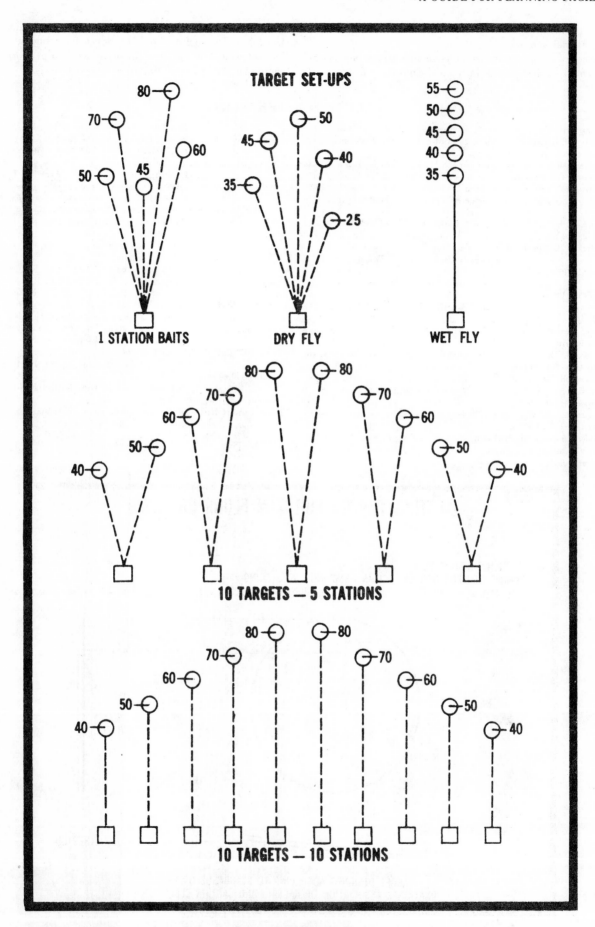

Figure 16
Area Arrangements for Various Types of Casting

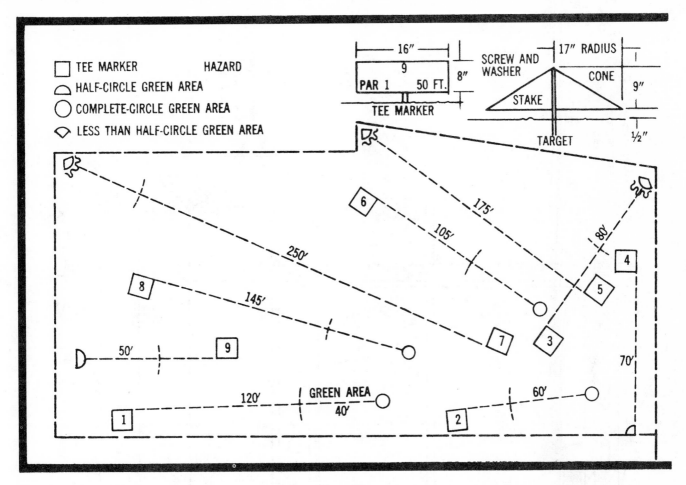

Figure 17
The Plug Golf Course

SPECIAL AREAS AND FACILITIES

ANGLING AND CASTING AREAS

Casting is simulated rod-and-reel fishing. This activity may be a part of the regular physical education, after-school, intramural, recreation, adult education, or club activity program. Practice casting on a playing field or in a gymnasium is possible the year round. If a pond or lake is nearby, a beach or dock affords an excellent facility for the casting program.

In order to teach all phases of the activity, an area 300' x 100' is desirable. A football, soccer, hockey, or lacrosse field is ideal for class instruction. Smaller areas can also be utilized. Accuracy-type casting may be done in a classroom-size facility, while the distance and game-type activities require greater space areas.

Casting targets, which are 30" in diameter, are easily constructed and can be an excellent project for any school industrial arts woodshop program. It is recommended that at least ten targets be made. Others can be added as the program expands. Targets for use on the water are also 30" in diameter and are made of hollow metal tubing. They float and can be easily anchored.

In order to eliminate the problem of fouled rods, lines, and plugs for class instruction, a gear box is recommended. This will hold several ordinary assembled bait and spinning rods and partially-assembled longer fly, surf-casting, and spinning equipment. The box can be carried to the instructional area and, with the utilization of two pieces of wood 1" x 2" and one piece of 1" x 4", a rack for rods is available.

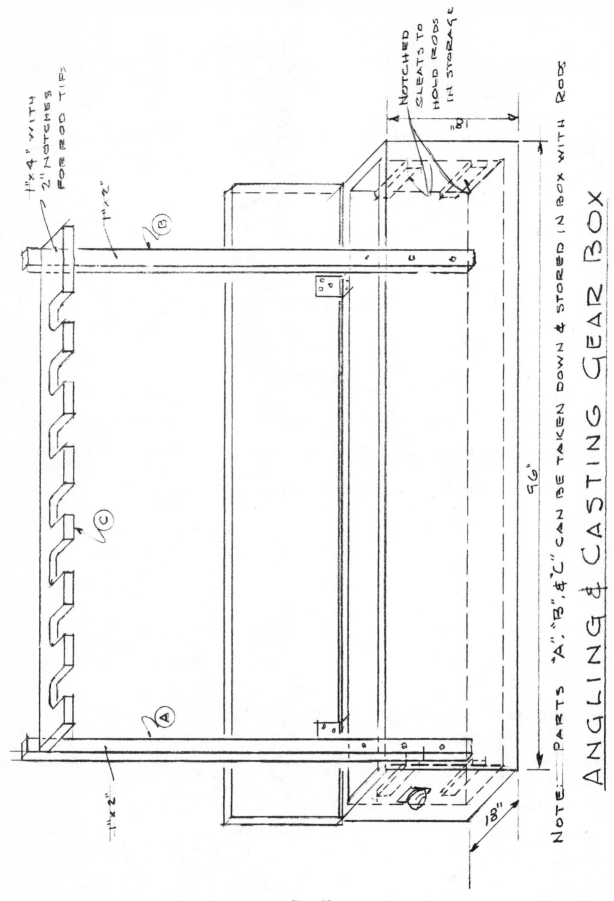

Figure 18
Angling and Casting Gear Box

BICYCLE PATHS

Cycling is becoming an increasingly popular form of recreation for all age groups, especially since the development of geared bicycles, which makes it possible to cycle over moderately rolling terrain without too much effort. In the larger community, citywide, district and regional parks, consideration should be given to providing separate bicycle paths. In addition to making possible a pleasant experience, these paths also serve to separate bicycle riders from vehicle and pedestrian traffic.

Bicycle paths can meander through wooded areas, skirt the edges of open areas, and may, in many instances, parallel existing roadways or walks where it is possible to provide a suitable median or buffer strip. The paths do not need to be highly engineered and can generally follow closely the existing ground surfaces so as to reduce grading to a minimum. Paths should be a minimum of 6' in width, hard surfaced, and, on cut or fill sections, provided with a minimum shoulder of 12". Bicycle stands should be provided adjacent to buildings or other points of interest or activity.

In larger parks, and especially those somewhat distant from urban areas, rental facilities are not only desirable, but also provide a source of income for the concessionaire or park operating authority. Facilities need be no more than a large stand to which cycles not in use can be securely chained or locked.

BRIDLE PATHS

Horseback riding is popular with all age groups, but is generally restricted to the larger park areas because of space requirements. Riding trails are usually a minimum of 10' in width to permit riders going in opposite directions to pass in safety. Except in very steep hillside terrain, very little is required in the way of construction. Clearing, a small amount of leveling, removal of large rocks and boulders, and trimming or removal of low-hanging tree limbs constitute the major items. Most small streams can be forded, but an occasional bridge may be required as well as cross drainage on steep gradients. No special surfacing is required except that a gravel base may be needed in wet or boggy areas that cannot be avoided. Tanbark, cinders, and other materials are also used frequently on heavily used trails and in areas of concentrated use around hitching racks and in riding rings.

Stables and adjoining facilities, such as feed racks, holding corrals, riding rings, and hitching racks, should be located a minimum of 500' from the nearest public-use area because of the fly-and-odor problem. The size of these facilities will, of course, depend on the number of horses being used in the operation. However, the stable will ordinarily contain a limited number of horse stalls, a feed-storage room, a tack room, a small office, and toilet facilities for men and women. A fenced enclosure, commonly called a holding corral or paddock, into which the horses can be turned at the end of the day is required. A surfaced riding ring, sometimes encircled with a rail fence, is frequently provided for training novices in the fundamentals of riding.

GARDENS

Gardens of various kinds serve a definite leisure-time function in a park system. They should be developed to provide for visual, cultural, and educational equipment.

FORMAL GARDENS

Formal gardens are designed to create certain accent points and to play up certain features. They are laid out in a sym-

metrical or asymmetrical manner. A formal garden may be composed entirely of one type of plant (such as roses), may consist of various types of assorted plant materials, or may be made up of a series of individual gardens comprised of single types of plant units. Features such as a water fountain and statuary can be incorporated into the design.

INFORMAL GARDENS

Informal gardens should have long, sweeping lawn areas to serve as a setting for plants and flower beds. Plants may include large specimen trees, flowering trees, shrubs, and vines. The flower borders can be of varied plants.

All the plants should be of interest to the average homeowner and should be useful in helping him select plants for his own yard. Attempts should be made to keep abreast of the latest introductions and to display those types of plants which are hardy to the particular region in which the garden is located. This aspect of planting for the homeowner should be stressed in both formal and informal gardens, and occasional demonstrations of plant cultural practices should be provided.

NATURALISTIC AND NATIVE GARDENS

Naturalistic and native, or wildflower, gardens are established in a wilderness location where the plants native to the region can be assembled in one area so they are easily accessible to the citizens. This may require an area of varied topography—lowlands, highlands, and prairies—and also an area that has varied soil conditions—all the way from alkaline to acid—to accommodate the various types of plants.

GOLF COURSES

The design, construction, operation, and maintenance of golf courses is too vast a subject to be covered in detail in this publication. The information herein is presented to introduce the reader to the basic requirements for the successful development of golf-course facilities.

Existing topography, vegetation, soil conditions, water courses, and property outline will dictate the amount of land required for a golf course. The following space requirements generally apply:
- Standard 18-hole golf course—120 to 160 acres
- Standard 9-hole golf course—70 to 90 acres
- 9-hole par-3 golf course—45 to 60 acres (including one or two par-4 holes)

These areas are normally sufficient to include a practice putting green, a practice driving range, the clubhouse area, and parking facilities.

The practice putting green should be equal in size to the largest putting surface on the course. Putting surfaces may vary in size from 3,000 to 15,000 square feet.

Where possible, fairways should be oriented in a north-south direction. Fairways with a line of play into the northwest are especially bad and should be avoided wherever possible.

The clubhouse is the control center for the golf course. Its primary function is to serve as the place where golfers register daily and pay fees for the use of the golf facilities. It is necessary that the clubhouse be located as near as possible to the 1st and 10th tees, the 9th and 18th greens, the practice putting green, and the tee for the practice driving range. The size of the clubhouse and the services it provides may vary with local conditions and intensity of use. The services may include various combinations of the following:
- Locker rooms
- Shower rooms

- Toilet facilities
- Dining room or snack bar
- Lounge
- Manager's office
- Pro shop (where golf merchandise may be purchased)
- Caddy-cart storage room
- Heating unit
- Maintenance storage room

Careful attention should be given to the location of the pro shop so that maximum supervision can be given all clubhouse and course activities.

In order to insure the maximum orderly use of the course, a "starter" must be provided to verify the golfers' registration on the course and to advise them when to tee-off. A shelter separate from the clubhouse is often provided for the starter. If such provision is made, it must necessarily be located immediately adjacent to the 1st and 10th tees.

MARINAS

America abounds in waterways. The myriad inland lakes, the rivers and streams, the vast Great Lakes, and the thousands of miles of coastline serve to invite America's citizens to take advantage of this natural resource. In increasingly greater numbers, people are finding boating to be a recreational outlet that captures a greater share of their attention than ever before. Today boating commands more of the recreation dollar than baseball, fishing, golf, or any other single recreation activity. In 1962, over 37,000,000 persons utilized over 8,000,000 boats. By 1980, the participation in recreational boating is projected to exceed 70,000,000. The magnitude of these and other figures related to boating brings into sharp focus the need for efficient, realistic, and functional planning for facilities to accommodate the present needs and the future growth that this recreational interest will precipitate.

The launching, mooring, and storage of yachts and rowboats are the function of a marina in a community—that waterfront area, publicly or privately owned and managed, that will serve the needs of the recreational-boat owner.

In planning the construction of a marina, certain principles can be used for guidance. Later in this chapter, certain types of marinas that have peculiar needs and characteristics will be surveyed. All marinas, however, are subject to the principles outlined in the pages to follow.

SIZE AND SCOPE

The size and scope of a marina will vary, depending on the requirements of the area involved. It is suggested that knowledgeable and experienced personnel be engaged to conduct a study of the number, types, and sizes of existing boats in the area, the number and size of existing berthing facilities, and the condition of such existing facilities. The survey should also include the potential population growth in the community and surrounding area to determine the future boat ownership. An accurate and comprehensive evaluation of such a study is the first step in planning a marina.

The data in the foregoing study will determine the next important consideration in laying out a marina: that of choosing the correct number of slips of each size that will be required. In most marinas, boats of many sizes will be served and efficient planning will foresee the necessary number of slips to accommodate boats under 18 feet long, those from 18 to 24 feet long, those from 25 to 36 feet long, and so on. The determination of the number and size of slips should be based on the needs of the community to be served.

SITE SELECTION

Factors that will influence the final choice of a site are: foundation material in both the land and the water area; tidal ranges (to determine types and detail of construction); possible wave hazards; prevailing winds; icing conditions during the winter; water depth (dredging is possible but quite expensive); and highways and transportation systems near the proposed site. Without this basic information, consideration of a site could well be wasted time and effort.

REGULATORY CONSIDERATIONS

After the site has been chosen and the type of marina determined, the planners must meet any legal requirements. A consultation with the district engineer is not only desirable but, in most cases, required. Local zoning, planning, construction, health, fire, and public-works ordinances must be satisfied before making large capital investments.

FINANCING

When the actual development of a marina is assured, accurate cost estimates must be prepared. Each of the different elements should be treated in detail to form a complete picture of the money to be spent on the project. These include such items as: dredging, filling, and similar work; bulkhead walls and other shore protection; piers, wharfs, catwalks, floats, hoists, and railways; buildings, sheds, service stations, and their equipment; utilities, roadways, walks, parking spaces, and landscaping; stock of merchandise for sale; engineering, planning, and supervision costs; and operation and maintenance costs.

The method of financing a marina is an important factor. This will vary considerably, depending on whether the planners are proposing a publicly-owned or privately-owned marina. In any case, careful consideration of financing methods will assure a sound fiscal foundation for a proposed marina.

FACTORS TO BE CONSIDERED IN PLANNING

The location, community needs, and proposed use should determine which of several types of marinas will be planned. The boating industry generally makes a distinction between the fresh-water marina and the salt-water marina. The operator of a salt-water marina must deal with the nagging problems of erosion, rust, and exposure more than the operator of a fresh-water marina, so compensation must be made for this in the initial planning. The planner must also solve the tide problem in designing the piers, slips, and ramps in a salt-water marina. Another distinction between salt-water and fresh-water marinas is that the salt-water marina must generally accommodate more of the large yachts and cruisers that are capable of seagoing trips.

Some marina operators prefer to serve the small-boat owner because the initial investment in the facility is much less, as are operating costs and general maintenance. On the other hand, some marina operators concentrate on the larger craft on the basis that there is more margin of profit in servicing the more expensive boats. A great many marina operators serve both small and large-boat owners and allocate space for each type of boat. In planning a marina, there are basic inclusions that must be figured in the way of equipment and facilities. Beyond these, there are extras which can be added.

The docks and piers of a marina can be constructed of wood, steel, or aluminum. They can be of the fixed, anchored type or the more popular floating type. If wood is used, it becomes subject to damage from a number of causes, such as rot, termites or other insects, or marine organisms. Preservatives are commercially available to treat these conditions, and care should be taken to treat those areas most vulnerable, such as where wood rests on wood, where wood rests on cement or on the ground, on the end grain, and in joints, cracks, or crevices. Most metal will give more satisfactory service if protected with proper finishes. Base coats of metallic oxide or aluminum paints will effectively guard against corrosion or oxidation. The fixed, anchored dock will have piles driven to a solid footing and the length of these piles will depend on the depth of water and penetration.

Most marinas have floating docks because these are more attractive and adapt more easily to expansions, changes, and rearrangement for varying boat sizes. To adequately support floating structures, a variety of materials and methods may be employed. Those most commonly used are: 55-gallon drums; wooden box floats; plastic foam (effective in salt water because it resists rust and corrosion); precast concrete floats; and wooden logs. In any design of floatation material, it is well to apply a safety factor that will give some reserve buoyancy. For stability, long, thin, wide shapes are preferable to short, narrow, high shapes.

Slips are the mooring spaces for boats and extend out from either side of the dock or pier. Each boat has its own allotted slip that must be easily accessible to the owner. Boat slips are the main revenue-producing facility at a marina, and rentals depend upon the size of the boat. Each slip must be equipped to secure the boat at both the bow and the stern. Many marinas offer catwalks on either side of the slip to facilitate the loading and unloading of passengers and cargo. Since many boats remain in their slip for days without being used, the marina operator may consider offering covered slips to boat owners. The coverings can be of wood, canvas, or aluminum and will vary in size with the boat being accommodated.

A launching ramp at a marina is a service facility that is in great demand by boating enthusiasts who prefer to keep their boats at home on boat trailers. The launching service becomes a source of extra revenue for the marina operator. The ramp may be of either the floating design or a permanent structure. The floating design has the advantage of being adaptable to tidewater locations by virtue of hinge plates that enable the far half of the ramp to rise and fall with the water-level variations while the near end is anchored to the shore and is held in place by piles. The permanent launching ramps are particularly suited to municipal waterfronts. This kind of ramp should be an extension of good access roadways and be near parking facilities for automobiles and trailers. Permanent launching ramps can be constructed of concrete, precast concrete, asphalt, cinders, or gravel. Determination of the material to be used should be based on such variables as soil conditions, climate, erosion, currents and waterfront conditions, availability of materials, and costs.

In the development of launching ramps, it is often desirable to cut back into a bank away from the shoreline to form the gradual slope of the ramp. To hold the earth embankment in place on each side of the ramp, small bulkheads can be con-

structed. In some cases, the bulkheads should extend into the water some distance in order to protect the underwater section of the ramp from erosion by currents and wave action. Bulkheads can be constructed of wood, concrete, or corrugated metal. Each of these materials has its advantage, depending upon soil and bottom conditions, tidal variations, seasonal changes in weather, and the possibility of floods and other abnormal conditions.

At marina locations that are bulkheaded and where space is limited, the launching of smaller boats can be handled by either a monorail and trolley hoist, or a launching derrick. With these arrangements, the boats are lifted directly from the trailer, placed in position over the water, and lowered. Many of the larger and more expensive marinas have a hoist over each slip to keep the boats out of the water when not in use. These can be operated either by hand or electrically.

At coastal and larger lake marinas, the planners must include provision for a breakwater to lessen the destructive sea waves and resulting beach erosion, and also to facilitate refueling and other normal dockside activities. The breakwater may be of the standard heavy stone-wall design or possibly the new "wave traps" of floating structures of fabric and plastic. In either case, breakwater engineering is skilled and precise work that requires consultation with professionals.

Another basic inclusion in a marina is some sort of structure to house administrative offices, the sales room for new motors and accessories, the repair shop, and perhaps a refreshment area. The extent of this building will depend on the needs of the marina as it serves its customers, and the lengths to which the owner-management of the marina wishes to go to provide more than basic services.

Parking space for cars and trailers must not be underestimated in the planning of a marina. Too often, drivers who are inexperienced at hauling trailers can cause monumental tie-ups and delays if parking space is less than the demand warrants.

The above inclusions are considered prerequisites for a successful marina operation. Beyond these, the planners of a marina can include numerous extras to enhance the service and beauty of their facilities. These extras include: private lockers; electricity for boats afloat or ashore; toilets and showers; restaurant services; overnight hotel accommodations; complete gas, oil, diesel-fuel, and boat-supply service; and complete year-round, onshore sheltered storage.

Because marinas vary so greatly in their design, function, location, and capacity, it is virtually impossible to arrive at standard conclusions and judgments concerning a model marina. For instance, quoted costs for constructing a marina vary from several thousand dollars for a small, skeleton-equipped facility to several million dollars for a plush West-Coast marina.

Each reader will be able to apply the general principles of planning a marina to his unique circumstances. From that point, however, he must adopt his marina to the peculiar needs and characteristics of his community and to the use for which the marina is intended.

Figure 19
Burnham Harbor Marina, Chicago Park District

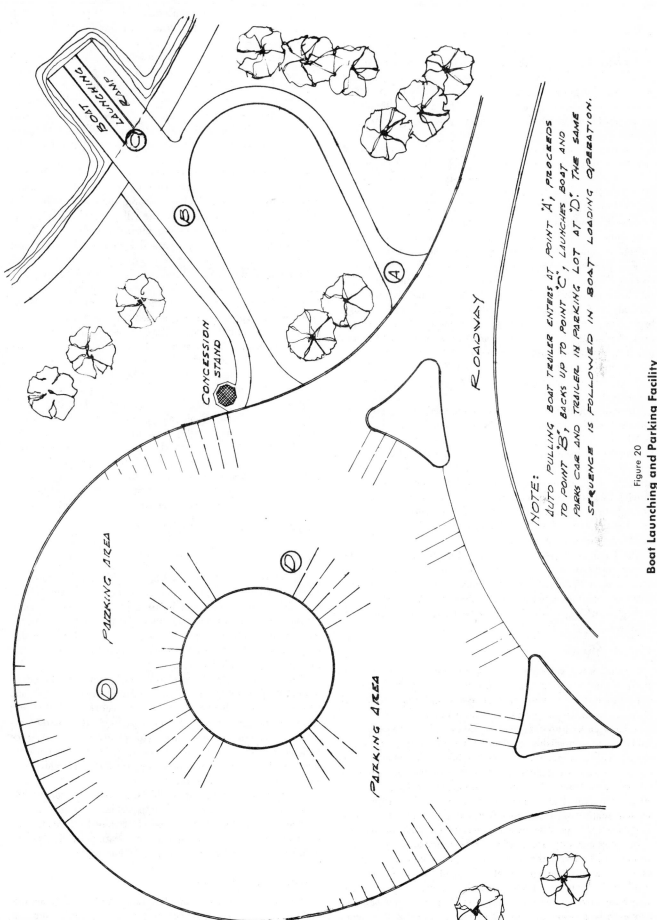

Figure 20
Boat Launching and Parking Facility

AMPHITHEATERS

The "cultural reawakening" that has been sweeping the country during the past few years has resulted in a demand for suitable facilities, both indoor and outdoor, for operas, plays, band and orchestral concerts, pageants, festivals, holiday programs, and civic celebrations. When performed outdoors, such activities usually require a stage or band shell with adjoining amphitheater capable of accommodating large numbers of spectators.

Selection of the proper site for an outdoor theater is of primary importance. It should have good acoustical properties and be located in a quiet place away from the noise of traffic or of groups at play. A natural bowl or depression on a hillside with a slope of 10 to 20 degrees, preferably bordered by slopes or densely-wooded areas, provides a fine location.

At some theaters, people sit on the turf of the slope comprising the amphitheater. At others, permanent seats are installed. Terraces with a turf surface are not recommended because they are too difficult to maintain. Sufficient level space should be provided at the rear of the seating area for the circulation of spectators, and aisles should be wide enough to facilitate the seating of large numbers in a short period of time. Public comfort stations and refreshment facilities are usually provided near the entrance to the amphitheater. Provision for the nearby parking of automobiles is essential, but parking areas must be located where noises and car lights do not disturb the theater.

The dimensions of the stage are determined by the proposed uses, but rarely should a stage be less than 50 feet in width or 30 feet in depth. The rear of the stage may be a wall or high hedge, or even a planting of trees, and the wings may be formed by natural plant materials. However, the band shell, or music shell, is more satisfactory for projecting voices and sounds free from echoes and interference to the people in the audience. A vertical rear wall with inclined ceiling is not only the simplest and most economical to construct, but affords excellent acoustical qualities.

The band shell usually contains dressing rooms, toilets, storage space, and rooms for the control of amplifying and lighting equipment, although sometimes these facilities are provided in separate structures near the back of the stage. An orchestra pit is generally located between the auditorium and the stage.

PICNIC AREAS

Picnicking use varies from a single-family picnic to a large-group picnic involving several thousand people. Accommodations range within these two extremes and require careful planning to ensure proper control and maintenance.

In large parks providing picnic groves and fireplaces accommodating an appreciable number of people, a large-size open shelter with a fireplace in one end is highly desirable to give shelter in case of sudden rainstorms. Shelters are built in varying sizes from 20' x 30', accommodating approximately 60 persons seated at picnic tables, to 30' x 50', which will accommodate about 150 people. It has also been found desirable in some areas to provide electrical service for night-picnic use.

In congested city areas where it is anticipated that picnic groups will be large, the development of a picnic area that is served by a portable type of table is highly desirable because these tables can be moved around, making it possible to distribute wear on the grass surfaces. If space is available, it may even be possible to close off certain sections of the picnic area for a season or two to allow the replenishment of the grass.

The areas where heavy concentrations will take place, such as near the picnic shelter, toilets, and drinking fountains, should be hard-surfaced. These sections, then, should have tables for large groups, and preferably, should be located near the parking area. The area for smaller gatherings and play equipment should be located beyond the facilities for large picnic groups. The groupings of picnic facilities, such as tables, easily-accessible trash receptacles, and fire grates, should be designed to take advantage of the topographical features, trees, fine views, and other similar factors that make an outing a pleasurable experience.

Tables of various kinds of material are available. In congested or metropolitan areas where picnic grounds are subject to continuous vandalism and destruction, and where there is not much supervision, picnic tables that will withstand abuses from the general public should be provided. Normally, this will require a table in a fixed location and with a hard-surface area under it.

In the more native or natural areas away from heavy populations, such as county or state parks, heavy rustic types of wooden picnic tables and facilities may be more desirable because of their appearance and the fact that they blend with the natural surroundings. Usually, these types of areas are not as heavily used, are not so susceptible to vandalism, and have more space available for the distribution of picnic uses so that the surfaces of these areas do not become worn out, as is frequently true of city parks.

Other features that may be incorporated in picnic areas are a council ring, barbecue pit, and picnic shelter. There seems to be a general trend toward people bringing their own cooking utensils, and it has also been the experience over past years that a small picnic grate for charcoal use is highly satisfactory and more economical to construct. A large fireplace made of stone or other similar material is subject to vandalism and deterioration due to weather conditions.

OUTDOOR SHOOTING AREAS

RIFLE RANGE

The advisability of constructing an outdoor rifle range on a school, college, or recreation site will depend on several factors: (1) the terrain and location of the parcels of land; (2) the availability of nearby outdoor ranges owned by sportsmen's clubs, military organizations, and other groups which might be used for instruction and recreational shooting; and (3) the location of indoor ranges.

If an outdoor range is developed, the target area should be protected, preferably by natural embankments. If the land is level, adequate banks of soil can be constructed that will reinforce the other types of backstops used. It is always desirable to have a good-sized area with plenty of unused space back of the target. A 50-foot range is sufficient for most instructional and recreational programs, since the .22-caliber rifle will be used in most instances.

In considering a range, it would be advisable to consult the National Rifle Association and, if possible, have the site inspected by a member of the NRA staff. Detailed information on specifications can be obtained from the National Rifle Association, 1600 Rhode Island Avenue, N.W., Washington, D.C.

SHOTGUN-SHOOTING AREA

Shotgun shooting and games like skeet are becoming increasingly popular. There may not be adequate facilities for trap and skeet in nearby gun clubs, police ranges, and military establishments. In such circumstances, an open area can be used for skeet by utilizing hand traps.

If the adjacent property, such as open fields, woods, or swamps, is not being used during the time of shooting, skeet can be conducted safely under the supervision of a qualified instructor. The National Rifle Association has detailed information on shotgun shooting and facilities.

STADIUMS

This consideration of stadiums is primarily concerned with a type of structure frequently needed for school and community use. It does not purport to discuss huge structures, of which there are or will be comparatively few. Rather, the treatment concerns the stadium of 10,000 capacity or less with limited spectator accommodations. It should be obvious, however, that the basic considerations for such structures will also apply to larger units. Those responsible for planning stadiums should keep in mind that their creation is an integral part of the physical education, recreation, and athletic programs of the school and community, not divorced from them.

In the early stages of planning for stadiums, there should be joint effort of all concerned. The professional staffs of the schools involved should furnish the curriculum and activity requirements. If the structure is also to be used by the community, representative civic and recreation leaders should be included in the planning. This process is necessary to enable architects and engineers to create functional facilities. In brief, those engaged in planning such structures should encompass all who will be expected to use them.

For the purposes of this chapter, the terms "spectator structure" and "seating structure" include both permanent and temporary outdoor-seating facilities, while the word "stadium" refers only to permanent accommodations. Spectator structures provide seating from which people can satisfactorily view athletic events without inhibiting the activities of the participants. However, the possibility of employing spectator structures and fields for other purposes also warrants careful consideration. Seating structures can be justified more readily if they have multiple use. In addition to serving athletic contests, these facilities are used for patriotic observances, plays and pageants, Easter sunrise services, anniversary celebrations, conventions, lectures, commencement exercises, mass meetings, demonstrations, exhibits, large religious assemblies, parades, drills, and band concerts.

The space underneath a stadium may provide physical education service and activity areas, such as dressing units, classrooms, rifle and archery ranges, bus storage, and handball courts. These facilities should supplement rather than duplicate existing units. To realize maximum utility, the possibility of satisfying the facility needs of other aspects of the physical education program should be considered. Representatives of groups affected and others who can contribute should participate in the planning.

SEATING CAPACITY

If possible, the seating capacity of a stadium should be sufficient to meet present needs, with plans for expansion to satisfy predicated needs for a period of at least 20 years. The number of seats required will be influenced by: the sports served; enrollment of the school or college; population and socio-economic status of the town, city, and region; available public and private means of transportation; and planned expansion of the program. The provision of an excessive number of seats should be avoided because construction and maintenance costs make it impractical to provide accommodations that are seldom used.

DESIGN

The crescent design places the greatest number of seats opposite the center of action. This design resembles a rectangular stand, with the back corners eliminated by a gradual arch extending from the front ends to the back center. Another design, which is a variation of the crescent, provides the greatest number of tiers between the two 40-yard lines of a regulation football field and then reduces the number of rows in a stair-step fashion between the 40-yard and 30-yard lines, and between the 20-yard and goal lines. Removable stands can be arranged in this manner, but the crescent shape is usually restricted to permanent construction.

The horseshoe and muleshoe stadiums are similar. The muleshoe design resembles a "U" with opposite sides parallel, and one end enclosed by the semicircle of the structure and the other end left open. Except for bowed tiers, the horseshoe and muleshoe stadiums are similar. The bowed tiers are intended to face spectators toward the center of activity. The open end permits inclusion of a 220-yard straightaway for track and provides additional space for field events.

The bowl-type stadium completely encloses the playing field, and the tiers may follow the curve of an ellipse or they may be parallel on the sides and semicircular on the ends. This design is used most commonly to accommodate large crowds. Some planners, however, have preferred to erect a second deck rather than to enclose both ends of a structure, thereby making possible the inclusion of track facilities and locating a greater number of seats nearer the center of the field.

The "V" or modified "L" design orients two rectangular structures to form a right angle. Often the two are joined by a curved portion. This design is especially applicable for baseball seating.

TYPES OF SPECTATOR STRUCTURES

The various shapes or designs previously mentioned should be applied to meet specific needs in terms of activities to be served and desired seating capacities. The use of fields and spectator structures for more than one sport affords maximum utility for money expended. Some sports are particularly adapted to the use of common areas and facilities. The single spectator structure for the combined football-track area is common. Spectators at games such as soccer, field hockey, speedball, and lacrosse may also be served by seating facilities for football. Such multipurpose use is desirable except for those activities which are not adaptable to this usage. Planners should make certain that the activity field area is large enough to satisfy the space requirements set forth in the official rules for the various sports.

FOOTBALL-TRACK AREA

All of the designs mentioned previously, except the "V" or modified "L", can be adapted to seating structures for football and track. When less than 10,000 persons are to be accommodated, the rectangular design is desirable. For small crowds, the structure should occupy the centermost portion of the area opposite the field, but as capacity increases, the structure is extended toward the goals. In no event should the structure be placed closer to the boundary or playing area than provided for in the official rules.

SHAPES OF OUTDOOR SPECTATOR STRUCTURES

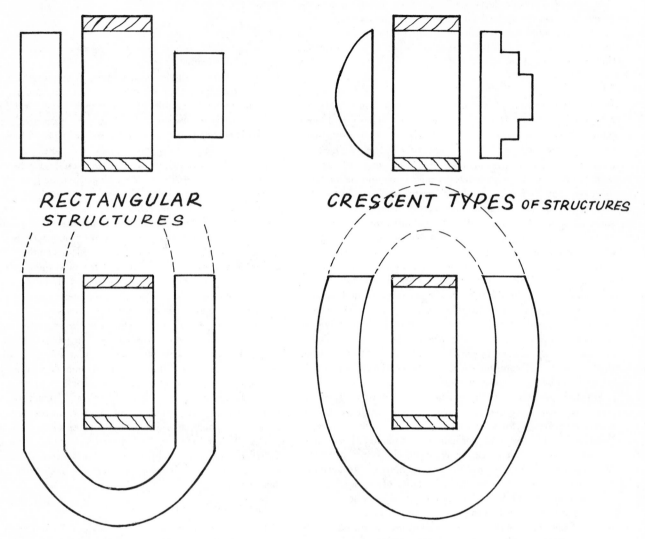

RECTANGULAR STRUCTURES

CRESCENT TYPES OF STRUCTURES

MULESHOE STADIUM   HORSESHOE STADIUM
(THE BOWL SHAPE ENCLOSES BOTH ENDS AS INDICATED)
BY THE DOTTED EXTENSIONS

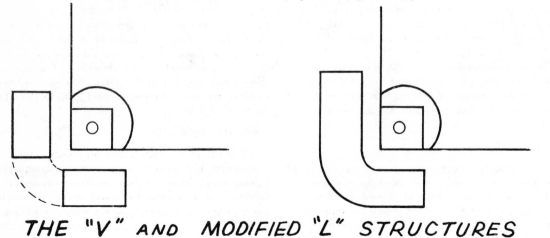

THE "V" AND MODIFIED "L" STRUCTURES

Figure 21
Shapes of Outdoor Spectator Structures

Stands can be erected on the opposite side of the field to provide for additional and more favorable seating. If necessary, seating accommodations can also be provided at the ends of the field. Rectangular spectator structures can be permanently located, be demountable, or be mobile. Demountable or mobile units are sufficient for small crowds or when used as supplementary to permanent facilities. These units may be transferred to other areas where seating is required, thus affording maximum utility.

Rectangular spectator structures provide the most practical seating accommodations for: baseball, softball, soccer, lacrosse, and other field games; tennis, outdoor basketball, volleyball, and other outdoor sports; and special events or demonstrations. For baseball, a structure can be located parallel to either or both the first-base and third-base lines. The most favorable view of tennis is from behind the ends of the courts. Seating facilities for other outdoor events should be adjacent to the activity area and as near as possible to the probable center of action consistent with the rules governing the activity.

Track-and-field spectator seating generally is parallel to the straightaway for the dashes. Some planners, however, have located spectator seating so that the structure angles in gradually toward the straightaway end of the track. The front end of the structure nearest the starting line should be farther away from the track than the front end nearest the finish. This arrangement faces the spectators toward the most common center of continuing action.

SOFTBALL-BASEBALL AREA

The combined use of a stadium for softball, baseball, and football often results from the desire to use existing floodlighting. In most instances, sufficient seating facilities can be provided with a small permanent structure or by relocating demountable or mobile bleachers used for football.

The combination baseball-football field should be avoided if possible. The superimposing of an infield upon a portion of the gridiron makes playing conditions undesirable for sports such as football and soccer. A baseball area that overlaps a track-and-field site presents safety problems. Competitors have had serious collisions on such combined facilities.

SITE AND LOCATION

Spectator structures should be easily accessible to the users. These facilities should be on the school or college site and near the gymnasium so that locker, shower, dressing, equipment, and other service facilities can be used. Duplication of existing adequate facilities increases costs of construction, operation, supervision, and maintenance. Traffic movement and parking requirements should also be considered in site location.

Cities with two or more secondary schools should consider the construction of one stadium for their combined use. Teams from each school may practice on their own fields but play their regular games at the stadium. If possible, the structure should be located on or adjacent to one of the schools' site for the reasons of greater accessibility, maximum use, and more efficient maintenance, operation, and supervision.

A primary requisite for a satisfactory site is adequacy of size. The site must be large enough to accommodate the play and safety areas for the sport or sports to be conducted, the proposed present and future seating, and service areas. The site should be flat or easily leveled. However, natural inclines of the topography can be used for support or partial support of a structure. Surface drainage of the site and adjacent areas, and the subsurface soils and geological formations should also be considered.

REMOVABLE AND PERMANENT SPECTATOR STRUCTURES

Permanent spectator structures are those designed and constructed to remain indefinitely at a given location. Removable seating structures are designed and constructed to permit dismantling and/or moving for storing or use at different sites. The most common temporary structure is the type that can be dismantled and moved in its component parts.

Wheels have been attached to small sections of spectator structures so that the entire section, without disassembling, can be rolled to the desired location. Several units can be placed together to create the required number of seats. Temporary bleachers can also be moved to meet the seating requirements of seasonal sports.

DECKS AND DECK SUPPORTS

Wood, steel, and concrete, or combinations of them, are the most common materials used for the construction of decks and their supporting members. The materials used are governed by the expected capacity, intended use of the structure, availability of funds, climatic conditions, and desired aesthetic qualities. If service and other facilities are included underneath a stadium, a solid, continuous, and waterproof deck of either metal or concrete is necessary. Wooden treads and risers often form the deck when the underneath area is not utilized.

A hard surface under free-standing structures will improve sanitation and expedite cleaning after stadium use. Where the topography permits, construction costs may be reduced by building the stadium deck on an embankment. Stadium decks resting on the slope of an incline may average 1/3 to 1/2 the per-seat cost less than those with similar decks built on concrete or steel-frame construction on level sites.

SIGHT LINES

Seating facilities are constructed to provide spectators with a good view of the performance. Nearness and an unobstructed sight line to the desired points affect the quality of the accommodations. A sight line is a straight line from the eyes of the seated spectator, over the heads of others below, and to a point on the field that represents the spot nearest the structure that should be in his field of vision. Recommended focal points for sight lines are as follows: for football, the nearest side boundary line; for track, about knee-height of the runner in the nearest lane; for baseball, several feet behind the catcher; for side tennis seating, four feet in toward the seats from the doubles boundary line; and for end seating for tennis, ten feet behind the base line. These are minimum recommendations. Light poles, fences, and rails should not obstruct the sight lines.

SEATING ARRANGEMENTS

The design of seating facilities is related to comfort, the kinds of events to be viewed, and economy of construction, operation, and maintenance. Seats for football spectator structures are usually without back rests. The space allowed for each seat, lengthwise in a row, is generally between 16 and 18-1/2 inches. For reserved seating, and in climates requiring heavy clothing, the seat width should be a minimum of 18 inches. The preferable minimum depth of a seat is 10 inches. The height of the seats above the foot-support treads should be between 16 and 18 inches. A new development in seating is to cover the seat benches with Fiberglas, which provides for better maintenance and durability.

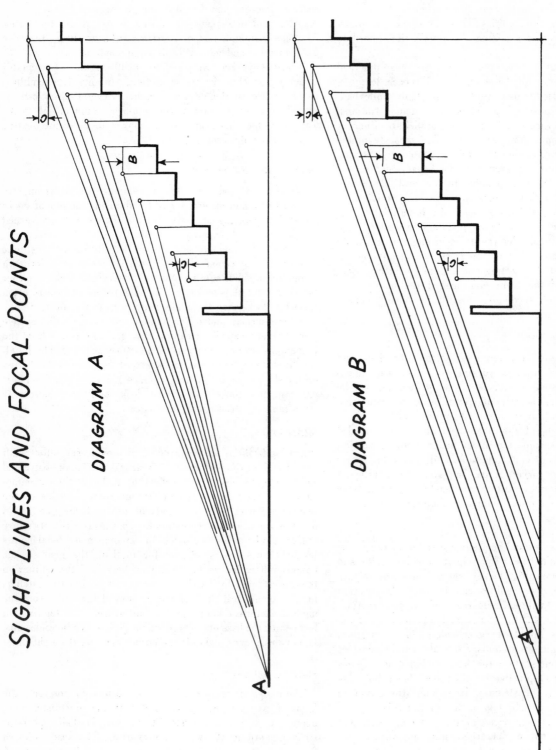

SIGHT LINES AND FOCAL POINTS

DIAGRAM A

DIAGRAM B

Diagram A shows a seating section with a gradual increase in riser heights. The focal points, "A", are the same from all seats. "B" represents height from a seat eye level. "C" represents the distance from eye level to the top of a spectator's head.
Diagram B shows a seating section with constant riser and tread heights. As the seating tiers progress upward, each focal point is closer to the field.

These diagrams are adapted from *Concrete Grandstands*, Portland Cement Association, Chicago, 1948.

Figure 22
Sight Lines and Focal Points

TREADS AND RISERS

The treads and risers should be as small as possible, but sufficient to provide for comfort and good view. Riser heights may vary, increasing from front to back in large stadiums.

The height of the first riser should be kept to a minimum because it affects the ultimate height of the entire structure, and, therefore, the cost. The width of the treads is governed by factors of economy and comfort. A minimum depth of 24 inches is recommended for treads with backless seats. For structures without continuous seating decks, this measurement should be taken between the front edges of the seating surfaces of successive tiers. The minimum depth for treads supporting seats with backs is 30 inches. Tread widths remain constant except for the first tier, unless there is a railing, low wall, or fence in front, in which case, additional space is required for spectator movement.

Drainage must be considered in the design of treads for solid-deck stadiums. A slope toward the front provides for rapid drainage. A gradual lateral tread slope away from entrance portals and expansion joints will minimize the flow of water into them. Water can flow off the front of small spectator structures, but gutters and drains should be included for large structures, and should be located so as to serve a section between expansion joints. The size of the drain should be based on the minimum ratio of one square inch to each 300 square feet of deck surface served.[1]

State and local building codes often establish standards for aisles, entrances, and portals for spectator structures. Planners should be cognizant of such codes. Aisles may not be necessary in small seating structures. For structures with many rows and large capacities, however, aisles are necessary. Sections between aisles should contain tiers with 24 to 32 seats. The first aisles should be located 14 to 16 seats from the ends of the structure. Horizontal walks are generally undesirable because persons using them will obstruct the sight lines of others. If such walks are used, the next tread above should be high enough to permit the occupants to look over those persons walking in front of them.

Aisles should have a minimum width of 36 inches, and, if divided by a portal or an obstruction, each side should be at least 24 inches wide. Whenever the riser height exceeds 9 inches, an intermediate step is necessary.

ENTRANCES AND EXITS

The number of portals and exits for a stadium deck depends upon the seating capacity as well as the number of seats in each section. They should permit the dispersal of a large crowd within a minimum period of time. Where possible, it is highly desirable to have exit ramps leading from the stepped aisles.

Entrances and exits for structures should be located for accessibility and be adequate in size and number for crowd dispersal. When entrances and exits are located at the front of a structure, a low fence or wall should separate the walkway from the playing-field area. The first tier of seats should be high enough to allow the occupants an unobstructed view.

DECK WALLS AND RAILING

The ends, backs, and, in some instances, the fronts of the seating structures should be bordered by walls or a railing. These walls or railings should extend at least 42 inches above the treads and be designed so as to prevent spectators from sitting on them.

[1] *Concrete Grandstands*, Portland Cement Association, Chicago, Ill., 1948, p. 27.

COMMUNICATION FACILITIES

Inasmuch as schools, colleges, and recreation departments endeavor to maintain close and friendly relations with the public, facilities to accommodate the press, radio, television, and motion-picture groups are essential in modern stadiums. Facilities for public-address and scoreboard operators, spotters, scouts, and other officials or dignitaries should also be included.

The football press-box unit should be located opposite the 50-yard line high in the west stand to eliminate interference from sunlight. Baseball press boxes usually occupy some portion of the stand behind the home plate.

SCOREBOARDS

Scoreboards are essential for football, softball, and baseball fields. Time clocks are also desirable for football.

It is advisable to have the scoreboard designed as an integral part of the structure, especially in the case of larger stadiums. For activities attracting a small number of spectators, mechanical or movable scoreboards may be practical.

UTILITIES

The availability of electricity, gas, water, and sewer connections significantly affects the use and validity of a spectator structure. The concession center, press-box area, rest rooms, scoreboard operation, field illumination and watering, and many other functions depend upon one or more of these utilities.

ICE-SKATING RINKS

Ice-skating facilities are feeling the impact of modern technology in more and more communities each year, with artificially-frozen ice replacing naturally-frozen skating areas. With this change, people are finding a new pleasure in out-of-doors recreation on the ice. Artificial rinks provide smooth ice in moderate weather, a combination especially desirable for older skaters. No longer is it necessary to brave the bitter cold to enjoy good ice for skating. With the advent of mechanical freezing, the skating season has been extended from a 20- to 60-day average season to a 140-day season, depending on climatic conditions.

This does not mean that natural-ice rinks have gone out of style, but it does mean artificial rinks are replacing natural rinks as central or regional facilities. Natural-ice rinks are continuing to serve as a supplemental neighborhood facility in many communities. Skaters have not become completely disenchanted with a natural-ice facility, and a considerable number prefer the rugged pleasure of an old-fashioned skating experience.

ARTIFICIAL-ICE RINKS

The function of an artificial-ice rink will determine many of its characteristics, such as size, cover, seating, and service rooms. If it is planned to include hockey as an activity of the rink, the size should be 85' x 185' or 200'. A general-purpose rink is usually an outdoor rink of 85' x 185' surrounded by dasher boards and with warming-house facilities for large numbers of skaters. It is generally agreed that the area per skater should be 30 square feet. Thus, the safe capacity of a general-purpose rink of the size mentioned would be 524 skaters. There are many variations of the general pattern to accommodate individual needs and limitations.

After the function of the ice rink has been determined, considerable planning is necessary to ensure an efficiently-operating facility. This can best be done by engaging an experienced designing engineer who has a number of successfully-operating

58

A GUIDE FOR PLANNING FACILITIES

rinks to attest to his skill. Some feel that the engineering and supervision of construction should be the responsibility of the same person to ensure a quality facility.

The proposed rink should be carefully located to gain the best position relative to sun exposure, wind velocity, and the blowing of litter, such as dried leaves, dust, or papers. If an open rink is built, plans may provide for a cover or enclosure at some future date.

Transportation and parking accommodations should also be considered in selecting a site. Preliminary planning may include such supporting services as skate rental and sharpening, a sport shop, and concessions. High-quality music for the rink should be ensured in the planning stage. If hockey is to be a part of the rink program, lighting will require advance consideration. During the planning period, subsoil should also be tested to ensure adequate drainage.

RINK CONSTRUCTION

A number of choices must be made in the construction of a refrigeration system. They include: (1) type of engine room; (2) extent of automatic controls; (3) number and size of compressors; (4) type of power supply; (5) number of brine pumps; (6) type of heat-rejection system; (7) type of refrigerant; (8) type of brine; and (9) type of floor construction.

Engine rooms—For the past few years, there has been a trend toward the purchase of engine rooms which are assembled in the factory and installed as a complete unit on the job. These engine rooms have replaced the "site-built" engine rooms, which require greater space and are more expensive. It is easier, however, to maintain and repair equipment in a site-built engine room.

Automatic-control systems—Machines may be automatic or manually controlled. Automatic safety devices may be required by codes governing this type of installation. The slight additional cost for fully-automatic operation will be amortized in a short time. Automatic controls can start the compressors when brine temperatures start to rise, and shut them off as brine temperatures fall. The starting temperatures of the compressors can also be staggered for a more economical use of power. In addition, a brine-pump control can be set to stop brine circulation if the air temperature falls below the brine temperature, a condition that occurs often in the colder climates.

Compressors—To illustrate this choice, assume that an outdoor ice rink of 85' x 185' needs 150 tons of refrigeration to maintain the rink surface. This refrigeration can be obtained with one 150-ton compressor, two 75-ton compressors, or three 50-ton compressors. When sunshine or rising air temperature causes the brine temperature to rise above the level set to start the chilling process, the compressors will start to work. In the case of one compressor, maximum power will be utilized, and when electricity is the power source, maximum demand rates will be charged even though a minimum of refrigeration is required. This expense is greatly reduced when two compressors are used, and a still greater saving is effected when the capacity is divided among three compressors. The greatest power-cost saving occurs during long periods of cold weather when minimum refrigeration is required.

Power supply—The refrigeration plant may be operated by either electricity or natural gas. Natural-gas engines may be more expensive to install, but may operate at considerably less cost. Gas engines can be put under service contracts that assure a life expectancy comparable to that of electric motors. Gas engines also provide heat energy that can be used for space

heating through a heat-recovery system.

Brine pumps—The brine pump is the heart of the refrigerating process. When it breaks down, everything stops and the ice surface is at the mercy of the sun and weather during the period of repair. Some brine pumps have quick-repair features which can shorten the time the system is out of operation. For all practical purposes, the breakdown time due to brine-pump failure can be eliminated by building two brine pumps into the system. With this arrangement, one pump will give stand-by service in case the other fails.

Heat-rejection systems—Heat removed from the ice must be eliminated in the refrigeration process. This is accomplished by the condenser which removes heat from the refrigerant. The condenser may use either cold water or the evaporation principle to accomplish heat rejection. An evaporating condenser costs more to buy, but if water is an item of expense, it will be cheaper to operate. Many competent rink designers insist on evaporative condensers where city water alone must be used for cooling. The refrigerant, which has absorbed heat in cooling the brine, must be cooled in this cycle of operation. This is done by circulation through coils exposed in the air. When the air temperature alone cannot cool the refrigerant to the proper level, water is sprayed on the coils and then fans blow air over the wet coils to cause evaporation. This process provides the necessary additional cooling.

Refrigerants—Two types of refrigerants are available: ammonia and Freon 22. Although operation with ammonia has been efficient, it is both toxic and explosive, and, for these reasons, the trend has been toward the use of Freon 22, which is neither toxic nor explosive. There is little difference in the initial cost of refrigeration machinery designed for either ammonia or Freon gas. The cost of the refrigerant does differ, however, with Freon costing about five times as much as ammonia. This cost is equalized since an ammonia system will use nearly five times the refrigerant necessary in systems using Freon gas. Since Freon is odorless, leaks in the system may go undetected and expensive replacement of refrigerant becomes necessary. This is not the case with ammonia. However, safety is an overriding factor that dictates the preference of Freon for ice-rink refrigeration. This does not mean that there are not applications where ammonia should be recommended, but local laws should always be consulted before using ammonia.

Types of brine—Calcium-chloride brine is used in most ice-rink refrigeration systems. It is not expensive, but it is highly corrosive and must be closely watched. It is possible to purchase salt (for brine) that contains a chromate which acts as a rust inhibitor. This inhibitor does not last long, however, and additional chromate must be added from time to time to maintain the rust-inhibiting factor. Although corrosion is reduced by the chromate, it is not eliminated. There is a growing trend toward the use of ethylene glycol or metholene alcohol as a brine. Once stabilized, these brines usually require no further attention.

Floor construction—The following types of floor construction are used in building artificial-ice rinks:
• Steel piping in post-stressed concrete
• Steel piping in reinforced concrete
• Open steel piping (or in sand)
• Open plastic piping (or in sand)

These choices are listed in the order of their cost, with the most expensive listed first. In addition to the choices listed, aluminum-finned tubes have recently made their appearance as piping for rink floors. The newly-developed construction of steel piping in post-stressed concrete floors is the most costly of the choices listed, but the least likely to develop cracks or heaving. It is reliably calculated that a post-stressed floor can endure, if necessary, at least twice as much frost heaving as conventional reinforced concrete floors.

Plastic is lightweight and easy to handle, especially in portable and take-up installations. However, plastic acts as an insulator and does not transfer heat from ice to brine as rapidly as steel does. Plastic is cheaper than steel, but may not last as long. The main preference for steel seems to be the efficiency in maintaining ice temperatures.

The floor pipes are connected to headers attached to the supply and return lines. There are two basic header designs, each with several variations. One system employs a header at each side of the rink, or at each end, with the floor piping joined to these headers at each end. The advantage of this design is that ideal uniformity of ice can be maintained. The disadvantages are that it is the most expensive design, and temperature-expansion variables can be a problem. In the second design, both headers are at the same side or end, and the rink grid surface is made up of hairpin pairs of pipes. This is the more common modern design.

Grid-construction practices in building rink floors call for good drainage around foundation footings to cut off ground-water seepage into the floor area. The installation of a slip-joint consisting of two or more dry, lubricated membranes between the grid and foundation slabs of concrete is essential. The concrete slab that encases the grids should be poured in one continuous operation which will permit the grid slab to contract or expand as a unit rather than in sections. The return header should be at a slightly higher elevation so that there can be no trapped air in the cross pipes. The floor should be pressure-tested after construction and after assembly if it is a take-up rink. This will eliminate brine leakage due to faulty assembly.

Other considerations—Although a majority of outdoor rinks have no cover, a variety of covers are available. A netting is available to provide a sunshade on bright days. It is drawn across the rink on high cables as a curtain, greatly weakening the melting effect of sunlight. An inflated bubble of fabric material has been used as a rink enclosure. Permanent covers have also been constructed of steel, concrete, and wood. All of these types of covers reduce power costs and snow-removal expense. A variety of permanent buildings have also been used to house ice-skating studios, general skating rinks, and ice arenas.

Whether the skating area is open or enclosed, a warming room or skate-changing room is necessary. This room contains a maximum number of benches and often has checking facilities for shoes. Adjoining the warming room in many rinks is a concession serving hot and cold drinks, sandwiches, candy, and popcorn. Besides providing a service required by the public, a concession's profit is often considerable. A first-aid room provides for the efficient handling of skating falls and injuries. A skate rental is another service found in many artificial rinks. Having skates available is not only a profitable service, but highly desirable in the campaign to keep skaters on the ice as they grow older.

Choices and problems will not cease to exist with the construction of the rink. They will continue in the programming and in the assuring of protection and pleasure to those using the facility. To get the fullest use out of as expensive and complex a facility as an ice rink, it will be necessary to program its use. General skating sessions during which skaters just go round and round is not enough. Interesting and challenging situations must be present to attract older skaters and keep them on the ice. The social side of ice skating must be exploited to maintain a sufficient enjoyment level to keep people skating. It would seem that the job is just beginning when the rink has been completed.

NATURAL-ICE RINKS

Preseason Preparations

If the rink is to be laid on the ground, sufficient moisture will be needed to provide ground frost. Water the area if a dry condition prevails. If a temporary dike is needed, it should be made in the fall so that settling can take place. If the rink is to be made on a concrete surface such as a tennis court, all drains should be sealed. Hoses, hydrants, nozzles, and scraping and snow-removal equipment should all be checked out prior to rink-building time. Ponds, streams, and lakes should be considered as possible ice-skating sites and necessary safety precautions taken in regard to ice thickness.

Rink-Construction Procedures

Site characteristics control in part the procedures necessary to build natural-ice rinks. If the ground is level and water can be contained by means of grade or dike, flooding is possible. If these conditions do not prevail, it is necessary to spray the water into the rink area. Flooding is faster and more economical, while spraying provides ice when flooding fails. Either process calls for temperatures of 20 degrees or colder, and the colder the temperature the faster an ice rink can be made.

In either method, the temperature of the water must be taken into account. Water coming from the main contains sufficient heat to melt ground frost. Therefore, it is advisable to flood at a slow-enough rate to permit water to chill before the frost melting point is reached. If spraying is necessary, the hose should be fitted with a spray nozzle and the water should be directed high in the air. Since lower temperatures occur in the evening, many communities do their flooding or spraying at night to obtain a faster build-up of ice. The periods of delay, when it is necessary to wait for the sprayed coat of water to freeze, are shorter at night.

The rate of build-up in a spray operation may be accelerated by diking the base ice with snow to reduce runoff. Care should be taken not to melt into the snowbank with too much water at one time. Shell ice will result.

Shell ice occurs when water seeps away after the surface is frozen over. Seepage can occur if the ground frost melts, a leak in the dike develops, or water melts away a part of the snowbank. Shell ice will remain a problem until it is removed.

If air pockets develop in the process of flooding, they should be punctured and filled with water before flooding is completed.

Natural-ice skating rinks can be created on tennis courts or other hard-surface areas, although costly additional construction is necessary. Some types of tennis courts do not hold up well if water is frozen on their surfaces.

LINER-TYPE RINKS

In many areas of the country, the traditional method of building natural-ice skating rinks is almost impossible because of constant freezing and thawing. In order to have success with the usual natural rink, temperatures must remain near or below freezing.

Many communities have 30 or 40 days of appropriate skating

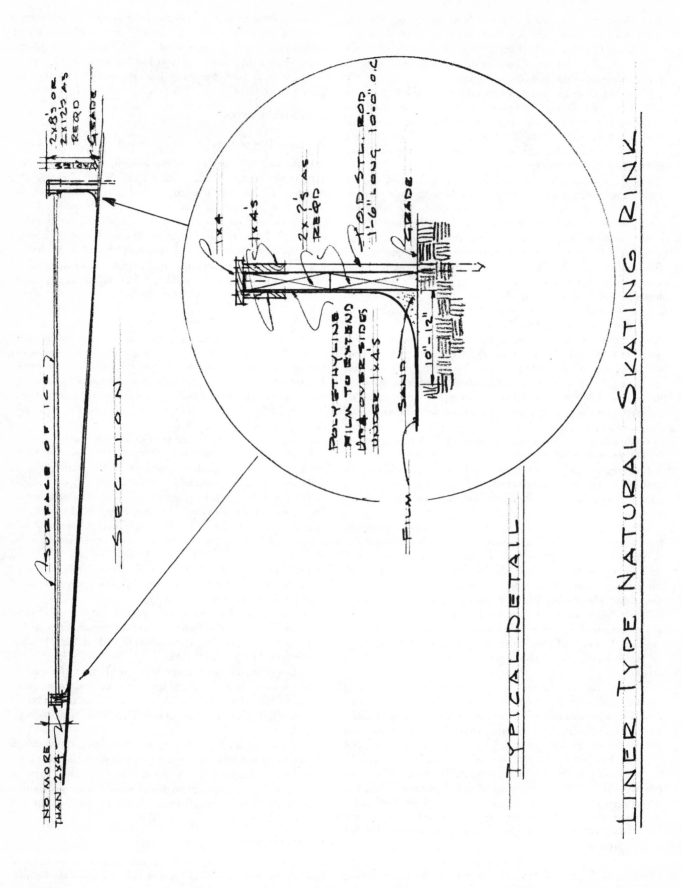

Figure 23

weather, but fluctuating temperatures cause the ice to melt and the ground to thaw. Under these conditions, the natural-ice-rink construction is impractical. In order to provide a skating facility under these circumstances, the liner-type rink is a possibility.

A plastic-type liner (polyethylene) is used to prevent water seepage and to waterproof the floor and sides of the rink. This material can be obtained in large sections—100' x 100', 200' x 200', and variations of these sizes. A framework to contain the liner should be constructed on flat ground, or possibly around the edge of a hard-surface area (see Figure 23). Sand is placed on the inside for a distance of 10" to 12" from the bottoms of the boards and shaped to form a cove. The liner is placed on the inside of the framework and up over the top. A cap of 1" x 4"s, which will extend below the ice on the inside, is necessary around the structure in order to prevent skates from puncturing the liner. The rink is then filled to the proper level with water.

Fencing and a ramp and rail are recommended. Temporary lights and music will add to skating pleasure.

RESURFACING

Once the ice surface is used for ice skating it should be resurfaced when needed. This can be accomplished by scraping away or sweeping the cuttings and spraying a light coat of water over the ice. If some cuttings are left after scraping, a little additional water should melt them and a good skating surface will result.

GENERAL CONSIDERATIONS

Safe Practices

Safety regulations should be posted. Rules should prescribe the direction of skating and conduct of skaters, and forbid games of a rough nature, such as tag, as well as objects on the ice, such as sleds and other coasting devices. Hockey sticks and pucks should also be banned during general skating sessions and times when small children are using the facility.

The thickness of ice is critical on ponds, streams, and lakes used for ice skating, and proper safety precautions should be taken to prevent accidents. Warning signs, barriers, and the dissemination of warnings through public communications media are desirable.

Sport Adaptations

Ice rinks may have a sport function as well as providing a recreation service. Figure skating requires nothing more than a smooth unobstructed ice surface. In some parts of the country, curling is a popular ice sport.

If ice hockey is to a part of the rink's activity schedule, goals will be needed and dasher boards will have to be installed to enclose an area as near 85' x 185' as possible. Dasher boards are heavily reinforced to stand the shock of players being pushed against them. They stand 4' high and come in lengths of 8' or 10'. The dasher-board enclosure should have round corners since square corners are found to be dangerous. A kick board 6" or 8" wide is fastened at the base of the dasher boards and is replaced as often as necessary. Dasher boards will reflect sunlight and cause melting of the ice. For this reason, they should be painted a dark color. Because it is difficult to follow the puck if the dasher boards are too dark, a shade of gray is recommended. If the hockey rink is indoors, the dasher boards can be painted a light color without causing a melting problem. If night hockey is anticipated, adequate lighting to insure seeing the fast-moving puck is essential for safety reasons.

Colored hockey lines on an outdoor rink create a melting problem on sunny days. This can be reduced by using vegetable dye in a water solution. The Ice Skating Institute of America has published a detailed technical paper on marking ice-hockey rinks and has developed a routing head for cutting lines in the ice.

Racing may be made a part of the natural-ice rink program by laying out a track of 4, 6, 8, or more laps to the mile. The track boundaries can be designated by drilling holes and inserting flags on short staffs. Many communities hold annual racing derbies for general participation. In some instances, skating clubs develop and the competition intensifies. As the quality of competition improves, so must the quality of the facility. Such refinements are explained in manuals of the Amateur Skating Union, an affiliate of the Amateur Athletic Union.

Warming Houses

Consideration should be given to the use of existing park buildings for warming houses in conjunction with skating rinks. Portable buildings may be used as warming houses as well as for other seasonal purposes.

SKI COURSES

Skiing is an activity which has become exceedingly popular in the past few years, and it is, indeed, a fine outdoor sport. If climatic conditions are suitable and desirable topogaphic features available, a school or a park and recreation department should look into the possibility of developing the facilities needed to foster this sport.

The provision of skiing in a school or public recreation system should be approached from an instructional standpoint, the theory being to give participants some basic instruction in the sport so they can enjoy it as a leisure-time activity in the resort areas that have more ideal facilities. If the park system contains ideal skiing hills with plenty of room, regular ski courses may be developed. Some of the basic facilities required for the instructional type of ski development are: proper topographical features; a headquarters building to be used for rental of equipment, a refectory, etc.; a ski tow; and slopes which may be used for instructional purposes for the various types of classes.

Normally, the series of classes is broken into three units: beginners, advanced, and expert. It is the opinion of ski instructors that the beginners' ski class, in relation to recreational skiing, is by far the most important.

Basic instruction in skiing may be conducted in classes not exceeding 25 to 30 beginners. For this group, a gentle and short slope with a relatively large flat run-out area is desirable. This permits a beginner to have complete control of himself and allows him to gain confidence in the use of his skis. In the advanced group, classes are much smaller, and in the expert group, instruction becomes almost individual. In each "promotion", hills become longer and a little steeper.

Beginners' Classes—The following criteria are recommended for the selection of facilities for beginners' classes:
- Flat-top hill area, 50 sq. ft. per skier, 25 skiers per class
- Slope about 75' to 100' long, drop in grade of 15', or 4:1 slope
- Starting line at top of slope, 100' wide
- Run-out at bottom of slope should be flat or uphill
- Slope should face east or northeast
- Instructional area should be free of stones, woods, etc.

- Protective cover, such as trees or brush, around the area is desirable

  Advanced Classes—The following criteria are suggested for the selection of facilities for advanced classes:
- Top of hill about same as for beginners
- Slope is most important; should be about 3:1, and 100′ to 150′ long
- Width of hill or slope should be minimum of 150′ because of speed and space required for turning movements
- Classes may use only a portion of slope in instructional processes

  Expert Classes—The following criteria are recommended for the selection of facilities for expert classes:
- These classes can use same hill as advanced classes, longer and steeper hill desirable
- Should be enough downhill length to permit a minimum of three turning movements—for example, 250′ on a 3 to 1 slope
- Greater width required than that of slope for advanced classes

  Skiing is so popular that many ski centers utilize artificial snow-making equipment when weather conditions threaten to halt the program.

COASTING HILLS

Often a community has a hill, or hills, suitable for coasting, which become meccas for children with sleds, toboggans, and other coasting devices after every snowfall. In the absence of a natural coasting hill, some park and public works departments have built a coasting hill. These hills are usually located in a park safely guarded from the hazards of street traffic.

In developing local coasting areas, care should be taken to incorporate adequate safety features. Plenty of room should be provided between sled runs, and up traffic should be isolated from the down traffic. The area should be as free as possible from hazards, such as nearby trees, grills, benches, or other park paraphernalia.

Communities that develop an extensive response to coasting or skiing may want to counter adverse weather with the use of artificial-snow equipment, or improve the activity with a ski lift. Most resort areas have such equipment and know its capacities and limitations.

SELECTED REFERENCES

A Cutting Tool for Making Ice Hockey Lines, (Technical Paper 101). Ice Skating Institute of America, P. O. Box 955, Fort Myers, Fla., April 1961.

A Round Table for New and Prospective Rink Managers. Fort Myers, Fla.: Ice Skating Institute of America, P. O. Box 955, July 1964.

Boating Facilities. Periodical published by the Outboard Boating Club of America, 307 North Michigan Ave., Chicago, Ill.

Burnett, W., How to Make an Ice Rink, **American City.** Vol. 68, September 1953.

Chaney, C. A., **Marinas: Recommendations for Design, Construction, and Maintenance.** New York: The National Association of Engine and Boat Manufacturers, Inc.

Christiansen, Milo, **Stadium Reference Material.** Washington, D.C.: Department of Recreation, 1944.

Concrete Grandstands. Chicago: Portland Cement Association, 1948.

Field, Jacob, How to Orient for Sun or Shade, **The Engineering News Record.** Vol. CXLIV, February 1950.

Gabrielsen, M. A., and Miles, C. M., **Sports and Recreation Facilities for School and Community.** Englewood Cliffs, N.J.: Prentice-Hall, Inc., 1958.

Launching Ramps and Piers. Chicago: Outboard Boating Club of America, 307 North Michigan Ave.

Outboard Marinas. Informational booklet published jointly by the Outboard Boating Club of America, 307 North Michigan Ave., Chicago, Ill., and the Socony Mobil Oil Company, Small Craft Division, 26 Broadway, New York, N.Y.

Rink Covers and Enclosures, **Proceedings, Fifth Annual Conference, 1964.** Fort Myers, Fla.: Ice Skating Institute of America, P. O. Box 955, l964.

Scott, Harry A., and Westkaemper, Richard B., **From Program to Facilities in Physical Education.** New York: Harper and Brothers, 1958.

Skiing Information, Eastern Ski Association, Littleton, N.H. [.

The Athletic Institute, **Cycling.** Color-Sound 35mm. Film Kit, Instructor's Guide, and Student Handbook. Chicago, Ill.: The Institute, 805 Merchandise Mart, 1965.

————, **Fishing.** Color-Sound 35mm. Film Kit, Instructor's Guide, and Student Handbook. Chicago, Ill.: The Institute, 1964.

————, **Golf.** Color-Sound 35mm. Film Kit, Instructor's Guide, and Student Handbook. Chicago, Ill.: The Institute, 1964.

————, **Skating.** Color-Sound 35mm. Film Kit, Instructor's Guide, and Student Handbook. Chicago, Ill.: The Institute, 1963.

————, **Skiing.** Color-Sound 35mm. Film Kit, Instructor's Guide, and Student Handbook. Chicago, Ill.: The Institute, 1964.

Chapter 6

OUTDOOR EDUCATION – RECREATION AREAS and FACILITIES

OUTDOOR EDUCATION and outdoor recreation are occupying an increasingly important place in school and college curriculums and in the programs of recreation, camping, and youth agencies. An unprecedented growth of all types of outdoor activities necessitating land areas and facilities can be anticipated in the next decade. A sudden awareness on the part of education and recreation leaders that the present generation and those to come are far removed from the land and the rural life of their forebears has caused much interest and concern in the development of outdoor education programs. It must be assumed that school-age children and many adults know little about the outdoors; and programs and facilities must be designed to educate them in, about, and for the outdoors. An ecological approach to outdoor education has both recreational and educational implications.

Recent national developments, such as the ORRRC report, the creation of the Bureau of Outdoor Recreation, and state and federal programs in conservation, have created a favorable climate for the rapid growth of outdoor education and have stressed the urgent need for lands and facilities. The passage of the Land and Water Conservation Fund Act and the establishment of the Open Space Program and the Area Redevelopment Administration are examples of recent activities of the Federal Government to facilitate outdoor education and outdoor recreation. Education and recreation organizations have accelerated their efforts in developing programs to meet the urgent need for educating the public concerning the protection and use of our natural resources. The Outdoor Education Project of the American Association for Health, Physical Education, and Recreation is an illustration of a nationwide education effort in leadership preparation for outdoor education and in providing services and materials to stimulate the development of more effective programs.

"Outdoor education" is a term which has reference to learning activities in the outdoors, and for the outdoors, that can be provided in the curriculum of schools, colleges, and universities, and in the programs of recreation, camping, and community agencies. Outdoor education has been broadly described as follows:

Outdoor education is a means of curriculum enrichment through experiences in and for the outdoors. It is not a separate discipline with prescribed objectives like science and mathematics; it is simply a learning climate which offers opportunities for direct laboratory experiences in identifying and resolving real-life problems, for acquiring skills with which to enjoy a lifetime of creative living, for attaining concepts and insights about human and natural resources, and for getting us back in touch with those aspects of living where our roots were once firmly established.[1]

There are many patterns for outdoor education programs which can be conducted in a variety of outdoor settings, such as school sites, camps, field campuses, parks, recreation areas,

[1]Julian W. Smith et al, *Outdoor Education*, Prentice-Hall, Inc., Englewood Cliffs, N.J., 1963, p. 19.

sanctuaries, museums, lakes, ponds, streams, forests, farms, or other land areas and facilities. Consequently, in considering facilities, much attention must be given to the types of outdoor programs that are now developing. The following principles are important in this connection:

- Maximum use should be made of the unique qualities of the natural environment without destroying its integrity.
- The areas and facilities should be designed to serve the needs of all age groups on a year-round basis.
- The program and facilities should supplement and enrich the community's education and recreation resources.
- The program should determine the structures and site treatment.

Outdoor education, when applied to schools and colleges, is a means of curriculum enrichment, involving the use of the outdoors as a laboratory and the teaching of skills, appreciations, and attitudes for the wise use of the outdoors and natural resources. Consequently, outdoor education facilities should serve the entire educational program and should be designed to supplement the other resources of the school plant and the "community campus". All community agencies concerned with education and recreation should be involved in the planning of adequate outdoor resources.

AN OUTDOOR EDUCATION-RECREATION COMPLEX

Outdoor education and outdoor recreation encompass a great variety of activities, many of which can be conducted on a single, large acreage of land. With careful planning, facilities and site treatment can have multiple use. It is recognized that, in many instances, there will be a cluster of sites and facilities, some in or near an urban area and others in more distant places. An outdoor-education complex on one piece of land or in several plots in close proximity has many advantages in the best use of leadership, equipment, and transportation. Such a site lends itself to wide community use, with responsibilities for leadership and finances shared by several agencies. Obviously, the size and physical characteristics of an outdoor-education complex will depend on the geographic location and the topography of the land.

Some of the facilities and types of site treatment for a complex that would accommodate a broad program of outdoor education and outdoor recreation, and which would constitute an outdoor laboratory or field campus, are briefly described. It is assumed that there will be many areas and facilities, public and private, that can also be used in a comprehensive program.

The areas and facilities which should be included in an outdoor education-recreation complex are as follows:
- An outdoor laboratory which would include:
    nature trails;
    plots for various conservation projects, such as water run-off, cover, and erosion control;

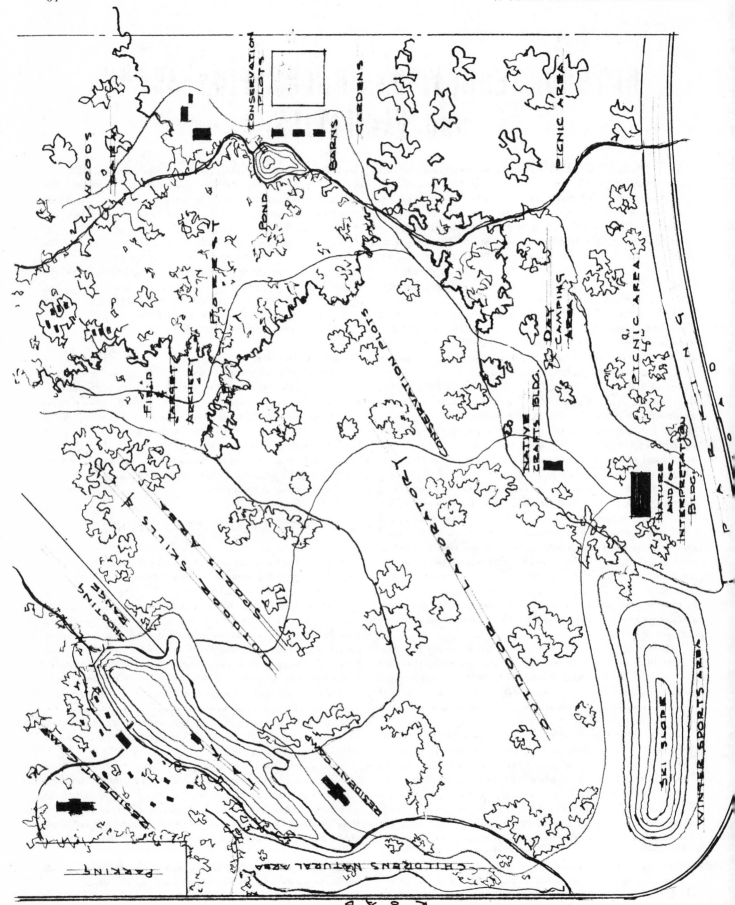

Figure 24
Outdoor Education-Recreation Complex

garden plots;
wildlife management.

- A resident camp for year-round use that will accommodate 60-120 people and which can be used by schools and youth agencies.
- An interpretation center and/or nature center and/or trail-side museum.
- A pioneer and/or modern farm, which would include farm animals, raising of crops, woods, garden, farm pond, etc.
- A forest area.
- A camp skills and natural crafts center—a·simple structure where small tools would be used.
- A day-camping area with ample shelter.
- An outdoor cooking and picnicking area.
- An outdoor skills and sports area, to include water activities, winter sports, and Youth Hostel building.

CONSIDERATIONS IN SELECTING AND DEVELOPING SITES

The type of program planned should determine the size and characteristics of the site. Size alone does not necessarily mean much except that it does affect the numbers of certain species of wildlife that might live in the area. A large area does not necessarily have a diversity of physical features. It may just be level land, harboring only a few species of trees, with no particularly outstanding features. This does not mean that such an area cannot be made interesting from an educational point of view, provided good leadership is available. It does mean that size alone should not necessarily be the determining factor in selecting a site for an outdoor education program. Many schools, recreation departments, and community agencies already have school sites, parks, and recreation areas that should be developed for outdoor programs. Schools in some sections of the country also have forest lands that could be developed and used in a broad education and recreation program.

SITE CHARACTERISTICS

It should be emphasized that the site and facilities should be determined by the type of program planned. If plans call for a resident camp, many more requirements must be met than if the site will be used only on a daily basis. If the land and facilities are to contribute to all aspects of the educational curriculum, or if there is to be special emphasis on science, conservation, and outdoor skills, many characteristics will need to be considered, such as:

- A location to give some privacy and solitude.
- Year-round accessibility by road.
- A minimum of natural and man-made hazards.
- Interesting geologic features, such as rock outcroppings, open field, flat terrain, and a variety of soil types.
- A variety of native vegetation, including woods.
- Wildlife that can be maintained with good management.
- A pond, stream, seashore, or large body of water.
- Demonstration areas for conservation practices.
- Woods for practicing outdoor skills and use of native materials.
- Sanitary facilities, including good drainage and good drinking water.
- Simple shelters in the event of inclement weather.
- Proximity to adequate medical and hospital services.

CAMPS

The word "camping" implies living outdoors and engaging in those activities that are primarily related to the outdoor environment. "Resident camps," "day camps", "group camps", and "family camps" are the common designations used for the various types of camps.

Camps have been developed by public agencies at all levels of government and by many voluntary youth-serving organizations. The rapidly increasing participation of children and adults in camping necessitates careful consideration of desirable areas and facilities.

CAMPS FOR OUTDOOR EDUCATION AND OUTDOOR RECREATION PROGRAMS

Organized camping and the use of resident camps by schools continue to grow. If adequate facilities are to be provided to meet the needs of both organized camping groups and schools, the facilities must be designed for year-round use. Cooperative planning is not only necessary in order to get the most from the community dollar, but is imperative if suitable lands and sites are to be obtained.

Camps for year-round and multiple use must be winterized and so constructed as to be adaptable to different types of programs. While the agency use will be heavy in the summer months, the schools, particularly elementary and junior-high classrooms, will be conducting "outdoor schools" from fall through the spring months. Another development is ′teacher and leadership preparation in outdoor education by colleges and universities, which requires camps designed to accommodate adults as well as children and youth. The suggestions concerning sites and facilities for resident camps are, therefore, made with this extended use in mind and are different from the more simple and primitive structures that would have only summer use.

GUIDES FOR THE DEVELOPMENT OF RESIDENT CAMPS

The term "resident camp" or "established camp" is used to designate an area that provides for 50 to 150 people, with facilities for cooking, sleeping, and program development. There are three major considerations in the development of resident camps: (1) selecting the camp site; (2) planning the layout and development; and (3) constructing the buildings and facilities.

SELECTING THE CAMP SITE

The selection of a site for a camp in which children and adults can live and learn is no small task. Both vision and technical knowledge are required. The type of camp which is finally decided upon will be the result of a series of processes. First, the area must be located; then the layout must be planned; and, finally, the camp must be constructed.

The availability of existing public lands as possible camp sites should be explored. Some states permit state-owned lands to be turned over to schools and other public agencies for their use. Often, privately-owned land borders on or is interspersed with state-owned land. These private lands, because of their proximity to large tracts of state-owned property, may be desirable for camp use.

Competent camp planners, architects, engineers, surveyors, and others with special knowledge and skills should be consulted. Maps and aerial surveys as well as "on-the-ground" investigations should be used. An examination of present and proposed roads and of population growth will help determine future crowding and solve questions of access. Water resources, both for domestic use and program purposes, must be carefully investigated.

It is advisable to secure a large-enough tract to provide for future growth. At least an acre per camper, in terms of predicted future use, is a minimum. Land with a varied topography and many outdoor-type program possibilities is highly desirable.

PLANNING THE LAYOUT AND DEVELOPMENT

Good planning means dollars saved. Such planning should be cognizant of certain principles of camp layout, some of which will be briefly discussed in the paragraphs which follow.

Roads and Paths

In selecting the entrance to the camp, the designer would do well to keep in mind the ease and safety of leaving or entering the public thoroughfare.

The camp should have a parking lot sufficient for the number of vehicles that would normally be accommodated. A relatively flat, open, and well-drained area nearby can serve as an overflow parking area.

A spur drive from the main entrance road should be constructed to the kitchen and other basic facilities. It would be advisable to seek the advice of a qualified road engineer in developing roads and trails.

Waterfront

Swimming and other water-related activities are desirable for a good camp program. Waterfront development is discussed in detail in Chapter 14.

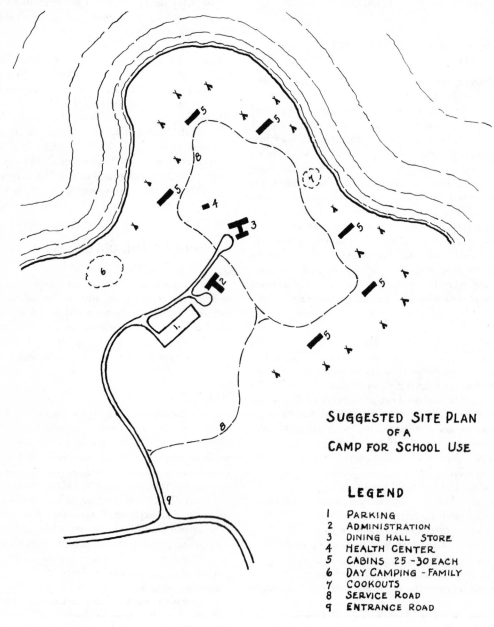

SUGGESTED SITE PLAN
OF A
CAMP FOR SCHOOL USE

LEGEND

1	PARKING
2	ADMINISTRATION
3	DINING HALL STORE
4	HEALTH CENTER
5	CABINS 25-30 EACH
6	DAY CAMPING - FAMILY
7	COOKOUTS
8	SERVICE ROAD
9	ENTRANCE ROAD

School and other groups which are close enough to come for a day cookout
Water and toilets

Families related to the school or other camping group
Large group cookouts and barbecues for the camping group and camp-related community groups.

Figure 25
Suggested Site Plan

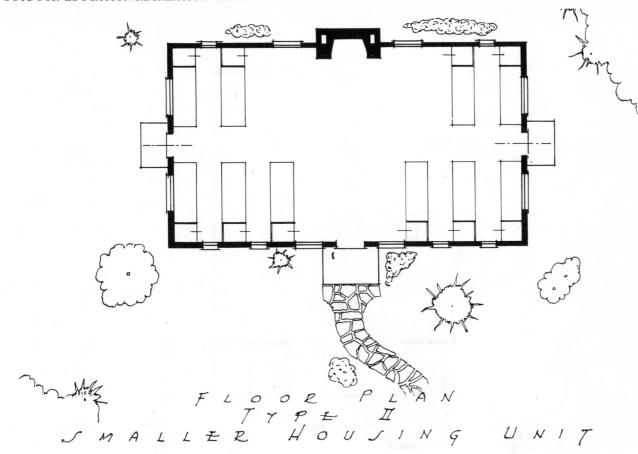

FLOOR PLAN
TYPE II
SMALLER HOUSING UNIT

Figure 23

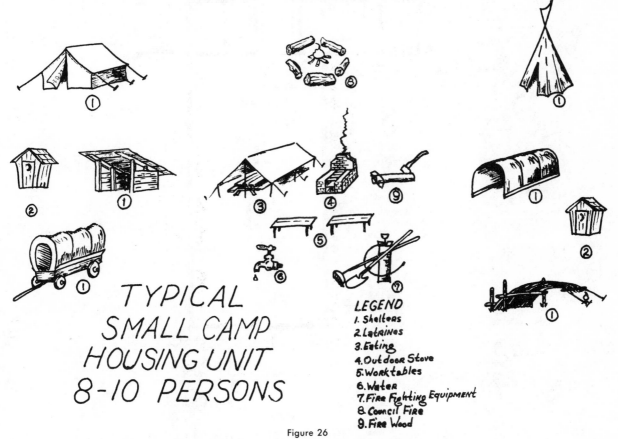

TYPICAL
SMALL CAMP
HOUSING UNIT
8-10 PERSONS

LEGEND
1. Shelters
2. Latrines
3. Eating
4. Outdoor Stove
5. Worktables
6. Water
7. Fire Fighting Equipment
8. Council Fire
9. Fire Wood

Figure 26
Typical Small-Camp Housing Unit

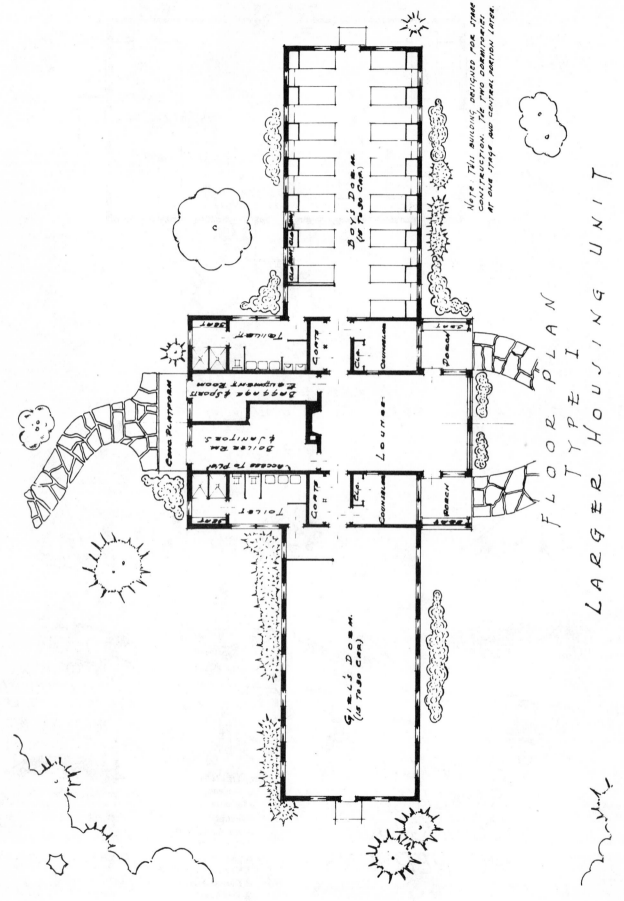

Figure 27
Floor Plan of Larger Housing Unit

Figure 28
Camp Riley Winterized Lodge and Dining Hall

General Features

The first building approached when one enters camp should be the administration building, and the next should be the dining hall. These buildings are main points of interest, for it is around and in these facilities that many camp activities will be centered. The buildings should be placed within easy access to both the parking area and the living units.

Wherever several housing units are grouped together for program or supervision purposes, they should be, if possible, at or near the same elevation. Enough room should be left between buildings so that activity in one does not interfere with the activities in others. Care should be taken to locate the buildings on the natural contours widely separated, not in lines, squares, or compact groups. The actual location of each structure should be planned so as to enhance the architecture of the building.

CONSTRUCTING THE BUILDINGS AND FACILITIES

Since camp structures represent a large investment, they require the best of planning energies and abilities. It is wise to retain a professional camp consultant and develop a master plan. Not only do these structures provide for the basic need of shelter, but they also create an atmosphere about the camp that can be a definite aid to the camp program.

The designer's objective should be to develop an exterior appearance that is suited to the region, the site, and the camp program. Contrary to popular belief, nearly all of the standard building materials can be used to produce an attractive building. The problem of annual maintenance, as well as appearance, must be considered. Native materials should be used wherever feasible and practical. In every way, the architectural treatment of the exterior and interior of buildings and other structures should be in harmony with the motif of real camping and with the natural environment.

The structures should be planned to meet all presently-known and anticipated needs. It is helpful to study plans of existing facilities and to interview present camp directors. However, one should never assume that a camp plan applicable to one site should be duplicated exactly on a different site or for a different camping use. Each camp designer will have to adapt such plans to the needs of the local program. The desirable camp structures will be described in the paragraphs which follow.

Administration Building

The administration building will house all the administrative functions of the camp. There should be office space for the camp director and assistants, a conference room, a secretarial room, a workroom for mimeographing and mailing, and toilet facilities for men and for women. Provision should be made for processing the entering and departing campers.

Dining Hall, Kitchen, and Store

The dining and food-preparation building should be large enough to accommodate the campers, staff, and occasional guests. These facilities should be designed so that the campers may be served at their respective tables. The layout should include: a separate room or enclosure for dishwashing; an exhaust system; a walk-in refrigerated room; a food-storage room; food-preparation counters with enclosed shelving; a loading platform; a garbage crib; the dietitian's or head cook's office or desk space; a camp store for supplying food to cookout groups, the camp post office, and the bank. Toilet and lavatory facilities should be provided for the kitchen staff. Adequate and evenly-distributed heat should also be provided. The type of heating will vary in different parts of the country. Fuel for cooking should be electricity or gas.

Coat and hat racks should be provided. Garbage and refuse should be disposed of in such a manner as to meet any local health regulations. If an authorized public garbage place is not available, the camp should have its own approved incinerator or garbage-disposal burial plant.

The dining hall should be friendly and restful. The lighting should be adequate and well distributed, without glare. Ease in cleaning is also essential. Light-colored asphalt, rubber, vinyl asbestos, or terrazzo tile makes an acceptable floor covering, although a hardwood floor is to be preferred. In the kitchen, a greaseproof asphalt tile makes an acceptable floor covering.

Housing Units

There are several approaches to the housing-unit design, depending upon the needs of the group and the program. Some school-camp administrators prefer to house an activity group together at one time in a large unit, while others prefer the smaller, decentralized unit. A large housing unit is a group of 25 to 30 persons, while a small-group unit includes 8 to 10.

Large Housing Units. For the large housing-unit arrangement, both boys and girls, or men and women, could be housed in the same building, with sleeping rooms separated by a common living room. It is desirable to locate each counselor room adjacent to the lounge and sleeping room so that adequate supervision can be maintained. In a school camp, this arrangement makes possible a good teacher-camper or counselor-camper living relationship.

In an established camp designed for the use of schools, each housing unit should accommodate 25 to 30 campers. Single beds are recommended. It is also desirable to have kitchenettes in case the central dining hall is not used. Kitchenettes are especially convenient if the camp is to be used for small adult-education groups, conferences, or workshops. Flush toilets and showers should be adjacent to the sleeping rooms. Not only is this style of building suitable for adult groups, but it is highly recommended for winter camping ,for young children.

Architectural design, insulation, and the heating plant will vary with the climatic conditions peculiar to the area. Comfortable beds, springs, and mattresses with water-repellent mattress covers should be provided. There should also be storage cabinets for clothes, suitcases, and personal items. Mirrors should be provided in the sleeping room and washrooms. Each sleeping room should have one writing table and chair per eight children, if these are not provided in the living room or lounge. The general lighting should be subdued, but there might be a student lamp for the writing table.

Small Housing Units. Some groups prefer to have smaller housing units more widely dispersed. This plan lends itself better to unit construction, which makes it possible to build some camp facilities with limited funds, adding more units from year to year. In addition to the well-placed and well-spaced housing units, there should be a central main building containing the food-preparation and dining facilities.

Small housing units should be equipped with minimum utilities. Each housing unit or cabin will accommodate approximately eight to ten campers and staff. In certain sections of the country, it is desirable to provide toilet and shower facilities in each housing unit. This is especially true in a year-round school camp in a cold climate. In other parts of the country, unit-type toilet and shower buildings could be provided to serve more than one housing unit. The number to be served would depend upon the unit site and location.

The simplest types of housing are tents, teepees, and shelters made of canvas and native materials. If pit latrines are to be used, they should be properly constructed to meet sanitary requirements.

Health Center

A health center should provide separate toilet and shower facilities for boys and girls, an isolation room, ward space for four persons, the nurse's quarters, an examining room, a reception room, and minimum kitchenette facilities. The accommodations offered by this building are only to supplement medical aid provided in the area where the camp is located.

Staff Quarters

Living quarters for the staff should be provided. This building should contain toilet and shower facilities, a common lounge and reading room, bedrooms, and a recreation room. In some instances, separate housing units may be needed for married staff members.

General Maintenance Building

A building of sufficient size to store the necessary equipment for maintaining the camp is desirable. This building will include space for trucks, a tractor, ground maintenance machinery and tools, repair materials, and a room for miscellaneous repair work. The design of the building will depend upon the type of equipment to be stored.

Toilet-and-Shower Building

This building is needed for the separate-unit-housing type camp and should be located so as to serve more than one housing unit. Heating facilities should be included. The toilet and hot-water showers should be adequate for the numbers to be served and should meet any state health regulations.

Utilities

It is essential that an adequate supply of potable water be provided for the total camp population and for any future expansion. An adequate reserve supply should be maintained for fire and other emergency use. Drilled wells are recommended except where other sources are approved by health authorities. Data on available water supplies may be secured from state hydrogeologists, local well-drillers, or nearby residents. Adequate and approved drinking fountains should be installed at strategic places of need.

Sewage Disposal

The geologic nature of the camp area will dictate the best type of sewage-disposal system. This disposal system will normally consist of a septic tank, dosing chamber, and tile disposal field. The location, construction, and maintenance of the sewage-disposal system should comply with regulations of the State Department of Health. In outpost camping, where pit latrines are used, they should be constructed and maintained in compliance with health regulations.

Electricity

The electrical-distribution system for the camp should be carefully planned for present and future needs. Whenever possible, all lines in the camp area should be placed underground.

DAY CAMPS

A day camp is an area and facility intended to provide a program similar to that of the resident camp except that campers sleep at home. Some considerations relative to desirable areas and facilities for a day camp will be outlined in the paragraphs which follow.

SITE

Reasonable isolation and a varied topography with outdoor program possibilities are essential. Natural parks, park-school areas, and community forests often lend themselves to use as day-camp sites. Some communities have developed special day-camp areas; others make appropriate picnic areas available for this special use.

TRAVEL

Buses are often used to transport campers to the day camp. If more than a half-hour is consumed in daily travel each way, the effectiveness of the program is reduced.

UNIT DEVELOPMENTS

Day-camp groups are divided into units or counselor groups ranging from 8 to 20 campers. Most day camps provide simple facilities for each unit, including a fireplace for cooking, storage cabinets, and tables. Some day camps serve a daily meal in a central dining hall, reducing or eliminating the need for unit cooking facilities.

GENERAL FACILITIES

Storage is needed for equipment, food, and program supplies. Some day camps use trailers or trucks for storage, hauling them back and forth each day.

A first-aid station, with first-aid supplies, and a rest-area facility are necessary.

GROUP CAMPS

Many public agencies today provide special camp sites for small groups, such as Scouts, church groups, and school classes. These sites generally accommodate from 10 to 40 persons. In most cases, the groups stay from 1 to 5 days.

Simple fireplaces for cooking, picnic shelters for use in bad weather, toilets, and safe drinking water are necessities.

FAMILY CAMPS

Family camps offer facilities for individual families or small groups who bring their own shelters and other equipment and who cook their own meals. There has been a phenomenal growth in the demand for this type of camping during the past ten years. Public agencies, particularly state and national forest and park agencies, have found it difficult to meet the demand.

Although there are no definite standards at present for family camping, some practices recognized as desirable have emerged.

GENERAL FACILITIES

A relatively undeveloped camp site might provide only pit latrines, water, and a stone circle for a fire. The more common pattern for family camping, however, is the camp ground which cares for from 40 to 500 families.

A large camp ground should have a headquarters building with a check-in station, an office, and a residence for a camp manager. The program facilities might include an amphitheater or indoor hall for evening programs, with equipment for slides and movies.

Large camps generally have wash houses with hot and cold running water, toilets, and, in some cases, hot showers. Trash and garbage containers should be close to the camp sites and should be adequate to care for the maximum number of campers.

TENT CAMP SITES

A camp ground for tent campers should contain four to eight camp sites per acre, each with a table, a fireplace, level ground on which to erect a tent, and a car-parking area with barriers. There should be a one-way road through the area. Water spigots should be available within 300 feet of each camp site. Pit latrines or wash houses with flush toilets should also be provided.

TRAVEL TRAILER SITES

Generally, travel-trailer sites should be separate from tent sites. Most public areas do not provide hookups for electricity, sewage, or water. Developments for water, washing, and toilets are similar to those for tent-camp areas. Many camp grounds now include sewage-dumping facilities for self-contained trailers and campers.

Drive-through sites for trailer parking are desirable.

FEES

The camping public seems to be seeking more and more comfort and more and more elaborate facilities than were offered in the past. Most family campers are willing to pay extra fees for these conveniences.

OTHER AREAS AND FACILITIES FOR OUTDOOR EDUCATION

OUTDOOR LABORATORIES

The term "outdoor laboratory" is being used for a piece of land (including wet lands, lakes, and seashores) set aside by a school for learning experiences directly related to land and its resources. It may be located close to an individual school or it may serve a group of schools. It may be a part of the school grounds or a section of a park-school development. It may consist of only a few acres nearby or of several hundred acres, nearby or many miles away. It may serve individual elementary schools, high schools, or universities, or all of them jointly. Because outdoor laboratories are extremely varied in their site possibilities and their purposes, no rigid format for their development is possible.

The term "land for learning" has been applied to the school laboratory. It implies the opportunity of school groups to study, explore, and experiment with land and its resources. Outdoor study, field trips, and experiments with water, soil, plants, and animals constitute its major functions.

Developments may range from nothing more than a few trails

with the area left natural, to nature trails, class and museum buildings, horticultural plots, developed ponds, forest plantations, gardens, and small-farm operations. The creativity of the school teacher or outdoor education specialist, the potential of the available site, and funds available may be the only limiting factors in the development of program facilities.

If a laboratory is heavily used, water and toilet facilities might be essential. A storage building for tools and supplies might also be desirable.

NATURE CENTERS

The term "nature center" is used to designate a particular type of development that will facilitate learning in the outdoors and the growth of recreational interests. The establishment of nature centers is being promoted extensively by the National Audubon Society and the Science for Young Americans Association. Several hundred such centers have been developed in the United States during the past 20 years. Children's museums may be considered a part of this development, although some of these museums lack adjacent lands for outdoor education.

Nature centers have been developed principally by three types of financing and management: schools, private associations, and public park and recreation departments.

Figure 29
Junior Museum, Greensboro, N.C.

GREENSBORO JUNIOR MUSEUM FLOOR PLAN
SCALE 1" = 20'

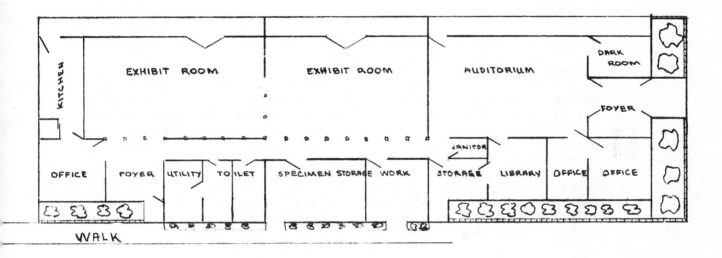

Figure 30

THE SITE

Some of the suggestions for the school outdoor-education laboratory are applicable here. Nature trails, ponds, bogs, gardens, forest plantings, and the like may provide the variety essential for a rich outdoor education program.

THE NATURE-CENTER BUILDING

The building should be designed so as to permit expansion as the program grows and as more funds become available. In its initial stage, the building should contain a minimum space of 2,500 square feet. This would be large enough to contain one class fairly adequately. The building should be designed according to the needs set by the program. The following general facilities are recommended:

- **Office for staff.**
- **Toilet facilities.** One for boys and one for girls. Access should be provided to the outside as well as to the interior of the building.
- **Large meeting room.** The wall space can be utilized for exhibits. Low cabinets along the walls should be provided for storage of educational aids. A long counter providing work and display space should be constructed on top of the cabinets.
- **Classrooms.** Two classrooms should be provided so that the class may be broken up into smaller groups if necessary.
- **Workroom.** This room would be used for constructing displays and for arts and crafts.

- **Science laboratory.** A room should be equipped with microscopes, soil and mineral testing equipment, and other materials necessary for scientific studies.
- **Library.** The large meeting room can contain the library, which would occupy one section of the room. The library should contain reference material, field guides, magazines, and novels concerned with the outdoors.
- **Storage room.** Adequate space should be provided for this facility.

It should be emphasized again that it is not essential for one center to have most of the facilities described here. Dynamic leadership is, to a large degree, more important, and not even the ultimate in good facilities can ever satisfactorily replace the need for effective leadership.

INTERPRETIVE CENTERS

Although the name "interpretive centers" might well be applied to the outdoor laboratories and the nature centers mentioned earlier, it has a specific use in describing certain facilities of public parks offered as a service to the general public and, in some cases, to school groups. The National Park Service has the most extensive development of such centers, although state and metropolitan parks have, in recent years, been expanding the number of their interpretive centers. The U. S. Forest Service is beginning to develop information centers that are essentially interpretive centers.

The primary purpose of interpretive centers is to help visitors understand and appreciate the natural, historical, or archaeological features of the areas in which the centers are located. Inasmuch as the problems of interpretation of each area are different, facility developments are likewise varied.

Interpretive centers frequently contain a trailside museum or interpretive-center building. This may vary in size from a ten-by-twenty-foot building to a large multiroomed structure. The size depends on the groups to be accommodated, the interpretive materials available, and the types of programs to be presented. A large building may contain:

- Display rooms with habitat cases and other exhibits;
- Office space for staff members;
- A laboratory for research and the preparation of display materials;
- Meeting rooms for lectures, slides, or movies;
- Lavatories and toilets;
- A counter for the sale of books and the distribution of pamphlets;
- An outdoor amphitheater or campfire area for lectures and movies;
- Trails to points of interest—sometimes these are self-guiding nature trails;
- Parapets or other special observation points—pointers indicating places of interest, and mounted telescopes are often included;
- Interpretive devices at points of interest—including bulletin boards, maps, diagrams, and displays;
- Parking areas.

School groups often visit interpretive centers, usually by school bus on a one-day basis. In some cases, picnic areas are provided for such groups. Work space, where children can work on projects at the center, is often a desirable feature.

SCHOOL AND COMMUNITY GARDENS, FARMS, AND FORESTS

Gardens, farms, and forests provide direct experiences with growing plants and, in some cases, with domestic animals. Schools, park and recreation agencies, and a few private agencies have been responsible for the development of facilities. Even when facilities are developed and operated by park and recreation departments or private agencies, some direct relationship with schools is often provided through an instructional program in which the school children are enrolled.

TRACT GARDENS

In a tract garden, which is the most common type of school or community garden, a piece of property, ranging in size from one to ten acres, is divided into small tracts for the use of individuals. Individual gardens may range in size from six-by-ten-foot plots for younger children to twenty-by-thirty-foot plots for older youth. Planting is generally done in accordance with a specific plan, and gardeners come during the summer months on a regular schedule of four to six hours per week to work in their plots. Supervision and instruction are essential for success.

Some of the necessary or desirable features of the tract garden are:

- **Garden building.** This may be a small building for the storage of tools and equipment, or a building large enough for class meetings and indoor activities during the bad weather.
- **Toilet facilities.** These should be adequate to care for the

maximum number of participants expected on the garden plot at one time.
- **Green house for plant propagation.**
- **Ready access to water.** Spigots and hoses should be available for limited irrigation.
- **Fencing for protection of the garden.**
- **Pathways and walkways to provide easy access to all plots.**
- **A demonstration home yard, with grass, flowers, and shrubs.**
- **Good landscaping.**

Preferably, the tract garden should be located within walking distance of the homes of the participants. In many cases, gardens are developed on or adjacent to school grounds.

Tract gardens for adults and families have been established in some communities. They are usually intended for people living in crowded urban centers or apartments who would not otherwise be able to garden. In some communities, these gardens are located at some distance from homes, and transportation is left up to the individuals concerned.

FARMS

Community or school farms are becoming increasingly important, especially near metropolitan centers, and offer opportunities for a rich and varied program. No single pattern of development can be indicated, although generally the farm is a place where children from schools or recreation agencies can observe diversified operations and, sometimes, do farm chores and help with planting and harvesting.

In addition to the buildings that are generally found on a diversified farm, there are meeting places and exhibits that make it possible to carry on indoor instruction. Picnic areas, farm ponds, day-camp facilities, campfire circles, and hiking trails are often developed also.

FORESTS

Over 1,200 school and community forests are to be found in the United States. Many of these were acquired through tax-delinquent land, through gifts, or through protection programs for community watersheds. Their use has followed diverse patterns. Some schools have carried on field trips, forest improvement projects, and other outdoor education activities. In general, however, schools have not made the maximum use of such areas.

Many of these forests could be developed as outdoor education laboratories. Some might be suitable sites for nature centers, day camps, or even resident camps.

School and community forests may serve valuable purposes even without extensive development. Water, trails, and toilets may be all the developments needed to provide useful educational facilities. Such areas may serve their best functions as places in which to study the ecological changes taking place over a period of years.

OUTDOOR SKILLS AND SPORTS AREA

Outdoor skills or sports areas should be included in the outdoor education-recreation complex, but it may be necessary to acquire special sites, depending on the topography of the land. These areas should provide opportunities to learn and to practice skills, but they may also be used as outdoor laboratories.

The following are some of the specialized program activities that might be conducted in the outdoor skills and sports area:
- **Casting and angling**—platforms and open level spaces.
- **Outdoor shooting range.**

- **Archery range**—target field course, archery golf, and other games.
- **Campcraft skills area.**
- **Overnight camping area.**
- **Outpost camping**—Adirondak shelters.
- **Facilities for water sports**—including swimming, canoeing, boating, sailing, skin diving and water skiing.
- **Area for crafts with native materials**—including carving, lapidary, weaving, and ceramics. A simple craft structure should be constructed for inclement weather and to house equipment.
- **Winter sports**—ski slopes and tow, ski shelter, tobogganing, and ice-skating rinks.

SPECIAL FEATURES IN OUTDOOR EDUCATION AREAS

Many kinds of developments are found in various types of outdoor education areas. Some of these are appropriate for camps, some for outdoor laboratories or nature centers, and some for outdoor recreation and sports centers. An outdoor education and outdoor recreation complex would include many site plans and facilities not possible in more limited areas. The adaptability of the area to the proposed program, the cost of construction, maintenance problems, aesthetic considerations, and available leadership are all factors in determining what facilities might be developed in a particular land area or cluster of acreages.

Listed below are some of the special developments that might be included in appropriate sites. Some of the features listed are discussed elsewhere in this report and are merely mentioned here. Others, not mentioned in other places, are discussed in more detail.

- **Grass, shrubs, and trees.** They provide shade, prevent soil erosion, provide food and cover for wildlife, serve as windbreaks, mark the boundary of the property, act as a buffer zone to insure privacy against an adjacent (presently or potentially) populated area, demonstrate principles of plant growth, serve as a resource for ecological studies, and give practice in forest management. A school forest offers popular activities in many schools.
- **A vegetable garden** or a bog garden.
- **Soil-erosion demonstration areas.** This should be an area rich in vegetation, and featuring good conservation practices, situated on an inclined area, and located next to a piece of land denuded of its vegetation and also located on an incline. Comparisons can then be made over a period of time to determine what happens to the quantity and quality of soil in both areas.
- **Snake pit.** A variety of reptiles found in the local area could be kept in a circular pit about 20 feet in diameter and constructed of concrete and stone. Concave walls and a water-filled moat surrounding an island will prevent the snakes from escaping.
- **Wildlife sanctuary.** Provide mixed plantings and construct birdhouses, feeders, and bird baths to attract a variety of birds.
- **Weather station.** This is for the study of meteorology and should be located in an area that can be fenced off and locked.
- **Council ring.** This facility provides a place for campfires, for conducting orientations before field trips, and for other special programs. The council ring should be located in a wooded area to insure a feeling of isolation. Use logs for seats.
- **Nature trails.** Develop, if space permits, a variety of trails, each serving a different purpose. One may be a geology trail which winds its way through an area rich in geologic features. Another trail may emphasize the study of erosion, while still another may lead to an historic spot, etc.
- **Develop a pioneer living area.** Social studies can be nicely tied in with such an area. Dramatize the life of the pioneer, including such things as making dyes from plants, cooking outdoors, constructing shelters, learning to identify edible plants, and learning other survival practices.
- **Observation platform.** This platform can be used for observing birds and for studying astronomy. It should be located on the highest point of the property.
- **Outdoor zoo.** Animals indigenous to the local area are featured. Be certain that arrangements can be made to care properly for the animals caught.
- **Miniature gardens.** Each garden features a particular grouping of native plants found in the typical setting in which they normally grow.
- **Plant grafting.** A demonstration area which provides interesting studies in genetics.
- **Animal-baiting area.** Put a salt lick and some meat in a cleared area. Place loose dirt around the baited spot, spread it, press it down with the feet, and smooth it out. Animals attracted to the area will leave their footprints, which can then be observed and studied.
- **Natural preserve.** An area could be set aside in which no developments would be made. It would be given complete protection and would provide a spot for the observation of ecological aspects.
- **Orienteering courses.** The development of several courses for map and compass use would stimulate educational and recreational use of the area.
- **Greenhouse.** A place for the propagation of plants, some of which may be used for area improvement, is important. A greenhouse would make possible an acquaintanceship with plants and would be a means of providing projects for study during the off season.
- **Winter-sports area.** Places for skating, skiing, and coasting would be desirable in those parts of the country that have sufficient snow and cold weather to make these sports feasible.
- **Natural play area.** An area set aside for children, which contains such elements as climbing logs, ropes for swinging across low areas, sand banks, and hide-and-seek areas, can provide play that is different from that in the city.
- **Turtle pit.** An attractive pit with water and plantings would make possible the study and observation of turtles and other amphibians.
- **Rifle and skeet ranges.** Such an area will provide opportunities for instruction in gun safety as well as for participation in rifle and skeet shooting.
- **Casting and angling area.** Developments for casting and angling would serve both school instruction and recreation uses.
- **Amphitheater.** For large group programs, an amphitheater would be important. It could be used for lectures, drama, music, and a variety of demonstrations.
- **Astronomy area.** A special area for astronomy may be developed on a large open area, waterfront, dock, or even a roof. Seating facilities are desirable, and sometimes a telescope is permanently mounted to facilitate observations.
- **Bird-feeding station.**
- **Historical markers.** Sites of old farms, early settlers' homes, Indian trails and village sites, and pioneer roads are illustrations of the kinds of historical sites that might be used for

projects for students using an area.

- **Shelters.** Adirondack or picnic shelters can serve day-camp groups and day-use groups during inclement weather.
- **Tree stump.** Locate a fairly well-preserved tree stump, make a sloping cut, smooth the top by sanding, and treat it with a clear waterproofing material, such as Fiberglas resin. Much can be learned about tree growth from carefully studying a tree stump.
- **Herb garden.** This garden features food seasoning and medicinal plants and serves as a useful teaching aid for a home economics class.
- **Photographic blind.** Construct a blind near a bird-feeding station for taking pictures of wild birds.
- **Evergreen-tree nursery.** Trees can later be transplanted to desired areas.
- **Field archery.** Targets are set up in wooded areas or fields, simulating actual hunting conditions.
- **Natural areas.** Such areas are left relatively undisturbed, and man-made modifications should be avoided as much as possible. These places serve as excellent resources for scientific studies of natural phenomena.
- **Picnic site.** It is desirable to locate the picnic site on the periphery of the property.
- **Seashore areas.** Communities adjacent to seashores may have areas set aside for study and observation. Developments might include ramps or walks to facilitate observation. Walkways through tidelands may be developed as nature trails. One of the national parks has an underwater nature trail.

SELECTED REFERENCES

American Camping Association, **Camping Standards.** Martinsville, Ind.: The Association, Bradford Woods, 1964.

Better Homes and Gardens, **Family Camping.** Des Moines, Ia.: Meredith Publishing Company, 1964.

Freeburg, William H., and Taylor, Loren E., **Programs in Outdoor Education.** Minneapolis: Burgess Publishing Company, 1963.

Hillcourt, William, **Field Book of Nature Activities.** New York: G. P. Putnam's Sons.

Jaeger, Ellsworth, **Wildwood Wisdom.** New York: The Macmillan Company, 1957.

Mitchell, Grace L., **Fundamentals of Day Camping.** New York: Association Press, 1961.

National Association of Biology Teachers (Richard Weaver, Editor), **Manual for Outdoor Laboratories.** Danville, Ill.: Interstate Printers and Publishers, Inc., 1959.

Outdoor Recreation Resources Review Commission, **Outdoor Recreation for America.** Washington, D. C.: U.S. Government Printing Office, 1962.

Salomon, Julian Harris, **Campsite Development.** New York: Girl Scouts of the U.S.A., 1959.

Shomen, Joseph J., **A Nature Center for Your Community.** New York: National Audubon Society, Information Education Bulletin No. 1, 1962.

Smith, Julian W.; Carlson, Reynold E.; Donaldson, George W.; and Masters, Hugh B.; **Outdoor Education.** Englewood Cliffs, N.J.: Prentice-Hall, Inc., 1963.

Stapp, William B., **Integrating Conservation and Outdoor Education into the Curriculum.** Minneapolis: Burgess Publishing Company, 1965.

The Athletic Institute, **Campcraft Series I.** Color-Sound 35mm. Film Kit, Instructor's Guide, and Student Handbook. Chicago, Ill.: The Institute, 805 Merchandise Mart, 1965.

Young, Paul R., **Elementary Lessons in Gardening.** Columbus: The National Garden Institute, 1953.

Many excellent resource materials are available from state and federal agencies. These include maps, diagrams, leaflets, and booklets.

Chapter 7

GENERAL FEATURES of OUTDOOR AREAS and FACILITIES

FENCES AND WALLS

THESE INSTALLATIONS are frequently required around facility units for the purposes of isolation, enclosure, separation, and traffic control (pedestrian and vehicular), and for the protection of participants, the general public, spectators, and property. Walls or living barriers may be used as sound controls and for screening out undesirable features.

FENCING

Some characteristics of good fencing are stability, durability, economy of maintenance, attractiveness, and effectiveness. Among the many types of suitable fencing available, woven-wire fencing of the chain-link type (minimum thickness—11-gauge), using H-type line posts or circular posts, have been found to meet requirements satisfactorily. All chain-link fencing should be installed so that the smooth edges are at the top and the sharp edges are at the bottom. In some cases, however, it may be desirable to have smooth edges at both top and bottom. A hard-surface strip about 12" wide may be placed under the fence to facilitate maintenance (grass cutting, etc.).

Fences may be painted for beautification purposes. The brush method of painting produces acceptable results but is exceedingly expensive. The spraying of paint on the fences may be objectionable because of the drifting action of the fine spray. The roller method seems to be the most efficient and economical.

Plastic-covered fences are attractive. These fences are available in several colors and are used in different parts of the country.

WALLS

Walls can be constructed of many kinds of masonry material or, in some cases, may be made of poured concrete. While they are usually extremely expensive, they may be necessary for sound control, visual control, or as a method of solving the problem of change of elevation of the ground from one area to another.

Oftentimes, walls can be used for such program activities as tennis and handball.

GRADING AND DRAINAGE

The development of any site should include the preparation of an overall grading and drainage plan prepared by a competent professional. This will assure proper attention to these very important considerations.

SURFACE DRAINAGE

Surface drainage on unpaved areas should be controlled by slope grading to natural or artificial surface-water collectors, to carefully-located surface inlets, or to catch basins connected to a storm-water drainage system. In order to facilitate surface drainage of activity areas, a good general rule is to establish and maintain a minimum slope of one per cent in noncompetitive sports areas. As a rule, the surface slope of paved areas should be a minimum of one per cent except when used for competition. Exceptions to the above may be necessary. When certain soil and area-use conditions exist, the degree of slope may be lessened.

SUBSURFACE DRAINAGE

Subsurface drainage should be effected by using either porous subsoil foundations or perforated drain tile. In regions of severe frost, where surfaces are to be paved, natural or tile subsurface dainage is essential. All drainage tile should be installed after rough grading is completed.

LIGHTING

The lighting of outdoor areas, particularly those used for various sports activities, involves many problems not encountered in other types of lighting.

A good lighting installation can only result from careful blending of the proper quantity of light, which is relatively easy to provide, with a good quality of light. The poorer the quality of lighting installation, the greater the quantity of light required to obtain a given degree of visual performance.

The importance of competent technical consultation in dealing with outdoor lighting cannot be stressed too strongly. This is of paramount significance if a satisfactory facility is to be secured. Private consultant firms, local utility companies, and manufacturers of lighting equipment are available in all sections of the country, and their help may be invaluable in preventing costly mistakes.

The extension of the use of outdoor facilities through lighting should be considered on the basis of better meeting the needs of a greater number of people. The availability of such facilities in the evening hours, after the often unfavorable heat of the day, can greatly increase patronage and interest and the possibilities for the reduction of facility costs per participant.

LIGHTING OF SPORTS FACILITIES

The most complete and reliable sources of general and specific information on the subject of sports-facility lighting is the Illuminating Engineering Society's publication entitled "Current Recommended Practice for Sports Lighting". This publication covers all aspects of sports lighting in considerable detail, including recommended illumination levels and recommendations for lighting sports areas of all types.

GENERAL AREA LIGHTING

Where specific sports-facility lighting is not available, a modified or general area lighting of the park or playground can be provided. Generally mounted on poles or structures on the perimeter of the area, this type provides sufficient lighting for movement throughout the area and is usually arranged so as to cover as much territory as possible with the greatest economy. Time clocks can be incorporated into the system so that the lights turn off at a specified time.

Stairways, ramps, building entrances, and secluded angles of the buildings should be illuminated to help prevent accidents and to discourage misuse. It is the practice in many cities to light the walkways throughout a park from power systems which are tied into the citywide lighting system and its regulated control.

The lights should be located to serve their primary function without creating a nuisance to the neighborhood residents. For both sports-facility lighting and general area lighting, underground service through conduits is recommended.

HOUSING FOR ELECTRICAL CONTROLS

A vital part of any outdoor lighting system is the protective and control equipment necessary to make it function. The very nature of this equipment is an attraction to children, and it represents a real hazard to anyone not completely familiar with its operation and the characteristics of electricity.

The development of new light sources has resulted in more frequent use of high voltage for larger outdoor lighting systems. Distribution systems of 240 and 480 volts are no longer uncommon and, in some instances, a primary distribution system utilizing 2,400 or 4,160 volts to strategically-placed distribution transformers can be justified.

Whenever such equipment is located in areas frequented by children or the general public, the controls must be adequately housed and padlocked. Where buildings or bleacher complexes are adjacent to the lighted area, consideration should be given to locating such controls inside a control room where they can be properly protected from access by unauthorized persons.

ORIENTATION OF AREAS

Courts and fields should be oriented to give protection to both players and spectators, with major consideration to those players who need it most. It may not be possible to get the best orientation of a particular court or field because such factors as topography, shape of the area, and location of other facilities may dictate some variations.

Outdoor courts and fields should be oriented so that the late-afternoon or early-morning sun rays will intersect the general path of the flight of the ball at an angle of approximately 90 degrees. Otherwise, players on the eastern end of the fields or courts will have to face the sun during afternoon play. In rectangular fields and courts, the general pattern of the ball's flight is parallel to the long axis of such areas. Therefore, the long axis should generally be at right angles to the late-afternoon sun rays. Locate the sunset position at midseason of the sport and orient the field or court accordingly.

On baseball, softball, and similar fields, the general pattern of the ball's flight does not parallel any axis. Instead, it covers an arc of more than 90 degrees. Since the field cannot be oriented to give equal protection to all players and spectators, a choice must be made. Because the batter, pitcher, and catcher are in the most hazardous positions, they should receive first consideration. Thus a line through these positions should be the axis for orienting the field. The field may be properly oriented by ensuring that the imaginary line from home plate to second base is at right angles to the rays of the late-afternoon sun.

PARKING

The need to provide off-street parking for automobiles is a major consideration in the design of school recreation facilities. A careful study should be made to determine the space requirements. Careful attention to the design of school and recreation

facilities is necessary so as not to locate the parking area where it conflicts with pedestrian use of the building and outdoor facilities. Parking lots should be placed so as to best serve the shop and custodial staff, the teaching staff, and the ever increasing number of student cars.

Each parking space should be marked. In larger recreation centers and parks, it is often more desirable to construct parking areas in several locations near the facilities which have the highest concentration of users. This will also make it easier to blend the parking areas into the landscape. Where possible, parking areas should be located near the perimeter of the park and should be designed so as not to interfere with normal pedestrian use of the area. In the case of large parking areas, it is necessary to make a study of the traffic pattern in the surrounding area in order to facilitate the movement of traffic to and from the parking area.

The off-street parking areas should be hard-surfaced and, when wisely planned, may be used for sports, free-play activities, driver education, marching band maneuvers, and other activities. Either post sleeves, flush with the surface, or portable standards will make it relatively easy to conduct a variety of net games on these areas.

An individual parking space is figured at 10' x 20'. To this must be added circulation roads, entrances, exits, walks, and planting islands.

PLANTING AREAS

Plans and specifications for landscape plantings should be prepared at the same time as those for the original site development. This will ensure that the plantings will be in keeping with the total development.

In any recreation space or park, there should be planted areas which serve both a functional and aesthetic purpose. Plantings in the larger parks and parkways should be arranged to form a pleasing pattern, with open areas, walks, drives, and highways. Plantings are not only used for enclosures for certain spaces, but also serve as excellent buffers to cut down on noise within the recreation area as well as the adjacent neighborhood. Good planting design in the development of buffer strips, enclosures, screening, and planting for areas previously mentioned should provide a pleasant pattern of overall landscape treatment.

SURFACING

There is no one surface which will satisfactorily meet the needs of all outdoor activities. Each activity has its own surface requirements, which will dictate what type or types of material can be used.

In the selection of surfacing material for any outdoor area, certain qualities should be sought. These include:

- Multiplicity of use
- Durability
- Dustless and stainless
- Reasonable initial cost
- Ease of maintenance
- Low maintenance cost
- Pleasing appearance
- Nonabrasiveness
- Resiliency
- All-year usage

Obtaining the proper surface for outdoor recreation areas continues to be a perplexing problem for school administrators, play supervisors, designers, and those responsible for maintenance. Over the years, there have been significant developments in surfacing, especially under and around playground apparatus. There has been a gradual change from earth, mud, sand, and turf to bituminous surfacing, which is presently being used throughout the country. This change has come about because of the concensus that bituminous blacktop surfacing is an improvement over other types which have proved unsatisfactory.

Figure 31
Illustration of Several Types of Surfacing

TABLE 2
TYPES OF SURFACING MATERIALS

Group	Type
Earth	Loams; sand; sand-clay; clay-gravel; fuller's earth; stabilized earth; soil-cement
Turf	Bluegrass mixtures; bent; fescue; Bermuda
Aggregates	Gravel; graded stone; graded slag; shell; cinders
Bituminous (asphalt-tar)	Penetration-macadam; bituminous or asphaltic concrete (cold and hot-laid); sheet asphalt; natural asphalt; sawdust asphalt; vermiculite asphalt; rubber asphalt; cork asphalt; other patented asphalt mixes
Synthetics	Rubber; synthetic resins; rubber asphalt; chlorinated butyl-rubber; mineral fiber; finely-ground aggregate and asphalt; plastics; vinyls
Concrete	Monolithic; terrazzo; precast
Masonry	Flagstone (sandstone, limestone, granite, etc.) brick; etc.
Miscellaneous	Tanbark; sawdust; shavings; cottonseed hulls

TURF

The advantages of using grass as a surface are its attractiveness, resiliency, and nonabrasiveness, and the fact that it is relatively dust-free. Such a surface lends itself very well to activities that require relatively large areas, as most field games do.

Turf is difficult to maintain in areas where there is intensive usage. In some parts of the country where watering is essential, maintenance costs are high. Turf surfaces are not practical for most activities when the ground is frozen or wet and, in addition, must be given time and care to restore themselves after heavy use.

Since climatic conditions and uses should determine the species of grass selected for a particular locality, careful consideration should be given to the several varieties available.

SOILS

The use of earth as a surfacing material has been widespread, particularly under apparatus, primarily because it is porous and inexpensive.

Among the difficulties encountered in the use of earth and surfacing materials are dust, and the tendency to become rutted, which, in turn, creates drainage problems and relatively high maintenance costs. These difficulties can be partially overcome by mixing the earth with clay or sand. When this is done, the resulting surface is often less resilient and somewhat abrasive.

Natural soils can also be stabilized by the addition of asphalt, resin, or cement, which are the most commonly-used stabilizers. The use of stabilized soils is a possibility in many areas where turf is impractical or cannot be grown.

MASONRY

Natural-stone slabs, or blocks, and manufactured brick can be used for such installations as walks and terraces, where interesting and attractive patterns, colors, and textures are desired.

CONCRETE

Concrete surfaces provide year-round and multiple usage. The costs of maintenance are very low and the surface is extremely durable.

BITUMINOUS

The common bituminous surface has many of the advantages which are sought in any surfacing material. It provides a durable surface which can be used on a year-round schedule. The maintenance of bituminous surface is comparatively easy and inexpensive. Such a surface can also be used for many different activities. When properly installed, the surface is dust-free and drains quickly. Asphalt surfaces can be marked easily and with a relatively high degree of permanence. Asphalt also provides a neat-appearing, no-glare surface that will blend well with the landscape.

The disadvantages of bituminous surfaces are their relatively-high installation costs and lack of resiliency as compared to some other types of surfaces. However, the high installation cost will be offset by low maintenance costs.

Bituminous surfaces will vary as to firmness, finish, resiliency, and durability in direct relation to the kinds and proportions of aggregates and other materials used in their mixture.

Asphalt can be combined with a variety of other materials to provide a reasonably resilient or extremely hard surface. The use of such materials as cork, sponge, or rubber in combination with asphalt will yield a fairly-resilient surface. Aggregates such as slag or granite will produce an extremely hard surface when combined with asphalt.

SYNTHETICS

Many different types of surfacing materials have been placed in experimental use, particularly under fixed equipment. Materials such as sponge, sponge rubber, rubber mats, cork, aircell materials, and combinations in conjunction with covers of rubber vinyl, canvas, and asphaltic binder coatings are in experimental use.

Some synthetic materials appear to meet the requirements for durability. Track spikes or cleats do not leave holes in the material. Rather, the material closes around the puncture. Very little maintenance of synthetic materials is required, thus maintenance costs are low. Most synthetics have a very pleasing appearance and are available in different colors. They are non-abrasive and suitable for year-round use.

There are a number of commercially-manufactured synthetic compounds, such as chlorinated butyl-rubber, rubber asphalt, synthetic resins, mineral fiber, finely ground aggregate and asphalt, plastics, and vinyls. They come in a variety of textures, colors, weights, and thicknesses. Most synthetic surfaces have a high degree of resiliency, which makes them desirable for many types of athletic activities. Research is needed, however, to develop a vandalproof resilient surface.

MISCELLANEOUS

Often there is a need for an especially-resilient surface, such as that needed beneath certain types of apparatus from which falling or jumping is frequent. Materials such as tanbark, sawdust, wood shavings, and cottonseed hulls have been used for this purpose.

Tanbark is often mixed with sand in an 80-20 ratio and spread beneath the apparatus to a depth of up to six inches. When sawdust is mixed with sand, it is frequently mixed in equal parts and spread to a depth of four to six inches.

Satisfactory surfaces can be had only by:
• Obtaining the best product or material for the surface desired
• Preparing a good design and complete specifications
• Retaining qualified technicians and skilled workmen
• Using proper equipment
A deficiency in any of these factors may result in seriously-impaired usefulness of the surfacing, or the need for costly reconstruction.

WALKWAYS

All-weather walks should be confined to a minimum in open play areas and should be provided only where the foot traffic is heavy enough to warrant their need. Circulation walks serve as guideways to interesting features and may be of many kinds of surfacing material.

The walks should vary in width in accordance with the anticipated traffic density and should not cross through game courts. It may be necessary to use signs, pavement lines, and fixed or planted barriers to accomplish the desired circulation movement. The degree of slope, and subsurface drainage should be given careful study.

In developments where it is impractical to service features and facilities with drives, or from adjacent street pavements, selected walks should be of heavier construction and of sufficient width to accommodate service-truck loads.

SELECTED REFERENCES

Cate, John, **Playground Surfacing.** Pittsburgh, Penna.: National Association of Public School Business Officials, 1940.

Gabrielsen, M. A., and Miles, C. M., **Sports and Recreation Facilities for School and Community.** Englewood Cliffs, N.J.: Prentice-Hall, Inc., 1958.

Herrick, J. H.; McLeary, R. D.; Clapp, W. F.; and Bogner, W. F., **From School Program to School Plant.** New York: Henry Holt and Co., 1956.

University of the State of New York, **Planning the Outdoor Physical Education Facilities.** Albany: University of the State of New York, Division of School Buildings and Grounds, November, 1954.

Part Three
Indoor Facilities

Chapter 8

INDOOR FACILITIES for ELEMENTARY and SECONDARY SCHOOLS

INDOOR FACILITIES for health education, physical education, athletics, and recreation should be planned and constructed so that the desired educational programs can become a reality. In an era of acceleration of change in national and world cultures, responsible persons must endeavor to anticipate needed program changes in both the near and distant future.

The task of planners is to ascertain the indoor space requirements of the school and the community for health education, physical education, athletics, and recreation, and to translate these needs into the number, size, type, and location of facilities. This requires a working relationship between local and state personnel, the school, public and private agencies, and city or county planners regarding the proposed uses of such facilities.

In this chapter, consideration is given to the facilities necessary to accomplish the educational objectives of the physical education program, including adaptations of these facilities needed to serve the added demands made by athletic activities, both intramural and interschool, and the recreation program for both school and community. This is not to suggest that all schools should have identical or even closely similar programs. Recommendations are both general and specific. Responsible persons must determine how to benefit from the general recommendations and decide which specific facilities are applicable to the particular needs of their programs.

The planners of indoor facilities should give attention to the following general concepts:

• The involvement of both men and women staff members of the physical education, recreation, and health education departments is considered essential in planning for all related facilities.
• To provide adequate variety in the physical education curriculum, it may be necessary to plan more than a gymnasium, depending upon the kinds of skills, knowledges, and attitudes which are to be emphasized. In a school for kindergarten through third grade only, a room smaller than a gymnasium may be used unless it is also a neighborhood center where older members of the community gather for recreation.
• While a single facility may meet the instructional needs of the physical education program, additional space will be necessary if all students are to be given an opportunity to participate in an intramural and/or interschool program.
• To expand the basic program in physical education, it is desirable to have such additional special facilities as bowling alleys, swimming pools, and archery and rifle ranges. It may be possible for the school to secure some of these facilities through the cooperative use of existing or proposed facilities owned and administered by some other agency.
• As planning for recreation is considered, the entire school plant becomes a potential space resource, and all units should be scrutinized and planned with recreational adaptability

in mind. Traditionally, the role of the school has been to educate the whole child. The community school, which is an extension of this role, is based on the belief that the provision of opportunities for continuing education and recreation for adults as well as children is the best means of improving the life of the entire community. Since community schools are centrally located in each neighborhood, they provide excellent facilities in which to carry out a wide range of educational and recreational activities. Isolation and retained accessibility of units to permit recreational use during a variety of hours is important.

• The best planning of indoor facilities will require a careful study of the community's unique characteristics—its attitudes, economic conditions, climate, topography, population, existing facilities, program demands—and the use of creative imagination by the planners.
• The location of facilities is important to efficiency in their use:

The location of areas most frequently used for community recreation purposes should be considered in relationship to each other for safety, economic operation, program expansion, and the adequate protection of school property.

The location of teaching stations or play areas in relation to each other, and each to its appropriate service unit, should be such as to permit coeducational activity and to meet other program needs.

The location of indoor service facilities should be such that they are readily accessible to persons using the outdoor areas during the school year as well as during vacation periods.

The location and adequacy of sanitary and storage facilities to accommodate spectator or recreation groups should be carefully planned.

The locker, shower, and dressing-room area should be planned for the safety, comfort, and convenience of its users.

TEACHING STATIONS

A fundamental concept with respect to the facilities of any school is that the unit of primary importance is the room or space where teaching occurs. All other parts of the school plant are, in a real sense, secondary. In physical education, therefore, the determination of the number and character of the teaching stations is basic to the planning process.

The term "teaching station" is used to mean any room or space where one teacher can instruct or supervise the learning experience of one class or group of students. For instance, a gymnasium would constitute a teaching station, or if divided, it would provide two or more teaching stations. Swimming pools, auxiliary physical education teaching stations, and rhythm rooms are examples of other kinds of teaching stations. The number of students accommodated by a teaching station is controlled by the nature of the specific activity as well as the size of the facility.

NUMBER OF TEACHING STATIONS

The total number of teaching stations required is dictated by enrollment, policies pertaining to instructional physical education, average class size, diversity of program, number of periods in the school day, and other uses of the facilities. It should be forcefully pointed out, however, that indoor facilities for health education, physical education, athletics, and recreation are difficult and costly to expand at some future date. The ultimate enrollment potential should be determined by research procedures used by school planners. The anticipated enrollment of the school in five to ten years after completion of construction should serve as a basis for determining the required number of teaching stations to be provided in the original construction. Long-range planning is imperative to provide for the logical and most economical expansion to accommodate the ultimate enrollment potential. The initial design should make provisions for the anticipated construction. This practice will enhance the acceptance of future building programs.

Thorough studies to determine ultimate enrollment potential also serve as the basis of identifying the desirable site size. Otherwise, expansion will create a loss of outdoor space at a time of actual increase in need. Immediately upon completion of construction, planning should begin to identify expansion needs.

TEACHING STATIONS FOR THE PROGRAM OF INSTRUCTION

By determining the number of teaching stations essential for the formal program of instruction, planners will have a basis for calculating other needs. Computation of the numerical minimum requirement is achieved by the following formula:

$$\text{Minimum Number of Teaching Stations} = \frac{\text{Number of Students}}{\text{Average Number of Students per Instructor}} \times \frac{\text{Number of Periods Class Meets Each Week}}{\text{Total Number of Class Periods in School Week}}$$

If a school with a projected enrollment of 700 students has six class periods a day with an average class size of 30 students, and physical education is required on a daily basis, the formula application is as follows:

$$\text{Minimum Number of Teaching Stations} = \frac{700 \text{ Students}}{30 \text{ per Class}} \times \frac{5 \text{ Periods per Week}}{30 \text{ Periods per Week}}$$

$$= \frac{3500}{900} = 3.9$$

Since construction of a fraction of a teaching station would be impractical, four teaching stations would be required. This number of units would afford flexibility in class scheduling. Only in unusual cases would the required number of teaching stations not involve fractions. Figures should be rounded off to the next higher whole number.

In computing teaching-station requirements, the desired class size must not be set so low as to require an impossible number of teachers and facilities, nor should it be so high that effectiveness is impaired. An average class size of 30 students is recommended for secondary schools. **Daily instruction** for all girls and boys is recommended.[1,2]

Elementary-school physical education classes may be organized by a number of methods. The average class size is usually based on the number of pupils in the classroom unit. Because of pupil-maturation differences, physical education periods generally vary from 20 minutes for kindergarten and first grade to 40 minutes for fifth and sixth grades, with the school average (for computation purposes) being 30 minutes per class.

The formula for computing the number of teaching stations needed for physical education in an elementary school is as follows:

$$\text{Minimum Number of Teaching Stations} = \frac{\text{Number of Classrooms of Students}}{} \times \frac{\text{Number of Physical Education Periods per Week per Class}}{\text{Total Periods in School Week}}$$

Thus if an elementary school with six grades has three classes at each level (approximately 450 to 540 pupils), with ten 30-minute physical education periods per day, since physical education is required on a daily basis, the teaching station needs can be calculated as follows:

$$\text{Minimum Number of Teaching Stations} = 18 \text{ Classroom Units} \times \frac{5 \text{ periods per week}}{50 \text{ periods a week}}$$

$$= \frac{90}{50} = 1.8$$

Under the circumstances set forth above, the need is indicated for two teaching stations which will accommodate the 18 daily classes and allow two periods for club activities, special groups, and other enrichment experiences.

TEACHING STATIONS FOR OTHER ACTIVITIES

The next step for planners is to determine the degree to which the number of teaching stations for the program of instruction will meet the needs for voluntary recreation, extramural and intramural activities, and interscholastic athletics for girls and boys, as well as the possible use of facilities by the community. The needs must be based upon the season of the year representing the greatest demand for facilities.

The following guide can be used to determine the number of teaching stations needed for activities other than the formal program of instruction in physical education:[3]

Minimum number of teaching stations, or fractions thereof, needed for interscholastic-team practice at peak load, plus

Minimum number of teaching stations, or fractions thereof, needed for intramural and extramural activities, plus

Minimum number of teaching stations, or fractions thereof, needed for student recreation, plus

Minimum number of teaching stations, or fractions thereof, needed for community recreation, equals

The total number of teaching stations needed for any specific after-school period.

To illustrate, assume a school has two interscholastic squads, an intramural program, a voluntary recreation group, and no community recreation use of facilities immediately after school during a specific season. The total needs are as follows:

Required teaching stations = 2 interscholastic + 1 intramural + 1 voluntary recreation = 4 stations

The need for four teaching stations for the after-school program must then be compared to the number necessary for the formal program of instruction in physical education. If the after-school needs are in excess of those for the regular periods of instruction, the additional teaching stations should be provided. Careful administrative scheduling results in maximum utilization of facilities.

VARIETY OF TEACHING STATIONS

A great variety of teaching stations is possible, depending

[1] *Physical Fitness Facts*, President's Council on Physical Fitness.
[2] Resolution by House of Delegates, American Medical Association, Miami Beach Meeting, 1960.
[3] H. A. Scott and R. B. Westkaemper, *From Programs to Facilities in Physical Education*, Harper and Brothers, New York, 1958, p. 33.

on the number of different activities that would appropriately be included in the physical education program. Among the possible types of indoor teaching stations which might be included are gymnasiums, rhythm rooms, rooms for gymnastics, adapted-physical-education rooms, wrestling rooms, classrooms, swimming pools, archery ranges, rifle ranges, and handball courts. Of these types, the gymnasium, auxiliary gymnasium, and pool might be included for elementary-school use, while all of those mentioned above are used at the secondary-school level.

The problem for some schools is not one of a lack of an adequate number of teaching stations, but rather one of facilities to accommodate the desired variety of activities. For a secondary school with 360 students, a divisible gymnasium will create an adequate number of teaching stations for the program of instruction in physical education, but may not meet the peak-load requirement for after-school activities. The facility must be planned and designed to serve all program needs as adequately as possible.

Whenever a school's teaching requirements are such that a basic gymnasium is inadequate, planners should consider special-purpose stations, such as an auxiliary physical education teaching station, a natatorium, or a dance studio. Teaching-station needs must be studied in terms of the number of students to be accommodated and the desired variety in an excellent physical education program.

ELEMENTARY-SCHOOL FACILITIES

The biological demands of the body require that the normal child engage in at least three hours of vigorous motor activities daily. Not only does the instructional physical education program endeavor to fulfill part of this basic need, but it also seeks to develop motor skills that will lead to enjoyable physical activities during leisure.

The elementary-school physical education program centers around the teaching of fundamental skills, rhythmics or dance, games and sports, gymnastic-type activities, combatives, self-testing activities, and aquatics. The design and scope of physical education facilities should be based upon these activities. They should also consider the needs of the disabled child.

THE CLASSROOM

The self-contained classroom can provide for limited indoor physical activity for the primary grades, but should not be used for instructional physical education. The floor should provide a nonslip surface. Because of the many breakable items in the room, games calling for the use of balls must frequently be excluded or restricted. The self-contained classroom, therefore, supplements rather than replaces traditional physical education facilities. Twenty-five square feet of storage space should be provided for balls, ropes, pins, and other equipment that is classroom-controlled.

THE GYMNASIUM[4]

The elementary-school gymnasium is used primarily, but not exclusively, by the upper grades. A minimum of 100 square feet per pupil and a total area of at least 4,000 square feet is recommended. Spectator seating, if provided, and storage rooms require additional space. Many of the general considerations recommended for secondary-school gymnasiums also apply to elementary-school facilities.

The specific dimensions of the gymnasium should provide

[4]See Appendixes G and H.

for a basketball court of 42' x 64', with a minimum safety space of six feet around the perimeter. An area of 54' x 76'—4,104 square feet—would be adequate. The ceiling should be a minimum of 18' high. This space is adequate for activities normally included in the elementary-school program. If the gymnasium is to serve the community recreation program, the ceiling height should be increased to 22' and the playing floor enlarged to accommodate older groups (see Table 3). The area could be divided into units of 38' x 54' and thus provide two teaching stations for primary-grade classes or for activities that do not require large areas.

A storage room of 175 square feet should be directly accessible from the gymnasium floor through a double-door without a threshold. At least one wall should be free of obstruction for ball and target games and skill practice. Attachments must be provided for backboards, ropes, and apparatus. Basketball backboards should be adjustable so that the height of the basket rim can be adjusted according to the maturation of the participants.

SERVICE FACILITIES

Shower and dressing rooms should be provided to enable students to change clothes and to take a shower after physical education classes. These facilities are also required for community utilization of the gymnasium or outdoor play areas. Shower-dressing-locker facilities are considered in detail in Chapter 11.

Storage space for equipment used in the auxiliary gymnasium is discussed later in this chapter. Additional space is required for equipment used outdoors. The room for the equipment should be easily accessible to the outdoors and should also be near the staff offices. Space to store out-of-season equipment is essential to prevent loss or misplacement between seasons. Storage areas should have bins, shelves, racks, and hangers for the best utilization of space and the proper care of equipment and supplies.

An office for the physical education staff should be located near the gymnasium and equipment-storage rooms. It should be a minimum of 100 square feet in size, with an adjoining room containing a shower, toilet, and lavatory. This unit could be used by the physical education staff, whether permanent or visiting, and persons directing noon or after-school recreation programs. Schools having two teaching stations should provide separate offices for a man and a woman.

AUXILIARY PHYSICAL EDUCATION
TEACHING STATION

The elementary-school auxiliary physical education teaching station supplements the main gymnasium. It is most practical when the main gymnasium cannot fulfill all of the school's needs for teaching stations. The auxiliary unit should be planned to accommodate apparatus and tumbling activities, games of low organization, rhythmics, and other activities for the primary grades. This room will, for the most part, be used by the lower grades and, therefore, should be accessible to their classrooms. If the area is to serve the after-school recreational program for pupils or is to be used by community groups, a drinking fountain should be located nearby in a corridor, and accessible toilet facilities are desirable. Extended use of the area would be enhanced by some degree of isolation.

At least 60 square feet per primary pupil, with a total minimum of 1,800 square feet of space, is suggested for this unit. A ceiling height of 18' in the clear is preferred. One wall should be free of obstruction so that it may be used for

TABLE 3

SPACE FOR SELECTED INDOOR ACTIVITIES IN SECONDARY SCHOOLS

Activity	Play Area in Feet	Safety Space in Feet*	Total Area in Feet
Badminton	20 x 44	6s, 8e	32 x 60
Basketball			
Jr. High instructional	42 x 74	6s, 8e	
Jr. High interscholastic	50 x 84	6s, 8e	
Sr. High interscholastic	50 x 84	6s, 8e	62 x 100
Sr. High instructional	45 x 74	6s, 8e	57 x 90
Neighborhood El. Sch.	42 x 74	6s, 8e	54 x 90
Community Junior H. S.	50 x 84	6s, 8e	62 x 100
Community Senior H. S.	50 x 84	6s, 8e	62 x 100
Competitive—DGWS	50 x 94	6s, 8e	62 x 110
Boccie	18 x 62	3s, 9e	24 x 80
Fencing, competitive	6 x 40	3s, 6e	12 x 52
instructional	3 x 30	2s, 6e	9 x 42
Rifle (one pt.)	5 x 50	6 to 20e	5 x 70 min.
Shuffleboard	6 x 52	6s, 2e	18 x 56
Tennis			
Deck (doubles)	18 x 40	4s, 5e	26 x 50
Hand	16 x 40	4½s, 10e	25 x 60
Lawn (singles)	27 x 78	12s, 21e	51 x 120
(doubles)	36 x 78	12s, 21e	60 x 120
Paddle (singles)	16 x 44	6s, 8e	28 x 60
(doubles)	20 x 44	6s, 8e	32 x 60
Table (playing area)			9 x 31
Volleyball			
Competitive and adult	30 x 60	6s, 6e	42 x 72
Junior High	30 x 50	6s, 6e	42 x 62
Wrestling (competitive)	24 x 24	5s, 5e	36 x 36

*Safety space at the side of an area is indicated by a number followed by "e" for end and "s" for side.

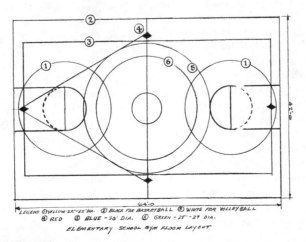

LEGEND ① YELLOW-22'-25'DIA. ② BLACK FOR BASKETBALL ③ WHITE FOR VOLLEYBALL
④ RED ⑤ BLUE -30' DIA. ⑥ GREEN - 25'- 27' DIA.
ELEMENTARY SCHOOL GYM FLOOR LAYOUT

Figure 32

target and ball games, or throwing practice. A smooth masonry wall will provide an adequate rebounding surface. If included, windows should be of breakproof glass or be protected by a shield or grill and be located high enough so as not to restrict activities.

The equipment could include items such as climbing ropes and poles, ladders, mats, stall bars, rings, large wooden boxes, horizontal bars, and peg boards. These should be located so as not to interfere with other activities, or so they may be easily moved out of the way. A storage room for equipment and supplies should be included. A section of wall can be equipped with hangers for mat storage. Electrical outlets are required for the use of record players and similar sound equipment.

NEIGHBORHOOD OR COMMUNITY ELEMENTARY SCHOOL[5]

Five basic facilities are desirable for carrying out a well-rounded program at the elementary level. These include a versatile community room, a large gymnasium, a well-lighted playground, a fully-equipped auditorium, and a branch library.

THE COMMUNITY ROOM

The community room is probably most representative of the community-school program in that it is designed specifically to meet community needs. The community room should be at least as large as a regular classroom. Kitchen facilities, including stove, refrigerator, cupboards, tables, and chairs, help to make it an ideal meeting place for civic and social organizations.

Since community schools are centrally located in each neighborhood, the community room is readily accessible for use by all residents of the area. Here, under auspices of the community school, neighbors become acquainted and plan the activities in which they would like to participate. The community room may be used during the day for adult club meetings or casual recreational activities. In the evening, it may be used for adult recreation classes or as a meeting place for community groups. Frequently, the community council, made up of representatives of all groups in the neighborhood, meets in the community room to discuss programs for the area served by the school.

THE GYMNASIUM

Recognizing the value of supervised recreation to the well-being of a community, the recreational facilities of community schools should be planned so that a maximum number of persons can benefit from their use.

Although the community room is perhaps the most versatile room in the school, a well-equipped gymnasium has the highest usage ratio. When the people in a community feel that recreation is important, the gymnasium has potential for many uses.

A gymnasium large enough to accommodate a 42′ x 74′ basketball court and folding bleachers can be adapted to a great many recreational activities (see Table 3 for space needs). It can be used for physical education classes during school hours and for community recreation during after-school hours.

Immediately after school hours, the gymnasium serves as a youth center. Besides basketball, the youngsters can take part in activities such as volleyball, shuffleboard, and badminton. In addition, by using special composition wheels to minimize floor wear, schools have been able to introduce roller skating as a family activity. On evenings in which the gymnasium is not devoted to family roller skating, it may be used for adult

[5] Ibid.

square dancing or other neighborhood or family activities.

THE LIGHTED PLAYFIELD

The playfield has long been a popular school facility. Throughout the school year and during the summer as well, youngsters have traditionally made the most of the open space provided for them. Steps should be taken in the initial planning of the community school program to make the playfield as accessible and functional as possible.

Basically, three improvements could be made to encourage wider community use of the already-popular playground. Paving an outdoor basketball court probably does more to encourage use of the playground than any other single improvement, since a large number of recreational activities are best carried out on a hard surface.

A lighted baseball or softball field is a second improvement which will increase playground usage. Adults as well as children can use the field in the evenings for both organized and casual recreational activities.

A third improvement found to be valuable is the provision of washroom facilities accessible from the playground as well as from inside the building. This arrangement makes these facilities available when most of the school building is not in use.

THE AUDITORIUM

An auditorium is a highly-desirable facility in a community school. Leaders who recognize its flexibility can make this facility available daily for a great variety of activities. In order to obtain the widest and most effective use of the auditorium, a seating capacity of approximately 200 to 300 persons is recommended. This will vary with the school and community needs.

During the school day, the auditorium, like the gymnasium, is used mostly by students. Music groups are able to take advantage of auditorium acoustics to practice, and speech students can make use of the stage to gain experience in their art.

When school is not in session, adults in the community have the same opportunity as children to use the auditorium for dramatic and musical events. One of the attractive features of this facility is that it can be used for many different kinds of activities. For example, the well-equipped backstage areas double as workshops for upholstery groups, and the dressing rooms serve as game rooms for children when not being used for other purposes. The extra seating capacity of the auditorium makes it an ideal meeting place for large community groups.

LIBRARY

Providing a school library adequate to serve the whole neighborhood is more economical than building separate library structures. This kind of planning is a good example of multi-use of facilities for the benefit of the entire community.

The central location of community schools makes the library easily accessible to the entire neighborhood. During the day, the book collections are available to teachers and students. Story hours for preschool children can also be scheduled in the library, making it possible for mothers to join in activities held in the community room or other areas of the school.

PROVIDING COMMUNITY-SCHOOL FACILITIES

Three methods can be used to provide community-type facilities in elementary schools:
- Planning new elementary community schools with the facilities that have been discussed above

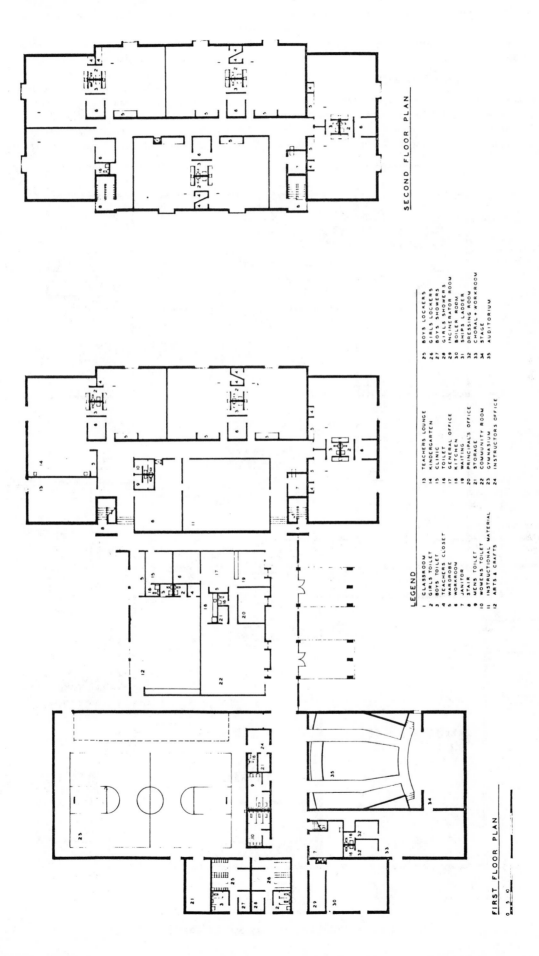

Figure 33

Miller Road Community School

- Building community-type additions to older elementary schools
- Modernizing existing structures to include the special facilities needed

PLANNING NEW ELEMENTARY COMMUNITY SCHOOLS

A one-story structure can be planned so that the community areas and the regular school area are separable from each other. Corridor gates permit the community area to be divided from the classroom area, thus making it possible for one person to supervise the entire community area when the total building is not in use.

Floor plan A shows the design of an elementary school with eight classrooms on one side of an open court, and the community room, auditorium, and gymnasium on the other side. Corridors within the community area may be closed off with portable or wall gates so that any one of the special facilities may be used without opening up other parts of the building.

Plan B shows the community facilities at one end of the building and regular classrooms at the other. In either plan,

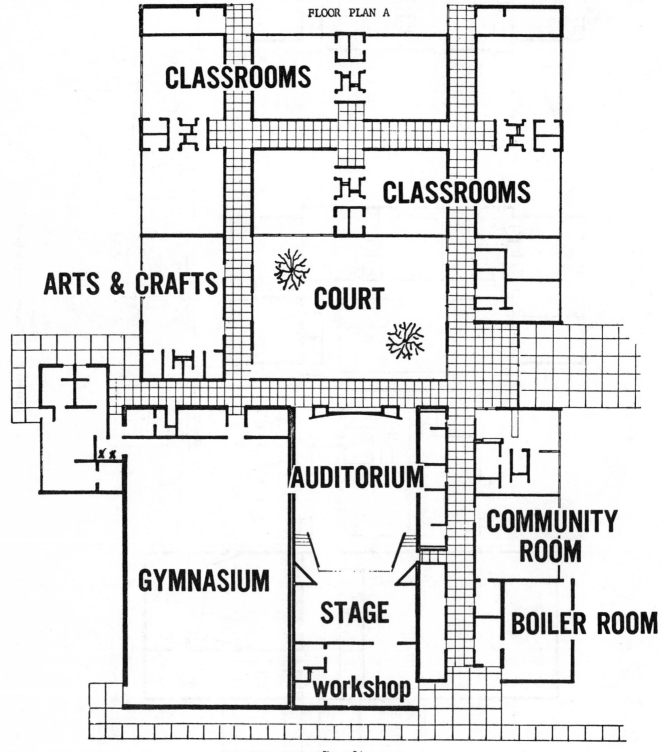

Figure 34
Neighborhood Elementary School Floor Plan A

toilet rooms in the gymnasium are available from the outside so that they may be utilized when the classroom area is not in use.

PLANNING THE COMMUNITY-TYPE ADDITION

Building additions to existing schools is the second method used to incorporate special facilities for implementing a community-school program. Although community-type additions do not provide facilities for as many activities as do the facilities in a new community-school building, they may be adequate for an effective program.

Additions to older elementary schools have included a community room, library and administrative office, and combination gymnasium-auditorium. Equipping a gymnasium with a folding, movable stage and curtain makes it usable for school assemblies and community meetings.

Building an addition to an existing school plant may be an effective and economical alternative to designing and constructing a new building. The cost of an addition will vary depending upon the construction costs in a particular area.

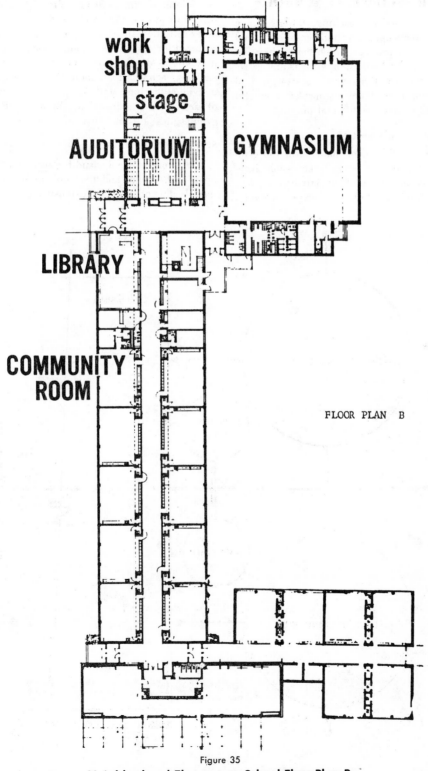

Figure 35

Neighborhood Elementary School Floor Plan B

MODERNIZING THE EXISTING STRUCTURE

Modernization may be an adequate method of providing community-school facilities at a low cost. Existing elementary schools may have facilities which might be adapted, and unused areas that might be converted, for use in developing a community-school program. A classroom, for example, might be converted to a community room; a movable stage with curtains might be added to one end of an existing gymnasium; and a hard-surface, lighted area might be added to the playground.

FACILITIES FOR SECONDARY SCHOOLS

The type and number of indoor teaching stations for a secondary school is dependent upon the number of girls and boys enrolled and the specific program of physical education and related activities. In all situations, a gymnasium is required. Other teaching stations, if necessary, are planned to supplement the gymnasium, but all are planned after careful consideration of the facility needs of the total program.

SECONDARY-SCHOOL GYMNASIUM

The building or portion of the school that houses the gymnasium should be located so that it is easily accessible from classrooms, parking areas, and the outdoor activity area (see Figure 36). A proper location not only provides accessibility,

but can be used after school hours or during weekends or holidays without having to open other sections of the school.

SIZE AND LAYOUT

For general purposes, allow a minimum of 125 square feet of usable activity space for each girl or boy in a physical education class at peak load. The space requirements and dimensions of a gymnasium floor are most significantly influenced by the official rules governing court games, particularly interscholastic basketball, and the extent of spectator seating. The minimum dimensions required of a gymnasium for basketball, however, should be expanded, if necessary, to accommodate other activities. In some instances, an entire gymnasium is not required for an activity. Folding, soundproof partitions can be used to divide the area and thereby provide two teaching stations, each of which should have the minimum area for an individual teaching station. Space requirements for a number of activities are listed in Table 3. Possible layouts for gymnasiums are included in Figures 37, 38, and 39.

SPECTATOR SEATING

The extent of the demand for spectator seating is dependent upon each school and the community it serves. Junior high schools do not have as extensive spectator activities as do

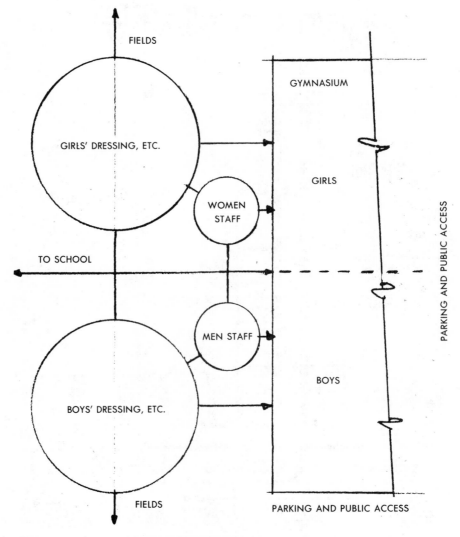

Figure 36
Orientation of Gymnasium to Related Areas

senior high schools. Under no circumstances should the program facilities be cut so that spectator accommodations can be financed. Modern design uses power-driven folding or roll-away bleachers which telescope and thereby require insignificant permanent space. If possible, the outer surface of folding bleachers should create a flat, wall-like surface so that it may be used for ball rebounding.

The number of seats which can be provided on the main-floor level by roll-away bleachers is directly related to the length of the floor, and the distance between the side of the court and the adjacent wall. The width of each seating space should not be less than 18″. Roll-away bleachers most commonly allow 22-inch depths for seats. A greater depth would provide

increased comfort. The number of rows available in roll-away bleachers varies among manufacturers, with 23 rows being the maximum for standard equipment. In some instances, bleachers with 30 rows can be secured by special order (see Figure 40). This illustration will serve as a space guide for planners. Planners should investigate local and state codes and those of the National Fire Protection Association, 60 Battery March Street, Boston.

Electrically-powered tractors with rubber tires are manufactured for pulling bleachers into position for occupancy and for folding them away. The tractor not only allows one man to do the job, but provides uniform and steady power, and avoids the danger that can result from having a group of

This Unit Provides:

Two teaching stations

One standard interschool basketball court

Two court areas for instruction and intramural basketball

Two court areas for volleyball, newcomb, etc.

Four court areas for badminton, paddle tennis, etc.

Two circle areas for instruction, dodge ball, and circle games

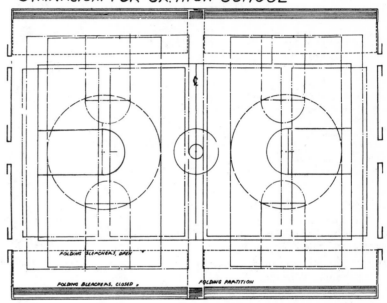

Figure 37

This Unit Provides:

Two teaching stations

One standard interschool basketball court

Two court areas for instruction and intramural basketball

Three court areas for volleyball, newcomb, etc.

Six court areas for badminton, paddle tennis, etc.

Four circle areas for instruction, dodge ball, and circle games

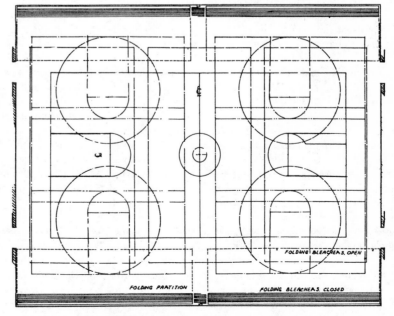

Figure 38

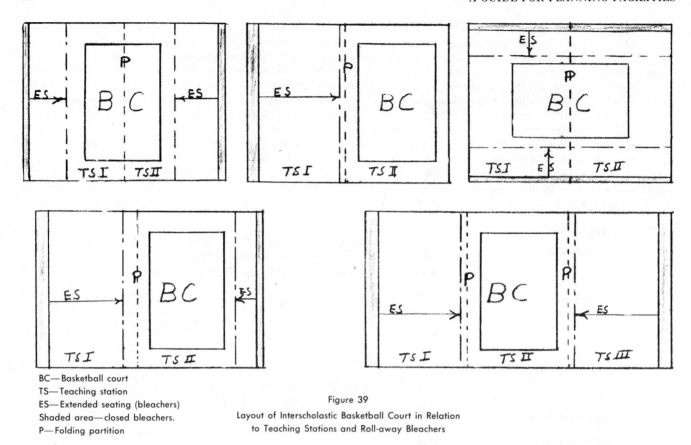

BC—Basketball court
TS—Teaching station
ES—Extended seating (bleachers)
Shaded area—closed bleachers.
P—Folding partition

Figure 39
Layout of Interscholastic Basketball Court in Relation
to Teaching Stations and Roll-away Bleachers

robust and energetic youth apply their efforts to the task. Other types of power-driven devices are available.

The maximum number of removable seats that can ordinarily be provided at floor level is from 3,000 to 3,400, using 23 rows 100′ long on both sides of the basketball court. An area of 110′ x 165′ could house these facilities. Balconies can be used to increase the total seating capacity beyond the maximum permitted at floor level. The space at both levels should be considered as activity area when the bleachers are closed. It may be desirable, in some instances, to provide less than maximum seating at floor level so that a balcony will be wide enough to serve as a teaching station for specific activities (see Figures 41, 42, and 43). Balcony bleachers can be installed to telescope from the back to the front so that in the closed position they stand erect, creating a divider wall at the edge of the balcony. This arrangement affords partial isolation of the teaching station and enhances the safety of participants.

OTHER INDOOR FACILITIES

Some activities require specialized equipment and areas that may be provided in a main or auxiliary gymnasium. Even with careful planning, it is difficult to make adequate provisions without some compromise. In some activities, such as aquatics or riflery, the very nature of the activity necessitates a separate facility for the sport. The natatorium is considered in a later chapter. Bowling lanes have been provided in a number of public and private schools, most commonly in boarding schools. These facilities have also been provided in schools located in small communities where the school is the center of social and recreational affairs. Planners should consult the manufacturers of bowling equipment if bowling lanes are considered. Some other specialized needs that planners should consider are discussed in this section. The chapter on "Indoor

Facilities for Colleges and Universities" describes specialized facilities that some schools may also provide (see Chapter 9).

THE AUXILIARY GYMNASIUM

A multipurpose auxiliary gymnasium can be designed to supplement the gymnasium by accommodating activities such as badminton, fencing, fundamental skills, calisthenics, gymnastics, tumbling, wrestling, dance, volleyball, and one-wall handball, whether instructional or recreational. This facility provides flexibility in programming and can be used during inclement weather by classes scheduled for outdoors. Each school must determine the general use of the unit and select dimensions adequate to serve its needs.

An auxiliary gymnasium of 75′ x 90′ will house two volleyball courts, three badminton courts, three one-wall handball courts, two half-court tennis areas using adjacent walls, and other courts and areas. In addition, this unit can serve a variety of other activities in the intramural, recreational, or interscholastic program, all of which cannot be accommodated immediately after school in the main gymnasium. Some auxiliary gymnasiums are large enough to be divided into two teaching stations for certain activities. Special considerations or characteristics of this facility, such as those relating to floors, walls, ceilings, and lighting, are similar for the gymnasium and are included in Chapter 11.

FACILITIES FOR GYMNASTICS AND TUMBLING

Two areas are imperative for gymnastics: one for storage and one for actual participation. Horses, rings, mats, ropes, bucks, springboards, bars, ladders, and trampolines are some of the items of equipment that may be used and which will require floor and storage space. For participation in competitive tumbling, a floor space of at least 70′ in one direction is required to house the 5′ x 60′ mat used. Instructional tumbling

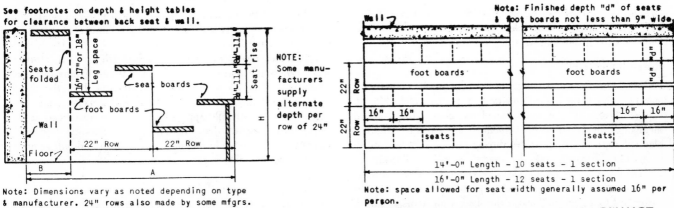

SECTION – SEAT RISE & LEG SPACE

ROW SPACING & SEAT WIDTH ALLOWANCE

DEPTH & HEIGHT – SPACE REQUIREMENTS FOR PRELIMINARY LAYOUT

Note: For exact dimensions, consult manufacturers catalogues. Manufacturers in addition to those given in dimension tables are: Beatty, Berlin-Chapman Company, Hussey Mfg. Co. and Leavitt Bleacher Co. Seats available to 30 rows by some manufacturers.

Note: Dimensions in different rows are not interchangeable — so select dimensions all in the same horizontal row.

NO. OF ROWS	ROLLING TYPES — STRAIGHT FRONTS Depth A Open	Depth B* Closed**	Height H Open-Closed	SLOPING FRONTS Depth A Open	Depth B† Closed††	Height H Open-Closed	FOLDING TYPES — STRAIGHT FRONTS Depth A Open	Depth B Closed	Height H Open	Height H Closed
3	4'-6" / 4'-6½"	2'-8" / 2'-8½"	3'-1½" / 3'-2"	4'-8" / 4'-9"	1'-9¾" / 1'-8¾"	2'-11" / 3'-0"	4'-8"	2'-1"	3'-2"	3'-8"
4	6'-4" / 6'-4½"	2'-8" / 2'-8½"	3'-11¾" / 4'-0½"	6'-6" / 6'-7"	2'-2" / 2'-0½"	3'-7½" / 3'-9"	6'-6"	2'-4½"	4'-1½"	4'-4½"
5	8'-2" / 8'-2½"	2'-8" / 2'-8½"	4'-10" / 4'-11"	8'-4" / 8'-5"	2'-6¼" / 2'-3½"	4'-4" / 4'-6"	8'-4"	2'-8"	5'-1¼"	5'-1¼"
6	10'-0" / 10'-0½"	2'-8" / 2'-8½"	5'-8¼" / 5'-9½"	10'-2" / 10'-3"	2'-10½" / 2'-6½"	5'-0½" / 5'-3"	10'-2"	2'-11½"	6'-0½"	6'-0½"
7	11'-10" / 11'-10½"	2'-8" / 2'-8½"	6'-6½" / 6'-8"	12'-0" / 12'-1"	3'-2¼" / 2'-10¼"	5'-9" / 6'-0"	12'-0"	3'-3"	7'-0"	7'-0"
8	13'-8" / 13'-8½"	2'-8" / 2'-8½"	7'-4¾" / 7'-6½"	13'-10" / 13'-11"	3'-7" / 3'-1¼"	6'-5½" / 6'-9"	13'-10"	3'-6½"	7'-11½"	7'-11½"
9	15'-6" / 15'-6½"	2'-8" / 2'-8½"	8'-3" / 8'-5"	15'-8" / 15'-9"	3'-11¼" / 3'-5"	7'-2" / 7'-6"	15'-8"	3'-10"	8'-11"	8'-11"
10	17'-4" / 17'-4½"	2'-8" / 2'-8½"	9'-1¼" / 9'-3½"	17'-6" / 17'-7"	4'-3½" / 3'-8¾"	7'-10½" / 8'-3"	17'-6"	9'-1½"	9'-10½"	9'-10½"
11	19'-2" / 19'-2½"	2'-8" / 2'-8½"	9'-11½" / 10'-2"	19'-4" / 19'-5"	4'-7¾" / 3'-11¾"	8'-7" / 9'-0"	19'-4"	4'-5"	10'-10"	10'-10"
12	21'-0" / 21'-0½"	2'-8" / 2'-8½"	10'-9¾" / 11'-0½"	21'-2" / 21'-3"	5'-0" / 4'-3½"	9'-3½" / 9'-9"	21'-2"	4'-8½"	11'-9½"	11'-9½"
13	22'-10" / 23'-0½"	2'-8" / 4'-8½"	11'-8" / 11'-11"	23'-0" / 23'-1"	5'-4¼" / 4'-6½"	10'-0" / 10'-6"				
14	24'-8" / 24'-10½"	2'-8" / 4'-8½"	12'-6¼" / 12'-9½"	24'-10" / 24'-11"	5'-8½" / 4'-9¾"	10'-8½" / 11'-3"				
15	26'-6" / 26'-8½"	4'-6" / 4'-8½"	13'-4½" / 13'-8"	26'-8" / 26'-9"	6'-0½" / 5'-1¼"	11'-5" / 12'-0"				
16	28'-4" / 28'-6½"	4'-6" / 4'-8½"	14'-2¾" / 14'-6½"	28'-6" / 28'-7"	6'-5" / 5'-4¼"	12'-1½" / 12'-9"				
17	30'-2" / 30'-4½"	4'-6" / 4'-8½"	15'-1" / 15'-5"	30'-4" / 30'-5"	6'-9¼" / 5'-11¼"	12'-10" / 13'-6"				
18	32'-0" / 32'-2½"	4'-6" / 4'-8½"	15'-11¼" / 16'-3½"	32'-2" / 32'-3"	7'-1½" / 5'-11¼"	13'-6½" / 14'-3"				
19	33'-10" / 34'-0½"	4'-6" / 4'-8½"	16'-9½" / 17'-2"	34'-0" / 34'-1"	7'-5¾" / 6'-2¾"	14'-3" / 15'-0"				
20	35'-8" / 35'-10½"	4'-6" / 4'-8½"	17'-7¾" / 18'-0½"	35'-10" / 35'-11"	7'-10" / 6'-6¼"	14'-11½" / 15'-9"				
21	37'-6" / 37'-8½"	4'-6" / 4'-8½"	18'-6" / 18'-11"	39'-7"	6'-9½"	16'-6"				
22	39'-4"	4'-6"	19'-4¼"	41'-5"	7'-0¾"	17'-3"				
23	41'-2"	4'-6"	20'-2½"	43'-3"	7'-4½"	18'-0"				

Figure 40

Bleacher Seats and Dimensions

does not require as long a mat, but about 75 square feet of space per student is desirable. The space and mats can also be used for instructional wrestling.

Rings, Ropes, and Bars

Climbing ropes are attached to a height of 24' and drop to about 3' above the floor. Apparatus may be attached to the exposed beams. If the ceiling is placed below the structural members, the location of suspended equipment should be planned and eyebolts provided during the construction of the gymnasium. Ropes should be spaced 5' apart, allowing one for each five students in class. Flying and still rings are attached at a height of 18', are spaced 18" apart, and are suspended to a point 92" above the floor. Side walls should be a minimum of 5' away from the rings. End walls at least 35' from the point of attachment will afford safety for the participants. Traveling rings are supported from a height of 18' to 26' and are located 7' apart along a continuous line. Lines should be provided so that ropes and rings not in use can be drawn to the overhead so as not to interfere with other activities.

High bars require both floor and wall or ceiling attachments which should be considered in planning. Adjustable bars for class instruction can be arranged in a linear series. Bars vary from 6' to 7' in length and require 12' of unobstructed space extending perpendicular to their long axis. Bars for interscholastic competition are most commonly located as individual units.

Equipment Storage

By planning in detail the equipment layout for gymnastics, attachment hardware for floors, walls, and ceilings can be included in the original design and construction. The manufacturers of gymnastic equipment will supply details for the attachment of their products. Not only will proper installation be achieved, but it is less expensive than similar work which occurs at a later date.

Equipment not permanently attached will require storage space unless the teaching station is limited to gymnastics. An adjoining storage room with double doors and flush threshold is recommended. The space required will depend upon the extent of each school's apparatus. In many instances, mats can be stored on wall hangers. The competitive-tumbling mat, which is 5' x 60', should be rolled for storage and will require about 30 square feet of space.

RIFLE RANGE

Courses in firearm safety are becoming increasingly popular. Interest in recreation or competitive target shooting, and federal legislation expanding secondary-school ROTC programs further indicate the possible justification of a rifle range. The National Rifle Association provides details for construction of firing ranges. The information that follows will assist planners in determining general space requirements for a range.

Targets are located from 54" to 66" apart and are placed 50' from the firing line. From 3' to 8' of space is required behind the targets for bullet-trap construction, and at least 12' should be provided behind the firing line to give ample space to those firing. A ceiling height of 8' is recommended. The width of the range will depend upon the number of firing points. The minimum width recommended for each point is 4'. A teaching-station range should provide one firing point for every three students. Pulley devices should be used to place targets in the firing position and for returning them to the firing line. If rifles and supplies are to be stored in the range, and if rifle maintenance and repair are to occur in the range, additional space should be provided. For participant comfort and sound isolation, careful consideration should be given to

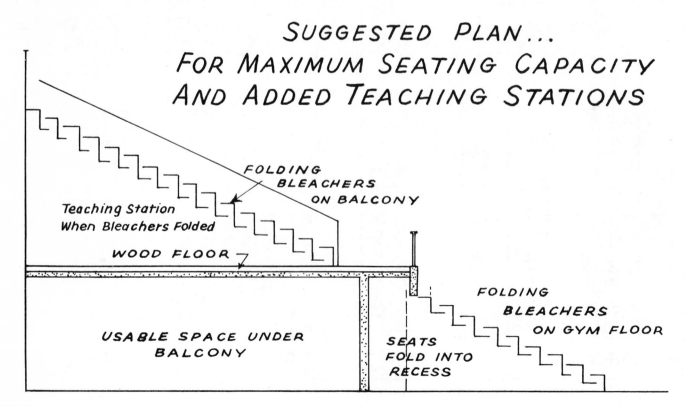

Figure 41
Suggested Plan for Maximum Seating Capacity and Added Teaching Stations

Figure 42

THE SECOND LEVEL of the Long Beach gymnasium offers complete facilities for gymnastics and physical-fitness work. Two fitness classes can be held in the gymnasium while the main area is used for competitive sports. This is one of the recommended features for schools needing a maximum number of teaching stations.

Figure 43

THE LONG BEACH HIGH SCHOOL gymnasium has been designed to handle huge crowds comfortably at its public sports events. Here you see a basketball game in progress before a capacity audience. Seating has been arranged in three levels, with two-level entrances for easy-flow of spectators. Additional features include a press box, easy-access rest rooms, snack bar, acoustical paneling, and sky lighting.

ventilation and acoustics. The proper illumination of targets should also be provided. In schools where it is not possible to provide a range, a program can be administered in a gymnasium with portable bullet traps. Information can be secured from the National Rifle Association.

FACILITIES FOR DANCE

Few schools have the program or number of interested students to justify a studio to serve only dance. In some instances, permanent facilities are provided for dance, but are also designed to accommodate other activities. In other situations, teaching stations used primarily for other activities are also planned to serve the dance program. The basic information which follows must be adapted to the circumstances of a specific school. (Also see Chapter 9.)

A minimum of 100 square feet per student is suggested for dance. For modern dance, one dimension should exceed 60′. Full-length mirrors extending a minimum of 30′ along one wall and 20′ along the adjoining wall will afford analysis of

skill from two directions by the participants. Some teachers, however, prefer all mirrors along one wall. Acoustics are improved by concealing mirrors with drapes when they are not in use. Mirrors located in teaching stations used for ball games must be protected.

A speaker system designed and located to distribute sound evenly throughout the room is preferred to a single loud-speaker. A control center can provide jacks for record players and microphones, as well as switches for selective utilization of speakers. These outlets and equipment could be provided in a built-in cabinet. Additional outlets located around the perimeter of the room could also be used to an advantage.

A tackboard could be used to post notices and to display pertinent information. A portable or permanent chalkboard is essential for class instruction. Practice bars, if provided, may be located on one wall at the recommended heights of 34″ and 42″. Wood floors are most satisfactory for dance. For modern dance, the floor should be of hard northern maple which has been sealed and then buffed with a fine abrasive. New materials currently being developed may warrant future consideration.

FIELD SERVICE BUILDING

The field-house concept for many secondary schools is a structure housing dressing rooms, showers, equipment-storage rooms, and coaches' and trainers' rooms. A separate building is recommended for the field house. Where permanent concrete stands are installed, the units of a field house are often provided under the concrete stands.

The field house should provide:

- One varsity dressing room—40 to 50 players (for football and track).
- One varsity dressing room—40 to 50 players (for soccer, cross-country, baseball, and lacrosse).
- One junior-varsity and freshman dressing room—50 to 60 players (to be used by visiting team on game day).
- Equipment drying room—accessible to all (should accommodate uniforms for all sports in addition to providing storage for towels).
- Laboratory facilities—for each dressing room.
- Shower and toweling facilities—may be a combination for all dressing rooms.
- Trainers' rooms.
- Coaches' rooms.
- Storage for both the current season and out-of-season equipment.
- Spectator toilets and refreshment stand (optional).

Dressing Rooms (Varsity, Junior-Varsity, and/or Freshmen)

This room is used daily during the outdoor-sports season. Consideration should be given the following:

- High windows to provide maximum space for lockers.
- Personal lockers, if possible, on a concrete base. Lockers should be a minimum of 12″ x 12″ x 60″. Avoid placing lockers in the center of dressing rooms. If no lecture room is provided, the varsity rooms will be used for conferences on rainy days and between halves in football, soccer, and lacrosse games. A chalkboard should be available on the wall or on a stand. Floor drains as well as faucets for hose connections should be provided for hosing down.
- Rooms should provide (particularly for football, with the amount of gear needed) approximately 15 square feet per player, exclusive of locker area. This size may be reduced to 12 square feet for rooms housing soccer, cross-country, baseball, and track.
- Mirrors (wall) should be installed.
- Drinking fountains should be provided.
- Benches (permanent type) should be installed in front of lockers.

Equipment Drying Room

One of the most important features of a field house is the equipment drying room. Uniforms improperly stored overnight are not thoroughly dry for use by players the next day. This area should provide:

- One large area to service all seasonal sports teams.
- Space enough for 100 or more uniforms. Usually a team will carry approximately 60 to 80 players on all squads. Extra provisions should be made for varsity-squad game uniforms. These uniforms must normally be dried after each game.
- Separate heat and ventilation. Air circulation is necessary for proper drying. Large circulating fans provide the best method of drying equipment, together with moderate heat.
- For drying equipment. The following methods are used:
  Special equipment hangers (most practical for handling). One to each player, hung on pipe rods for free air circulation.
  Rods in walls at different height levels for hanging equipment.
  Special hangers on movable carts that may be rolled out into the dressing room.
- Shoe storage boxes. These may be built of wood, with cubicles of 12″ x 12″ x 8″ high. Frequently during practices, shoes are the only equipment used, and if shoes are separated from other equipment, they can be obtained easily. They can also be cleaned more easily after muddy-day use.
- An entrance to the room by Dutch door, with shelf, so players may expedite the check-out and return of equipment.
- Towel storage for towel issue from this room.

The size of the equipment drying room should be determined by the number of uniforms to be stored. A room for 100 uniforms should be approximately 20′ long by 15′ wide by 10′ high, or approximately 3 square feet per player.

Shower and Toweling-Body Drying Facilities

- This area should be large enough to accommodate all players at the same time. It is difficult to stagger the use of showers.
- A large shower area connected to the toweling areas of each team dressing room can best service the participants. Such practice helps for better socialization between home and visiting teams.
- Athletic teams require soap baths, necessitating approximately four players to a shower head. A shower room of 20 to 25 shower heads should be installed.
- The entrance to showers should always be through the toweling area to prevent carrying water on bodies into the dressing room. Towel rails should be installed.
- Cake soap often presents a custodial problem. Liquid soap dispensers, when properly cared for, are the most serviceable.

Toilet Facilities

- Separate units should be provided for each dressing room.
- They should be located near the shower area.
- One water closet to each 30 players, one urinal for each 20 players, and one hand lavatory for each 30 players are recommended.

Trainers' Room

- A room every field house should have.
- The room should be large enough for cabinets for medical supplies, rubbing tables, a cot, heating units, a whirlpool bath, a toilet facility, a lavatory, and a tub lavatory.
- A drainage outlet for the whirlpool bath should be provided. A tub lavatory will serve many purposes, such as cold soaking, ice packing, etc.
- Electrical outlets for various types of mechanical medical apparatus should be installed.
- A room of approximately 15′ x 20′, exclusive of toilet facilities, is recommended.

Coaches' Room

- This room services both the coaching staff and officials for games.
- Lockers or clothes closets should be provided. Extra lockers should be provided for game officials.

- One water closet and one hand lavatory should be provided.
- One or two showers should be installed, depending upon the size of the coaching staff.
- A storage closet, with lock, is recommended for the storage of emergency athletic equipment, such as extra footballs, new bats, baseballs, timing devices, movie projectors, etc.
- A wall chalkboard, tackboard, and screen are desirable.

Equipment-Storage Room

This may be located on the top floor of a field house, or it may be a combination of a storage-and-issue room separated by a heavy-wire or solid partition. It should provide storage area for excess equipment, cold-weather and rain gear, game uniforms which have been cleaned and dried, and other equipment not used each day.

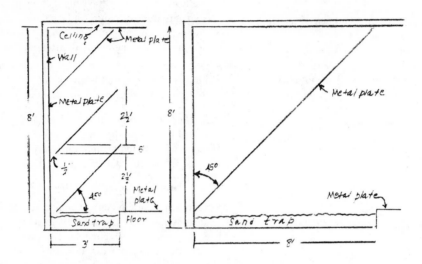

Multiple- and Single-Plate Bullet Stops. The multiple-plate design allows the section receiving the most fire to be replaced without removal of the other sections.

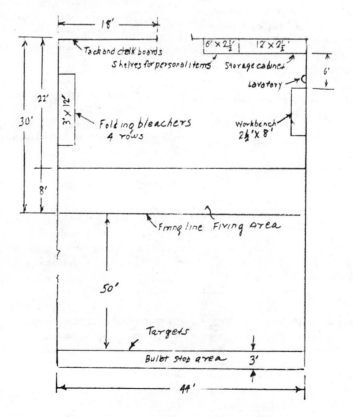

Figure 44
Hand Gun and Rifle Range Layout and Bullet Stop Designs

Lecture Room

This room provides opportunity for rainy-day conferences, chalkboard drills, movies, etc. It may serve as a lounge for lettermen, a social center for teams after a game, etc. However, if the cost of construction prohibits proper sizes for other rooms, such as dressing, shower, trainers', and toweling rooms, then the lecture room should be sacrificed first.

Maintenance-Equipment Storage Room

The size of this room will depend upon the amount and type of equipment to be stored. The usual equipment includes lawn mowers, a roller, wheelbarrows, hose, etc. Space for a work-and-repair center is recommended. This area should be at ground level with double or garage-type doors.

Spectator Rest Rooms

All outdoor athletic events which attract large crowds produce a need for rest-room facilities. Rest rooms should be designed for proper light, ventilation, and sanitary care. The size should be determined by the number of spectators at athletic events.

Spectator rest rooms can be located in the field house unless the number of spectators requires more and dispersed locations.

Concessions

Concessions have come to be considered a necessary public service in relation to public gatherings. Appropriate space and distribution as well as adequate fixtures for concession stands within the field should be planned. Since plumbing and electrical services are already available in the field house, the concession stand might be located as a part of the field house or adjacent to it.

GENERAL CONSIDERATIONS

Chapter 11 considers general plant features, such as heating, ventilation, electrical services, illumination, fenestration, utilities, and materials. The information below will cover specialized features specifically related to teaching stations.

WALLS AND CEILINGS

The walls of the gymnasium should be of a material that is resistant to hard use, at least to door height. The finish should be resistant to marking and scarring, and should have a smooth, nonabrasive surface. All corners below door height should be rounded and there should be no projections into playing areas. Lower portions of the walls should be finished with materials that can be easily cleaned without destroying the finish.

The following are recommended gymnasium ceiling heights for various school levels: elementary, 18'; junior high school, 20' for instruction and 22' for interscholastic athletics; and senior high schools, 22'. All heights should be to the lowest point of the ceiling. Ceilings should be insulated to prevent condensation of moisture and should be of a light color to enhance light reflection. Acoustical ceiling materials are necessary in all areas, especially in dance studios and areas accommodating spectators.

FOLDING PARTITIONS

Folding partitions make possible two or more teaching stations in the gymnasium. They should be power-operated, insulated against sound transmission and reverberation, and so installed as to permit compensation for building settlement. The control should be key-operated. The design and operation must ensure student safety. Partitions should extend from floor to ceiling and may be recessed when closed. Floor tracks should not be used. A pass door should be provided at the end of a partition. When installing partitions in gymnasiums with open truss construction, the space between the top of the folding doors and the ceiling should be insulated against sound transmission.

FIXED EQUIPMENT

If suspended equipment is planned, provision for its attachment should be made before the ceiling is installed.

All basketball backstops will need special care in their installation to ensure rigidity and safety. An adapted mechanical device can be helpful in the operation of swing-up or fold-up types. In addition to the main-court basketball backstops, provision should be made for other backstops on clear sidewalls. All basketball backstops should be attached to ceilings or walls, and they should be the swing-up or fold-up type where they will interfere with other activities.

In the interests of safety, suspension apparatus, such as bars, rings, and climbing poles and ropes, should be placed so they have sufficient clearance from basketball backstops and walls. If wall apparatus is desired in the gymnasium, a strip of metal or hardwood firmly attached to the wall at the proper height is recommended. Wherever necessary, floor plates should be installed for fastening movable equipment such as horizontal bars and volleyball standards.

If mats are to be hung in the gymnasium, appropriate hangers should be provided. For safety reasons, padding should be installed on all walls in back of baskets. Rubber-tired mat trucks which may be wheeled into a storage room have been found quite satisfactory in many places.

TRAFFIC CONTROLS

Good traffic control should permit the efficient movement of students to and from the gymnasium, locker rooms, and other related service areas. Traffic planning should also include provision for the controlled movement of spectators. When there are balconies as well as seating on the main floor, each balcony should be made accessible by separate ingress and egress.

All traffic arrangements for spectators should provide direct movement to and from bleachers with a minimum of walking on gymnasium floors. Spectators should have access to drinking fountains, refreshment counters, and toilets without crossing the gymnasium floor. Steep, high stairways should be avoided.[6] Ramps with nonslip surfaces might be substituted in appropriate places. Local and state building codes and standards of the National Fire Protection Association should be consulted.

FOYERS

Where finances and space will allow, foyers should be placed so they will serve as entries to gymnasiums and will guide spectators as directly as possible to seating areas. Building codes and the spectator capacity of the gymnasium will have a bearing on the size of the foyer. Toilet facilities for men and women, ticket-sales windows, ticket-collection arrangements, checkrooms, public telephones, a refreshment-dispensing room with counter, and lockable display cases should be provided, opening directly to the foyer. In some gymnasiums, these services might be omitted or reduced.

Floors should be of a type that will withstand heavy traffic and some moisture. It is appropriate to create a pleasing appearance in foyers through the use of special building materials, colors, lighting, and other means.

6 *Ibid.*

OTHER FACTORS

Provision should be made for the installation of: electric scoreboards; a central sound system and public-address system; picture projectors; a radio; television; high-fidelity equipment; and cleaning machines. Special consideration should be given to floor outlets for scoreboards and public-address systems so that they are placed according to the location of the scoring table. Wall outlets should be installed near cupped eyes to permit special lighting as needed. Controls for gymnasium lighting should be conveniently located, recessed, and keyed.

Drinking fountains and cuspidors should be accessible without causing a traffic or safety problem. It may be desirable to provide a drained catch-basin, grilled flush with the floor, to care for splash and overflow. Drinking fountains may also be located adjacent to the entrance of the gymnasium or in the foyer.

Cupped eyes should be installed in all walls at approximately a 15-foot height and 10-foot intervals for decorating convenience. They may also be used for attaching nets and other equipment to walls at appropriate heights. Bulletin boards and chalkboards should be provided in places where needed. If wall space is available, such boards may be provided for each teaching station in the gymnasium.

SELECTED REFERENCES

American Association for Health, Physical Education, and Recreation, **Administration of High School Athletics**—Report of a National Conference. Washington, D.C.: AAHPER, 1201 Sixteenth St., N.W., 1962.

American Association of School Administrators, **American School Buildings.** Washington, D.C.: The Association, 27th Yearbook, 1949.

American School Board Journal. Published monthly by the Bruce Publishing Co., 540 North Milwaukee St., Milwaukee, Wis.

Bucher, Charles A., **Administration of School Health and Physical Education Programs.** St. Louis: The C. V. Mosby Co., 1963.

Caudill, William W., **Toward Better School Design.** New York: F. W. Dodge Corporation, 1954.

Daniels, Arthur S., **Adapted Physical Education.** New York: Harper and Brothers, 1954.

Educational Facilities Laboratories, 477 Madison Avenue, New York, N.Y. Several helpful materials available.

Forsythe, Charles F., **Administration of High School Athletics.** Englewood Cliffs, N.J.: Prentice-Hall, Inc., 1961.

Gabrielsen, M. Alexander, and Miles, Caswell M., **Sports and Recreation Facilities for School and Community.** Englewood Cliffs, N.J.: Prentice-Hall, Inc., 1958.

George, Jack F., and Lehmann, Harry A., **School Athletic Administration.** New York: Harper and Rowe, 1965.

Herrick, John H.; McLeary, Ralph D.; Clapp, Wilfred F.; and Bogner, Walter F., **From School Program to School Plant.** New York: Henry Holt and Co., 1956.

National Council on Schoolhouse Construction, **Guide for Planning School Plants.** East Lansing, Mich.: The Council, c/o Floyd G. Parker, Secretary, Michigan State University, 1964.

School Sites—Selection, Development, and Utilization. Washington, D.C.: United States Department of Health, Education, and Welfare, 1950.

Scott, Harry A., and Westkaemper, Richard B., **From Program to Facilities in Physical Education.** New York: Harper and Brothers, 1958.

Chapter 9

INDOOR FACILITIES for COLLEGES and UNIVERSITIES

GYMNASIUM BUILDINGS

BASIC CONSIDERATIONS

THE TYPE and size of gymnasium facilities needed for a given college or university will depend upon many factors, one of the most important of which is the anticipated enrollment of the institution. A gymnasium planned to serve 2,000 students will, obviously, be considerably smaller than, and different in design and construction from, a facility planned for a university of 10,000 or more students. In other words, planning must be done with future enrollment in mind, and as part of the master plan for the college or university. If a college or university has a definite enrollment ceiling, the building may be planned for this enrollment. If the enrollment ceiling is indefinite, however, the structure should be planned so that additions to the building are feasible. Most universities or colleges should plan for and build for expansion. Gymnasium space is usually planned to take care of enrollments for at least ten years in advance. Universities of 15,000 or more students may find it desirable to build more than one gymnasium structure, each servicing an area of the campus.

Another factor that will affect the type of building constructed is the philosophy of the administration concerning athletics and physical education. Many questions need to be answered before planning begins. Some of these questions are:

- Will all students be required to take physical education for one, two, three, or four years?
- Is the required program in physical education to be broad in scope, i.e., will a great many opportunities to develop sports skills be extended to students?
- Is teacher education in physical education to be part of the program?
- What responsibility does the college or university take for the physical education, recreation, and fitness of its faculty?
- Is it anticipated that research in physical education, health, and recreation may become an important aspect of the program?
- What is the scope of the varsity athletic program? (The facility requirements are considerably different if varsity teams are to be fielded only in the major sports.)
- What will be done to provide facilities for an expanded program of intramurals and extramurals?

PRINCIPLES OF GYMNASIUM PLANNING AND CONSTRUCTION

Indoor facilities for sports and athletics should be planned so that all activity areas will be available to both men and women. It is unwise to identify facilities as men's or women's athletic areas. Good planning will permit easy access to all areas from both the men's and women's locker rooms. This type of planning permits the flexibility necessary for efficient utilization and control.

The space used for permanent seating of spectators at athletic events should be kept to a minimum unless space and funds present no problem to be considered. Roll-away or folding bleachers should be used in order to utilize efficiently the space available. Most colleges and universities cannot afford to invest large sums of money nor give large areas of space to permanent seating which is used only a few times each year.

The health and safety of those using the building should be a prime consideration in the planning of all activity areas. The disabled and the aging should also be considered.[1,2]

The construction of the types of facilities and the allocation of adequate square footage to handle a broad athletic and intramural program will provide more than enough gross space for a two-year physical education requirement for all students.

The traffic patterns for a building should be carefully studied. Lockers, showers, and toweling rooms should be centrally located in the building so that they may serve all activity areas. Easy access should be provided from the locker rooms to the playing fields adjacent to the building.

Storage rooms for equipment and supplies should be carefully planned and functionally located. These rooms should be of three types:

- Central receiving storage room, to which all equipment and supplies are delivered. The warehouse storage room should be accessible by truck.
- Utility storage rooms located adjacent to gymnasiums so that bulky equipment may be moved to the floor and back to storage with limited difficulty. Overhead doors or double doors should be large enough to permit free movement of heavy equipment.
- Supply rooms with an attendant's window opening to the locker rooms.

Off-season storage rooms are critically needed. The type of equipment to be moved and stored will define the dimensions of the room and size of the doors needed. Reserve storage should also be provided.

LOCATION OF THE GYMNASIUM

If physical education and athletic facilities are used by all of the students at a college or university, the gymnasium facility should be centrally located in order to be easily reached from both the academic buildings and student housing. Physical education facilities, to serve as teaching stations, must be close enough to academic buildings to make it possible for students to move from the classroom into the gymnasium and back within the time provided between classes.

Buildings used only for intramural and intercollegiate activities may be located farther from classrooms and housing than a general-use gymnasium would be. This is especially true if the activities promoted in these buildings are scheduled. If the building is to be used for unscheduled participation of students, however, the amount of use will vary inversely with the distance from housing and other campus buildings.

[1] See Chapter 11.
[2] See Appendixes G and H.

THE MAIN GYMNASIUM

The criteria for determining the size of the gymnasium are: (1) the nature of the total physical education program; (2) student load as determined by enrollment and attendance requirements per week; (3) spectator interest; and (4) anticipated enrollment growth.

The physical education building should include one main gymnasium to be used for general physical education class work, intramurals, and intercollegiate athletic activities in basketball and wrestling. Ideally, the size of the main-gymnasium floor for an enrollment of 4,000 students would be approximately 140′ x 140′. (Use a rectangular dimension if the facility will be heavily used for spectator sports.) This size would provide for one official and three junior-size (35′ x 84′) basketball courts, with adequate space between the courts and between the courts and walls. If desirable, folding partitions can be used to provide three practice gymnasiums, each 48′ x 140′. For the basketball courts, backboards that swing up to the ceiling are needed since nonfolding backboards would interfere with the court usage for volleyball and badminton. In order to increase the number of other instructional units, electrically-controlled wooden partitions or nets (nylon or Fiberglas) should be installed.

If the gymnasium is to be used for intercollegiate athletics, seating must be provided for spectators (3 square feet per person). Portable folding bleachers which can be easily moved are recommended for seating. Portable knock-down bleachers are not recommended because they interfere with class work while they are being erected, used, and removed. Cost is also an important factor.

The number of seats to be provided will be determined by the size of the student body, the college community, and the degree to which there is public demand for admittance. The seating capacity should be set at a minimum of one-half to two-thirds of the student-faculty population. In larger institutions, it may be necessary to install roll-away bleacher seats in the balcony, which, when combined with the bleachers on the main floor, will provide the required number of seats.

The varsity basketball court should be laid out lengthwise in the center of the gymnasium. If the dimensions of 114′ x 145′ are provided, 25′ is left on either side for bleachers. A minimum of 5′ should be left between the first row of seats and the outside boundary line of the court.

Where a permanent balcony is required, it is necessary to plan the line of vision so that the sidelines of the varsity-basketball court are plainly visible to the spectators. In this case, the folding bleachers on the floor should be planned to conform to the same line of vision. With the use of roll-away bleachers, added teaching stations can be provided in the balcony area.

If the gymnasium is to be used for intercollegiate sports, the number of entrances and exits equipped with panic hardware should meet fire regulations and be ample in number to control spectator traffic. Spectators should be routed in such a manner that they do not cross the playing courts or other activity areas in the gymnasium.

The height from the floor to the beams in the main gymnasium should be such that in normal use of any of the courts, the balls or badminton birds will not strike the lowest ceiling beam. This height should be a minimum of 22′ to accommodate the rope climb, basketball, volleyball, and badminton.

Where intercollegiate basketball is played, there should be adequate provision for sportswriters. A press box is recommended if conditions permit. The placing of tables adjacent to playing courts is not a good practice. Provision should be made

for telephone and telegraph connections, for reception and transmission lines for television, for timing and scoring devices, and for the operation of a public-address system, including stereophonic music.

When an area is designed for an activity which will require the use of a piano, phonograph, or tape recorder, a space should be provided for storing this equipment. It is preferable to have a space recessed in the sidewall near the place where the instructor will stand to lead the class. Electrical outlets which will provide current at all times will be needed for such equipment as amplifiers. A locking, sliding door should be installed for the protection of the instruments as well as the students. All instructional equipment should be on movable carts.

In addition to the niche described above for the storage of the piano and phonograph, there should be a storage room adjacent to the main gymnasium of sufficient size to accommodate the storage of all types of equipment, such as roll-away standards, mats and gymnastic apparatus, and chairs.

Other audio-visual aids can include still and movie projectors, daylight-projection screens, television sets, a scoreboard, a clock, chalkboards, and an intercommunication system.

Concrete is commonly used as a base in constructing the floor of the main gymnasium. Sleepers of 2″ x 2″ up to 2″ x 10″ are laid on edge. Maple tongue-and-groove is the most popular type of wood finish.

It is suggested that a glazed-tile wainscot be carried up to a height of 7′ or 8′. From that point to the ceiling, the concrete or cinder block should be painted with a light-colored paint.

Experience has shown that, in general, natural lighting methods have not proved satisfactory. Mercury-vapor or fluorescent lights with diffusion panels have provided satisfactory illumination.

There is some evidence that suspended tracks are no longer favored by physical education directors. However, if there is no balcony in the main gymnasium, a track serves as space for spectator seats and also for additional teaching stations.

If a track is constructed, it should be at least 8′ wide and 10′ above the gymnasium floor. The surface should provide good traction, and the curves should be banked.

THE LOBBY

The purpose of the lobby is to furnish an area for the control of admission and distribution of traffic and the provision of information. It should contain well-lighted and locked display cabinets, bulletin boards, and directories. These units should be recessed and flush-mounted. Public telephones should be located in or adjacent to the lobby. Other service facilities needed, as defined by the program, should be provided. Examples of these needs are: ticket booths, planters, and special decorations. The lobby should be attractive and of sufficient size to accommodate traffic needs. Vestibules should be included for climate control.

The general administrative offices of the building should be located near the lobby. Corridors should lead from the lobby to locker rooms and spectator areas. Probably the most serviceable and attractive floor for the lobby is terrazzo or a material of similar quality (see Chapter 11). The walls should be constructed of durable material (see Chapter 11).

A large checkroom for outer wraps should be placed adjacent to the direct line of traffic, but in an alcove or a side room in order to prevent congestion. The location and arrangement of the checkroom should serve the daily needs of the building as well as the needs of special occasions. The room should have a long, low counter covered with brass or stainless steel, and it should be possible to lock both the room and counter opening when the facility is not in use. Racks permanently numbered for checking coats and hats should be installed. Shelves should also be provided for storing packages and bags.

Toilet and washroom facilities for men and women should be located near the checkroom. Adequate stairways or ramps should lead from the main lobby to balconies or other spectator areas above the first floor (see Chapter 11).[3]

OFFICES

The central administrative offices serve as the nerve center of the entire physical education plant. They should be located near the entrance of the building since all who have business with the department will first come to these offices. The office of the director and those of the various faculty members should be adjacent to a large central office which will serve as the workroom for the secretarial and clerical staff, as a repository for all departmental records, and as a reception center and waiting room for persons who have business with the department.

The work area of this central office should be separated from the reception-waiting room area by a counter. The reception-waiting room should open into the main corridor of the building. A large closet should be provided adjacent to the work area for the storage of office supplies and records. The administrative head should have his office in or near the central administrative suite. His office should be of sufficient size to accommodate such things as an executive desk, a number of chairs, a file cabinet, and a small work table. This will require approximately 200 square feet. The central administrative office unit should include a conference room. This room should be near the office of the administrative head of the department. It should be furnished with a truncated conference table large enough to seat the entire physical education faculty, if possible, or the administrative staff in a larger university.

A small cloak room and rest rooms should be located near the conference room. The chairs for the conference room should be upholstered in attractive colors of vinyl materials so they can be kept clean. The conference room should be finished in light, attractive colors. It is desirable to have a small murphy-type kitchen for refreshments.

Each member of the faculty with major responsibilities should be provided a private office. Ideally, each of these offices should occupy a minimum of 120 square feet and be equipped with necessary office furniture. A workroom with space for a secretarial pool should receive serious consideration.

CLASSROOMS

The physical education complex should include sufficient classroom space designed primarily for lectures, discussion, and demonstrations. The number, size, and types of rooms will depend upon the anticipated enrollment and curricular offerings. Institutions offering teacher-training programs in health, physical education, recreation, and safety will have need for more specialized rooms than will those concerned primarily with service and basic instruction courses and varsity athletics.

The sizes of classrooms may well vary to accommodate from 10 to 150 persons. The space per student may vary from approximately 20 square feet per student in smaller rooms to 12 square feet per student in rooms for 100 or more persons. Standard classrooms normally seat an average of 40 students. The smaller rooms lend themselves more readily to seminars, conferences, and informal discussions, while an assembly room

big enough to combine large groups for professional lectures, clinics, and demonstrations is essential.

Where class size warrants, a wall clock visible from all seats should be installed. Acoustical treatment, adequate lighting, and thermostatically-controlled mechanical ventilation should be considered for all classrooms. Each classroom should be provided with chalkboards, tackboards, and hook strips. Electrical outlets for audio-visual equipment should be strategically located with due regard for the convenient placement of controls.

Windows should be equipped with effective room-darkening devices which are easily operated. A speakers' platform or podium is frequently desirable in rooms designed for larger groups. Large assembly rooms might well be equipped with a projection booth. A rectangular room is more satisfactory for film projection. Transmission and reception of television, including closed-circuit programs, should be considered when planning modern physical education facilities.

In locating room entrances, due regard should be given to traffic control. The rooms themselves should be placed where they are conveniently accessible, yet removed from disturbing noise and distraction.

In smaller classrooms, movable tablet or desk armchairs may be used, or conference tables and straight chairs may be preferred. Large lecture halls and assemblies should be equipped with numbered tablet or desk chairs secured to the floor and so arranged as to provide visual efficiency. It is highly desirable that convenient recessed cabinets and closets be provided for storing instructional materials and personal effects.

AUXILIARY GYMNASIUMS

In addition to the large general gymnasium, or gymnasiums, several other gymnasiums may be required for:
- Exercise therapy
- Gymnastics
- Weight exercise
- Wrestling and personal defense
- Street-shoe usage
- Dance studio
- General games

EXERCISE-THERAPY FACILITIES

Two separate areas should be planned for this specialized program: (1) an exercise-therapy room, which can be used as a clinic, designed for individual ameliorative exercises, is the basic requirement; and (2) a gymnasium for adapted activity is necessary for students assigned to this program.

The exercise-therapy room should be on the ground floor, if possible, or accessible to an elevator. It should be well lighted, and the walls and floor attractively finished to lend a cheerful atmosphere. The size of the room is determined by the number of students needing this special attention. Approximately 70 square feet of floor space is required per student. To accommodate equipment, the minimum size of the room should be 1,600 square feet. Office space should be located within this area, and the office should be equipped with large glass windows for adequate supervision of the room. The room should be well ventilated, with air conditioning provided where necessary. The dressing and toilet facilities should be close to the exercise-therapy room and should be adjusted to the needs of the handicapped.[4] A sink or wash basin should be provided in this facility. Doors and windows to the room should be designed for privacy. A curtained area should be provided for changes of equipment or appliances when privacy is desired.

[3] Ibid.

[4] See Chapter 11 and Appendixes G and H.

Permanent equipment installed in the exercise-therapy room should include: stall bars, wall weights (pulley), press bar, weight racks, shoulder wheel, finger ladder, hanging bars, overhead ladder, push-up bars, wall charts and anatomical drawings, mirrors (single), mirrors (triple), and walking rails.

Removable equipment should include: plinths (treatment tables) 26″ x 72″ x 30-1/2″; stall-bar benches; incline boards 7′ x 30″ x 3″; ankle exercisers; a bicycle (stationary); weights (dumbbells); weights (barbells); exercise mats; iron boots (single); iron boots (double); parallel bars (low); orthopedic stairs; rowing-machine stools; scales; an Elgin table (or improvisation of quadriceps exercise table); wrist rollers; neck-traction halters; cushions or pillows; crutches; a wheelchair; dynamometers (hand, spring cable); goniometers; a chalkboard; and a skeleton.

The equipment in an adapted-activities gymnasium should be the same as in a regular gymnasium, with necessary adaptations. This gymnasium should be in close proximity to the exercise-therapy room so that a student can utilize both facilities.

GYMNASTIC FACILITIES

With the recent nationwide surge of interest in physical fitness, there has been a renewed support of instruction in gymnastics. Gymnastics make a unique contribution toward overcoming a lack of development of the upper body, which is often neglected in other sports. Gymnastics contribute to building strength, agility, flexibility, coordination, balance, and posture. They also contribute to: the mental qualities of alertness, daring, and precision; the character trait of self-discipline; and fun and enjoyment. These values, together with those of preventative and corrective action, place gymnastics in a position of major importance in physical education.

In addition to the main gymnasium where gymnastic meets, exhibitions, and other competitions are held before a viewing public, a separate gymnasium should be provided for the permanent installation and storage of apparatus and equipment and for instruction in gymnastics. The dimensions of this gymnasium should be determined by space requirements needed to accommodate the apparatus and equipment to be installed, by space needs for performance in gymnastics, and by total school enrollment and interest in gymnastics. Ideally, the size of this gymnasium should be 120′ x 90′, with a minimum ceiling height of 23′. This height permits a clearance of 22′ for the rope climb and is ideal for hanging the various mechanical systems used in gymnastics. Some have found it desirable to install tracks on the ceiling supports to make it possible to use trolleys for moving equipment and for attaching safety belts used in the instruction of trampolining and tumbling.

The safety of performers and instructors should receive major consideration in planning the location and installation of apparatus, equipment, and wall fixtures. Apparatus used in performance should be located so that performers do not interfere with each other when going through their routines. Flying rings should be located so that there is at least 15′ of free

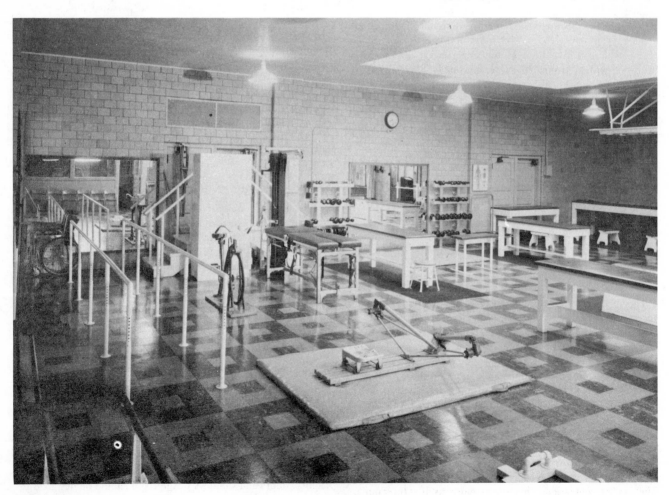

Figure 45
Therapeutic Exercise Room, University of Illinois

space allowed at each end of the swinging arc. All equipment should be installed according to a plan that will permit, without interference, a full range of movement, including the approach. Mats should be laid completely around the area of performance on horizontal and parallel bars.

Floor plates for attaching equipment should be recessed and flush with the floor. It may be necessary to reinforce the floor to install floor plates adequately where tension is unusually severe. Wall boards should be securely installed to the wall when equipment is attached to it. Apparatus suspended from the ceiling should be securely attached to metal supports.

The ceiling should be acoustically treated (see Chapter 11). Lights should be shielded and adequate for the program (see Chapter 11). Doors should be constructed wide enough and without a threshold so as to accommodate the movement of equipment to other areas. Maple has many advantages over other types of flooring (see Figures 75 and 76). The facility should be air-conditioned in accordance with standard specifications. Wall construction should be of the same materials as recommended for other gymnasiums.

A common failure in planning is to overlook the need for adequate and conveniently-placed storage space for gymnastic equipment. If multiple use of this equipment is expected, transportation carts and dollies should be provided. Specifications on size and installation of the various pieces of apparatus and equipment may be obtained from the manufacturers. Ideally, the gymnasium for gymnastics should be equipped with the following types of items: side horses, horizontal bars, long horses, parallel bars, bucks, trampolines, mats, rings, and other special apparatus.

A gymnastic landing pit, 10' wide, 20' long, and 30" deep, filled with sponge rubber—for use with parallel bars, horizontal bars, still rings, and tumbling—is a new development in construction for gymnastics.

WEIGHT-EXERCISE ROOM

This room should contain a minimum of 2,500 square feet of floor space. Such space will provide a weight-training area and space for the practice of official events in competitive weight lifting. It is recommended that the floor of this room be covered with a durable, resilient material. A flooring of this type makes it unnecessary to use weight platforms, which are essential to protect a maple or other wood flooring.

The weight-lifting area should be roped off and should be approximately 15' x 15' for the practice of official lifts. The rest of the room may be used for exercise with barbells, dumbbells, isometric cables, etc. Several full-length mirrors should be installed on the walls. Barbell and weight racks should be attached to the walls so that the room may be kept tidy.

WRESTLING AND PERSONAL-DEFENSE ROOM

This room is designed for wrestling, judo, and personal-defense activities. The ceiling should be of acoustical material and should be a minimum height of 12'. It should be rectangular in shape and should contain two square 40' x 40' mats. The floor area not covered by the regulation mats should be covered wall to wall with the same type of mat material. The room should be at least 40' x 80'. A satisfactory standard is 40 square feet per student during peak usage.

The floor of the wrestling room should be constructed of, or covered with, resilient materials to prolong the life of the mats. These materials may be rubberlock products, other newly developed resilient materials, or wood. Concrete is not recommended. The mats should be of plastic-type materials and the walls should be covered with resilient materials up to five feet above the floor on all sides. Adequate lighting which is properly screened, and forced ventilation are essential in this room.

STREET-SHOE USAGE ROOM

This room should be of sufficient size—70' x 90'—to care for the groups for which it is needed. A floor for street-shoe usage may be needed in any size college or university, or in a program with a variety of offerings. The floor most commonly used for this purpose is hard maple, tongue-and-groove, conventional gymnasium flooring. Square dance, folk dance, social dance, physical education for elementary teachers, marching and band practice, and similar activities can be conducted on such a floor. The demand of special college and community events which need to be served, such as musical and drama production, fairs, and carnivals, may be met. The "make-up" room or "warming room" for department and college outdoor programs can be housed in this area and can be served through a door leading to a corridor and immediately to the out-of-doors.

This street-shoe room, when not scheduled in some manner as indicated above, can serve the purposes of any regular gymnasium if so planned in its equipment and floor markings. The floor will need some extra maintenance for the hard use it will receive, but the desirability of the activities which may be scheduled on it will justify the usage and resultant wear.

DANCE STUDIOS

Dance areas should be provided to serve the departmental and student needs and to afford opportunity for individual and departmental development. Some of these areas are specific and may be limited to forms of dance activity. Other dance areas are versatile and may serve several purposes. Large colleges and universities with a variety of courses may need to plan for one or more of each of several dance-activity rooms. Classes should be advantageously scheduled for the purposes of floor maintenance or equipment moving. The types of dance areas suggested are discussed in the material which follows.

Main Dance Studio

This studio, which should measure no less than 56' x 56', will provide for a class of up to 36 students in modern dance, ballet, or some other dance form performed in bare feet or with soft-sole dance shoes. The floor, which should be of conventional gymnasium construction—tongue-and-groove, select maple—should be free of floor plates, plugs, and other installations. The ceiling height should be 22' to be proportional with the room and to give the feeling of height in leaps.

The room should have wall mirrors along one wall—24' in length, 6' high, and with the bottom being 2' from the floor. The mirrors should have a draw drapery controlled by cord pulls. Ballet bars (hand rails) should be installed on two opposite sides of the room at ascending heights of 3', 3-1/2', and 4' above the floor.

Audio-visual equipment should include a tackboard, a chalkboard, a hook rail, and a lockable glass-front bulletin board. An amplification system—for a record player and tape recorder—on a roll-away table should be recessed into a lockable cabinet with a sliding door. Other cabinets should provide space for musical instruments, records, music, costumes, and other properties. Some dance studios may have a grand piano in the room. It may be desirable to have an area where a grand piano or an upright piano can be stored when removed from the floor. Storage cabinets for stage equipment, levels, and other items should be provided since floor storage of materials not actively used markedly diminishes the floor space usable for dance activities.

Main-Dance-Studio Balcony

Current plans of some major institutions may be considered desirable in the provision for a hanging balcony or a balcony over other class or service areas. This balcony can provide 100 or more seats for viewing activity on the floor of the main dance studio or in the auxiliary dance studio, which can be used as a stage area for the main dance studio. Access to the balcony may be gained from the dance-studio floor through a lockable control door, or from the second-floor service hallway. The balcony will provide opportunity for practice-performance viewing from the balcony level by the members of a dance group, or will make it possible to seat visitors for an invitation performance.

Auxiliary Dance Studio

An auxiliary dance studio of 56' x 40', with a ceiling of 22', can be located adjacent to the main dance studio on the side opposite from the balcony and can be separated by appropriate folding doors and draperies. This studio can serve as a stage for small concert productions or class projects. Several institutions have successfully constructed such a facility. Traveling draperies suspended from the ceiling can be run on tracks and can be controlled electrically to serve as the traditional "flats" used in staging and in making up a backdrop behind which dancers can cross over. When not used, the draperies can be withdrawn from the staging area and can be stacked along one wall. Stage lighting can be developed to give illumination from the ceiling, from the stage side of the divider, from "projecting" semi-cones in the ceiling of the main dance studio, and from "spots" in the balcony.

This dance studio will need to include those features desirable for the program needs as are included in the main dance studio: ballet bars, mirror, cabinets for classroom materials, and a roll-away table with record player and tape recorder. In addition, there may be a need for piano and equipment storage rooms.

Dance-Rehearsal Room

One or more dance-rehearsal rooms of a minimum of 400 square feet each will contribute to the development of students in dance who need small-group practices and extra rehearsals. A chalkboard, tackboard, and rolling table for tape recorder and record player should be provided in such rooms. The table should be housed in a recessed, lockable cabinet. Other lockable cabinets will provide needed storage space for dance-practice materials. Ballet bars and mirrors will add to the usefulness of such a room.

Dance Property Construction and Storage Room

Flats, levels, and other properties can be made and stored in a room of approximately 25' x 30'. This room should be located adjacent to the main dance studio and should have wide double doors with a removable mullion so sets and properties can be moved in and out. The room should have a high ceiling to allow sets to be constructed and moved to a vertical position or to the finished position for painting. Drawers and cabinets, some lockable, a sink with hot and cold water, lumber racks, work counters and tables, and electrical outlets are essential in the planned structure of the room. Tackboards, bulletin boards, and lockable, glass-front display bulletin boards are desirable.

Dance Costume Construction and Storage Room

The size of this room will vary according to the program needs for costume construction and the storage needs for costumes made and retained in the department. The room will probably be best used by having cabinets in close-order banks, somewhat as bookcases are placed in the stacks in a library. This will free one end of the room for clothing construction. Costume-storage cabinets should have racks for hanging and bins and drawers for storage. Units can be planned so as to be comprised of several components, which may be used as desired for separate assignment to clubs, groups, or projects.

Cabinets for material and equipment storage, wall-attached ironing boards, an automatic washer-drier, a three-way mirror unit, a washroom basin, a large cutting table of 4' x 8', and a counter sink are additional necessities.

GAME ROOM

This is a multiple-purpose room, and its use will determine its dimensions. It should be large enough to accommodate at least six table-tennis tables. A ceiling height of 12' is adequate. The room should be equipped with a public-address system and record player for instructional and recreational activities, including social and square dancing. This room should be accessible from the lobby or from a building corridor. It should have small-kitchen facilities and a hard-usage-type floor. The disabled should be considered in the planning.[5]

SPECIAL INSTRUCTIONAL AND ACTIVITY AREAS[6]

HANDBALL COURTS

Handball is a vigorous competitive sport long recognized as an essential activity for a college physical education program. Depending on the size of the institution and the expressed interest in handball, one or more batteries of four-wall handball courts should be provided. The official size of a handball court is 20' wide by 40' long by 20' high. Specifications for handball courts can be found in the official handball rule book.

When more than a single battery of courts is to be constructed, the batteries should be arranged so the back walls of each battery are separated by a corridor approximately 10' wide and 8' high. A corridor located immediately above, and at least 12' high, may serve an instructor or be used as a spectator gallery. Corridors and galleries should be illuminated with indirect light.

The back wall of a single court need not be higher than 12'. Shatterproof glass may be used to enclose the remainder of the back wall. The use of wire mesh for this purpose is of questionable value. Many courts are satisfactorily used with an open upper rear wall.

Handball courts may be constructed of hard plaster, concrete, shatterproof glass, or a nonsplintering, durable wood. While plaster is sometimes recommended, it would be wise to consider courts constructed of other materials because of maintenance costs. Glass courts provide maximum spectator participation, but the initial cost may be prohibitive. Hardwood construction is most satisfactory. Courts constructed with a high proportion of glass walls obviously allow for a large number of observers. Open-balcony construction interferes with individual-court air-conditioning.

Front walls may be constructed of hard maple laid on diagonal

---

[5] See Appendixes G and H.

[6] The aging and the disabled should be considered in the planning. See Chapter 11 and Appendixes G and H.

wood sheathing. Studding should be placed close enough to prevent dead spots. A maximum of 16-inch centered studs is recommended. A costly but desirable front-wall construction is to lay hard maple on edge grain.

Side and back walls may be of non-splintering, durable wood, such as yellow pine or hard maple. Some side and back walls constructed with one-inch, tongue-and-groove, marine plywood have been satisfactory and economical. Hardwood floors of standard gymnasium construction are recommended. Plaster ceilings have proved satisfactory. All interior surfaces should be painted with egg-shell-white enamel.

Entrance doors should open toward the corridor and be provided with flush-type pulls and hinges. A small shatterproof window installed flush with the interior surface of the door should be located at approximately average-adult-male eye level.

No fixtures, such as heat pipes, ventilating ducts, lights, or any other mechanical equipment, should project into the playing area. Ventilating ducts and lighting fixtures are best located flush with the ceiling surface. Lighting specifications are available for handball courts. Provision for replacement of burnt-out light bulbs from above is a desirable feature.

A single light switch to control all lights in each court should be placed on the corridor side and near the entrance door. Warning lights, located outside each court, should indicate when a court is being used. By use of a sturdy push button, lights can be turned on when an entrance door is closed.

Refrigerated air conditioning, or at least forced ventilation, is essential for individual courts. The ventilation switch can operate in conjunction with the light switch. Climatic conditions may dictate separate switches.

SQUASH COURTS

Squash is very popular in some localities and should be provided for in the physical education program. It is recommended that at least one single and one double squash court be included in a physical education complex. A singles court is 18'-6" wide by 32' long by 16' high. A doubles court is 25' wide by 45' long by 20' high. The number of courts should be determined by the interest in this activity in a given community.

It is possible to install movable metal "telltales" across the front of handball courts so they can be used for squash. Construction features of squash courts are similar to those of four-wall handball courts relative to floors, walls, ceilings, lighting, heating, and ventilation.

The official rules of the United States Squash Racquets Association and the National Squash Tennis Association should be consulted in planning and constructing squash courts.

ROWING-PRACTICE FACILITIES

In certain colleges and universities, it may be desirable to construct facilities for indoor crew practice. Colleges engaging in competitive rowing will require either fixed rowing machines with accompanying mirrors to reflect the action of the rowers, or a rowing-practice tank. The rowing machines may be installed in a special activity room. If there is space underneath the spectator area in the main gymnasium, they may be installed there. In every case, the area should be well lighted and ventilated.

The rowing tank, when used, should simulate the conditions to be found in open-water rowing. The water should be mechanically circulated in such a manner as to make possible the actual introduction of the oar into the water, and the completion of the stroke. The crew should be seated on a rigid platform which spans the pool at actual shell height.

All of the specifications for indoor rowing equipment may be obtained from the manufacturers, and the details of the construction of a rowing tank are available through the office of the Intercollegiate Rowing Association.

INDOOR ARCHERY RANGE

An indoor archery range is much needed in modern college gymnasiums. The popularity of the Chicago Round has made indoor ranges feasible because of the decreased shooting distances, requiring less space than formerly required for the American and York Rounds. A satisfactory indoor range should be 45' in width and 78' in length. This will provide space for 15 shooters on the line at the same time, each facing a separate target. The length suggested will provide a distance of 60' for the Chicago Round, two feet for backstop material, and 16' behind the shooting line for instructors, observers, and those preparing to shoot.

Backstops may be constructed of baled straw treated with fire-resistant materials, or may be purchased from archery-equipment manufacturers. The targets may be fastened to the backstop or placed on easels in front of it. The floor in the archery room should be constructed of hard-usage materials to permit street shoes to be worn. The room should be well lighted. (see Chapter 11). The target line should be illuminated by floodlights which shine only on the target area.

RESEARCH LABORATORY

College and university health, physical education, and recreation programs are becoming increasingly involved in research. Graduate studies and faculty research cannot thrive unless space is allocated for this work in the gymnasium building where exercise and sports areas are convenient.

Research in physical education may be of many different types. Some colleges and universities emphasize one or more areas. The research taking place in physical education programs is in the following categories: kinesiologic, tests and measurements, organic (metabolic, cardiovascular, and chemical analysis), and statistical.

A laboratory providing opportunities in the kinds of research mentioned requires a minimum of 2,800 square feet of space for the basic equipment needed. The maximum space needs will depend upon the number of faculty and students involved and the complexity of the research program. Resarch-laboratory space may be provided in one large room or in several smaller rooms. It is suggested that a separate room of 300 square feet be used for a statistical laboratory.

STEAM ROOM

Some college gymnasium facilities include a steam-bath installation. This may be desirable if supervision is present when the steam room is in use. Unsupervised steam baths or sweat boxes are not recommended.

If a steam room is constructed, a satisfactory size is eight feet square, with a ceiling 10' high. A lockable door containing a window should open outward. The room should be equipped with two or three movable benches of sturdy wood construction. The steam valve used should be a type that can be set to prevent the temperature in the room from exceeding 130°.

GROUP STUDY ROOMS

If the gymnasium is to serve the needs of students enrolled in a major professional program, the inclusion of small-group study rooms is recommended. Study rooms should occupy approximately 150 square feet and should be equipped with a large table and sufficient chairs to accommodate a maximum of eight students. These rooms may serve a variety of educational needs in addition to small-group on-campus study.

"IN-UNIFORM" STUDY-HOUR ROOMS

In gymnasium buildings, there is a need for rooms where men and women students who have one free hour between two activity classes, may go in uniform to read or study.

The use of this room will conserve student time, encourage their reading or studying habits, and will clear the dressing rooms. Rooms for "in-uniform study" should be separate for men and women and should be located near the appropriate dressing rooms.

WORKROOM

Each physical education department may wish to concentrate several work or repair functions in one or more areas according to the program and equipment, and dependent upon the secretarial and office needs. Two types of areas are described below. In some colleges, it may be considered practical to combine most of the functions of these two workrooms into one plan.

Secretarial Workroom

Secretaries, machines, and typewriters are assigned to some individual offices or to a group of offices, but it may not be practical to have all individual offices so staffed and equipped. Office supplies, typewriters, duplicating machines, and some other needed and desirable office machines can be concentrated in one or more department or college workrooms where services can be performed for faculty members who have limited or irregular need of secretarial help. In such a room, a workroom manager can receive assignments, distribute and allocate this work, receive it from the workers, and return it to the appropriate faculty members.

The room should have area enough to accommodate desks, tables, and cabinets, which must be planned according to the anticipated demands. Acoustical treatment and a generous supply of electrical outlets are essential to the orderly functioning of such a service area. A wall-installed wash basin and a hand-towel cabinet are important to the economy of time in the work area.

Repair-and-Service Workroom

The need for repair and service of equipment will dictate the size of the repair-and-service workroom. Some departments will perform only minor repairs which can be accomplished in a small, modestly-equipped workroom, or in a part of some other area already provided. Other faculties will wish to plan to repair archery-target stands, covers, field carts, and other larger pieces which require the use of tools and space. This plan to service and repair large pieces, then, will require space for the equipment to be repaired and tools with which to perform the needed repairs.

A well-equipped workroom will contain such constructional and built-in features as cabinets, a sink, wood and lumber storage racks, shelves, a blower discharge fan, a work shelf, and drawers. Many, or most, of the storage areas should be locked individually or as a group with a master-key system.

THE FIELD HOUSE[7]

FUNCTION

The field house provides enclosed and unobstructed space

[7] Ibid.

adaptable to indoor and outdoor sports activities. It is not intended as a substitute for the gymnasium; it is complementary and supplementary to other facilities for indoor and outdoor physical education and recreation activities. The enclosure may also serve purposes other than physical education and recreation.

Typical functions of the field house for a college are as follows: instruction in the service program in physical education; practice for intercollegiate athletics (football, track and field, baseball, basketball, tennis, soccer, lacrosse, and other sports); intramural and intercollegiate competition; informal play; horseback riding; demonstrations and exhibitions which attract large crowds of spectators; commencement exercises; registration; and final examinations. In addition, community uses may include: interscholastic games, matches, meets and tournaments; band concerts; school commencement exercises; exhibits; and mass meetings.

The total physical education program, including co-physical education and co-recreation, should be considered when plans are developed so that facilities for activities such as tennis, volleyball, badminton, and golf practice may be provided. Unless provided in the gymnasium, handball and squash courts should be constructed in the field house. A survey of available facilities for activities common to modern physical education programs will serve to determine the number and kind of activity units to include in the field house.

LOCATION

If needed for class instruction, the preferable location for the field house is adjacent to the main gymnasium building and the natatorium. If space is not available in proximity to the gymnasium, the field house will serve well for intramural activities and intercollegiate sports, even though it is constructed in a peripheral area of the campus. It should, however, be placed in an area contiguous to athletic fields and where parking problems are not critical.

SIZE

The size of the field house should be determined by careful study of its functions; consideration should be given to the size and number of groups (classes, squads, teams) likely to participate simultaneously in the program. There should be a minimum of interference of groups with each other. The area surrounded by a one-eighth-mile track can include the following facilities: a regulation basketball court; a tennis court on each side of the basketball court; broad-jump, high-jump, and pole-vault runways and pits; and a shot-put area.

The minimum length of the field house should accommodate a 60-yard straightaway for men's track plus sufficient distance for starting and stopping. A wide door at the end of the straightaway to permit competitors to run outside the field house would prevent injuries and eliminate a mental hazard where space is limited. Six regulation lanes are desirable. The track around the portable, or permanent, basketball floor should be of such size as to be a convenient fraction of a longer standard distance.

BALCONIES AND BLEACHERS

When permanent balconies are planned, they should be constructed without supporting pillars which would interfere in any way with the playing or visual area. Balconies should be served by ramps which connect directly, or by means of wide corridors, with convenient entrances and exits.[8] Temporary bleachers, when placed in front of and below the permanent balconies, should continue the sight lines of the balconies. Bleachers can be placed inside a one-eighth-mile track on both sides and ends of a basketball court to accommodate approximately 5,000 spectators. Such bleachers should be inspected thoroughly before they are used; their capacity should never be taxed.

The field house should be so designed that the normal flow of traffic will not encroach upon the activity areas. It is essential that this be done in order to avoid interference with instruction and participation, and to decrease maintenance costs.

PRESS, RADIO, AND SCOUT ACCOMMODATIONS

Accommodations for reporters, sports broadcasters, and scouts should be planned in the original design. Soundproof broadcasting and television booths should be provided for these services when the field house will be used for attractions of considerable public interest.

ENTRANCES

Entrances to the field house should be located with reference to parking facilities and traffic approaches. The main lobby should be large enough to accommodate anticipated crowds seeking tickets and admission. This is particularly important in northern climates, The lobby should be so designed for ticket selling and collecting that the traffic will flow in a straight line, or nearly so, from the entrances to the box offices to the ticket collectors. To avoid congestion, approximately two-thirds of the lobby should be planned for accommodating box offices and ticket purchasers; the remainder should be reserved for ticket holders, who should have direct access to admission gates.

DRINKING FOUNTAINS[9]

Drinking fountains should be sufficient in number and so located that they do not interfere with the circulation of the crowd.

SERVICE UNITS

If the field house is adjacent to the main gymnasium building and the natatorium, the requirements for lockers, showers, and toilets[10] can, in some instances, be reduced. An underpass from the gymnasium to the field house may be desirable in order to make the gymnasium service units available to some participants in the field house. If the field house is not adjacent to the gymnasium, consideration should be given to the erection of a small building or a basement, simple in design, with dressing, shower, and toilet facilities, rather than use space for such purposes which might be utilized more advantageously for activity units.

Convenient and accessible dressing units equipped with chalk and tack boards for the home and visiting teams should be provided. When the field house is to be used for interscholastic basketball tournaments and indoor track meets, consideration should be given to providing separate locker rooms with adjoining shower and toilet facilities. These units could be used regularly throughout the year by intramural participants and intercollegiate squads.

It is desirable to provide passageways from dressing rooms directly to the basketball floor to avoid crowd interference.

A dressing room with adjoining shower and toilet facilities should be provided for staff members. These accommodations can also be used by game officials.

Separate toilet facilities[11] in sufficient number for men and for women spectators should be provided in close proximity to the seating areas. Toilets should be provided near traffic lanes. Where large crowds attend games, it is advisable to place supplementary toilet facilities off the main lobby.

FIRST-AID AND TRAINING ROOMS

A room for first-aid treatment should be provided if the field-house program is planned to attract spectators. This room may also serve the purpose of a training room for emergency treatment of participants, and the prevention of injuries.

LOUNGE AND TROPHY ROOM

Provision for a lounge room may be advisable after consideration of such factors as available space and funds, and the functions of such a room for clubs, members of athletic squads, letter men, officials and coaches, and visitors. An adjoining kitchenette is desirable.

STORAGE SPACE

Sufficient storage space should be provided to accommodate physical education and maintenance supplies and equipment. Supply rooms, built so that supplies and equipment may be cared for within them and issued from them, should be provided where they are needed.

CONCESSION BOOTHS

When the field house is planned to accommodate large crowds, concession booths should be constructed. They should be equipped with electric or gas stoves, sinks, running water, and sewer connections, and should be located where they do not interfere with the normal flow of traffic.

SCOREBOARDS AND TIMING DEVICES

Scoreboards and timing devices should be of sufficient number and be so placed that they can be seen readily by players and all spectators. They should be easy to operate and readily accessible for maintenance purposes.

PUBLIC-ADDRESS SYSTEM

Provision should be made for the installation of a public-address system. Acoustical treatment of the building is desirable.

LIGHTING, HEATING, AND VENTILATION

Windows should be equipped with means to prevent the interference of sunlight with player performance at any time during the day. Walls and ceilings should be light in color. Catwalks are necessary for servicing the ceiling lights, spotlights, and net.

Condensation problems should be given major consideration, particularly where there are extremes of temperature, where sprinkling of surface or dirt areas is required, and where large crowds witness events in the field house. As a means whereby some of the excess condensation may be reabsorbed, the building should be heated by the circulation of warm air, in addition to fixed radiation. Adequate means should be provided to supply fresh air and to exhaust foul air. The walls inside and outside should be impervious to vapor pressure. Technical heating, ventilating, and lighting problems should be referred to a specialist.

[8] See Appendix H.
[9] *Ibid.*
[10] *Ibid.*
[11] *Ibid.*

In consideration of the typical shape of field houses, which includes a tunnel vault roof, there should be no parapets.

FLOORS

The floor of the field house should be of an all-weather-resistant construction. Rubber asphalt and several patented rubber-like synthetics should be considered. A portable wood floor for basketball may be used. Dirt floors are not recommended.

GUIDE LINES FOR COLLEGE AND UNIVERSITY FACILITIES

The colleges and universities of the United States are facing the greatest decade of expansion in history. Predictions indicate that these institutions will have to build as many new buildings in the next ten years as they have constructed during the past 300 years. The magnitude of this problem has made the development of a master plan essential to college and university development. Space requirements of various programs of the institutions of higher learning have caused those responsible for master-plan development to request standards for facilities in terms of square feet per student. Standards in these terms are meaningful to campus planners, since relating standards

to predicted enrollment results in assured space for all disciplines involved.

The following standards are recommended for consideration by those involved in planning college and university facilities for physical education, intramural sports, intercollegiate athletics, and recreation.

TYPE "A"—Indoor Teaching Stations

Space requirements: 8.5 to 9.5 sq. ft. per student (total undergraduate enrollment)

Including: Gym floors, mat areas, swimming pools, courts, etc. (adjacent to lockers and showers and within ten-minute walking distance of academic classrooms)

Uses: Physical education class instruction, varsity sports, intramural sports, unorganized informal sports participation, student and faculty recreation, etc.

Breakdown of Type "A" Space

A1—Large gymnasium areas with relatively high ceilings (22' minimum) for basketball, badminton, gymnastics, apparatus, volleyball, etc. (approximately 55 percent of Type "A" space)

A2—Activity areas with relatively low ceilings (12' minimum) for combatives, therapeutic exercises, dancing,

Figure 46
Field House, Illinois State University

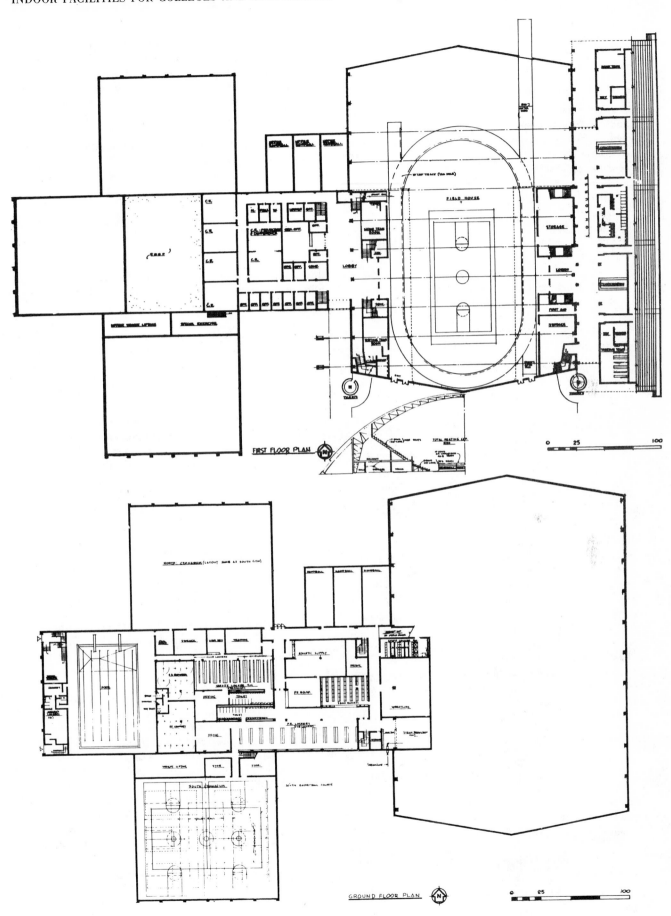

Figure 47

Floor Plan of Field House, Illinois State University

weight lifting, etc. (approximately 30 percent of Type "A" space)

A3—Swimming and diving pools (approximately 15 percent of Type "A" space)

TYPE "B"—Outdoor Teaching Stations

Space requirements: 70 to 90 sq. ft. per student (total undergraduate enrollment)

Including: Sports fields of all types (adjacent to lockers and showers and within ten-minute walking distance of academic classrooms)

Uses: Physical education class instruction, varsity sports, intramural sports participation, student and faculty recreation, etc.

Breakdown of Type "B" Space

B1—Sodded areas for soccer, touch football, softball, etc. (approximately 60 percent of Type "B" space)

B2—Court-type areas for tennis, volleyball, flicker ball, etc. (approximately 15 percent of Type "B" space)

B3—Specialized athletic areas for track and field, baseball, archery, varsity football, golf, camping demonstrations, etc. (approximately 25 percent of Type "B" space)

B4—Swimming pools (included in B3 approximation)

TYPE "C"—Sports Fields and Buildings; Intramural and General Outdoor Recreation Areas

Space requirements: 120 to 140 sq. ft. per student (total undergraduate enrollment)

Including: Playing fields and athletic buildings of all types; softball diamonds, tennis courts, arenas, field houses, etc. (too far removed from general student lockers, showers, living quarters, and academic buildings for use as teaching stations) (maximum distance from major residence areas—one mile)

Uses: Intramural sports, varsity sports, unorganized informal sports

Breakdown of Type "C" Space

C1—Sodded areas for soccer, touch football, softball, etc. (approximately 40 percent of Type "C" space)

C2—Court-type areas for tennis, volleyball, flicker ball, etc. (approximately 10 percent of Type "C" space)

C3—Specialized athletic areas for track and field, baseball, archery, varsity football, golf, camping demonstrations, etc. (approximately 45 percent of Type "C" space)

C4—Swimming pools (included in C3 approximation)

C5—Sports and intramural buildings providing lockers, showers, play space, office space, lounge rooms, etc. (approximately 5 percent of Type "C" space)

TYPE "D"—Informal Recreation Areas

Space requirements: included in C3

Including: On-campus picnic areas (maximum distance from residence areas—1-1/2 miles) (approximately 15 percent of total Type "C" space)

Uses: Picnics, outing activities (including outdoor cookery, evening songfests, storytelling, etc.)

TYPE "E"—Off-campus Outdoor Education, Camping, and Recreation Areas

Including: Outdoor camping and outdoor education center, off-campus golf course, University country club, etc. (maximum distance from heart of the campus—25 miles)

Uses: Overnight camping, picnics, outing activities, camp-

ing demonstrations, golf, archery, boating, canoeing, outdoor swimming, formal classes taught outdoors

Estimate of space needs of this type area: It is difficult to state these needs on a square-feet-per-student basis. Such areas contribute materially to the outdoor education and outdoor recreation of both men and women students, but the many variables in climate, in topography, in distance from the heart of the campus, and in emphasis on outdoor education, make a square-feet-per-student standard difficult to establish.

It has been estimated by intramural leaders that graduate students participate in physical recreation 25 percent as extensively as undergraduates. Consequently, it is suggested that planners add 25 percent of the graduate enrollment in using the standard.

ANCILLARY AREAS

Investigation indicates that a reasonable standard for determining the space needed for lockers, showers, toweling rooms, equipment storage, supply rooms, and offices associated with Type "A" space is a square footage equaling approximately 40 percent of the play or activity area in a gymnasium facility. As an example of how this figure may be used, assume that a gymnasium is being planned which will provide 100,000 square feet of activity space. In other words, the square footage in the swimming-pool surface and deck, and all gymnasium floors, including high and low ceiling areas, equals 100,000 square feet. This would mean that the square footage needed for ancillary areas would be in the neighborhood of 40,000 square feet. Architects generally speak of the combination of play space and ancillary areas in a gymnasium as "net usable area." Consequently, the net area in the building would be approximately 140,000 square feet.

All other space in a building, including hallways, stairways, wall thicknesses, lobbies, public toilets, bleachers for public use, custodial space, and space needed for service conduits of all types, is spoken of by many architects as "tare." The space needed for tare varies greatly from building to building, depending upon the function and architectural design. A rough estimate of the area needed for this item is a figure equal to 80 percent of the activity or play area in a gymnasium. By adding tare, ancillary, and play space, a rough estimate of the gross square footage of a gymnasium plan can be computed. This figure is helpful in preliminary discussions of costs involved.

ENROLLMENT RELATIONSHIPS

When standards in terms of square feet per student are used as guides in college or university planning, it is natural to ask where the cut-off begins. At what point, from ten students up, do the standards become meaningful? Obviously, for a college of 200 students, nine square feet per student of indoor area for sports and athletics would be woefully inadequate. It would not even provide one basketball court.

A university or college meeting the space standards for 1,500 students represents the minimum physical-recreation space needs of any collegiate institution. As a college or university increases in size, these standards are applicable regardless of enrollment.

PEAK LOAD AFTER SCHOOL HOURS

Through study of utilization problems at the various universities, it was found that the greatest load on facilities each day occurred between 4:00 p.m. and 10:00 p.m. In all of the universities studied, either one or two years of physical education was required of all students. As long as the requirement in basic physical education is not greater than two years, it seems that the greatest demand for space comes after the usual school hours. This may not be true in universities which require all students to register for physical education each year they are in residence.

A few universities have dropped required physical education in the belief that this will reduce the pressures on facilities for sports and athletics. The futility of this move is obvious. In fact, the elimination of a physical education requirement may increase the demands for this type of space, since all students will then tend to use after-school hours to meet their physical-activity needs. This concentration of student activity will likely make it necessary to provide greater play and exercise space than needed for a balanced program of basic instruction, free-play opportunities, and intramural-sports competition.

APPLICATION OF STANDARDS

Standards are guides for the use of planning committees and administrators. They are not substitutes for creative planning. They help a great deal in early computations of cost estimates and are also helpful in checking preliminary drawings to determine whether or not enough space has been provided in different categories to meet the program needs of the student enrollment for which the facilities are planned.

RECREATION BUILDINGS

Several large universities have constructed, or are considering the construction of, buildings which have a wide variety of physical and social activities of a purely recreational nature. No intercollegiate sports contests are held in the building. The disabled should be considered in the planning.[12]

The stated objectives of campus recreation buildings are: to provide on-campus leisure recreation; to develop social and ethical qualities; to develop physical and mental fitness; and to develop skills and interests for future leisure-time pursuits.

Student fees support the building so that only a few special activities require a charge. Towels, lockers, and equipment are free.

THE COLLEGE UNION[13]

A college or university union is a complex service center for members of the college community. A center of college life, this organization provides through its staff a program of cultural, social, and recreational activities as a part of the total educational program of the college. The union is considered a recreational building on campus, but may provide services and facilities beyond those of a recreational nature.

The Association of College Unions International has classified unions by total enrollment of the college and by the type of institution (medical, technical, community, church, etc.). The nature of the building varies with each college, and reflects the philosophy and traditions of the institution. Typical recreational facilities include bowling lanes, billiards rooms, game rooms, craft shops, and quiet areas.

For a complete treatise on functional planning for the construction or expansion of a college union, the reader is referred to the publications of the Association of College Unions Inter-

national, which are available from Willard Straight Hall, Cornell University, Ithaca, N.Y.

AIR STRUCTURES FOR SCHOOL SPORTS

HISTORY

Air structures—buildings blown up by air pressure—were introduced as school facilities about 1961. The military used them before this date as supply depots and hangars. Industry has acquired them for warehouses. Resort hotels and private athletic clubs use them as cold-weather covers for outdoor swimming pools and tennis courts. Participants in the New York World's Fair utilized them to house exhibits. A giant "bubble" outside Chicago is used as a stadium for sports ranging from ice hockey to wrestling.

The Educational Facilities Laboratories[14] has encouraged schools seeking additional and more economical facilities to experiment with this novel-type structure. The bubble is a possibility for much cheaper and quicker construction to provide additional physical-activity space. The basic structural envelope —a skin that serves as both walls and roof—plus attachment hardware to hold the structure down, and inflation equipment to hold it up, costs under two dollars a square foot. It can be anchored in place, blown up, and readied for use in one day. In even less time, it can be deflated, freed from its moorings, folded like a tent, and stored or moved to another site. Safe and easy to care for, it will last at least five years in continuous service— twice that if used only part of each year, or treated to a factory reconditioning.

PRESENT SCHOOL USE

Because of its economy and versatility, the air structure fits neatly into the specifications of many schools for facilities for physical education, athletics, and recreation. In 1961, the Forman School of Litchfield, Conn., experimented with the bubble for an all-weather facility. A traditional gymnasium was not possible because of the cost. A tennis court was covered and the bubble proved most satisfactory. Forman has since incorporated other air structures for a swimming pool and other play areas.

In 1965, the Homewood-Flossmoor High School of Homewood, Illinois, completed a physical education bubble station. It is 34' high with a ground area of 115' x 110'. Two electric blowers move 6,120 cubic feet of air per minute for the purpose of keeping the structure erect. Cables, which anchor the structure, are imbedded in a concrete base. The plastic material is 70 percent iridescent and artificial lighting will not be used. Heaters are provided to afford comfortable temperature. Two revolving doors control air pressure inside to maintain the structure. This area will provide two basketball courts of 80' x 45', or six volleyball courts of 30' x 45'. The floor will be pulverized red brick mixed with 2" of existing soil. The total cost of $25,000 averages two dollars per square foot.

This kind of construction could be a tremendous asset to schools which need facilities quickly and cannot afford the traditional type of building. Some of the uses of such a structure could include:

• For elementary-school gymnasiums—to be erected over existing land-surface areas
• For low-cost instructional swimming pools
• For auxiliary facilities in school and college—wrestling rooms, dance rooms, etc.
• For an extended area for the intramural program

12 See Appendixes G and H.
13 The disabled and the aging should be considered in the planning of the Union. See Chapter 11 and Appendixes G and H.
14 Educational Facilities Laboratories, Inc., 477 Madison Ave., New York, N.Y.

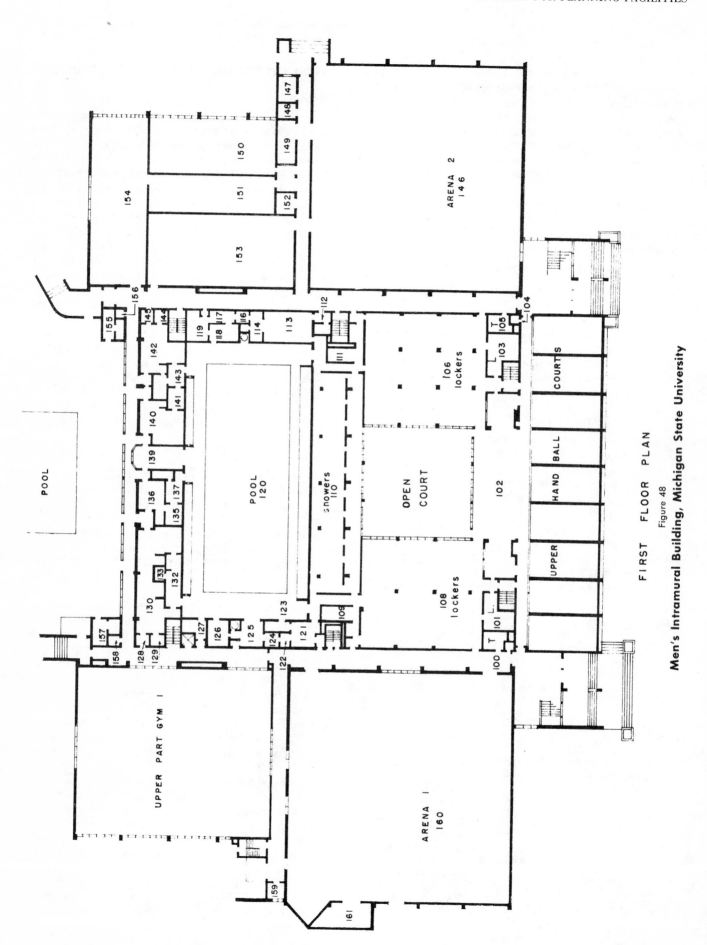

FIRST FLOOR PLAN

Figure 48

Men's Intramural Building, Michigan State University

SELECTED REFERENCES

Berry, Chester A., **Planning a College Union Building.** New York: Bureau of Publications, Teachers College, Columbia University.

College Physical Education Association, **College Facilities for Physical Education, Health Education, and Recreation.** Flushing, N.Y.: The Association, 1948.

Crawford, Wayne H., **A Guide for Planning Indoor Facilities for College Physical Education.** New York: Bureau of Publications, Teachers College, Columbia University, 1963.

Engelhardt, N. L.; Engelhardt, N. L., Jr.; and Leggett, Stanton; **School Planning and Building Handbook.** New York: F. W. Dodge Corp., 1956.

Focus on Facilities: Planning Space for Physical Acitivity, **Journal of Health, Physical Education, and Recreation.** April, 1962, Vol. 33, No. 4, April, 1962.

Kenney, H. E., Facilities Standards for Physical Education in Colleges and Universities, **The Physical Educator.** Vol. 21, No. 4, December, 1964.

Sapora, Allen V., and Kenny, H. E., **A Study of the Present Status, Future Needs and Recommended Standards Regarding Space Used for Health, Physical Education, Physical Recreation and Athletics at the University of Illinois.** Champaign: Stipes Publishing Co., 1960.

Scott, Harry A., and Westkaemper, R. B., **From Program to Facilities in Physical Education.** New York: Harper and Brothers, 1958.

Chapter 10

RECREATION BUILDINGS

RECREATION BUILDINGS should be functionally designed to make possible a varied program of activities for all ages and both sexes. These buildings should be designed and dedicated to meet the needs of all people in their respective neighborhoods and communities.

Recreation buildings should provide a safe, healthful, and attractive atmosphere in which every person in the community or neighborhood has the opportunity to enjoy his leisure by participation in activities of a social, creative, cultural, or physical nature.

Due to advances in medical science, people live longer. Thus, the percentage of the aging in our population is increasing. In addition, it is approximated that one out of seven people in our

nation has a permanent disability. Therefore, there is a greater challenge than ever before to prevent the construction of architectural barriers which make it difficult for the aging and the disabled to participate in the recreation program.

Almost without exception, recreation areas require some type of structure which will fulfill program needs and, yet, blend aesthetically into its surroundings. In terms of function, building types may range from the simple picnic shelter to the complex community recreation building with its variety of special service facilities. Such buildings may vary in design from the rustic, depicting the style of early colonial days, to the contemporary, representing the most modern architectural concepts.

Figure 49
Westport-Roanoke Community Center, Kansas City, Mo.

In many neighborhoods and communities, school facilities are adequately equipped to provide recreation programs for youth, but other existing age groups are not always served. In such instances, the community must depend upon public recreation facilities which are planned and operated independently to accommodate a recreation program for the total community. Since the school is an integral part of the community, it should have a part in the planning of public recreation facilities. Conversely, when school buildings are being designed, cooperative planning with community recreation authorities is essential in order to assure that the new structures will include facilities needed for joint school and community use.

PLANNING OBJECTIVES

The planning and designing of a recreation building demands a precise and logical approach. Since a recreation building reflects the unique needs of a neighborhood or community, the specific plans and design will vary, but the preliminary considerations and planning objectives will be the same.

The successful incorporation of accepted planning objectives will insure maximum utilization of the building. The preliminary plans and the continuous reevaluation of the functional design of the building prior to its construction should be considered in terms of the following questions:

- Has the most effective use of the entire area been determined, and does it utilize all of the natural resources?
- Does the preliminary plan include all of the essential areas and facilities necessary to fulfill the program objectives?
- Does the design provide for flexibility in use and for future expansion?
- Does the floor plan permit convenient access to, and facilitate circulation within, the building?
- Does the floor plan provide for ease in supervision and administration of the building?
- Have individual rooms been located and designed so as to encourage multiple use within safety limits?
- Has the building been designed so as to insure opportunity for its use by all members of the community, including the aging and disabled?

- Does the design encompass accepted aesthetic qualities that relate harmoniously with the surroundings?
- Is the building designed and constructed so as to insure joint use with other public or private agencies?
- Is the building so designed that it will permit economy in construction and maintenance?

CLASSIFICATION OF RECREATION BUILDINGS

Growth in the scope and complexity of the recreation program has created a need for buildings which will provide facilities adapted for a wide variety of recreation activities. Unlike many of the early structures, present-day buildings provide for adaptability and multiple use. This change from the simple to the complex has stimulated the development of a variety of recreation buildings. These are classified by function and then categorized by size.

The standards used for determining the size requirements of recreation buildings are usually based upon a square-footage-to-population ratio. This may be determined by allowing one to two square feet per person to be served. For example, if the building is to serve 8,000 persons, it should be approximately 12,000 square feet in size. This footage ratio may vary where cities build one center to accommodate the entire population.

TYPE I RECREATION BUILDINGS

Figures 50 and 51 illustrate a Type I recreation building. These buildings are usually constructed in larger subdivisions or suburban areas of a metropolis. However, recent trends reveal that many smaller cities (30,000 or less) have constructed such facilities to serve the total community.

This type of building encloses 20,000 square feet or more and usually includes the following facilities:

- Multipurpose room
- Gymnasium
- Shower and locker rooms
- Club rooms
- Arts and crafts room
- Lounge and lobby
- Game room
- Photography room
- Office (administration)
- Office (staff)
- Rest rooms
- Kitchen
- Large storage areas

Figure 50
Collett Street Recreation Center, Morganton, N. C.

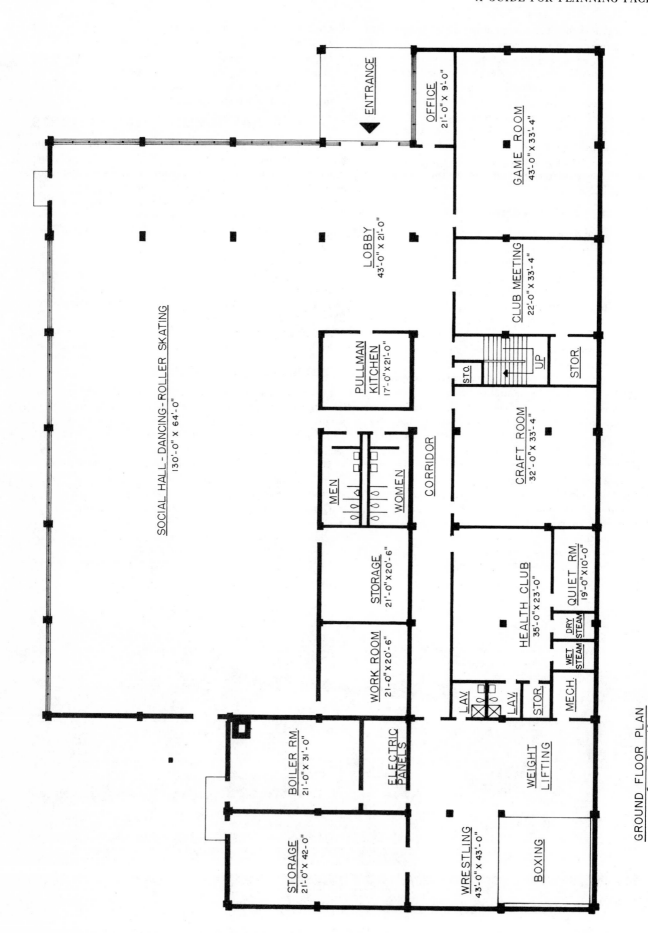

Figure 51

Floor Plan of Collett Street Recreation Center, Morganton, N. C.

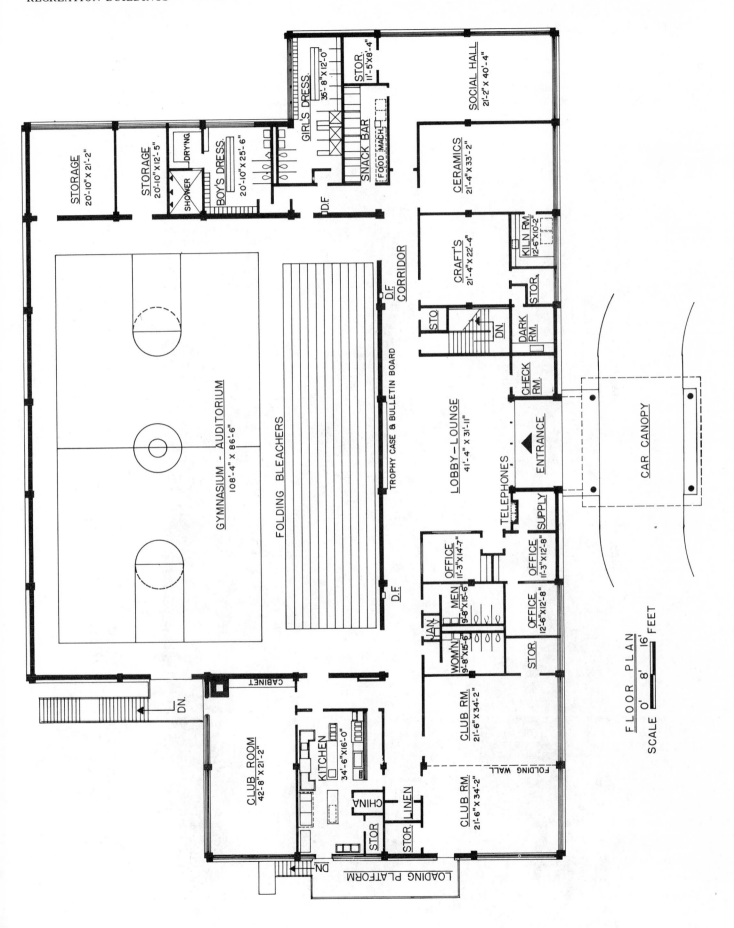

STORAGE
20'-10" X 21'-2"

STORAGE
20'-10"X12'-5"

DRY'NG.

SHOWER

BOY'S DRESS.
20'-10"X 25'-6"

GIRL'S DRESS.
35'-8"X12'-0"

STOR.
11'-5'X8'-4"

SNACK BAR

FOOD MACH.

SOCIAL HALL
21'-2' X 40'-4"

CERAMICS
21'-4"X33'-2"

CRAFTS
21'-4"X 22'-4"

KILN RM.
12'-6'X10'-2"

STOR.

D.F

CORRIDOR

D.F

STO.

DN.

DARK RM.

GYMNASIUM - AUDITORIUM
108'-4" X 86'-6"

FOLDING BLEACHERS

TROPHY CASE & BULLETIN BOARD

LOBBY—LOUNGE
41'-4" X 31'-11"

CHECK RM.

TELEPHONES

ENTRANCE

SUPPLY

CAR CANOPY

D.F

OFFICE
11'-3"X14'-7"

MEN
9'-8"X15'-6"

OFFICE
11'-3"X12'-8"

JAN.

WOMN
9'-8"X15'-6"

OFFICE
12'-6"X12'-8"

STOR.

CLUB RM.
21'-6" X 34'-2"

FOLDING WALL

CABINET

DN.

CLUB ROOM
42'-8" X 21'-2"

KITCHEN
34'-6"X16'-0"

CHINA

STOR

STOR.

LINEN

CLUB RM.
21'-6" X 34'-2"

DN.

LOADING PLATFORM

FLOOR PLAN
SCALE   0'   8'   16'   FEET

TYPE II RECREATION BUILDINGS

The Type II recreation building is illustrated in Figures 52, 53, 54, and 55. This is the most common type and can be used in any city or community. It is believed by many recreation experts that the most efficiently operated building is the one designed to accommodate a neighborhood or area of approximately 8,000 persons.

This building encloses 10,000 to 20,000 square feet and includes basically the same facilities as the Type I structure. Room sizes may vary and emphasis may be placed on those facilities that will best serve the program objectives.

THOMASTON - UPSON COUNTY RECREATION CENTER
THOMASTON, GEORGIA

Figure 52

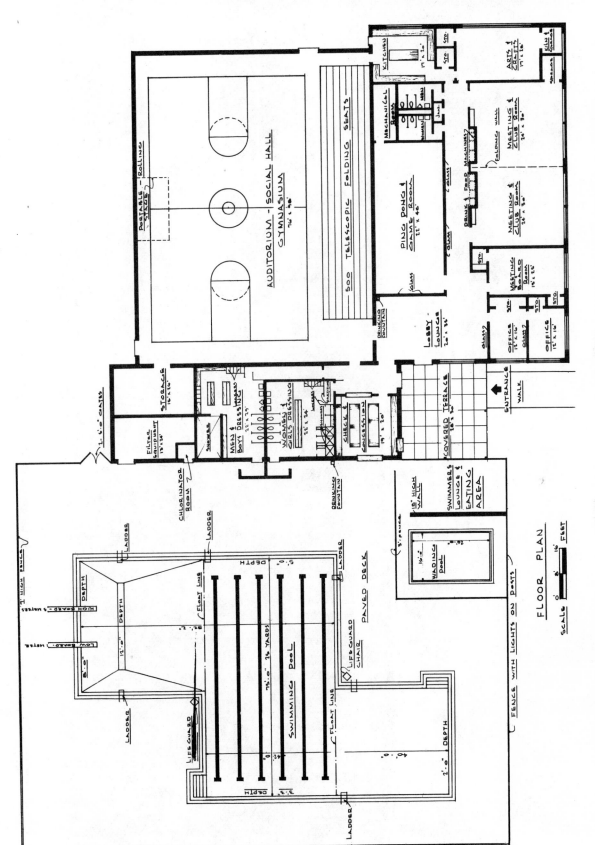

FLOOR PLAN

Scale 0 8 16 FEET

THOMASTON - UPSON COUNTY RECREATION CENTER
THOMASTON, GEORGIA

Figure 53

Figure 54
Glenwood Community Center, Greensboro, N.C.

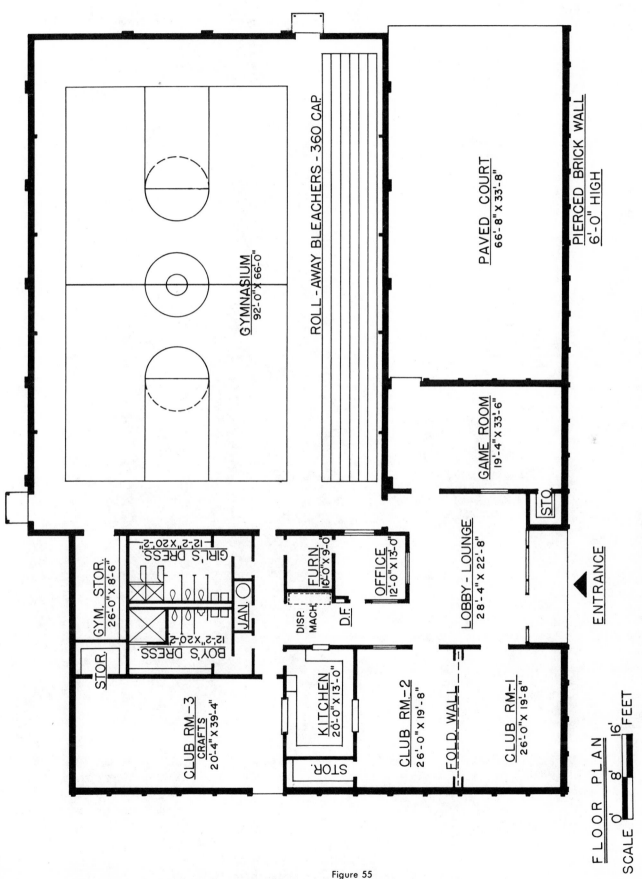

FLOOR PLAN OF GLENWOOD COMMUNITY CENTER, GREENSBORO, NORTH CAROLINA

Figure 55

TYPE III RECREATION BUILDINGS

Figures 56 and 57 illustrate a Type III recreation building. These buildings are used in many communities to satisfy the needs of less-populated areas, and usually include most of the following facilities:

- Social hall or gymnasium
- Shower-dressing room
- Club room
- Lobby-lounge

- Office
- Rest rooms
- Kitchenette
- Adequate storage areas

Figure 56
Warnersville Community Center, Greensboro, N. C.

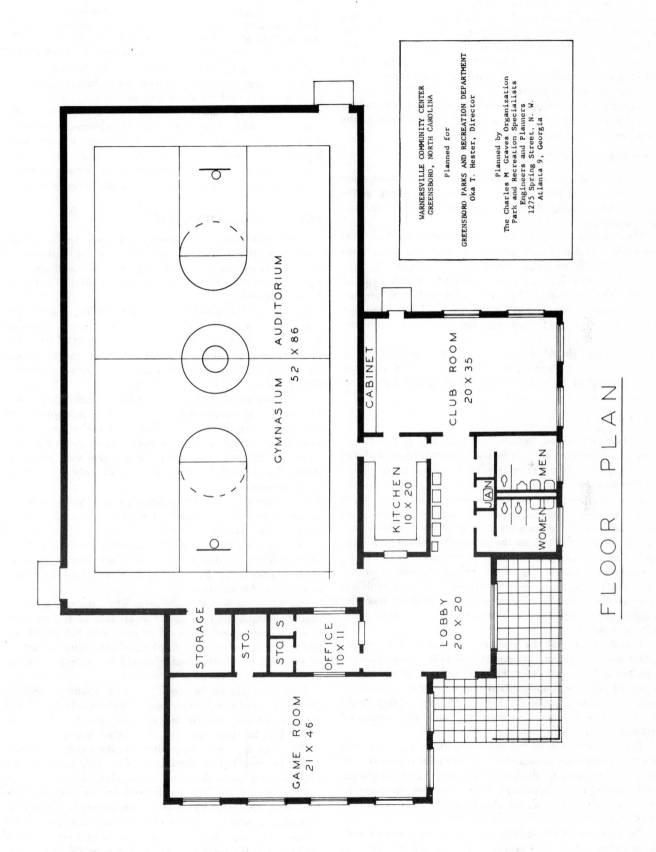

GYMNASIUM AUDITORIUM
52 X 86

CABINET

CLUB ROOM
20 X 35

KITCHEN
10 X 20

JAN.

MEN

WOMEN

STORAGE

STO.

STO S

OFFICE
10 X 11

LOBBY
20 X 20

GAME ROOM
21 X 46

WARNERSVILLE COMMUNITY CENTER
GREENSBORO, NORTH CAROLINA

Planned for

GREENSBORO PARKS AND RECREATION DEPARTMENT
Oka T. Hester, Director

Planned by
The Charles M Graves Organization
Park and Recreation Specialists
Engineers and Planners
1275 Spring Street, N. W.
Atlanta 9, Georgia

FLOOR PLAN

Figure 57
Floor Plan of Warnersville Community Center, Greensboro, N. C.

THE COMMUNITY RECREATION BUILDING

The community recreation building functions beyond the primary purpose of serving a single neighborhood. It is designed to offer a more diversified program in order to meet the complete recreational needs of all people in the community. The community building is normally larger than a neighborhood building and is usually located in a major recreation area such as a community park or playfield.

As stated previously, community recreation buildings vary in function and design, but, generally, they contain most of the facilities described on the following pages.

MULTIPURPOSE ROOM

The multipurpose room should be designed to accommodate such activities as general meetings, social recreation, active table games, dancing, dramatics, orchestra practice, concerts, and banquets.

The area of this room should be approximately 2,000 to 3,000 square feet. It should be rectangular in shape with a minimum width of 40'. The minimum ceiling height should be 16'.

Vinyl-asbestos flooring is recommended for this type of facility. The floor should have a nonskid surface to prevent many common accidents. The floor should also be level in order to permit multiple use for meetings, dancing, dramatic presentations, etc.

The entrance should contain double doors and should be at the end opposite the stage. Each door should have a minimum clear opening of at least 32".[1] The doors should have a removable mullion.

STAGE

A stage and related facilities are frequently included in a community center. They may be built in conjunction with the multipurpose room or, preferably, as a separate unit.

The stage proper should be about 20' in depth, and the proscenium opening should be at least two-thirds the width of the room. It is desirable that the approach to the stage from the floor of the main room be by inclined ramp with a nonskid surface to facilitate the physically disabled and aging and to accommodate the movement of equipment.[2]

Consideration might be given to the construction of an outdoor stage contiguous to the multipurpose room. Some buildings have been successfully constructed with a revolving stage for outdoor and indoor programs. Portable or recessed stages might also be considered.

It is desirable that the room be equipped with a modern public-address system, permanently installed with matched speakers and with outlets for additional microphones and phonographic equipment. Consideration should be given to a master control from the office of the building. All stage lighting should be modern and should be controlled from a dimmer-control cabinet equipped with a rheostat.

The base and wall of the room should be equipped with electrical outlets to accommodate floor and table lamps, motion-picture equipment, floodlights, vacuum and waxing machines, and other electrical apparatus. A heavy-voltage line may be necessary. Provisions should also be made for television installation.

The entrance should contain double doors. Stage doors should be of sufficient width and height to facilitate the movement of scenery. It is desirable to have a door at the rear of the stage area to permit the handling of stage properties and scenery. Adequate exit doors should be provided and should be equipped with panic hardware. Door frames and thresholds should be flush. All door openings should be in accordance with the specifications of the American Standards Association.[3]

Space should be provided for the storage of chairs, tables, and portable staging. This space can be under the stage or in an adjacent storage room provided with dollies having swivel ball-bearing fiber or rubber-covered casters.

Acoustics is an important factor in a multipurpose room and this should be kept in mind in the selection of materials for walls and ceilings. Wooden ceilings are not recommended. It is desirable to have rigid acoustical materials for ceilings instead of suspended acoustical tile. Rigid acoustical tile is not only more economical, but will help discourage vandalism.

SOCIAL HALL-GYMNASIUM

In order to obtain maximum benefit from the social hall-gymnasium, this facility is ordinarily used for a variety of social activities, such as folk, square, and social dancing, banquets, and roller skating, in addition to basketball and other forms of athletics.

The size of a community recreation building's social hall-gymnasium should be at least 90' x 100', with a minimum height of 22'. This will permit a basketball court of 50' x 84'. These dimensions will permit seven tiers of telescopic bleachers on one side of the social hall-gymnasium, seating approximately 325 spectators.

Provision should be made for a mechanical ventilating system (forced air). The wainscoting should provide clear, unobstructed wall space from the floor to a height of twelve feet. If the room contains windows, they should be placed above the wainscoting on the sides and should be provided with protective guards. There should be no windows at either end of the social hall-gymnasium.

It is preferable to have no windows in a social hall-gymnasium, as they have little functional value. If it is necessary to use windows, they should be placed on the north side, or if used on two sides, then on the north and south, never on the east or west. Where sky domes are installed, they should be waterproof, and the room should be equipped with vent domes and exhaust fans for ventilation.

Maple flooring is commonly used. The cork spring clip or other type expansion joint should be installed on all four sides. If suspended apparatus is used in the social hall-gymnasium and wall attachments for control ropes and chains are affixed to the wall, these attachments should be at least 7' above the floor level and should be recessed.

This room should be equipped with stainless steel or aluminum portable and removable handrails attached to all wall surfaces, and also along the face of folding bleachers to provide a hand hold for those participating in roller skating.

Whenever possible, noncontact (nonmarring) furniture should be used. Design characteristics of such furniture also facilitate safer use by the aging and disabled.

In a masonry building, particularly in one with concrete reinforced frame, stainless-steel eyebolts should be installed in each corner and at each column for the hanging of decorations for special parties. These bolts should be located within 12" of the ceiling in the smaller rooms, and at least 15' high in the social hall-gymnasium. The use of eyebolts will eliminate the necessity of driving nails or screws into the walls.

[1] See Appendix H.
[2] Ibid.

[3] Ibid.

Figure 58
Social Hall - Gymnasium, Chicago Park District

Figure 59
Social Hall - Gymnasium, Wildwood, N.J.

Recessed drinking fountains and cuspidors should be provided and should be located in areas where they will cause a minimum amount of interference. Water fountains should be hand or hand-and-foot operated, with up-front spouts and controls. Protective floor covering or drainage at the base of the fountain should be considered to avoid floor damage. For detailed specifications on the installation of drinking fountains, see Chapter 11.

DRESSING-LOCKER ROOM

A room for the purpose of changing clothes is necessary and should be in close proximity to the social hall-gymnasium. There are two accepted plans for checking personal apparel: (1) locker rooms with metal lockers; and (2) dressing rooms with a checkroom for checking clothing in wire baskets or nylon bags.

LOCKER ROOM

If the lockers are to be used in connection with outdoor sports, they should be located so the players will have access to them without going through the entire building. The suggested minimum requirements for the locker room in a community recreation building are: for men and boys, 200 lockers; for women and girls, 150 lockers. The placement of lockers should take into account the space requirements of the disabled. [4]

The floor of the locker room should pitch to a central drain, or drains, to facilitate cleaning and washing. The junction of the wall and floor should be coved. In the women's locker room, dressing booths should be supplied in the ratio of ten percent of the total number of lockers. Hair driers and nonbreakable liquid-soap dispensers are also recommended (refer to Figure 73).

DRESSING ROOM WITH CHECKROOM

The use of galvanized-wire baskets or nylon or plastic bags is growing in popularity. This system will accommodate the same number of users in about one-fourth of the space required for metal lockers. However, there is no saving of space required for dressing.

If there is a possibility of a swimming pool being constructed on this site at some future time, dressing rooms should be located and arranged so as to serve both the gymnasium and the pool.

SHOWER ROOMS

The size of shower rooms is dependent upon the extent of the facilities and the number of persons to be served at one time. Adequate ventilation should be a primary consideration.

For men and boys, it is suggested that approximately 12 shower heads be provided, spaced a minimum of 4' apart and 6' above the floor level. For women and girls, it is recommended that a minimum of 6 group shower heads and 3 individual shower-and-dressing booths be provided. Shower heads should be 4-1/2' above the floor level. Nonbreakable liquid-soap dispensers are recommended, and hair driers are suggested for the ladies' locker room.

To accommodate the disabled, two folding "L" seats should be placed in opposite corners of each group shower to facilitate both right-hand and left-hand approaches (refer to Appendix I).

In the construction of the shower-room floor, drainage gutters 4" deep and 8" to 10" wide placed around the perimeter of the shower room will provide a sanitary means of drainage. The central portion of the shower floor, raised above the depressed area, should drain toward the shower drains. A carborundum-impregnated ceramic tile, or its equal, will provide a nonslip surface.

The temperature of water feeding into the shower heads should be 120° F, controlled by means of a mixing chamber rather than by individual control. Vandal-proof shower heads should be used.

CLUB ROOMS

Experience indicates the desirability of providing a minimum of 500 square feet of floor space per club room. For community recreation buildings, at least 3 to 5 club rooms should be provided for multiple use. At least one large club room should be located adjoining the kitchen.

When windows in club rooms and lounges are placed high in a wall, they are not broken as often as low windows and they also provide more space for furniture, bulletin boards, peg boards, chalkboards, and exhibits. Since broken window glass is a major problem, a nonbreakable type of windowpane is preferable. Windows may be omitted and sky domes and vent domes used. By omitting windows, the need for drapes, Venetian blinds, and curtains—all items subject to vandalism—is also eliminated.

A chair rail or wainscoting to prevent the marring of walls should be installed to a height of 3' above the floor. Whenever possible, noncontact (nonmarring) furniture should be used.

ARTS-AND-CRAFTS ROOM

A separate arts-and-crafts room is desirable. However, if this is not possible, then at least one club room should be equipped for crafts, with provision for gas, compressed air, and a modern sink with hot and cold water. The sink should have a clay trap.

Ample storage cabinets, closets, or lockers should be included for the safe storage of craft materials, unfinished projects, and exhibit materials. Base and wall plugs should be provided in all club rooms for the operation of electric irons, sewing machines, power tools, movie projectors, etc. If a kiln is used, it should be placed in an adjoining room for reasons of safety, and should be equipped with a heavy-duty 220-volt electrical outlet. Bulletin boards and exhibit cases may be used to display completed projects.

LOUNGE AND LOBBY

The lobby of the community recreation building is the space just inside the entrance. The lounge should open off the lobby, and, if possible, should be close to the central office and to the multipurpose room and/or social hall-gymnasium. The lounge and lobby are often combined into one single room. When the rooms are combined, it is suggested that the size of the lobby-lounge be approximately 600 to 800 square feet.

This facility should be attractively lighted and should contain a wall-mounted, recessed drinking fountain and a built-in electrically-lighted trophy case and bulletin board. Appropriate space should be allowed for public telephones, and at least one telephone should be installed so as to accommodate a person in a wheelchair. [5] Provision should also be made for aquariums and for growing plants and flowers. Adequate space, preferably recessed, and electrical and water connections for automatic vending machines should be included.

The office, club rooms, game room, and rest rooms are usually adjacent to the lobby-lounge.

4 Ibid.

5 Ibid.

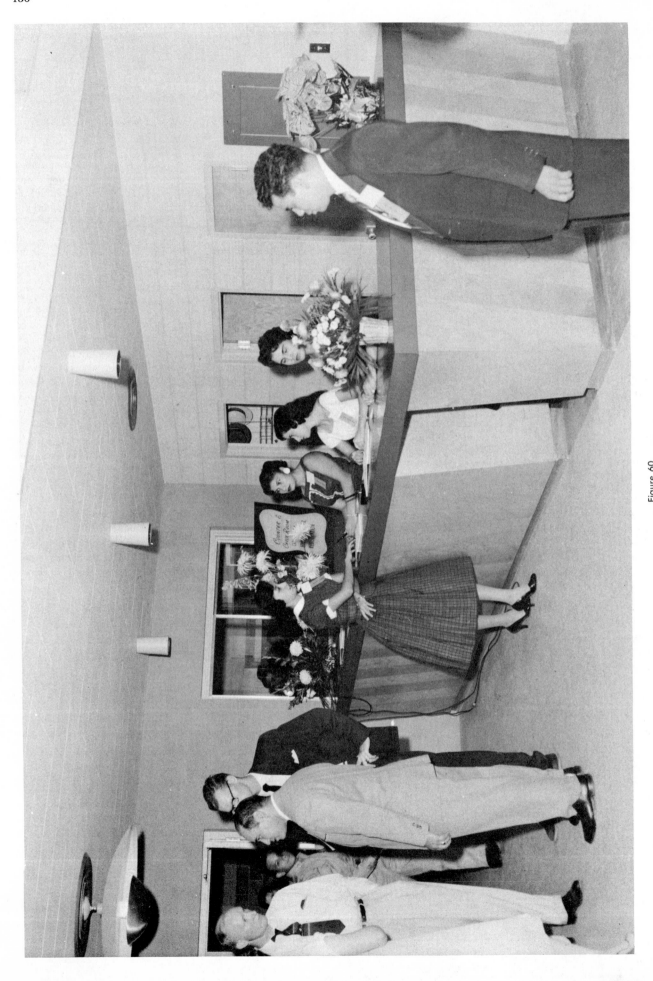

Figure 60
Lounge and Lobby in Recreation Building, Austin, Texas

Figure 61
Recreation-Center Lounge, Greensboro, N.C.

The entrance doors of the lobby present a problem from the standpoints of aesthetics, safety, security, and vandalism. Solid-glass panels—from ceiling to floor—and solid-glass doors are quite popular and attractive, but their use must be carefully studied. Since glass doors and panels can be easily broken, good aluminum doors with a minimum of glass are preferable.[6]

One of the main causes of damage to floors is the habit of many individuals of dropping a cigarette on the floor and stepping on it. This habit causes definite damage to asphalt or vinyl-asbestos tile, disfiguring and discoloring light colors, and, to some extent, marring even darker colors. Therefore, terrazzo, quarry tile, and patio tile are preferable.

GAME ROOMS

The game room, approximately 30' x 64' in size, is designed for a variety of games, including billiards and table tennis (see figure 62). In planning this room, sufficient storage space should be provided for various items of game equipment and supplies to be used.

 Ibid.

This room should be in close proximity to office supervision. It should also be acoustically treated, due to the noise factor.

The choice of floor material should be carefully considered because of the heavy traffic usually prevalent in this room. Windows should be placed high in the walls to reduce glass breakage. A chair rail or wainscoting to prevent the marring of walls should be installed to a height of 3' above the floor. Whenever possible, noncontact (nonmarring) furniture should be used.

PHOTOGRAPHY ROOM

A special room can be provided and equipped as a dark room. Ventilation should be provided through the use of light-proof ventilators. Hot and cold running water, special light plugs—both wall and base—and photographic sinks for developing and washing prints should also be provided.

A mixer is desirable to accurately control the water temperature. A filter should also be provided if the water quality is not good. Doors should be lightproof.

Figure 62
Game Room, Collett Street Recreation Center, Morganton, N.C.

DIRECTOR'S OFFICE

An office of approximately 120 square feet in size is suggested, with sufficient window space to provide maximum supervision of the lobby, lounge, club rooms, and social hall-gymnasium. At least three walls should have windows. If there is a window connected to the social hall-gymnasium, a nonbreakable-type glass is preferable.

It is often recommended that there be an adjoining shower-dressing unit with a floor-surface area of not less than 100 square feet. This unit should contain a shower, toilet and lavatory, clothes closet, and first-aid supply cabinet.

Opening off the director's office should be a storage closet with a burglarproof door for storing valuable supplies and equipment, such as the motion-picture projector and public-address system.

REST ROOMS

Rest-room facilities should be designed to serve both indoor and outdoor areas. Provision should be made for direct access from the exterior of the building at a point adjacent to such activity areas.

Rest rooms should include multipurpose units, combining automatic towel and soap dispensers, mirror and shelf, and a combination paper-towel dispenser and waste receptacle. These units should be recessed in the wall.

Mirrors should have metal frames and be recessed into the wall so they cannot be torn off. The preferred soap dispenser is built into the lavatory since this type is less subject to vandalism than the wall-installed type.

Dressing-room benches should be of a permanent type and should be securely anchored to the floor so they cannot be turned over, stacked against the wall, broken, or removed from the building. Toilet fixtures should be hung from the wall for ease in cleaning. In rest rooms where several fixtures are used, one fixture of proper height for young children and the disabled should be included. Lavatories should be of enamel-coated iron or other unbreakable material rather than vitreous china.

A flush-valve water closet with the valve 24 inches above the top of the fixture—or three feet above the floor—is preferred over a tank-type toilet fixture. Automatic valves for water taps in showers and lavatories are recommended to reduce water loss caused by taps being left open. Hose bibbs should be installed in each rest room and/or shower room, at a proper height so buckets can be placed under them.

Toilet facilities should be made accessible to the disabled.[7]

KITCHEN

The Pullman or kitchenette-type kitchen is usually desirable for most community and neighborhood recreation buildings (see Figure 63). If large dinners or banquets are to be served, provision should be made for a full-size modern kitchen that conforms to local health regulations and has a free floor space at least 54″ wide.

The kitchen should be located near the club rooms and the social hall-gymnasium. This will make the kitchen available to small gatherings in the club rooms and to large banquet gatherings in the social hall-gymnasium. The kitchen is often placed between two club rooms and made available to both rooms by the use of aluminum roll-up doors.

Adequate storage space, cabinet space, and electrical outlets for such appliances as the refrigerator, the range, the dishwasher, and can openers should be provided. Exhaust fans should also be installed.

STORAGE AREAS

One of the most common errors found in many recreation buildings is the lack of sufficient storage space for equipment, maintenance, and custodial purposes.

EQUIPMENT STORAGE ROOM

Provision should be made for storing apparatus and equipment. There should be an opening 6′ wide with flush doors with louvers between the social hall-gymnasium and the storage room. This will permit passage of the most bulky equipment. There should be no raised threshold.

The minimum size of the storage room should be approximately 250 square feet. Provision should be made for storage of inflated balls, bats, softballs, and other supplies, either in separate cabinets or a special closet. Appropriate bins, shelves, and racks are suggested. In addition, a recessed alcove for the storage of a piano is desirable.

MAINTENANCE STORAGE ROOM

The maintenance storage room varies in size, depending upon the adjacent outdoor space and the size of the building. The room is ordinarily located on the ground level, adjacent to the outdoor areas. An outside entrance should be provided by means of a burglarproof door sufficiently large to permit the passage of motorized and other maintenance equipment.

This facility is used as a headquarters for all outdoor maintenance. It may have to house rakes, shovels, hose, marking equipment and supplies, hand tools, power tools, and other equipment. A repair shop and its facilities are usually incorporated in this area. The room should have sufficient base and wall outlets to serve both the work-bench and power-equipment needs.

Recessed wall shelving and cabinet storage should be provided for tools, supplies, and equipment. This space should also contain hot and cold water, a slop sink, a lavatory, a water closet, and a clothes closet.

The floor should be concrete and should be pitched to a central drain. The junction of the floor and wall should be coved.

CUSTODIAL STORAGE ROOMS

A supply closet equipped with a slop sink and space for mops, pails, brooms, and cleaning supplies should be centrally located on each floor level.

NEIGHBORHOOD RECREATION BUILDINGS

The neighborhood recreation building will include many of the features of the community recreation building, as previously described. The neighborhood building, however, is usually intended to serve a smaller number of people. The size of the facility will ordinarily fall into the Type III (under 10,000 square feet) or Type II (10,000 to 20,000 square feet) classification. In all cases, the building should be so designed that rooms can be easily added.

[7] Ibid.

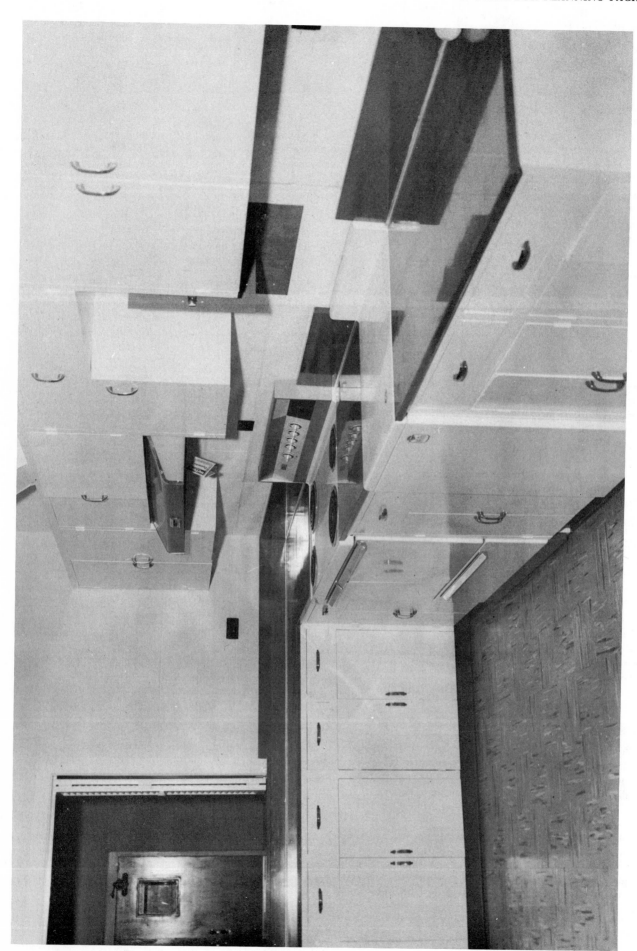

Figure 63

Kitchenette-Type Kitchen in Recreation Center, Greensboro, N.C.

ADDITIONAL FACILITIES FOR COMMUNITY AND NEIGHBORHOOD RECREATION BUILDINGS

The various facilities of the community or neighborhood recreation building function best as a complete unit and should be so planned, but, in some instances, conditions will not permit the erection of the entire building. Construction of the most necessary units should begin as circumstances will allow. Thus, those facilities which meet the most urgent needs can be provided first and additional units gradually added.

Besides the basic facilities usually common to neighborhood and community recreation buildings, there are many additional facilities to be considered. These additions are determined by the needs and interests of the people to be served, as well as the funds available.

SWIMMING POOL (NATATORIUM)

Many neighborhoods and communities have a considerable interest in swimming and demand that a swimming pool be included as part of the recreation building. For maximum year-round use, the indoor-outdoor type pool is recommended. The construction cost of this type pool is greater, but the value of having a year-round activity rather than a seasonal activity is more important to the community or neighborhood (see Chapter 12).

AUXILIARY GYMNASIUM

The auxiliary gymnasium is for such activities as wrestling, weight lifting, tumbling, fencing, and apparatus work. Acoustical treatment for this room is desirable.

The size of the room and height of the ceiling will depend on the various activities for which this facility will be used. The floor should be treated with special material due to the use of heavy weights, etc.

At least one well-ventilated storage room will be needed for equipment and supplies used in the auxiliary gymnasium. If the apparatus is to be cleared from this room, an additional apparatus storage room should be provided.

BOWLING LANES AND ARCHERY AND RIFLE RANGES

Some communities may have a need for such additional facilities as bowling lanes and indoor rifle and archery ranges. Expert technical advice should be secured before such facilities are included in the plan.

HANDBALL COURT

In the designing of a social hall-gymnasium, sufficient wall area for a one-wall handball court should be provided.

MUSIC ROOM

The size of the music room should be determined by the potential number in the choral or instrumental group using this facility at any given time. A guide commonly used is to allow 20 square feet for each participant. Provision should be made for the storage of music, instruments, band uniforms, and supplies. Shelves are commonly used for storage of musical equipment.

INSTRUCTORS' OFFICE

If the program is of considerable size, there should be an office for physical-activity leaders. It should be approximately 120 square feet in size and should be adjacent to the social hall-gymnasium.

A dressing room opening into this office should be provided for the activity leaders. This facility should contain a shower, water closet, lavatory, and clothes closet. Proper ventilation should be provided for all rooms.

CHECKROOM

The size of the checkroom will depend on the magnitude of the program. This room should open into the lobby and should be equipped with a Dutch door, shelves, and portable hanger racks.

PARK AND PLAYGROUND BUILDINGS

PLAYGROUND ACTIVITIES BUILDING

The playground activities building is a facility to provide opportunities for informal participation, group meetings, and such supervised activities as social recreation, dance instruction, table games, handicraft, art, and music. It will serve a small playground and may become the focal point for all recreation activities in the neighborhood. It will also stimulate outdoor activities, or may be used in a larger area where the inadequacy of the existing outdoor facilities makes it necessary to have additional building space separate from the community center or school building. Common practice suggests a minimum of 1,500 square feet of floor space for this facility.

ACTIVITIES ROOM

The activities room should have a minimum area of 1,000 square feet. It is designed to serve as a recreation facility for a variety of informal games, group meetings, and creative activities. An open fireplace is desirable. Wall electrical outlets should also be provided. In some cases, two activities rooms may be needed.

PORCH

The porch area should be free from obstructions and be provided with lighting. The floor surface should be level and smooth to permit the playing of table games and other activities and should be on a common level with the activities room. Access from outside should be by an inclined walk or ramp.[8]

REST ROOMS

The boys' room should contain an open-type water closet, two urinals, and a lavatory equipped with hot and cold running water. A 3/4-inch hose bibb with clear bucket height above the floor should be provided. The girls' room should contain two water closets enclosed by stalls,[9] and a lavatory with hot and cold running water.

The spring-closing type of water faucet has been found very satisfactory for lavatories. Wall containers for the dispensing of paper towels should be installed near the lavatories.[10]

8 *Ibid.*
9 *Ibid.*
10 *Ibid.*

Figure 64

Park Activity Building (Closed-Type), Greensboro, N.C.

DRINKING FOUNTAINS

Drinking fountains should be provided in and outside the building.[11]

OFFICE

An office of approximately 80 square feet in size is recommended. It is important that a sufficient number of electrical outlets be provided to meet anticipated needs.

It is recommended that a special storage room of 4' x 7', with opening off the office, be provided. This room should be equipped with a burglarproof door and with adequate lighting, but should have no windows. It should be used for the storage of valuable equipment, such as motion-picture projectors. Permanent shelving should be installed from a height of 4' up.

Flexibility in design and construction is important, but the size of this storage room should not be smaller than that recommended, and should be larger if possible.

PLAYGROUND ACTIVITIES BUILDING (OPEN)

This building is a small compact unit with an open porch, and is intended to serve primarily as a custodial and comfort-station building. It will include a place for the storage of maintenance and recreation equipment. Various activities may be conducted on the open porch on hot days or during inclement weather.

The building is designed for use on a neighborhood playground. It may also be used as an auxiliary building in larger areas, or in a housing project. It could be used to augment building facilities in those instances where water closets and storage facilities are needed some distance away from the main building.

This building should contain an enclosure of approximately 400 square feet, plus a porch of approximately 600 square feet.

ESSENTIAL FACILITIES

The building should contain two rest rooms, one for boys and the other for girls. Each of these rooms should be approximately 100 square feet in size and the rooms should be separated by the storage space. The boys' room should contain a water closet, a lavatory, and a urinal. The girls' room should contain two water closets in an enclosed stall,[12] and a lavatory. A 3/4-inch hose bibb in each rest room should clear bucket height above the floor.

A master-key switch in the storage room should control all lights. Base and wall outlets should also be provided. Electrical fixtures should be tamperproof insofar as possible.

A drinking fountain should be provided.[13] Floors should be of concrete and should be properly pitched to floor drains. Access from the exterior of the building should be by inclined walk or ramp.[14]

If funds are limited, this building could be constructed without the porch.

PICNIC SHELTER

In large parks providing picnic groves and fireplaces accommodating an appreciable number of people, a large-size open shelter with a fireplace in one end is very desirable to give shelter in case of sudden rainstorms. It has also been found desirable in

some areas to provide electrical service for night-picnic use.

Shelters are built in varying sizes from 20' x 30' to 30' x 50', and should accommodate approximately 60 to 150 persons seated at picnic tables.

OTHER COMMON RECREATION BUILDINGS

CENTRAL CRAFT SHOP

The central craft shop is designed to serve as a citywide center for the teaching of crafts to playground and community-center craft leaders, lay leaders, and individuals participating in a craft program for personal satisfaction. The building should include several rooms, be attractively designed, and be centrally located so as to be easily accessible to the entire community. The suggested size of this facility is 6,000 to 10,000 square feet, depending upon the number of people to be served.

LOBBY

This room should contain approximately 1,200 square feet, with space for circulation, lounge furniture, exhibits, displays, a drinking fountain,[15] and automatic food and beverage dispensing machines.

OFFICE

The office should be approximately 140 square feet in size, with space for office equipment and storage of administrative materials and supplies. This room should be located so that it will be adjacent to the lobby, corridor, and craft area. It is best to have large windows for ease of supervision when the director is in the office.

REST ROOMS

The women's rest room should have two water closets and one lavatory. The men's rest room should have one water closet, one urinal, and one lavatory. Each room should be approximately 90 square feet in size.[16]

MEETING ROOM OR CLUB ROOM

This room should be approximately 30' x 40' in size so as to accommodate at least 100 persons for lectures, illustrated talks, slides and movies, and similar activities.

CRAFT ROOMS

There should be three to six craft rooms, each containing 800 to 1,200 square feet. Each room should be planned and equipped for specific crafts and should have adequate storage space for supplies, equipment, and unfinished craft articles. These rooms can be used for such activities as ceramics, weaving (looms), leather tooling, braiding, knot tying, cord weaving, needlework, art, painting, finger painting, plaster casting, lapidary, metal crafts, and photography.

KITCHEN

A Pullman-type kitchen (kitchenette) should be provided since there will be a demand for food service in connection with craft clubs and other similar groups.

INDOOR ARTIFICIAL-ICE SKATING RINK

Indoor artificial-ice skating rinks are becoming quite popular in many sections of the country, particularly where climatic

11 *Ibid.*
12 *Ibid.*
13 *Ibid.*
14 *Ibid.*

15 *Ibid.*
16 *Ibid.*

Figure 65
Park Activity Building (Open-Type), Chattanooga, Tenn.

conditions are such that outdoor rinks are not feasible. For further information, refer to the detailed recommendations in Chapter 5.

GOLF CLUBHOUSE

Although the golf clubhouse is an indoor recreation facility, specific recommendations for its design and construction are covered in Chapter 5.

TENNIS-CENTER BUILDING

Tennis is a growing and popular sport in most communities. Often a large tennis center with a clubhouse is recommended. The size of the building will depend upon the potential maximum use by participants and spectators.

RECOMMENDED FACILITIES

Recommended facilities include a pro shop with lounge, rest rooms and dressing rooms, and storage room.

Pro Shop with Lounge

Provision should be made in the pro shop for drinking fountains[17] and automatic dispensing machines. This shop should be centrally located to facilitate supervision of the area. An office should also be a part of the pro shop. Adequate space should be allowed for the display of equipment.

Rest Rooms and Dressing Rooms

Provision should be made for men's and women's rest rooms and dressing rooms. These rooms should include lockers, benches, and shower facilities. Drinking fountains should be provided in both dressing rooms as well as on the outside.

Storage Room

Adequate storage space for materials, supplies, and maintenance equipment should be provided.

BATHHOUSE FOR LAKES AND BEACHES

In the bathhouse for lakes and beaches, the dressing and shower rooms, clothing checkrooms, and rest rooms should be arranged functionally in the same manner as those found in a bathhouse for an outdoor pool, except that they should be larger in order to accommodate more persons and should be constructed of inexpensive materials. The clothing checkroom, office, first-aid room, and lobby should be under cover, while dressing and shower rooms, although enclosed by walls, need not necessarily have a roof. This type of construction is less costly and allows for maximum sunlight and air. In many cases, grass and planting areas are included within the dressing and shower area. In cases where the building is completely roofed, adequate ventilation should be provided.

The structure should be functionally planned for efficient operation. The bag system or basket system is generally preferable over the use of lockers for clothes storage.

GENERAL CONSIDERATIONS FOR RECREATION BUILDINGS

Some of the features described in the pages which follow may be of value in the construction of neighborhood and community recreation buildings.

17 Ibid.

HEATERS

Heating costs should be carefully studied before the building is designed. Fuel cost is always an important factor. Unit heaters are satisfactory for rooms in which the ceiling is at least 12' high. If less than this height, a different type heating system is recommended.

Where unit heaters are used in club rooms, dressing rooms, the lobby, and other rooms, there should be a distance of at least 9' between the floor and the bottom of the heater. This distance is necessary in order to prevent unauthorized tampering with the heater controls. Thermostat and other electrical and heating controls located on a wall should be approximately 6' above the floor and should have metal shields and locks. Unit heaters can be gas, hot-water, or electric. Local fire codes should be taken into consideration.

AIR CONDITIONING

All recreation buildings should be designed with the idea that they will be air-conditioned. Forced-air heating systems can be designed so that the air ducts can also be used for air conditioning. If it is impossible to purchase air-conditioning equipment at the time of construction, provision should be made for its installation at a later date.

ZONE HEATING AND AIR CONDITIONING

All major areas and offices should be thermostatically controlled.

ELECTRICAL CONNECTIONS

Electrical wall outlets should be provided on all four walls of each room for lamps, vacuuming and waxing machines, craft machines, slide and movie projectors, and similar equipment. Outlets should be on separate circuits from the lighting. Outlets should be 30" to 36" above the floor and sized according to potential use. Be sure that electrical outlets for scoreboards in the social hall-gymnasium are installed in proper location for the scoreboard and that controls are near the location of the official scorer's table.

Check the location and type of installation of all conduits. If at all possible, place them in walls, floors, and ceilings. TV antennas and outlets should be installed when the building is constructed.

Conduits for phone outlets, including pay telephones, should be installed when the building is constructed. The wall stand-up-type pay phone is recommended rather than the sit-down booth type.

All conduits for sound distribution and the public-address system should be installed at the time the building is constructed. This system should be designed for proper distribution and coverage, with control panels in the central office. Jacks for microphones should be installed in the social hall-gymnasium near the scorer's table, at points where a stage might be located, and in other rooms where such equipment might be used. Speakers should be a minimum of 9' above the floor so as to prevent their being molested or torn from the wall.

In some buildings, a two-way room-controlled microphone and speakers, or remote TV, can be used for supervising or observing areas where personal supervision is not available.

Electrical outlets on the building exterior should be weatherproof. Local electrical codes should be met in all electrical construction.

EXTERIOR, INTERIOR, AND STORAGE DOORS

All exterior doors should preferably be hollow steel, except at entrances where aesthetics are important. In this case, aluminum frame doors with a minimum of glass can be used. All doors should have a clear opening of no less than 32″ and should be easily operated.[18]

For the interior, steel door frames should be used, with flush-panel solid-core (rather than hollow-core) wood doors equipped with kick plates extending from the bottom of the door to at least 16″ above the floor.[19] Where excessive moisture is present, wooden doors are not desirable.

Storage rooms should have double doors where possible and should have adequate louvers for ventilation. Doors of storage rooms, as well as those opening into the social hall-gymnasium, should be flush. In addition, the frame should be flush with the walls so as to avoid the possibility of sharp corners.

EXHAUST FANS

Exhaust fans, when used in the kitchen, social hall-gymnasium, or other rooms, should be belt-driven rather than direct-drive so as to ensure quiet operation.

CORNERS

Where masonry of any type is used in the interior walls, corners should be rounded or protected to minimize accidents and avoid chipping. The same applies to concrete columns.

ZONING

Buildings should be so designed that sections can be closed off when not in use. This will contribute to ease of maintenance, economy in operation, and protection of areas that need close supervision.

EXTERIOR WALLS

For economy purposes as well as better supervision, exterior walls should be as simple as possible, with no bays, wells, or projections.

FLOOR SAFE

A small floor safe for keeping small amounts of cash is desirable and should be located in the central office.

SAFETY TREADS ON STAIRS

Where stairs are used, safety treads on steps are desirable. Steps should not have abrupt (square) nosings. For construction details and drawings, refer to Appendix H.

CORRIDORS

Corridor alcoves, cubbyholes, or nooks which provide hiding places and maintenance problems should be avoided. Where corridors are used, they should be at least 60″ in width.[20]

TICKET BOOTH

Where appropriate, provision should be made for ticket sales. If adequate space for a booth cannot be incorporated in the building design, one of the office counters can serve this purpose. A Dutch door with a shelf should be provided if a ticket window cannot be installed.

HOSE BIBBS

Frostproof hose bibbs, for use in washing down walks and watering shrubbery, should be installed on the exterior of the building.

THERMOSTATS

Thermostats with guards should be located at least 6′ off the floor. These should be locked and securely fastened so they will not be controlled by unauthorized persons.

SIGNS

For permanency, interior door signs should be of cast-bronze, aluminum, or plastic type, with raised letters. The background surface should be of a fine-pebble-type texture. Signs should be installed with wood screws, toggle bolts, or matching screws, depending on the surface to which they are to be attached, and with decorative cover rosettes for each screw. Such identification should be placed on the wall to the right or left of the door at a height of approximately 5′ from the floor. Exit signs should be protected with wire guards.

FLOOR BASES

The base around all floors should be coved and should, preferably, be glazed ceramic tile or quarry tile. Rubber might be considered as a third choice.

LOCKS

All locks and cylinders should be keyed to a master key for each major building.

TRANSFORMER ROOM

The transformer room should house the transformer, main switches, and other electrical equipment. One of the doors of this room should be open to the outside. Consideration should be given to the possibility of underground utility service to the building.

LANDSCAPING

The need for, and importance of, landscaping around recreation buildings should not be overlooked. The environment of the facility is not encompassed by the walls of the building; it is the totality created, in part, by the building and its location on the site, but it is influenced in no small measure by patios, lawns, courtyards, flower gardens, driveways, planter boxes, and well-planted trees and shrubs.

Landscaping need not be expensive. All too often, striking features of a beautiful site are destroyed in the construction process or, in some instances, deliberately removed or distorted because people fail to appreciate their beauty and their enhancement of the site. Preserving a rocky crag, a cluster of trees, or a running stream may be more important in the long run than moving tons of earth and planting hundreds of dollars worth of cultivated shrubs.

All too frequently, landscaping is not considered an important item in the capital-outlay budget. A site is acquired that has outstanding potential, but for lack of funds it is left undeveloped, untended, and unused year after year. This is neither effective planning nor good economy. The expenditure for landscaping that adds elements of beauty, warmth, and friendliness is little enough compared to the cost of vandalism inspired by unattractive, uninviting facilities.

[18] Ibid.
[19] Ibid.
[20] Ibid.

SELECTED REFERENCES

American Standards Association, **American Standard Specifications for Making Buildings and Facilities Accessible to, and Usable by, the Physically Handicapped.** New York: The Association, 10 East 40th St., 1961.

Anderson, Jackson M., **Industrial Recreation—A Guide to Its Organization and Administration.** New York: McGraw-Hill Book Company, Inc., 1955.

Butler, George D., **Recreation Areas and Facilities.** New York: A. S. Barnes and Company, Inc., 1960.

Ledermann, Alfred, and Trachsel, Alfred, **Creative Playgrounds and Recreation Centers.** New York: Frederick A. Praeger, Publisher, 1959.

Meyer, Harold D., and Brightbill, Charles K., **Recreation Administration.** Englewood Cliffs, N. J.: Prentice-Hall, Inc., 1960.

National Recreation Association, **The Multiple-Use Recreation Building.** New York: The Association, 8 W. 8th St.

Playground Layout and Equipment. New York: A. S. Barnes and Company, Inc.

Scott, Harry A. and Westkaemper, Richard B., **From Program to Facilities in Physical Education.** New York: Harper and Brothers, 1958.

Williams, Wayne, **Recreation Places.** New York: Reinhold Publisher, 1958.

The Athletic Institute, **The Recreation Program.** Chicago, Ill.: The Institute, 805 Merchandise Mart, 1963.

Chapter 11

GENERAL BUILDING FEATURES

THERE ARE some features which are common to several units of the total plant. These include safety and the physical and psychological comfort of pupils, teachers, and spectators. The health and safety of participants in health, physical education, and recreation activities is a public responsibility of ever increasing significance, and any compromise with best health and safety practices in designing new structures should be firmly resisted.

In the design of the structure, provisions must be made not only for safety, but also for ease of egress and circulation. The features of design having safety significance necessarily include the total plant. These are discussed throughout this Guide in the places where they apply. The whole environment should be efficiently laid out, aesthetically designed, sanitary, and provide for visual, audio, and thermal comfort.

This chapter supplements much that is included elsewhere in this Guide, and consists of a discussion of lighting, heating, ventilation, electrical services, sanitary and service facilities, acoustical treatment, custodial facilities, provisions for traffic circulation, indoor-surfacing materials, and the importance of color and aesthetics. No attempt is made to provide complete technical information on these subjects. It is recommended that the advice of competent engineers and architects be obtained for the planning and construction of major facility projects.

LIGHTING

The quality and control of lighting are more important than the quantity of lighting.

DEFINITION OF TERMS

FOOTCANDLE

The footcandle is a measurement of light intensity at a given point. Light intensity, as measured in footcandles, is one vital factor in eye comfort and efficiency, but intensity must be considered in relation to the balanced brightness of all light sources and reflective surfaces within the visual field.

REFLECTION FACTOR

The reflection factor is the percentage of light falling on a surface which is reflected by that surface. In order to maintain a brightness balance with a quantity and quality of light for good seeing, all surfaces within a room should be relatively light, with a matte rather than glossy finish.

FOOTLAMBERT

The footlambert is the product of the illumination in footcandles and the reflection factor of the surface. For example: 40 footcandles striking a surface with a reflection factor of 50 per cent would produce a brightness of 20 footlamberts. These brightnesses are needed when computing brightness differences in order to achieve a balanced visual field.

BRIGHTNESS BALANCE

The brightness balance is the quality of light achieved by maintaining acceptable ratios of brightness differences within the total visual field. Brightness balance is very important to visual comfort and efficiency. Good lighting involves the proper interrelationships of surface brightnesses and lighting intensities from natural and/or electrical illumination. It is desirable to reduce brightness differences to a reasonable minimum by eliminating the sources of excessively high and low brightness and by increasing the brightness of the dark areas within the total visual environment.

Visual discomfort and poor visual discrimination can result from unbalanced brightness conditions. The National Council on Schoolhouse Construction has adopted the following brightness-difference goals for the total visual environment where critical seeing tasks are being performed:

- The footlambert brightness of any surface viewed from any normal standing or sitting position in the room should not exceed ten times the footlambert brightness of the poorest-lighted task in the room (the 10:1 ratio).

- The footlambert brightness of any surface viewed from any normal standing or sitting position in the room should not be less than one-third the footlambert brightness of the poorest-lighted task in the room (the 1:3 ratio).

- The footlambert brightness of any surface immediately adjacent to the task should not exceed three times the task brightness (3:1 ratio).
- The brightness difference between adjacent surfaces should be reduced to a minimum.

- The brightness goals stated above assume a lighting system that provides from 30 to 70 footcandles on the poorest-lighted task. The extent of the area of the surface producing brightness has a measurable effect upon visual comfort. Small areas of either extremes of brightness are usually less noticeable than are large areas of the same brightness. Figure 66 gives the recommended brightness goals for classrooms.

In the past, it was the practice to prescribe the footcandle level of the illumination desired for various areas in the school, including the typical classroom. Increasing the quantity of light, with little consideration for its quality, often resulted in extremely unfavorable visual conditions. For this reason, the emphasis in discussing school lighting has shifted from quantity to quality. The present discussion reflects this shift.[1] The

[1] IES Lighting Handbook, The Standard Lighting Guide, 3rd ed., Illuminating Engineering Society, New York, 1959, pp. 9-82.

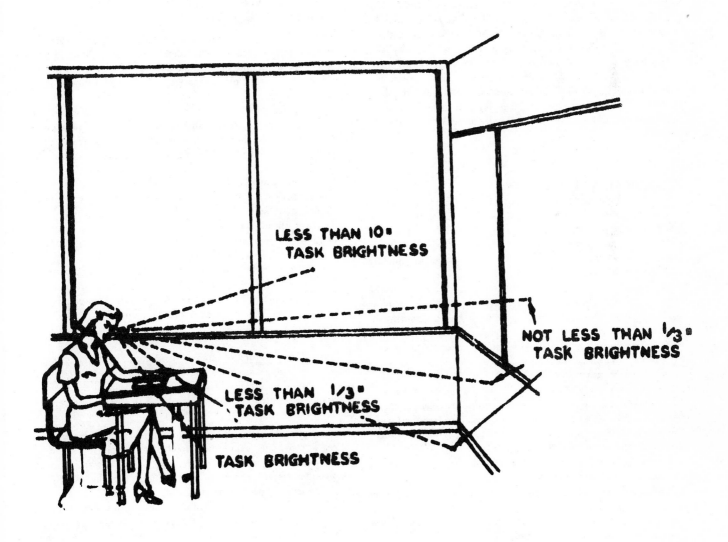

Figure 66
Brightness Goals for Classrooms

illumination levels now recommended by the School Lighting Committee of the Illuminating Engineering Society are found in Table 4.

FENESTRATION

Visual fatigue may result from facing windows while engaged in critical seeing. If natural light is the main source, it is often advisable to provide for daylight from multiple directions. This need not violate principles of brightness balance, provided the openings on all sides, except one direction which occupants do not face, are above the visual field, or if openings are protected by louvers or some other device for reflecting light to the ceiling.

Window sills should not be below the eye level of pupils engaged in critical seeing. If windows are used in dressing-locker suites, the sills should be above the lockers. Window tops should extend to the ceiling in order to provide light as far across the room as possible. Gymnasium windows should be at least 10' above the floor; 14' is often preferable. This provides a flat-wall area for such activities as handball. Regular window walls may be omitted entirely in gymnasiums, and the room lighted by: clerestory windows; north, saw-tooth skylight; or top lighting, if carefully designed and correctly engineered. Frequently, it is best not to use windows in these areas.

It is desirable to have blank building walls next to those portions of nearby playgrounds used for ball games. If this is not feasible, window guards are usually necessary to prevent breakage.

ELECTRICAL ILLUMINATION

The ideal lighting fixture has both a direct and an indirect component, throwing surface light on the ceiling to give it about the same brightness as the lighting unit itself. There is less need, however, to provide high-ceiling areas with direct-indirect fixtures. In recreation areas, the visual task is to see quickly and distinctly in any portion of the room. This requires an even distribution of light throughout the entire room. It may be advisable to provide supplementary lighting on such areas as goal and target areas, or to place dimmers on the lighting in spectator areas. Supplementary light sources should be shielded from the eyes of participants and spectators in order to provide the proper brightness balance.

In recreation areas where balls are used, it is necessary to protect lighting units by guards or transparent, nonbreakable plastic coverings. Vaporproof lighting units are recommended for all damp areas, such as toilets, showers, the dressing-locker suite, and the swimming pool. Locker-room lights should be spaced to light the areas between lockers.

When questions arise regarding the relative merits of incandescent and fluorescent fixtures, lighting authorities should be consulted. The incandescent light is instantaneous, burns without sound, and is not affected by the number of times the light is turned on and off. Incandescent lights and fixtures are considerably cheaper in initial cost, are easier to change, and the lamp, within limits, may be varied in size within a given fixture. Incandescent fixtures, however, have excessively high spot brightness and give off considerable heat, which becomes a problem when high levels of illumination are needed.

Fluorescent lamps have the advantage of longer life and give at least two-and-a-half times the amount of light for the same amount of current consumed. They may sometimes be used in

old buildings to raise the illumination level without installing new wiring.

ELECTRICAL SERVICE

GENERAL CONSIDERATIONS

All electrical wirings and connections should be installed in accordance with requirements of the National Electric Code of the National Board of Fire Underwriters,[2] and of state and local building codes and fire regulations.

The capacity of the wiring system should be determined accurately for reasons of safety and economy. Full consideration should be given to present and future program plans when designing the electrical system. The increasing use of electrically-operated equipment, higher standards of illumination, and special audiovisual equipment should be anticipated.

ELECTRICAL SERVICE ENTRANCE, PANELS, CONDUITS, AND SWITCHES

The service entrance should be installed so as to insure the safety of pupils, school personnel, and the public. Where practicable, it should be located at the side or rear of the building, away from play areas where balls and other moving objects are used.

Main service panels with main service switches, meters, and main light and power panels should be located so as to prevent tampering by unauthorized persons. The main electrical units should be protected against obstruction by storage or accumulation of trash.

Secondary control panels should be placed for the convenient use of persons who open or close the facility during hours of darkness or outside of regular school hours. Electric lighting and power should be fully available to all athletic, physical education, and recreation facilities during hours when the main building may be closed off.

The main distribution panel, all secondary panels, and all circuits should be protected by automatic circuit breakers. A number of spare circuits should be provided in panels for future use. Secondary panels, located in corridors, halls, and similar places, should be of the flush-front type provided with locks.

Wiring for program systems and communications should not be in the regular service conduits. Switches in instructional rooms should be arranged so that lights adjacent to the interior wall may be controlled independently of the lights adjacent to the exterior wall.

Stairway and corridor lighting should be on separate circuits. Three-way switches should be provided at the foot and head of stairs, near each end of corridors, and near doorways of large classrooms, activity rooms, or gymnasiums. Thus lights may be operated from two or more points.

All general lighting in lunchrooms, auditoriums, gymnasiums, multipurpose rooms, and similar facilities should be controlled by a switch located on the open side of entrance doors. Switches should be provided and should be located on the open side of entrances to all spaces in the building. Switches should also be provided in projection booths and on stages, to control some (or all) lights in rooms used for assembly. Remote-control switches should have pilot lights.

[2] *National Electric Code*, National Board of Fire Underwriters, 85 John Street, New York, N.Y.

TABLE 4

LEVELS OF ILLUMINATION CURRENTLY RECOMMENDED FOR SPECIFIC SCHOOL AREAS
(WHERE EXACT AREA WAS NOT LOCATED, VALUE DETERMINED FROM LIST AREA WITH SIMILAR TASK)

Area	Footcandles on Tasks*	Area	Footcandles on Tasks*
Auditoriums (see also Theatres)		College intramural and high school, with spectators	30
Assembly only	15	College intramural and high school, without spectators	20
Exhibitions	30	Volleyball	
Social activities	5	Tournament	20
Cafeterias		Recreational	10
Dining area+	30	Library	
Cashier	50	Reading room	
Food displays	70	Study and notes	70
Kitchen		Ordinary reading	30
Inspection, checking, pricing	70	Stacks	30
Other areas	30	Book repair and binding	50
Classrooms		Cataloging	70
Art rooms	70	Card files	70
Drafting rooms	100**	Check-in and check-out desks	70
Home-economics rooms		Lounges	
Sewing	150**	General	10
Cooking	50	Reading books, magazines, newspapers	30
Ironing	50	Offices	
Sink activities	70	Accounting, auditing, tabulating, bookkeeping, business-machine operation, and reading poor reproductions	150
Note-taking areas	70		
Laboratories	100		
Lecture rooms		Regular office work, reading good reproductions, reading or transcribing handwriting in hard pencil or on poor paper, active filing, index references, mail sorting	100
Audience area	70		
Demonstration area	150**		
Music rooms			
Simple scores	30	Reading or transcribing handwriting in ink or medium pencil on good quality paper, intermittent filing	70
Advanced scores	70@		
Shops	100**		
Sight-saving rooms	150**	Reading high-contrast or well-printed material, tasks and areas not involving critical or prolonged seeing, such as conferring, interviewing, and inactive filing	30
Study halls	70		
Typing	70		
Corridors and stairways	20		
Dormitories		Parking areas	1
General	10	Storerooms	
Reading books, magazines, newspapers	30	Inactive	5
Study desk	70	Active	
First-aid rooms		Rough bulky	10
General	50	Medium	20
Examining table	100	Fine	50
Gymnasiums		Swimming pools	
Exhibitions, matches	30	General and overhead	10
General exercising and recreation	20	Underwater	#
Dances	5	Theatres	
Lockers and shower rooms	20	During intermission	5
Badminton		During motion picture	0.1
Tournament	30	Toilets and washrooms	30
Club	20		
Recreational	10		
Basketball			
College and professional	50		

*   Minimum on the task at any time.

** In some cases, it is necessary to use local lighting to supplement the general illumination. These cases are generally found where it is economically unfeasible to produce the recommended footcandle levels from a general lighting system. Quite frequently, seeing tasks are on oblique rather than horizontal surfaces. This results in a reduction in illumination and a consequent loss in task brightness. Also, some of the seeing tasks are more difficult because the contrast between the paper and the printing may be very low. In both of the foregoing cases, supplementary illumination is sometimes required or indicated. Care should be used in the choice of supplementary lighting units so they will not direct objectionable glare into the eyes of any worker. The distribution of the light across the working surface should be as uniform as possible.

+ If used also as a study hall, a level of 70 footcandles is recommended.

@ When score is substandard size and notations are printed on the lines, a level of 150 footcandles or more is needed.

100 lamp lumens per square foot of pool surface.

FIRE ALARM

Electric fire-alarm systems should be separate and distinct from all program-signal or other signal systems and should be designed to permit operation from convenient locations in corridors and from areas of unusual fire hazards. All fire-alarm systems should be of the type approved by the Underwriters Laboratories[3] and by state and local fire laws and regulations.

EXIT ILLUMINATION

Electrically-illuminated exit lights, clearly indicating the direction of exit to the exterior, should be provided: over all exit doors from auditoriums, gymnasiums, combined auditorium-gymnasiums, multipurpose rooms, and other rooms which could be used for assembly purposes or by other large groups; over all exit doors from the building; and at the head and foot of exit stairways. All exit-lighting circuits should be installed in metal conduits and should be on a special circuit.

Emergency (white) lighting systems should be provided for exits—including exterior open spaces to which exits lead—in gymnasiums, auditoriums, recreation centers, multipurpose rooms, and other places of assembly or large-group activity. This lighting should be on a special emergency circuit. All controls should be located so as to be under the supervision of authorized persons, and all other aspects of the installation should be of the type approved by the Underwriters Laboratories, the Building Exits Code,[4] and state and local fire laws and regulations.

PROGRAM-SIGNAL SYSTEMS AND CLOCKS

Large school buildings should be wired for a signal system operated by a master clock or by push buttons from the main administrative office. Secondary controls should be placed in the administrative unit of the gymnasium, or other facility, in those situations where time periods are different from those of the regular school program, or where programs such as adult-education classes are held at times when the main administrative unit may be closed. Clocks should be provided in instruction and activity rooms, places of assembly, locker rooms, and offices.

Program signals should be independent of the fire-alarm system and should not be used as a fire-alarm system. Program signals usually include: buzzers or chimes in classrooms; bells in corridors, pool, gymnasium, fields, and dressing-locker suites; and large gongs on the outside of the building. In many instances, signals placed strategically in corridors, rather than in individual classrooms, are adequate. (See Appendix H.)

INTERCOMMUNICATION SYSTEMS

Means of intercommunication should be provided not only between the main administrative office and the health, physical education, recreation, and athletic facilities, but also between units of these facilities. Special consideration should be given to the need to communicate with instructors and leaders who have groups on outside areas. Secondary control panels and microphone-input equipment should be carefully planned so as to permit programs or other communication to originate in such places as music rooms, the auditorium, and the gymnasium.

The central sound system should include provision for radio reception. Special conduits should be provided, appropriately sized to accommodate television installation at a later date.

TELEPHONES

At least one "outside" telephone is needed in each school or recreation center. In larger centers, several extensions may be needed to certain units. For example, each swimming-pool office should have a telephone. When several extensions are to be provided, a central private-branch-exchange system may be used.

Independent telephone service should be provided to the gymnasium, pool, health unit, or other facilities to be used during hours when the school or recreation center switchboard is closed. One or more pay-telephone units should be installed for public and pupil use in convenient areas, such as in the gymnasium foyer or near activity areas serving adult groups. Telephones should be accessible to everyone, young and old, large and small, able and disabled. This can be accomplished easily, with economy in cost and space (see Appendix I).

PUBLIC-ADDRESS SYSTEMS

Built-in public-address systems are considered to be a basic service in indoor or outdoor facilities which accommodate sports events, demonstrations, large social- or square-dance groups, or similar activities. Special thought should be given to outdoor areas where large groups gather for occasions such as play days, demonstrations, outings, and intramural and extramural contests since these areas are often not accommodated by the public-address system which serves the varsity-athletic facility. Sound systems should be carefully designed by experts at the time the engineering and acoustical treatment of the facility is being planned.

Public-address systems should be designed for flexible use. Microphone inputs and secondary control panels should be located according to the variety of anticipated uses. For example, the built-in system for a large gymnasium or recreation center should be able to accommodate such needs as the following: (1) announcements and description of athletic contests and all other events, either from the main floor or press booth; (2) amplification of vocal and instrumental music or directions for group activities; (3) instructions or announcements from the floor in connection with large-group social recreation, demonstrations, contests, or meetings; (4) addresses or panel discussions at meetings; (5) directions for building control; and (6) amplification for an underwater speaker that can be tied in with the pool public-address system for synchronized swimming and other swimming instruction.

SERVICE FOR AUDIOVISUAL EQUIPMENT

Many of the units, especially classrooms, health rooms, auditoriums, gymnasiums, and multipurpose rooms, will require connections for projectors, tape recorders, record players, portable public-address equipment, and radio and television. The specific needs for such facilities should be determined before wiring and conduit layouts are designed. It is advisable to install ample conduits and wall plugs because audiovisual aids are increasingly used. Facility planners and designers should consult program specialists and the professional literature in the fields of health education, physical education, and recreation for current developments and the implications for audiovisual installations.

[3]Underwriters Laboratories, 222 West Adams Street, Chicago, Ill.
[4]*Building Exits Code*, National Fire Protection Association, 60 Battery March Street, Boston, Mass.

TABLE 5
SUGGESTED NEEDS FOR ELECTRIC SERVICE

FACILITY	Audiometer, Vision Testing	Electric Tools	Fans, portable or wall-mounted	Floor-cleaning Machines	Hair Dryers	Electric Shavers	Hot Plates, Urns	Small Appliances	Lamps	Special Lighting	Office Machines	Picture Projectors	Record Players	Tape Recorders	Refrigerators, Water Coolers, Food-Beverage Dispensers	Air Conditioner (220 volts)	Central Radio	Inter-com.	Television (Rec.)	Central Radio (Rec.)	Inter-com. (Rec.)	Radio (Send.)	Television (Send.)	Dental Chair	Display Cases, Bulletin Boards	Exit Lights	Kiln (220 volts)	Motors, heavy duty; Blowers, Exhaust Fans	Public-address System	Score Board	Stove or Grill, Electric (220 volts)	Telephone	Washer, Ironer, Dryer (220 volts)	Dishwasher, Disposall	Rheostat, Dimmers
Adapted Physical Education Room	D		X						X	X					X	X									X										
Administration — Office Suite		X	X					X	X	X	X	X	X	D	X	X	D	X						X								X			
Archery Range — Indoor			X					X		D					X																				
Audio-visual Room		X	X					X			X	X	X	X	X	X	X	X	X					X											
Auditorium		X		X					X		X	X		D	X	X	X	X	X	X	X			X		X	X								
Bathhouse		X	X	X	X			X		X					X									X	E				X	X				X	X
Bowling Alleys		X		X			X		X		X				X	X								X	E				X						
Cafeteria		X	X		X	X	X		X	X	X	X	D	X	X			X						X	E				X	X			X	X	
Classrooms		X	X	X					X	X					X	X																			
Clubrooms		X	X	X	X		X		X	X	X	D	X	X	X									X	E										
Corridors			X							X															E								D			
Craft Rooms		X	X	X					X		X	X		D	X	X	X							X		X									
Custodial Rooms		X	X	X					X						X																		X		
Dressing-Locker Rooms			X	X											X														X						
Equipment Rooms		X	X	X					X						X	X																			
Faculty-Staff Rooms		X	X	X		X	X		X		X	X	D	X	X	X																D			
Fine Arts Room		X	X	X					X		X	X	X	D	X	X	D							X											
First-aid Room		X	X	X	X				X				X	D	X	X																X			
Foyer			X						X						X									X	X								X			
Game Room (Ping-Pong, Billiards)		X	X					X	D	X		D	X	X	X									X	E										
Gymnasium & Fieldhouse		X		X					X	X	X	D	X	X	X	X	X	X	X					X		X	X	X	X						
Handball Courts			X																																
Health-Instruction Laboratory	X	X	X	X				X	X		X	X	X	X	D	X	X	X		X	X			X											
Health-Service Suite	X	X	X	X	X	X	X	X				X	X	X	X	X	D	X		X												X			
Home Economics Room		X	X	X			X	X		X	X	X	X	D	X	X	X	X		X										X	D	X			
Kitchen or Kitchenette		X	X	X	X																								X		X		X		
Laundry		X													X														X				X		
Library		X	X					X	X	X	X	X	X	X	X			X		X	X			X								X			
Little Theatre		X	X	X					X		X	X	D	D	X	X	X	X	X	X	X			X		X	X	X							
Lounge, Social Room, or All-purpose Room		X	X	X			X	X		X	X	X	X	D	X	X	X							X								X			
Multi-purpose Room		X	X	X			X	X		X	X	X	X	D	X	X	X	X	X					X		X	X	X							
Music Room		X	X						X		X	X	D	X	X	X	X	X	X					D											
Outside Areas	X							X			X			X	X	X	X	X	X					X	X										
Photography Room	X	X	X	X	X							D												X											
Rhythm Room			X						X	X	X			X	X	X								D											
Rifle Range — Indoor		X	X	X					X	X	X				X																				
Shops		X	X	X		D	X	X	X	X	D				X	X								X	E	D	X				D				
Skating Rink (Ice or Roller)		X	X	X				X	X	X		X			D		X			D	D			X	X	X	X	X						X	
Snack Bars — Refreshment Stands			X	X		X	X																	D	E		X			X					
Stadium	X								X					X			X	X	X	X	X			X	X				X	X		X			
Staff Office & Service Facilities		X	X	X				X	X		X				D	X	X															X			
Storage Rooms (In-season)		X	X	D																															
Storage Rooms (Out-of-season)			D																																
Swimming Pool		X	X	X					X		X	X			X	X	X	X	X					D	E		X		X	D		X		X	
Toilet and Shower Room			X	X																									X						

Legend:
X—This kind of service or equipment is either necessary or often found in the facility.
D—Desirable or sometimes found in the facility.
E—Exit lights needed if opening to exterior or if spectators or large groups assemble in the facility.

Power for audiovisual aids should be furnished through wall outlets independent of light switches. In fact, electrical codes do not allow outlets and light switches on the same circuit. Light switches should be placed, wherever possible, near the location where audiovisual equipment will be used. In recreation centers, auditoriums, gymnasiums, or other places of assembly having a stage or projection booth, at least some of the house lights should be controlled by switches located on the stage and in the booth.

For the use of individual radio receivers in classrooms, the gymnasium, or other units, it is desirable to provide connections to a cenfral antenna system because steel construction and electrical equipment often impede reception through the radio's built-in antenna. In audiovisual rooms, or any room to be used often for sound-motion pictures, it is desirable to run an appropriately-sized conduit, with polarized outlets on each end, from one end of the room to the other to carry the sound cable.

The desirability of providing a master television antenna from the roof to various points of the installation should be carefully studied. Electrical service for lights and special audiovisual effects should be provided for bulletin boards and display cases in the gymnasium foyer and similar locations.

SERVICE FOR RADIO-TELEVISION

Provision for radio-television reception has been mentioned in the preceding section on audiovisual aids. However, the schools and recreation centers, more and more, will need to provide for the origination of radio and television programs of several types: (1) public-service broadcasts, through commercial or educational radio-TV outlets, of school or community athletic events, demonstrations, study courses, or similar instructional, interpretive, or entertainment features; (2) closed-circuit instructional programs transmitted to other units or sections of the same building or campus; and (3) closed-circuit instructional programs transmitted to other schools or recreation centers through educational radio-TV facilities.

The design of electrical work for such facilities and equipment requires expert consultative assistance. School and recreation officials should give careful and imaginative consideration to the provision of facilities to accommodate radio-TV offerings in their present programs or in those for the near future.

SERVICE FOR OUTDOOR FACILITIES

The master plan should include the lighting of outdoor courts, play areas, fields, and stadiums. Increasing night use of school and community recreation, instructional, and athletic facilities should be anticipated. It is important that the aging and the disabled can get to and from adjacent indoor and outdoor facilities. (See Appendix H.) Particular considerations for outdoor lighting have been mentioned in Chapter 7.

SERVICE FOR APPLIANCES, MOTORS, AND OTHER EQUIPMENT

There are many needs for electrical wiring and connections which require careful program analysis and wise planning. The following are illustrative:
• Basic construction: motors to operate folding partitions; blowers for heaters and ventilating ducts; exhaust fans in gymnasium ceilings or walls.

• Custodial and maintenance services: receptacles for floor-cleaning equipment and power tools.
• Dressing-locker rooms: wiring for hair and hand driers and electric shavers.
• Lounges, kitchenettes, snack bars, and concessions; outlets for refrigerators, water or soft-drink coolers, electric stoves (220 volts), blenders, mixers, coffee urns, and hot plates.
• Office suites: wiring for individual air-conditioners (220 volts), business machines, and floor fans.
• Laundry rooms: wiring for washers, dryers, and ironers (some use 220 volts).
• Pools: provisions for underwater vacuum cleaners, pumps, and special lighting.
• Gymnasium-recreation center or gymnasium-auditorium: receptacles and other provisions for special lighting effects, spots and kliegs, and rheostats or controls to lower the illumination for dances, parties, and other activities.
• Auditoriums or little theatres: special wiring for lighting effects.
• Health suites: receptacles and provisions for audiometers, vision-testing equipment, floor fans, and air-conditioning units (220 volts).
• Craft rooms: provisions for small tools and kiln (220 volts).
Table 5 summarizes some of the needs for outlets and special wiring and connections.

CLIMATE CONTROL

STANDARDS OF DESIGN

The engineering design of heating, air-conditioning, and ventilating systems should be based upon the technical data and procedures as published in the latest edition of the Heating, Ventilating and Air Conditioning Guide.[5] The selection of the type of heating, air-conditioning, and ventilating system should be made with special consideration for economy of operation, flexibility of control, quietness of operation, and capacity to provide desirable thermal conditions. The design and location of all climate-control equipment should make ample provision for possible future additions. All fans used for climate control should be constructed of the physical proportions of commercial fans and should be rated in compliance with the requirements and the standard test code of the National Association of Fan Manufacturers.

The number of occupants in the gymnasium will vary. Special consideration should be given to the provision of variable controls to supply the proper amount of fresh air and total air circulation for minimum and maximum occupancies. The same condition exists in connection with auditoriums, swimming pools, recreation buildings, field houses, and similar facilities. Special design of equipment and controls is necessary in order that the climate control in some major areas may be regulated and operated independently of the rest of the building.

DESIGN FOR HEATING, VENTILATING, AND COOLING

Man is a heat-originating and heat-rejecting mechanism. Of the 500 British thermal units produced in the average healthy body every hour, 400 must be dissipated. Thus the problem is the orderly dissipation of the heat—not too fast and not too

[5]Published by the American Society of Heating and Ventilating Engineers, 51 Madison Avenue, New York, N.Y.

slowly. This requires a well-designed and delicately-balanced heating system in cold climates and air conditioning in warm climates.

Ventilation is necessary to remove odors, reduce humidity, and in some cases, to remove heat.

Since all three systems are interrelated and should be balanced together, it is necessary to secure the services of a competent engineer, not only for design, but also for making inspections during construction and for giving operating instructions.

Some of the problems involved in the installation of heating, ventilating, and cooling systems are as follows:

- Getting the proper and comfortable temperatures for both the spectators and game participants.
- Eliminating the down drafts on the spectators.
- Keeping the noise from the equipment to a minimum.
- Keeping all equipment recessed if below a height of 15', and shielded if below 7'.
- Marking and insulating all steam pipes, hot-water pipes, and cold-water pipes.
- Exhausting dry air through the locker room, and damp air through the shower room, directly outside.
- Getting at least four changes of air per hour without drafts.
- Keeping an air gradient differential of not more than five degrees at a height of 60" above the floor.
- Installing locking-type thermostats in all areas, with guards wherever they may be subject to damage.
- Placing the thermostats for highest efficiency.
- Zoning the areas for night and out-of-school use.

SANITARY FACILITIES

GENERAL

Adequate, well-arranged sanitary facilities are essential for comfort and convenience and for promoting desirable health habits. All plumbing and plumbing materials must meet the requirements of plumbing codes.

Safe water-supply and sewage-disposal systems are essential. Advice should be secured from local sanitarians and engineers to ensure the adequacy of the water supply and the suitability of the soil for sewage disposal for present and possible future needs. This is particularly important in areas where no public water and sewer are available. It is strongly recommended that possible school and recreation sites be thoroughly investigated before they are purchased.

TOILET ROOMS

Appropriately-located toilet rooms should be provided as follows: (1) near points of entrance to gymnasiums, field houses, recreation buildings, and other similar areas; (2) convenient to playgrounds; (3) in each locker-and-dressing room and in bathhouses; and (4) near offices of administrators, faculty members, and all other leaders.

The toilet-room sizes will vary with the conditions, depending upon the scope of the local program, the type of facility, the seating capacity, the general location of the facility within the plant, and whether the facility will be used by both participants and spectators. Private toilets for instructors and recreation leaders generally include a water closet, lavatory, and shower.

Entrances to toilets and other areas within the general dressing rooms should be protected with vision screens. It is not difficult to make toilet rooms equally accessible to, and usable by, the disabled and the aging[6].

MIRRORS

Mirrors should be placed in all toilet areas, preferably on walls next to exits. To avoid crowding around the lavatories, no mirrors should be placed over them.

In girls' locker-dressing rooms, mirrors can be installed on the ends of each battery of lockers, and full-length mirrors can be placed at locker-room exits.

DRINKING FOUNTAINS

Drinking fountains should be provided as follows: (1) at or near the entrance, or entrances, to activity areas; (2) in locker-and-dressing rooms; and (3) at strategic points for playgrounds and playfields, but secured to a building or permanent structure. Fountains should not be placed in foyers or entrance lobbies. If fountains are located in corridors, they should be recessed. Each fountain should be equipped with one sanitary-type bubbler head. The orifice should be above the rim of the bowl and should be of a type to prevent the mouth from coming in contact with the nozzle and to prevent water from falling back on the nozzle.

Indoor fountains should be installed not to exceed the following heights:
- Elementary age—28" to top of nozzle
- Junior-high age—32" to top of nozzle
- Senior-high age—36" to top of nozzle
- Adult use only—36" to 42" to top of nozzle.

Outdoor fountains should be of frostproof type, with the same sanitary and safety features, and heights as indicated above for indoor fountains. Drinking fountains should not be located in toilet rooms.

Fountains should be recessed to full depth where construction permits. Face-mounted or projecting fountains should not be installed in activity areas such as gymnasiums. With minimal planning, drinking fountains, which are critical to many aging and disabled persons, can be made equally accessible to all.[7]

Supply lines to drinking fountains should not run close to hot pipes or heated spaces. Each fixture should be equipped with an automatic pressure-control device.

LAVATORIES

Lavatories should be provided in each toilet room and each locker-and-dressing room. The type selected should be of vitreous china with backs and aprons. Floor-supported types are not desirable. Recent developments and experiences indicate that wall-mounted (or supported) lavatories are preferred because of ease of care and maintenance and diversity of use. Sinks with shallow aprons and with the deep part of the basin to the rear (also the drain) are most desirable, particularly in facilitating the aging and disabled.[8] Hot water is a necessity.

6 See Appendixes H and I.
7 Ibid.
8 See Appendix H.

A mechanical stopper is recommended for use in school and public lavatories. Liquid soap should be provided.

The mounting heights of lavatories should be as follows:

- Elementary age—25″ to top of basin
- Junior- and senior-high age—30″ to top of basin
- Adult use only—30″ to 36″ to top of basin

WATER CLOSETS

Water closets should be of the extended-lip or elongated-bowl type vitreous china, equipped with impervious open-front seats. Individual flush valves, located about 36″ above the floor, are recommended. Fixtures with a ten-inch rim height are recommended for the lower grades. Fixtures to be used only by adults should be 15″ in height. Wall-mounted water closets are recommended. These should have a rapidly-receding front design[9].

URINALS

Urinals constructed of vitreous china should be provided in each men's and boys' toilet room, and should be equipped with a hand-operated, foot-operated, or automatic flushing device. Floor-type urinals, when provided for small youth, should be flush with the floor. The lip height of wall-mounted urinals should not exceed 15″ from the floor for elementary- and junior-high-school-age children, and 19″ for high-school-age children.

Wall-mounted urinals are recommended. Floor-mounted urinals and trough urinals are very undesirable[10]. In the selection of urinals for women, the advice of an informed professional woman should be obtained.

CUSPIDORS

Recessed cuspidors of vitreous china should be provided in wrestling and team dressing rooms. Mounting heights should correspond to those recommended for drinking fountains.

HOSE BIBBS AND FLOOR DRAINS

Each public toilet, locker-room toilet, locker-and-dressing room, swimming-pool area, field house, recreation building, stadium, and custodian service sink should be provided with hose bibbs. They should be key-operated, with the exception of those for the service sink, and should be recessed in walls or located under lavatories.

Frostproof hose bibbs are desirable for the cleaning and maintenance of track equipment, hard-surface play areas, and other outside areas. Where provided, hose bibbs should be recessed or otherwise protected. Where hose bibbs are placed above ground adjacent to buildings, they should be high enough for filling buckets.

Floor drains should be provided in each of the following areas: toilet rooms, shower rooms, toweling areas, locker rooms, laundry rooms, team rooms, drying rooms, custodian closets, and the swimming pool area.

Scuff grills should be installed at entrances to buildings leading to such facilities as dressing rooms and gymnasiums. These grills should be the width of the door and long enough to be efficient.

ACCESSORIES

The following accessories should be provided in toilet rooms: (1) liquid-soap dispensers convenient to each lavatory; (2) toilet-paper dispensers for folded or roll paper (roll-paper dispensers should limit the amount of paper that can be removed at each operation); (3) mirrors (polished metal or glass) located so as not to interfere with the use of lavatories nor to reflect the interior view into corridors; (4) a shelf for personal items while using lavatories and water closets; (5) appropriately-located hooks for hanging garments; and (6) paper-towel dispensers or electric driers. (Advanced thinking on drying-room design suggests the principle of drying by circulating heated dry air through multiple jets. The saving on towel costs, together with other advantages, may justify a considered analysis of this possibility.)

SHOWER ROOMS

Shower rooms should be separated from dressing rooms by a drip passage, toweling area, and/or body-drying room. Adequate ventilation and humidity control is essential.

The width of shower rooms with heads on opposite walls should not be less than 9′-6″; for rooms with heads on one wall only, 6′-6″. Floors should be of nonslip ceramic tile, quarry tile, or terrazzo sloped toward the drain. The drain should be at or near the base of the wall, under the shower heads. The base should be coved of the same material as the floor. Wainscots should extend to a height of not less than 7′ and should be of quarry tile, ceramic tile, terrazzo, or glazed tile.

A soap dispenser should be located at each shower head if a soaping area is not provided. Liquid-soap dispensers are desirable.

To make showers usable by the disabled and aging, handrails or safety rails should be introduced along with folding "L" seats. The shower seat to facilitate individuals in wheelchairs, or individuals with comparable disabilities, will not interfere with use of the same space by able-bodied participants. The seat can be placed in a corner of a gang shower, although a stall shower is preferable. There should be at least two such seats, mounted oppositely, to facilitate a left or right approach. It is possible to combine gang showers with stall showers[11].

HOT-WATER SUPPLY

Hot water to shower heads and lavatories should not exceed a temperature of 120°F. Faucets should be of a type that delivers both hot and cold water. A mixer valve which equalizes the pressure should furnish hot water to faucets and shower heads. Hot water should be supplied to service sinks in custodians' closets.

PIPING, VALVES, AND FITTINGS

All piping, valves, and fittings should be selected to facilitate service and reduce replacement. The provision of pipe-access

---

[9] See Appendix I.
[10] Ibid.

[11] Ibid.

TABLE 6

HEIGHTS OF SHOWER HEADS AND MIRRORS*

Age Group	Grades	Mirror Height		Shower Height		Shower Valve Height
		Vertical Length	To Bottom of Mirror	Girls	Boys	
Elementary	2 thru 6	30"	32"	50"	55"	36"
Junior High	7 thru 9	30"	40"	54"	60"	40"
Senior High	10 thru 12	30"	44"	56"	66"	45"
Adults		30"	48"	60"	72"	48"

*Notes: 1. Mirror mounting heights apply only to mirrors of size listed. Smaller mirrors are not recommended.
2. Shower heights are for heads 8" from wall. Height should be adjusted if closer to wall.
3. Girls' shower heights are shoulder high.
4. Shower heights are from floor to face of shower head (not rough-in dimension).

space, the use of noncorrosive materials, and the identification of valves and fittings are in the interest of long-range economy.

All plumbing fixtures, water closets, and lavatories should have individual shut-off valves. Shower heads should have a tamperproof shut-off control available and convenient to the instructor. They should be of heavy-duty institutional type and should be securely fastened to the walls. Sinks or lavatories in health-service rooms, first-aid rooms, and food-preparation areas should be equipped with wrist-, knee-, or foot-operated fittings.

Water pipes on playgrounds should be protected against freezing or be installed so as to permit seasonal draining. All inside cold-water pipes need to be insulated to prevent condensation.

TOILET STALLS

Toilet stalls should be provided to shield water closets and urinals. The partitions should be of impervious material that resists marking and rusting. They should be securely anchored, and the hardware selected should be durable, noncorrosive, and easily cleaned. Standard modules and installations are recommended[12].

GAS LINES

When gas is used for heating, strict codes must be followed. Hot-water tanks and other gas-fired equipment should be vented to the exterior.

METERS

Coin-operated gas and water meters are needed where buildings are used by the public for limited time periods which require separate billing.

SOUND CONTROL—ACOUSTICAL TREATMENT

Some areas of the building, such as gymnasiums, swimming pools, band rooms, shops, and dressing-locker rooms, are noisier than others, but nearly every area in the building needs some acoustical treatment for efficient operation of the program. Two main objectives are to be met in proper sound conditioning: (1) sound absorption and reverberation control for good hearing conditions; and (2) sound attenuation to decrease

the transmission of unwanted sound (noise) from outside the room and to decrease the transmission of sound to other areas.

SOUND CONTROL

School buildings and recreation facilities should be located in quiet residential areas away from the distracting and fatiguing influences of railroads, factories, and major traffic arteries. The buildings and playgrounds should be arranged on the site to separate the areas of noisy activities, such as music rooms and gymnasiums, from the quiet areas such as classrooms, libraries, and study halls. When the prevailing winds are from the west, southwest, and northwest, it is best to have the noisy areas on the east side of the building. Special attention should be given to the possible telephonic effect of some ventilating systems and the prevailing winds.

ACHIEVEMENT OF GOOD HEARING CONDITIONS

Defects in sound transmission, such as objectionable echoes and/or dead spots, result from improper design. Any room with an interior space of smooth hard materials will have reverberations which will be distracting. Conversely, the absence of any sound reflection will deaden a room to an uncomfortable point. The services of an acoustical engineer should be utilized to make the necessary computations and supply the needed information. Floor coverings, wall surfaces, window areas, and the number of occupants must also be considered when designing a "sonic-balanced" area.

SOUND INSULATION

Sound insulation is a highly-technical matter requiring the employment of the best sound engineers. However, a few of the problems will be discussed here. Ventilating ducts frequently transmit noises from one area of the building to another. The transmission of sound through ducts can be reduced by the use of baffles or by lining ducts with sound-absorbent, fire-resistant materials. The improper location of doors and windows may create a serious noise distraction.

Reducing the transmission of air-borne sound is largely dependent upon the weight of partitions, and upon double-wall construction in which the studs or members supporting one side of the double wall do not touch or are not attached to the studs or members supporting the wall on the opposite side. Machinery-vibration or impact sounds should be cushioned by selecting a proper floor covering or by installing the machinery on floating or resilient mountings. "Sound locks", such as double walls or doors, are needed between any noisy area and adjoining quiet areas when separation is impossible. When fold-

[12] Mary M. Fredrick, Play Safe in Technicolor, Journal of Health, Physical Education, and Recreation, Vol. 27, No. 10, 1956.

ing partitions are used, caution should be exercised to assure adequate sound conditioning.

MATERIALS FOR ACOUSTICAL TREATMENT

Care must be taken in the maintenance of acoustical materials. Oil paint reduces the sound-absorbent qualities of most materials. Surface treatment will vary for different acoustical materials. The most common treatment of acoustical-fiber tile is a light brush coat of water-base paint. It should be noted that most acoustical materials lose their efficiency after several applications of paint.

CUSTODIAL FACILITIES

Well-planned quarters for the custodial staff encourage systematic management and routine, efficient, and economical use of supplies and tools, and, most important, a high standard of workmanship. The standards of housekeeping and maintenance must be high to do an effective job of teaching the observance of good health and safety habits. Custodians should assist in the planning of facilities for their own use.

CLOSETS

Custodians' closets should be planned in relation to the equipment and materials to be used. For example, closets near large general-use areas should be large enough to accommodate the equipment needed for maintenance purposes. At least one fire-resistant closet should be provided for each 7,500 to 10,000 square feet.

SINK

A custodial-service sink should be located either in the custodians' closet or nearby.

SUPPLY-STORAGE ROOM

The custodian may require a ventilated supply-storage space adjacent to toilets, dressing rooms, and shower rooms of gymnasiums and recreation centers. Such a space may provide nearby storage for such supplies as paper towels, toilet paper, light bulbs, soap, detergents, wax, and polish. A hook strip should be provided for hanging mops and brooms.

SPACE RELATIONSHIPS IN THE PHYSICAL EDUCATION SUITE

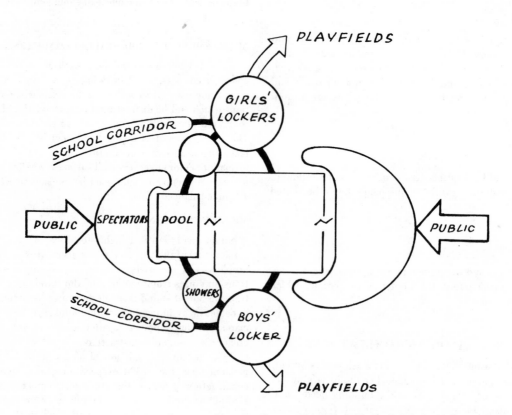

Source: Herrick, John H., Ralph D. McCleary, Wilfred E. Clapp, and Walter F. Bogner. *From School Program to School Plant.* New York: Henry Holt and Company. 1956. p. 325.

Figure 67

Space Relationships in the Physical Education Suite

VACUUM-CLEANING FACILITIES

Central vacuum systems have been found useful in some installations. Large portable cleaners, however, are less expensive and more flexible.

DRAINS AND HOSE BIBBS

Proper floor drainage is essential for good custodial care in cleaning toilet rooms and shower rooms. Floors must be pitched to the floor drains which lead into a sewer pipe. There should be hose-bibb connections for hot and cold water.

INCINERATOR

If it is necessary to plan for the disposition of waste by the use of incinerators, special precautions should be considered to control smoke and to eliminate fire hazards.

TRAFFIC CIRCULATION WITHIN THE BUILDING

The main objectives in planning for traffic circulation are: providing for minimum travel distances; reducing traffic congestion; minimizing the disturbance of class work; increasing the comfort and safety of occupants; providing for ease of supervision and desirable separation; and providing for connections to future additions.

FACTORS IN TRAFFIC CONTROL

The control of traffic is dependent upon the careful planning of all facilities, including classrooms and activity and service areas, and a careful study of their anticipated use by students and the community. This study should include the preparation of flow charts of the required movement of people, and the placement of services so as to aid in providing means of supervision of the circulation of persons engaged in activity and in the provision of services and equipment. The special circulation problems created by evening use and by summer recreation programs for children and adults should be studied.

SPACE RELATIONSHIPS

The relationship of spaces to the placement and size of corridors, lobbies, stairs, and doors needs careful consideration if the traffic flow is to move easily and safely. Spectator space, if provided, should be separated from the pool and deck areas and from the gymnasium floor. Entrances to the seating area should be direct from the out-of-doors or from school corridors without requiring travel through locker rooms or across the pool deck or gymnasium. In addition, student traffic to and from the locker rooms should not be across the gymnasium floor. A suggested plan for the entire unit, indicating traffic flow from the school corridors and within the various spaces, is shown in Figure 67.

The individual components of the dressing-and-locker rooms should permit access and exit from each area without cross traffic in wet and dry areas. The location of toilet rooms in relation to the pool and to outside facilities should be considered, especially with reference to community use.

Units within the building which require truck delivery service should be grouped so as to reduce to a minimum the number of delivery points. Delivery of supplies within the building should be planned so that there is no traffic through locker rooms or across gymnasium floors.

CORRIDORS AND FOYERS

In large buildings, the group-health and physical education units should be accessible from at least two corridors[13] or passageways leading from the principal classroom areas of the buildings to prevent traffic congestion at the change of periods. Provision should be made for heavy traffic from the dressing-locker suite to playfields. The designated corridor widths should be clear of all obstructions, including the maximum swing of locker and room doors. No corridor should be less than 60″ in width. All equipment, such as heating units, drinking fountains, and fire extinguishers, should be recessed. Each end of every corridor should terminate on an exit, or stairway leading directly to a point of exit.

Public-assembly rooms, including gymnasiums, used for large public groups should be designed with entrance foyers. The size of the foyer will depend upon the capacity of the seating space. The planning of this area should include consideration for ticket sales, public telephones, and a cloak checkroom. The foyer should be accessible to public toilets for men and women. If the gymnasium is part of a school building, the gymnasium lobby should connect with a corridor serving the main school building. In many situations, it is advisable to provide cut-off gates so it will not be necessary to supervise the entire building when limited areas are in use.

STAIRWAYS

Buildings of two or more stories should have no fewer than two stairways, remote from each other. All stairways should be of fire-resistant construction and should be in fire-resistant enclosures, and all main stairways should lead directly to grade exits. Two-lane stairways are recommended, and they should have a clear width throughout their entire length of a minimum of 44 inches between handrails (see local fire code).

Stairways should be divided into runs of not more than 16 nor less than 3 risers. Risers should not exceed 6-1/2″, and treads should be at least 10-1/2″ measured from riser to riser. The rounded nosings of all treads and landings should have nonslip, flush surfaces. Do not use abrupt overhanging nosing.[14] Winding stairways should not be constructed. In some cases, ramps are desirable to compensate for minor differences in floor levels. Ramps should have nonslip surfaces and should not have a rise of more than 1 to 12; 1 to 15 or 20 is preferred. It is desirable to have adequate stair aisles for all bleachers of more than three rows, movable or fixed.

EXITS AND DOORS

Exits should be located so that at least one exit, or stairway leading to an exit, will be within 100′ of a doorway of every room designed for occupancy. Every floor of the building should have at least two exits, remote from each other, and additional exits as prescribed by the National Fire Protection Association formula in the Building Exits Code. Exits should be located for convenience as well as for safety. It is important that the number of exits and their location be in proper relation to the public seating capacity and space in the gymnasium.

Folding bleachers are often provided along the sides of the long axis of the gymnasium playing court. When a second level of folding or fixed bleachers is provided on one or both sides of the gymnasium, there should be adequate exits at the four corners of the gymnasium. It should be possible for the

---

[13] Corridor widths should be checked against local and state building codes.
[14] For further information, write to: The Maple Flooring Manufacturers Association, 35 East Wacker Dr., Chicago, Ill. They will supply detailed information on the various recommended methods of maple-floor construction. Information on floor finishing and maintenance is also available.

spectators to reach the outdoors directly from the main floor without passing up or down stairs. With two levels of seating, this is hardly possible, at least on a level site, but stairways or passageways down long hallways should be reduced to a minimum.

All doors should open in the direction of exit, and should either swing into a recess or should swing 180°, with the entire door swinging free of the door opening (side-hinged). Double exterior doors should be provided with a center mullion so that each door will operate independently. At least one such mullion should be removable to permit the passage of large objects. Each exterior door and each door from occupied rooms to the corridor should be at least 36 inches wide. Every room should be provided with exit units as prescribed by the Building Exits Code, and doors should be equipped with anti-panic hardware.

Doors to the furnace room and to storage rooms where combustible materials are kept should be metal-clad and in accordance with Fire Underwriters' specifications. Exterior doors and all doors in damp areas, such as the swimming-pool area, laundry room, shower rooms, and dressing-locker suites, should be solid and moisture-resistant.

If exterior doors cannot be recessed, they should be covered by soffits for weather protection. Outside entrances should be provided with mud-and-dirt grates or mats for cleaning the mud and dirt from shoes. One method which has proved satisfactory is the use of a grate-covered sump about 6' long and the width of the door opening, so placed that persons entering the building must walk across it with both feet.

INDOOR SURFACE MATERIALS

The selection of indoor surface materials becomes a complicated problem because indoor facilities may be subject to hard usage and excessive moisture, and they must meet minimum light-reflection factors.

Small accessory rooms not treated in this discussion or in Table 7 may, in most instances, take finishes similar to the larger contiguous areas unless otherwise indicated. Other materials not mentioned in Table 7, such as patented resilient synthetic plastics now available on the market, should be considered. For example, a concrete glaze is being used for dadoes and, in some instances, for both the lower and upper walls of shower and dressing rooms.

FLOORS

In the treatment of floors, it is well to heed instructions of the manufacturer of the product being used. One rather-common satisfactory method for finishing wood floors is as follows: sand carefully to a smooth finish; clean thoroughly without water; apply a penetrating floor seal; allow to dry; buff; paint the floor lines; repeat the sealing process; and apply a coat of finish seal. Asphalt-tile floors should be treated with nonspirits wax. All waxed floors require frequent rewaxing. Wherever possible, and particularly in vestibules and corridors, a floor material of a nonslip nature, and one which cannot be made slippery by use or by janitor care, should be used. Suitable materials include quarry tile and ceramic tile, or comparable material, impregnated throughout with carborundum.

Flooring should be continuous through interior doorways if the floors are the same in both areas. If flooring materials change at the doorway, flush thresholds are recommended.

When floors are treated with borax or corn meal for dancing, they should be well cleaned with a treated mop before being used for games. The treatment of floors with a hard-seal finish, as described above, for multiple use in gymnasiums and recreation centers makes possible a higher percentage of utilization of the facility. Multiple use for dancing, skating, and games is recommended even though it may increase maintenance costs by requiring more frequent floor treatment. Borders around skating rinks, where skaters walk, should be made of wood flooring or resilient surfacing.

TACKBOARDS AND CHALKBOARDS

Chalkboards may be obtained in light colors which reflect light more efficiently than do blackboards. They reduce glare and thus relieve eye fatigue. Boards of 32″ to 42″ in height, top to bottom, are appropriate for areas where classes, discussions, research activities, and meetings are held. Recessed eraser and chalk trays are desirable.

In most rooms, there is an equal need for tackboards and chalkboards. Tackboards should be the same height and width as chalkboards. Tackboards used out-of-doors or in swimming pool areas should be weatherproof.

Chalkboards and tackboards should be equipped with hook strips or map rails.

WALLS AND CEILINGS

In the selection of materials for walls and ceilings, care must be taken that the area will have proper sound control and yet be impervious to moisture and rough usage. Ceilings in shower rooms may be made of moisture-resistant acoustical tile.

COLOR AND AESTHETICS

VALUES OF COLOR

One of the chief values of color lies in substituting beauty for monotony and drabness. School and recreation authorities should provide a cheerful, friendly atmosphere in which youth and adults live, work, and play. Daily contacts with good color and design help to give people an appreciation of aesthetic values which lead to a feeling of pride in their surroundings. Studies have shown that the psychological response of children to color and its use definitely affects their attitudes and work habits in school. The trend toward the use of light colors is most appropriate in planning gymnasiums, classrooms, play rooms, craft shops, little theatres, and recreation facilities.

FACTORS TO BE CONSIDERED IN USING COLOR

GEOGRAPHY AND ORIENTATION

Intense colors are used in bright, sunny locations because bright light tends to "wash out" color. In warm situations, cool (blue-green group) colors are desirable. In cool areas and exposures, warm (red-orange group) colors are preferred.

NEARBY STRUCTURES AND OUTSIDE DETAILS

If the reflections from nearby structures are too intense,

TABLE 7

SUGGESTED INDOOR SURFACE MATERIALS

ROOMS	FLOORS										LOWER WALLS							UPPER WALLS				CEILINGS	
	Asphalt, Rubber Linoleum Tile	Cement, Abrasive and Non-absorbent	Maple, hard	Terrazzo Abrasive	Tile, ceramic	Brick	Brick, glazed	Cinder Block	Concrete	Plaster	Tile, ceramic	Wood Panel	Moisture-proof	Brick	Brick, glazed	Cinder Block	Plaster	Acoustic	Moisture-resistant	Concrete or Structure Tile	Plaster	Tile, acoustic	Moisture-resistant
Apparatus Storage Room		1	2			1		2	1	C													
Classrooms	2		1				2		1		2					2	1			C	C	1	
Clubroom	2		1				2		1		2					2	1			C	C	1	
Corrective Room			1		2	1					2		2	2	1	2						1	
Custodial Supply Room		1		2																			
Dance Studio	2		1																	C	C	1	
Drying Room (equip.)		1		2	2	1	2	1	1				1		1								
Gymnasium			1		2	1					2		2	2	1	2		*		C	C	1	
Health-Service Unit	1		1		2				1		2					2	1					1	
Laundry Room		2		1	2	1	2	2			1	C	*						*			*	*
Locker Rooms		3		2	1	1	2	2	3	1			*	1		1	2				C	1	
Natatorium				1	2	1	3	2			1		*	2	2	1		*	*	C	C	1	*
Offices	2		1				2		1		1					2	1					1	
Recreation Room	2		1		2		2		1		1		2	1	2	2		*				1	*
Shower Rooms		3		2	1		1		2	1			*	2	1	2	2	*				1	
Special-activity Room	2		1				2		1		1				1	1	1				C	1	
Team Room		3		2	1	2	1	2	2	3	1		*	1		1	2				C	1	
Toilet Rooms		3		2	1		1	2	2	2	1		*	1		1	1					1	
Toweling-Drying Room (bath)		3		2	1		1		2	1			*	2	1	2	2	*				1	*

Note: The numbers in the Table indicate first, second, and third choices. "C" indicates the material as being contrary to good practice. An * indicates desirable quality.

these structures should be painted in darker, cooler colors. If the area is in a "pocket," then light colors, including sunlight yellow, are desirable.

SIZE AND SHAPE OF ROOMS

Tints make a room look larger and are "receding" in effect. Using a combination, one can change the apparent shape and size of a room.

LIGHTING

Both the type of lighting fixtures and the color temperatures of the lamps affect the final color rendition of an area. Man is accustomed to seeing color either in daylight or in a light high in yellow. One should select a color under the light under which it is normally seen. Otherwise, he may be in for a visual shock.

AGE OF OCCUPANTS

Children prefer bright, gay, exciting colors, while adults prefer tones and shades of less-intensive colors, except for accent purposes.

TYPE OF ACTIVITY

Colors may be considered depressing, stimulating, relaxing, and neutral. After the other factors are considered, the type of activity should determine the exact color, tint, shade, or tone. A bright red in a gymnasium, for example, is too stimulating, and a purple too depressing. On the other hand, a delicate peach or blue tint will probably best serve the purpose. The gymnasium should reflect an inviting, hospitable, and friendly atmosphere.

LIGHT REFLECTION

The reflectances of the surfaces in a room should approach the following:

Furniture	35% to 50%
Ceilings	70% to 90%
Walls	40% to 70%
Dado or wainscot	40% to 60%
Trim	30% to 60%
Floors, desks, and other equipment	30% to 50%
Chalkboards	5% to 20%
Tackboards	40%
Window walls	80%

Nongloss or matte finishes should be used.

WALLS

In general, walls should be darker than ceilings. Colors in a large area, such as a gymnasium, add interest and variety. Reasonable variations in color combinations from room to room and in corridors add to the attractiveness of the entire unit.

FLOORS

A natural-finish maple floor or tile floor will provide a reflection factor of 30 to 40 percent. Other synthetic materials may prove satisfactory.

FURNISHINGS AND COLOR

The selection of properly designed furniture is important. Chairs designed so as to prohibit chair backs from hitting or marring the walls are also of the nontipping type that facilitate use by the aging and the disabled.

The old institutional grays and browns are obsolete in an era of light wood finishes and pastel colors. However, it is important to be aware of glossy surfaces which may cause excessive glare.

Where draperies and upholstered materials are used, appropriate color combinations can be worked out in the decoration plan to achieve color coordination for the area. Lockers, files, cabinets, and sanitary fixtures may be obtained in colors.

EQUIPMENT AND COLOR

Colors are being widely used in coverings for exercise and tumbling mats, on protective materials placed on walls under basketball backboards, or around the supporting structure or framework of apparatus or movable equipment. Paint markings in simple design can be worked out in needed colors to specify danger or foul areas, but "busy" patterns should be carefully avoided. It is possible to identify areas for seating spectators in field houses or gymnasiums by using color zones or colored seats to denote sections and price range.

Bright hues add considerably to the general appearance of a facility. The use of color to cut down on the glare of the surface of such outdoor areas as tennis courts and multiple-use playground areas is an important consideration.

COLOR CODES

IDENTIFICATION

Pieces of apparatus and playground equipment may be painted different colors so they may be readily identified on a play area. Multipurpose use of gymnasium floors and other play areas for different games indicates the need for colored court markings, which may be achieved by permanently-painted lines or by using different-colored sensitized pressure tape. This tape may be applied easily and removed when necessary.

SAFETY

Recognition of hazards, such as close clearances, edges of openings, moving objects, and barriers, may be achieved more readily if associated with a specific alerting color. For example, red has always been associated with fire extinguishers, fire-alarm stations, and other fire-fighting equipment. Persons may be alerted to danger or emergency areas by using orange on power controls, rims of pulleys, gears, and switch boxes. A high-visibility yellow, or alternate yellow and black stripes, may be desirable for swing seats, the edges of teeters, the steps and guard rails of slides, the edges of merry-go-rounds, and giant-stride ladders.

Frederick[15] recommends the following safety color code for play areas and playground equipment:

- Red—Used for equipment and facilities for fire-fighting purposes. Red may be used on stationary playground equipment, such as horizontal-bar supports, slide supports, and slide ladders.
- Green—Denotes safety and marks first-aid equipment. Green may be used for benches or resting areas on the playground and for the first-aid box.
- Yellow—Identifies physical hazards and marks equipment one might trip over or strike against. Yellow may be used on moving equipment on playground areas, especially on swings, balance beams, chains for rings, clamps for ropes, swing supports, and guard rails.
- Blue—Light blue denotes an area where caution should be used, while dark blue is used for equipment or machinery temporarily out of service. Since dark blue is used primarily as a signal for a temporary condition, it is advisable to use this signal in the form of a movable sign. Light blue may be used on comparatively safe equipment, such as climbing-horse supports, sand-box shelves, horizontal-ladder supports, jungle-gym supports, seesaw supports, and the inside rails of slides.
- White—Marks good-housekeeping, sanitation, or traffic facilities. White may be used on playgrounds to denote bicycle-parking areas or pathways for walking.
- Orange—Used as a signal for caution or to be on the alert. Orange may be used on playground equipment that may cause injury if someone walks into the area, such as supports for rings and ropes, sand-box sides, seesaw boards, and swing seats.
- Black—Balance-beam supports may be in black.

SERVICE FACILITIES

Service facilities are spaces, structures, and features primarily for the health, safety, comfort, and convenience of the participants in a program of physical education, athletics, and school-community recreation. These facilities include the following types of rooms and areas: locker, shower, toweling, toilet, storage, custodial, trainer's, laundry, equipment-drying, staff-office, and health-service (see Chapter 15). The extent to which these facilities are provided will depend on the type, grade level, size, and location of the school as well as the community recreation needs.

LOCKER ROOMS

LOCATION

The locker rooms should be located so as to serve functionally the indoor and outdoor teaching stations and other service facilities related to dressing-room use. It is recommended that locker rooms be located on the gymnasium floor level directly adjacent to and leading into the gymnasium. Other teaching stations should be located so as to have easy accessibility to the locker rooms. Where possible, students should be able to pass from locker rooms to activity areas without crossing main

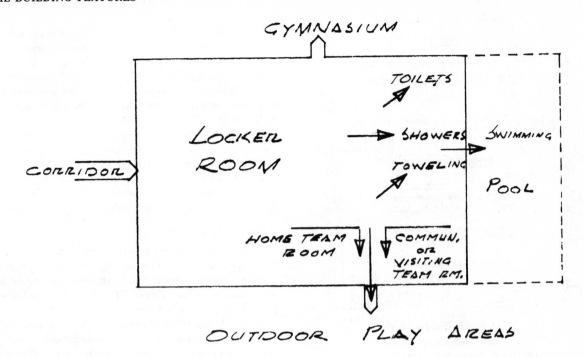

Figure 68
Suggested Traffic Flow Chart for Locker Rooms, Shower, and Pool

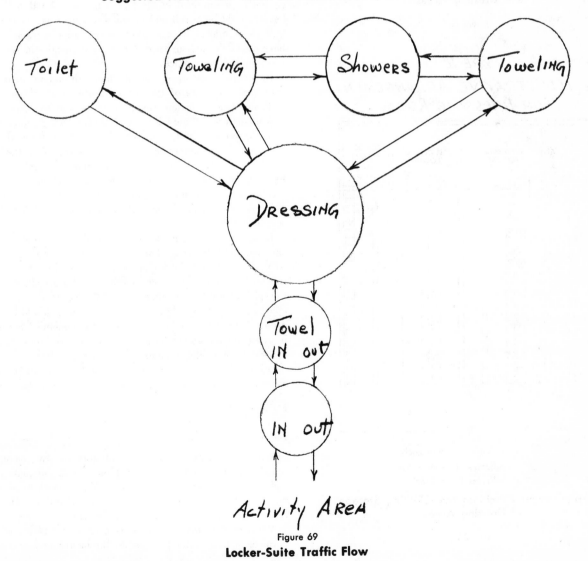

Figure 69
Locker-Suite Traffic Flow

TYPE I.
AN ILLUSTRATIVE ARRANGEMENT FOR DRESSING ROOM

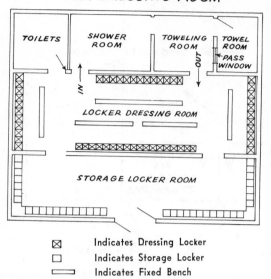

⊠ Indicates Dressing Locker
☐ Indicates Storage Locker
▭ Indicates Fixed Bench

This Arrangement Separates the Clothing Storage and Dressing Areas

Figure 70

TYPE II
AN ILLUSTRATIVE ARRANGEMENT FOR DRESSING ROOM

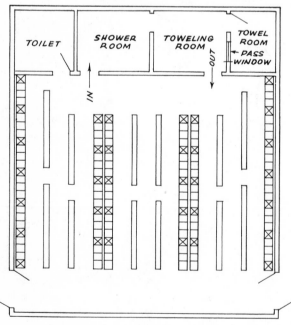

⊠ Indicates Dressing Locker
☐ Indicates Storage Locker
▭ Indicates Fixed Bench

This Arrangement Combines the Clothing Storage and Dressing Areas

Figure 71

traffic corridors. Locker-room entrance-exit doors are generally required by state regulation to have vision barriers.

Figures 68 and 69 indicate the flow of students from the rest of the school plant into the physical education teaching stations and service facilities. These figures also show a manner in which community recreation groups may have access to these facilities.

SIZE

The locker-room size should be based on the number of students using it during a peak-load period. The generally-accepted square footage required is 15 to 20 square feet per person, depending upon the number of people served.

PHYSICAL FEATURES

Consideration should be given to the factors which influence the shape and size of locker rooms and space requirements for benches, lockers, storage, toilets, showers, circulation of pupils, and toweling rooms. Figures 70, 71, and 72 indicate several possible arrangements.

Floors should be of impervious materials, such as ceramic or quarry tile, with a carborundum-impregnated surface, and should be properly sloped toward the drains. Concrete floors (nonslip surface), if used, should be treated with a hardener to prevent the penetration of odors and moisture. A dry climate should be maintained in the locker rooms. The 8-inch locker bases should be coved and of the same material as the floor.

Walls should be of materials resistant to moisture and should have easily-cleaned surfaces. All external corners in the locker room should be rounded.

Heavy-duty, moisture-resistant doors should be installed at entrances and exits of the locker rooms, and should be of sufficient size to handle the traffic flow and to form natural vision barriers. All outside doors from the locker rooms should be equipped with anitpanic bars of noncorrosive metal.

When natural light is desired for the locker room, the vented sky dome may be used where practical. Sidewall windows should be no larger than 24″ in height, with the lowest point of the window at a maximum distance of 36″ from the ceiling. Windows should be glazed with opaque glass and the window frames bonderized or galvanized.

Locker rooms should be well lighted with vaporproof and shielded light fixtures. The ceilings should be acoustically treated with a material impervious to moisture. The layout of the lockers should be such that the lights are directly over the spaces between the lockers. Wall outlets should be located approximately 3 feet above the floor level and should be vaporproof. Radiant heating in the floor is recommended because of its value in maintaining dry floors, foot comfort, and elimination of drafts. In colder regions, supplementary heating may be necessary. Floor drains should be properly placed in the locker room to permit complete drainage.

EQUIPMENT

Elementary Schools

When the physical education program in the elementary school involves both dressing and showering, adequate locker and shower areas are necessary. Many elementary-school physical education programs do not require a uniform. However, rubber-sole shoes should be worn for safety reasons.

A locker, dressing, and showering area should be available in the elementary school for use by the faculty and after-school

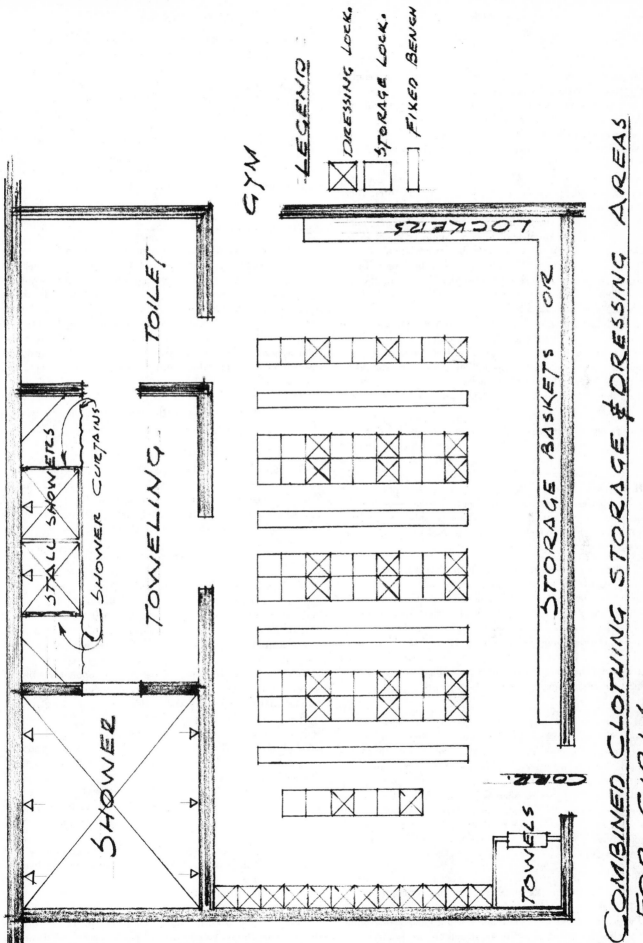

LEGEND:
⊠ DRESSING LOCK.
☐ STORAGE LOCK.
▭ FIXED BENCH

GYM

LOCKERS

STORAGE BASKETS OR

TOILET

TOWELING

SHOWER CURTAINS

STALL SHOWERS

SHOWER

CORR.

TOWELS

COMBINED CLOTHING STORAGE & DRESSING AREAS FOR GIRLS.

Figure 72

FIGURE 72

groups, including adult groups. Such an area should be not less than 600 square feet in size.

Secondary Schools

Lockers are needed for all pupils who will use the central locker room. Storage lockers should be provided for physical education uniforms, and dressing lockers for street clothing. The number of storage lockers should be equal to the total enrollment plus 10 per cent for expansion.

The following are commonly-used sizes of storage lockers for both boys and girls: 9" x 12" x 24"; 9" x 12" x 18"; 9" x 12" x 15"; and 12" x 12" x 12". The specific unit accepted should be based upon the needs of each school. Often there is a tendency to select a unit that is too small.

Dressing lockers should be large enough to accommodate street clothing. The number of lockers should be equal to the peak-period load plus 10 to 15 percent for variation in class size and scheduling, for intramurals, and for some interscholastic athletic participants. For secondary schools, the following locker sizes are recommended: 12" x 12" x 72"; 12" x 12" x 60"; and 12" x 12" x 54".

A combined storage-dressing locker arrangement should be planned as a coordinate unit to attain a uniform height. There should be a ventilation space of 2" to 4" between lockers when they are placed back to back. The same space should be provided between the backs of lockers and the walls. Aisle lockers should have heavy-duty sides to prevent excessive wear and damage.

Basket-type lockers of metal or wire may be used for storing physical education uniforms. There are several ways of storing these baskets. They may be stored on permanent shelves in a protected area or may be placed on movable racks.

If a separate community locker room is not provided, a number of dressing lockers in the central locker room can be equipped with lock and key. The key can be checked out from an attendant when the locker is used. The lockers would remain unlocked for pupil use during the school day.

Benches should be secured to the floor. A seat board of hardwood at least 8" in width, surfaced on four sides, with rounded edges and corners, is essential. The height of the bench should be 16" from the floor. Space relations of lockers to bench, and bench to bench should be planned for traffic control and dressing comfort. The recommended allowances are 30" from lockers to bench, 8" for bench width, and a 30-inch passage between benches. Benches should extend the full length of each locker bank, with traffic breaks at intervals of about twelve feet (see Figure 74).

Mirrors should be installed in both boys' and girls' locker rooms. The location, number, and size will depend upon the arrangement of lockers and wall spaces. The mirrors should be framed in noncorrosive metal frames and should be permanently mounted on the walls. Stainless steel mirrors have been found highly desirable. Recessed shelves beneath the mirrors are an added convenience. Full-length mirrors are recommended near the main exit for the locker room. A reasonable ratio of full-length mirrors is 1 to 100. Facial-tissue and sanitary-napkin dispensers are necessary in the girls' rooms.

Sufficient hair driers, conveniently located, are necessary for girls' locker rooms. Recessed-type drinking fountains should also be included. Cuspidors are desirable for boys in the team and wrestling rooms. A bulletin board and a chalkboard should be installed in each dressing room at appropriate locations.

AUXILIARY LOCKER ROOMS

In secondary schools, two separate auxiliary locker rooms should be provided. These may serve boys' and girls' interscholastic teams, the faculty, or community groups. A small room for coaches' use is also desirable. The central locker room may be partitioned by a ceiling-height noncorrosive wire enclosure. The dressing lockers within this enclosure may be available for pupil use during the school day. Large-size, full-length lockers are usually put in auxiliary locker rooms. The same-size lockers are desirable for adult use. If an auxiliary locker room is not provided, the central locker room should be increased in size and larger lockers added.

SHOWER ROOMS

All persons should have an opportunity to take a shower following participation in physical education classes, school athletics, or physical-recreation activities. The time available for showering and dressing is usually limited to 10 to 12 minutes. It is important that there be a sufficient number of shower heads. Ten shower heads are recommended for the first thirty people, and an additional head is recommended for every four persons thereafter. The shower heads should be spaced at least 4' apart. Temperature controls are necessary to keep the water from exceeding 120 degrees F. Both individual and master controls are needed for all group showers. The location of the master control should be near the showering area in a secured box.

LOCATION

The shower room should be directly accessible to the toweling room and the locker room which it serves. When a shower room is designed to serve a swimming pool, the room should be located so that pupils must pass through the showers prior to entering the pool. The entrance should lead directly to the pool deck.

PHYSICAL FEATURES

All showers for boys should be of the gang type. For girls, approximately 90 percent of the showers should be the gang-type and 10 percent the individual-type with related dressing cubicles. Where there is extensive use of showers by women, it may be desirable to increase the number of individual showers and dressing cubicles.

The size of shower rooms is predicated upon the type of showers (gang-type, or individual-type with cubicles) and the number and spacing of shower heads.

Floors should be of nonslip ceramic or quarry tile properly sloped toward the drains. In the construction of the floor, drainage gutters 2" deep and 8" to 10" wide around the perimeter of the shower room provide a sanitary means of drainage. All corners of the gutters should be rounded. Another method for drainage which has been found economical and satisfactory is to slope the floor to a recess approximately 30" x 30". The recess is covered by a removable nonferrous metal grating.

If walls enclosing the shower room are of ceramic or glazed tile units, or of marble, they should extend to the ceiling. Coved bases and rounded external corners are desirable. For ceiling construction, tile or portland-cement plaster are satisfactory.

Moistureproof fixtures should be installed. Lights in the shower room should be controlled by a key-type switch in the

TYPICAL COMBINED STORAGE-DRESSING LOCKER ARRANGEMENTS
and
LOCKER AREA REQUIRED FOR DIFFERENT TYPES OF STORAGE-DRESSING UNITS

ADAPTATION	SIZE OF LOCKERS AND BATTERY ARRANGEMENT	ARRANGEMENT OF LOCKERS ONE PUPIL EACH PERIOD	OVER-ALL HEIGHT WITH 8" BASE	NUMBER STUDENTS PER DAY	AREA REQUIRED INCLUDES 4" FOR VENTILATION
6-PERIOD DAY	A [6 STORAGE 9" x 12" x 24" / 1 DRESSING 12" x 12" x 48"] B [6 STORAGE 9" x 12" x 24" / 1 DRESSING 12" x 12" x 72"]	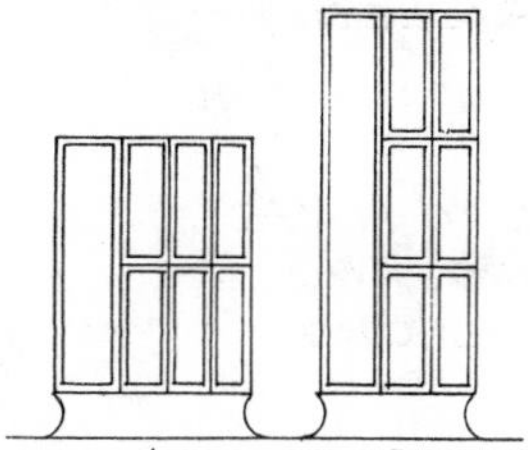	A. 56" / B. 80"	240	A [152 SQ. FT.] B [115 SQ. FT.]
6-PERIOD DAY	6 STORAGE 9" x 12" x 20" / 1 DRESSING 12" x 12" x 60"		68"	240	115 SQ. FT.
6-PERIOD DAY	6 STORAGE 12" x 12" x 12" / 1 DRESSING 12" x 12" x 48"	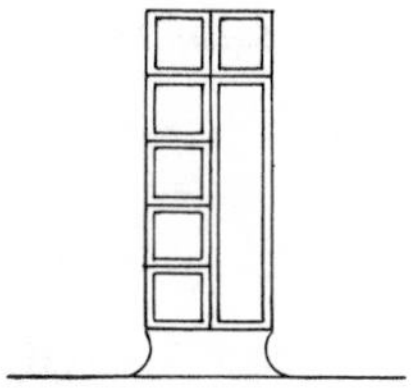	56"	240	93 SQ. FT.
6-PERIOD DAY	12 STORAGE 12" x 12" x 12" / 2 DRESSING 12" x 12" x 36"	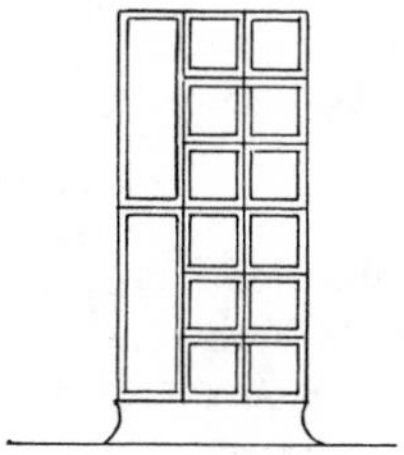	80"	240	133 SQ. FT.
7–8-PERIOD DAY	8 STORAGE 9" x 12" x 24" / 1 DRESSING 12" x 12" x 48"	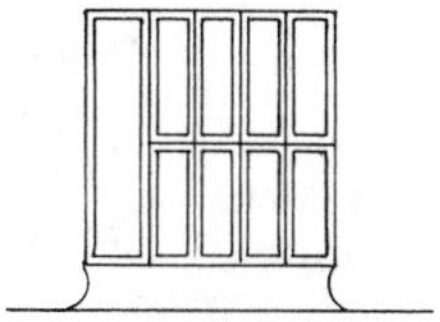	56"	320	187 SQ. FT.
7–8-PERIOD DAY	8 STORAGE 12" x 12" x 12" / 1 DRESSING 12" x 12" x 48"	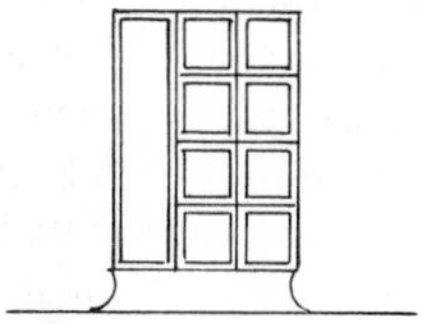	56"	320	133 SQ. FT.

Figure 73

DETAIL OF
LOCKER AND BENCH INSTALLATION

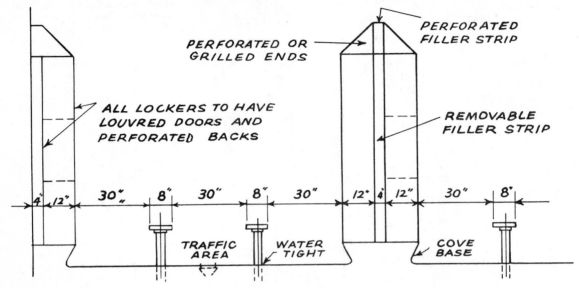

Note: Locker heights and widths are variable.

Figure 74

locker room.

A soap dispenser, preferably liquid-type, should be placed at valve height between every other shower head. The soap outlets should be supplied from a central reservoir of sufficient size to hold several days' supply.

TOWELING ROOM

The toweling room should have about the same total floor area as the shower room and be immediately accessible to both shower and locker rooms through an entrance to each. Floors should be of the same material as used in the shower room. Walls should also be of the same material as used in the shower room, except that the tile need extend upward only to a height of approximately 5'-6". Provision for drainage should be made in the toweling room.

If the wall between the toweling room and the dressing room extends to the ceiling, the ceiling should be of the same material as that used in the shower rooms. If there is a low wall between the toweling room and the locker room, the ceiling material may be the same as that used in the dressing room. Heavy-duty towel rails, approximately 4' from the floor and securely fastened to the wall, are recommended. A large foot-drying aid 18" high and 8" wide, and of the same materials as the walls, coved at wall and base, with bull-nose edge, is desirable. Benches should not be installed in this area.

ELECTRICAL FIXTURES

Adequate vaporproof light fixtures are needed in the toweling room. The lights in the toweling room should be controlled from the locker room by key-operated switches.

EQUIPMENT-DRYING ROOM

An equipment-drying room should be located immediately adjacent to the auxiliary team dressing room or in the locker-room area. A size of 200 square feet is usually sufficient. In larger schools, more space is needed. Sufficient air circulation and heat temperatures are necessary for proper drying. Rack or pipe installations are recommended for hanging equipment. Specially-designed hangers for athletic equipment may be used.

STORAGE ROOMS

TOWEL STORAGE

Towel service offered by the school is desirable. The towel room should have a window or Dutch door opening into the locker room. Soiled-towel storage is needed adjacent to the exit from the toweling room or the locker room. Large laundry receptacles are generally used.

SUPPLY-ISSUE ROOM

A supply room of about 200 square feet in area is needed for the storage of athletic clothing and physical education equipment issued daily. It should be adjacent to the locker room. A locking-type Dutch door for checking out supplies should be installed so as to serve those using inside as well as those using outside facilities.

OUT-OF-SEASON STORAGE AND REPAIR ROOM

This room should have sufficient space for the storage of all nonseasonal, new, and reserve equipment and supplies. Appropriate cabinets, drawers, hangers, and adjustable shelves are important items for good storage. Space should be provided for a work bench and repair unit. A solid partition with a door should separate this room from the seasonal-supply-issue room. A room of approximately 200 square feet is usually of sufficient size.

GYMNASIUM-EQUIPMENT STORAGE ROOMS

These rooms should be on the gymnasium level and directly accessible to the gymnasium. In divided gymnasiums, there should be one storage room on each side of the partition. The minimum area needed for the storage of apparatus, mats, and other equipment is 250 to 300 square feet for each teaching station. The door, or doors, should have heavy-duty hardware.

Piano storage space is best provided by a recessed area in the gymnasium sufficiently large (6' x 6' x 4') for the piano to be used. This will eliminate movement of the piano and the resultant markings on the floor.

COMMUNITY-RECREATION STORAGE

Provisions for storage of recreation equipment will depend on the type and sponsorship of the recreation program. Adequate storage space for community-recreation equipment and supplies should be added to the storage room, or separate facilities must be provided.

FIELD-EQUIPMENT STORAGE

If provision is not made for outside storage of equipment used out-of-doors, space for such storage should be located in the building, with immediate access to the outdoor playing areas. When so located, steep ramps should be avoided because of the size of the equipment used.

TOILETS

Toilet facilities must be provided in the following places: central locker rooms; auxiliary and community-recreation dressing rooms; and a small unit adjacent to shower, toweling, and trainers' rooms. Toilets for public use should be conveniently available to the foyer, auditorium, and gymnasium.

Toilet and lavatory facilities should be provided in proportion to the peak-period loads in the central locker rooms, as well as in auxiliary and community-recreation dressing rooms. In the planning of toilet facilities, provision should be made for direct access to outdoor activity areas.

In the boys' central locker-room area, there should be a minimum of two water closets, two urinals, and two hand lavatories for the first 30 students. Additional fixtures should be provided as follows: one urinal for 20 students, one lavatory for 20 students, and one water closet for 30 students. In the girls' central locker-room area, there should be a minimum of two water closets, two urinals, and two hand lavatories for the first 30 students. Additional fixtures should be provided as follows: one water closet for 15 students and one lavatory for 20 students. The placing of mirrors over hand lavatories should be avoided.

TRAINERS' ROOMS

Trainers' rooms should be located in close proximity to the locker facilities for athletics. In connection with these rooms, attention should be paid to the need for wide doors and convenience for ambulance service. The primary purpose of these rooms is to meet the particular needs of those engaged in the athletic program. They may also be used to serve those in community-recreation activities. Separate trainers' rooms should be provided for each sex when both boys and girls are engaged in an interscholastic athletic program.

These rooms should have the following physical characteristics: a minimum of 200 square feet; floors and wainscot of ceramic or quarry tile; adequate heating, lighting, and ventilation; electrical outlets to serve the equipment normally used in these rooms; hot- and cold-water connections for general use; and a refrigerator. Toilet facilities should be available to these rooms. A first-aid cabinet, cot, rubbing tables, and slop sink are some of the special requirements. For emergencies in physical education classes or elsewhere in the school requiring first aid, a health-service facility should be provided (see Chapter 15).

LAUNDRY

Laundry facilities or services should be provided for physical education and athletics. If there is a general school laundry, the particular needs of physical education and athletic groups may be met by this service. If special laundry facilities are installed for physical education and athletics, it is essential that they comply with local public-health regulations. In the latter case, the laundry should be located close to the area which it serves. It should be of sufficient size (about 200 square feet) to accommodate the equipment and personnel needed for the service it renders.

CUSTODIAL ROOMS

Rooms of sufficient size to house the custodial equipment and supplies are needed for properly servicing the physical education and recreation facilities. They should be located in or immediately adjacent to such areas. A slop sink and appropriate storage spaces are recommended. Office space for the custodians should preferably be located in one of these units.

STAFF FACILITIES

In order that men and women staff members can perform their functions most effectively, they should have certain facilities. These include adequate office space with proper furnishings, a conference room, a dressing room, showers, toilets, lockers, and moderate storage space.

If individual offices are provided, they should be approximately 120 square feet in size. When group offices are planned, 80 square feet should be added for each additional staff member. Offices should be as accessible as possible to existing teaching stations. They should be equipped with furnishings normally found in school offices, and a security cabinet or closet to lock up costly equipment. In large schools where there are several staff members, it may be advisable to plan multiple offices and a separate office for the department head. Related to these offices, there should be a conference room which may serve such purposes as staff meetings, student counseling, and conferences with other instructors and parents. Opening off the teachers' office, there should be a combination dressing, shower, and toilet room. Large-size lockers and moderate storage space should be included in this room.

THE DISABLED AND THE AGING

In addition to the consideration given the disabled and the aging throughout the text of this Guide and in Appendixes

G, H, and I, certain recommended standards are set forth below which are widely applicable in general facility planning.

DESKS OR WORK TABLES (FIXED OR SEMIFIXED)

- The minimum width of the kneehole space should be 20″, 24″ is preferred.
- The underside of the top should be 30″ above the floor.
- Aprons should be avoided on all desks and table tops, or should be recessed at least 8 inches.

FOOD SERVICES (PARTICULARLY CAFETERIA)

- The dining table should be a minimum of 30″ from the floor to the underside of the table top and should not have an apron.
- The height of the serving-tray slide can be the conventional height of 34″, 32″ is preferred.
- The clear width between the control railing and the tray rack should be 34″.
- The counter-balanced tray well should be at a height of 38″.
- Self-service water faucets should be placed so that the glass can remain on the counter surface while being filled.
- The counter surface should be 32″ high.
- Trays, where possible, should be wide enough to bridge the width of the wheelchair (20″ wide).

SHOWER STALLS

The following standards are recommended regardless of whether the shower stall is separated or incorporated into a gang shower to facilitate the disabled:[16]
- The size of the stall should be 3′ x 3′.
- The shower head for men should be mounted 6′-1″ from the floor.
- The shower head for women should be mounted 5′ from the floor.
- Soap trays should be 3′-6″ from the floor.
- Operating handles should be 3′-6″ from the floor.
- Grab rails should be 3′ above the floor outside the shower.
- Grab rails should be 1-1/2″ O.D. stainless-steel pipe installed on the side opposite the seat and halfway across the back of the compartment opposite the entrance. There should be 1-1/2″ clearance between the rail and the wall.
- When possible, the hand-testing outlet for men should be 5′ from the floor.
- When possible, the hand-testing outlet for women should be mounted 5′ from the floor.
- A diversionary valve to divert water to the hand-testing outlet, located toward the outside edge of the shower stall, should be installed. A flexible rubber hose 4′ long, with spray head, should be attached to the hand-testing outlet.
- The shower head, operating handles, diversionary valve, and hand-testing outlet should be mounted on the wall opposite the shower seat near the outside edge of the stall.
- Vandalproof shower heads should be used throughout.
- Each shower stall should have a folding seat as follows:

1. Seat frames should be constructed of 3/8″ x 1-1/4″ aluminum shapes, welded fabrication, 6063-T6 Alloy, chemically cleaned, given a "satinized" treatment by caustic-etch process, be anodized for 30 minutes, and given a protective coating of water-white lime-resistant

methacrylate lacquer. Metal parts of seats should have edges and corners rounded.

2. All other metal components, including round tubings, guide bars, brackets, keepers, retaining hooks, wall brackets, bolts, etc., should be stainless steel.

3. Seat pads shall consist of rubberized hair cushions 2″ thick, mounted on 3/8-inch marine-plywood bases, with all surfaces covered with "Elastic Naugahyde", heavyweight. This is to avoid decubitus ulcers (pressure sores) in many manifestations of disability—it is not a luxury or attempt to be plush.

4. Slotted holes in the aluminum frame to receive the seat keepers should be sloped to allow the seats to be held firmly against the frame. At pivot points, provided by bolts passing through bearing sleeves welded to the main supporting tubing, the aluminum frame should be tapped at the thread end of the bolts to receive the threads.

5. The seats should be constructed and installed so that they can be raised and lowered easily without binding or sticking, and so as to avoid excessive noise when dropped into position.

6. It is imperative that the seat be wider in the far corner, or in effect, turn the corner.

GENERAL CONSIDERATIONS

The material below will cover specialized features specifically related to teaching stations.

FLOORS

Gymnasium floors should be constructed so as to provide an even resiliency and still maintain a firmness that will provide a lively rebound quality. The floor should be smooth, tight, warm, dry, easily cleaned and maintained, resistant to marring, and light in color. Hard northern maple, properly installed, best satisfies these needs, although a good quality of birch or beech is acceptable. Flooring should be tongue-and-groove, of superior or second-grade quality, and at least 25/32-inch thick. Floors of 33/32-inches thick can be resurfaced a greater number of times than those of thinner stock.

It is recommended that gymnasium floors placed on concrete have sleepers of 2″ x 4″ or 2″ x 3″, treated with a preservative, placed not more than 16″ on center, and anchored at not more than 24-inch intervals with floor clips set in the slab.[17] The slab should be coated with 1/4″ to 1/2″ of hot asphalt pitch poured over membrane impervious to moisture. Subflooring of Douglas fir, hemlock, pine, or spruce boards not wider than 6″ should be placed on the sleepers at a diagonal and from 1/8″ to 1/4″ apart. A floor paper placed over the subflooring will aid in the control of moisture. Maple flooring can then be laid at 90° to the sleepers. Flooring should terminate 2″ from the walls to allow for expansion. An angle-iron strip or shoe should cover the gap between the floor and wall. The spacing for sleepers placed under sections of the gymnasium floor which will support bleachers should be calculated on the basis of the load to be supported. The boards on the finished floor should extend along the length of the basketball court.

Another floor designed for greater resiliency employs a series of floor joists and sleepers as illustrated in Figure 75. This

---

[16] See Appendix I.

[17] For further information, write to: The Maple Flooring Manufacturers Association, 35 East Wacker Dr., Chicago, Ill. They will supply detailed information on the various recommended methods of maple-floor construction. Information on floor finishing and maintenance is also available.

floor is more expensive than the one mentioned above. Another design eliminates both joists and sleepers by placing 1/2-inch cork board directly on a concrete slab with wood-block flooring (see Figure 76). Those having responsibility for approving the specifications of floor construction should keep in mind that new designs for floor construction and new procedures for laying floors are being developed.

Manufacturers provide detailed information for use of their products on gymnasium floors. The use of approved products in accordance with recommendations for their application insures a satisfactory floor in terms of function and prolonged life. A good finish seals the grains of the wood, which renders it impervious to dirt, water, and stains; is light in color without glare; is nonslippery; is resistant to marring and scratching; can be touched up easily; and is easy to clean.

Tiles of various kinds and quality, as well as other synthetic materials, are available for use in the construction of floors. Some of these are preferred to maple floors and should be investigated thoroughly before a final decision is made. Manufacturers of the various kinds of floor products are in a position to supply samples and specifications on quality, price, and installation.

Permanent markings on wood courts are painted after the first sealer coat. The lines should be chalked in by a surveyor or person with similar competence. All lines should be double-checked because errors are hard to correct once the lines are painted. The widths, colors, and locations of all lines should be based upon the current official rules for the various sports. Lines applied over the first sealer coat are much easier to remove if necessary because of rule changes, than those painted on an unsealed surface. A professional sign painter is qualified to paint the lines. Colored tape is being used satisfactorily in many buildings.

WALLS AND CEILINGS

The walls of the gymnasium up to door height should be of a material that is resistant to hard use. The finish should be resistant to marking and scarring, and should have a smooth, nonabrasive surface. All corners projecting below door height should be rounded. There should be no projections into playing areas or passageways. Lower portions of the walls should be finished with materials that can be cleaned easily without destroying the finish.

The following are recommended ceiling heights for various school levels: elementary, 18'; junior high school, 22'; senior high school, 22' at its lowest point. Local building codes and weather conditions in the various geographical areas will affect ceiling construction. Ceilings should be insulated to prevent condensation of moisture and should be of a light color to enhance light reflection. Acoustical ceiling materials are necessary in all instructional areas.

FOLDING PARTITIONS

Folding partitions make possible two or more teaching stations in the gymnasium. They should be power-operated, insulated against sound transmission, and installed to permit compensation for settling of the building. The door should be key-operated to ensure student safety. Such partitions should extend from floor to ceiling, and be recessed when closed. Floor tracks should not be used. A pass door should be provided at the end of the partition. When installing partitions in gymnasiums with open-truss construction, the space between the top of the folding doors and the ceiling should be insulated against sound transmission. If audiovisual isolation is not desired, a net may be used to divide the playing areas.

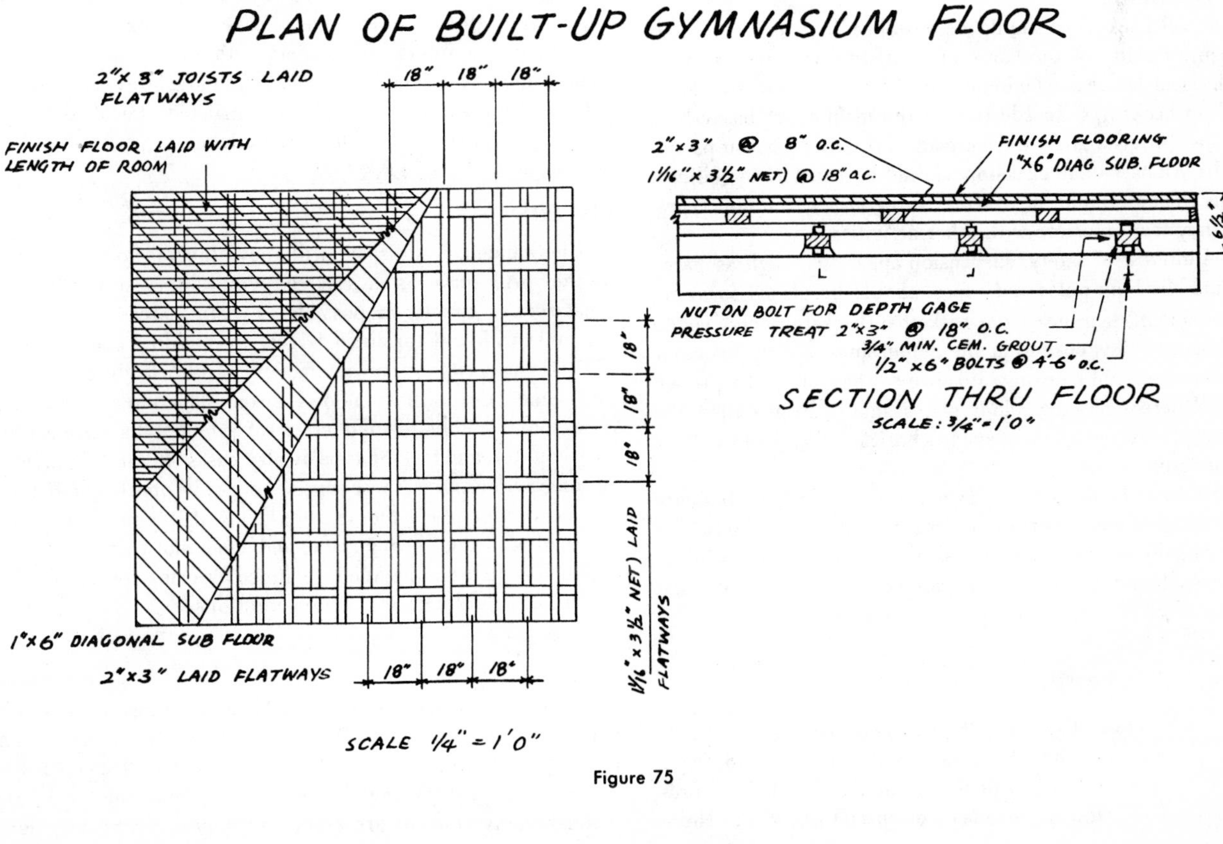

Figure 75

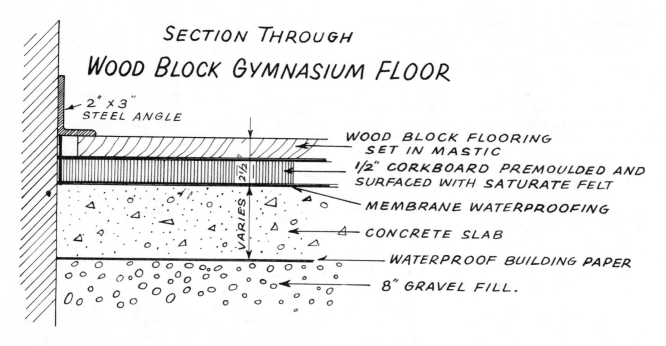

Figure 76

FIXED EQUIPMENT

If equipment is to be installed by being attached to the ceiling, provision for its attachment should be made before the ceiling is installed.

Basketball backstops should be installed in a manner that will ensure rigidity of the board and satisfy safety regulations. A mechanical device can be helpful in the operation of swing-up or fold-up backstops. In addition to the main-court basketball backstops, provisions should be made for other backstops on sidewalls. All basketball backstops should be attached to ceilings or walls. They should be of the swing-up or fold-up types where they may interfere with other activities.

In the interest of safety, suspension apparatus, such as bars, rings, and climbing poles and ropes, should be placed so as to have sufficient clearance from basketball backstops and walls. If wall apparatus is desired in the gymnasium, a strip of metal or hardwood should be firmly attached to the wall at the proper height. Where necessary, floor plates should be installed for fastening movable equipment such as horizontal bars and volleyball standards.

If mats are to be hung in the gymnasium, appropriate hangers should be provided. For safety reasons, padding should be installed on all walls in back of basketball baskets when needed. Rubber-tired mat trucks, which can be wheeled into storage rooms, have been found satisfactory for moving mats.

TRAFFIC CONTROLS

Good traffic control should permit the efficient movement of persons to and from the gymnasium, locker rooms, and other related service areas. Traffic planning should also include provision for the controlled movement of spectators. When there are balconies as well as seating on the main floor, each should be made accessible by separate ingress and exit passageways. All traffic arrangements for spectators should provide direct movement to and from bleachers without walking on gymnasium floors. Spectators should have access to drinking fountains, refreshment counters, and toilets without crossing the gymnasium floor. Steep and high stairways should be avoided. Ramps with nonslip surfaces may be constructed. Local and state building codes should be followed in detail.

FOYERS

Where finances and space will allow, foyers should be placed so they will serve as entries to gymnasiums and will guide spectators as directly as possible to seating areas. The size of the foyer will be determined largely by building codes and the spectator capacity of the gymnasium. Toilet facilities for men and women, ticket-sales windows, ticket-collection arrangements, checkrooms, public telephones, a refreshment-dispensing room with counter, and locking-type display cases should be provided. In some gymnasiums, these services might be omitted or reduced in size and number. Floors should be of a kind and quality that will withstand heavy traffic and some moisture. A pleasing appearance in foyers should be planned by using special building materials, colors, lighting, and decorations.

SECURITY

The school or recreation building is a structure of special complexity in developing features that lead to security. The facilities and program attract large numbers of people who move at all times during the day, throughout the week, and through many kinds of areas and in many different directions.

There is scarcely a real traffic flow and hardly a pattern, except for individuals. The building, viewed wholly, presents an intermeshing of movement. This is a large building into which people are entering through many outside doors, dispersing to offices, classrooms, or dressing areas, and distributing to different activity areas from the dressing rooms. Others may be spectators and are going to spectator galleries.

It is reasonable to believe that all students and visitors who come to the building are good subjects for public-relations accomplishments and, as such, should be welcomed. There should be some plan for pedestrian control and for the handling of visitors who wish to observe activities within the building.

Security within a building is accomplished in two ways, both of which are equally important. Each is necessary to the proper functioning of the other. These two ways in which security can be accomplished are:

- Constructing facilities according to a plan which makes for maximum security.
- Adopting an administrative plan for the direction and control of all persons using the building.

The physical layout will facilitate the accomplishment of security measures but will not guarantee them. A good administrative plan will, with a good physical layout, ensure the accomplishment of security. However, the implementation of a good administrative plan cannot completely accomplish effective security if the physical layout does not lend itself well toward the attainment of such security.

SECURITY FEATURES OF CONSTRUCTION

The doors at the entrances of the building constitute the first barriers against illegal intrusion. Outside doorways and entrances should be fairly wide and be exposed at the exterior surface plane of the building, rather than be recessed. Open and descending stairways, walled entries, and deep-set entrances should be avoided. The points of entrance to a building should be well lighted from dusk to dawn. The corners of the building should have floodlights which light the corners and face of the building. So-called "vandal lights" should be selected and protected to make them vandalproof.

Corridors which are continuous and straight, providing unbroken vision, add qualities of safety and security to the building, its contents, and its users. Corridors are often best lined up with entrance doorways, making possible a commanding vision of the doorway from the corridor, and of the corridor from the door. There should be an attempt to avoid angularities of corridors, and to eliminate small niches and cubbyholes. If such extra areas occur in planning, they should be included in the adjacent rooms or in the corridors so that a locking door will close off and control the space.

The use of night lighting within the building and at its entrances will give protection against vandalism and other forms of undesired conduct. Night lighting may necessitate some separate wires and switches to maintain a desirable amount of illumination. Switches for such lighting should be key-controlled to prevent their use by unauthorized persons. A building chart for day and night "on" and "off" lights should be developed. There should be additional directions for "on" and "off" at each switch, such directions to be changed according to need. A key-station system for night-watch checking is an appropriate inclusion for many buildings.

SECURITY OF THE BUILDING

To secure the building and its component rooms against illegal entry is the first and most logical consideration. Good door framing, substantial doors, and heavy-duty hardware and locks hold up against wear and abuse. In their long life and securing qualities, they constitute a reasonable investment. In reducing replacement costs for materials and labor, the installation of good hardware is an economy in the long run. In reducing loss by breakage and theft, the additional security factor of quality hardware should never be overlooked at any price.

A lock-and-key system, developed with the help of an expert in the field of building administration or keying, will usually result in a plan which considers some of the following features:

- A building master plan, including a lock-and-key system.
- Lock-tumbler adjustments so that an area may have its own control and authorization.
- Area division (vertical division) by responsibility or usage and, thus, for key assignment; or "level" division (horizontal division) for key assignment; or a combination of both vertical and horizontal divisions.
- A policy of not lending keys. The person to whom a key is assigned signs a pledge card for no lending. The keys for the facilities should be identified by a significant mark, and a policy should be established with key duplicators in the area that they shall refuse to duplicate keys carrying such identifying marks.
- A schedule or plan for door locking should be developed for a building. It may be practical or desirable to chart this on a master plan or to attach a plate or sticker to each door. Such instructional plates might be changed for temporary or permanent rescheduling of the facilities.
- An annunciator system in which outside or other doors of critical importance may be connected to an electrically-controlled system. The individual door can be connected in or out of the annunciator by a lock-controlled switch at the door, or a switch at the annunciator. Thus a door tampered with, or illegally opened after the annunciator for it is "on", will direct a warning signal. The annunciator may be developed to work in any of several ways:
  1. a light on a control box
  2. a sound at a control box
  3. an alarm sound of general broadcast in the building
  4. an alarm system with signals directed to the campus security office.

The nature of the annunciator response should be determined by whether it is wished to quietly apprehend the unauthorized person, or if it is desired to deter him or to frighten him away.

SECURITY OF THE POSSESSIONS OF PARTICIPANTS

The installation of lockers contributes an initial and basic security measure against loss. Heavy-gauge metal doors cannot be easily sprung, good-quality locks cannot be easily broken, or paired pierced lock tabs of good structural steel cannot be easily broken and removed.

The next reasonable step to take in establishing the security of the personal belongings of participants is to provide, or to require the participant to use, a lock of good quality. A good locker and good lock provide security only when the lock is closed on a fully-closed locker.

If the layout of a locker room is such that the lockers are in plain view of the checkers' office, the security factors are greatly strengthened. Large locker-and-dressing rooms ordinarily provide better security than small subdivided units. The presence of people and the lack of seclusion by room division contribute to security. Locker placement in which a sight line can be taken down all of the dressing aisles makes for ease of supervision and economy of time needed to check and control the dressing room.

A dressing-room inspection gallery with one-way glass simplifies the checking of the dressing room by authorized personnel. Separate galleries for viewing men's and women's dressing rooms should be planned if needed. These galleries should not be keyed to the building key system. A one-way glass allows the inspector to see the dressing-room area, but prevents the occupants of the dressing room from seeing the inspector. It probably does not matter whether or not it is known among the users of the dressing area that there is an inspection gallery. The gallery use can serve in both deterrent and detection action.

SECURITY OF PARTICIPANTS

In seeking the security of persons in the building, there are probably three main considerations: (1) security and safety in the use of the facilities, (2) security in normal and ordinary building use; and (3) security of persons in the building.

Security in Use of the Facilities

Security suggestions related to the use of a number of facilities ordinarily found in school and recreation buildings are outlined below.

- Gymnastics gymnasium and related trampoline activities— The room or certain pieces of the equipment must be locked except at times when an instructor is directly in charge.
- Swimming pool—All doors are to be locked unless unlocked by a person authorized to do so. When a door is unlocked for a purpose, the person unlocking the door is responsible for the accomplishment of the purpose in the pool area. Outdoor, and some indoor, pools may desirably be connected with a sonar detection system or a sound amplification plan which will announce illegal use or entry. The signal can go to one or several strategic control points.
- Steam room—The door must be locked from the outside when the room is unsupervised. Those persons who have keys and are authorized to lock the door need specific directions to do so before locking the door. The door should have an instruction plate by the door lock, bearing directions to those who have a key to lock the door. The steam-room control should be set at the maximum room temperature of 130°. This control should be tamperproof. The steam room should have a bar latch of the antipanic type (noncorrosive hardware) to make exit readily possible under any conditions, even if the door should be locked from the outside.
- Stairs in the viewing balconies should have handrails and lights at the sides, or luminous reflectorizing material on the edges.
- Bleacher seats should have aisles and exits to allow rapid clearing other than to the playing field or playing floor.
- Hot water available through shower heads should have a maximum temperature of 120°.
- Shower-room and dressing-room floors should be kept free of objects and obstructions which may cause foot injury.
- Activity-room floors must be free of objects, or floor plates which set up above the floor level.
- Shower rooms should be equipped with liquid-soap dispensers to avoid having bar soap on the floor.
- Areas for vigorous activity, where combatives or competitive sports are engaged in, need floor and/or wall covering to protect the participants. No specifications or classifications are given here, but every consideration is urged and every precaution should be taken.

Security in Normal and Ordinary Building Use

All accepted standard building practices which consider safety should be employed. State and local requirements and regulations for stair width, ingress and exit openings, fire escapes, fire alarms, fire extinguishers, and exit lights should be met. Open and straight hallways leading straight to outside doors can be clearly marked and used for exits. Antipanic hardware should be on all doors which lead from areas of assembled persons to corridors or to the outside.

Security of Persons in the Building

The participants' safety and security must be given some consideration in planning for the location of entrances to dressing rooms and to toilet rooms. Dressing-room entrances should be away from the main traffic and in the area where only participants go to change clothes. Toilet rooms should be away from direct view of the lobby, yet in service corridors rather than in isolated parts of the building.

SECURITY OF EQUIPMENT AND SUPPLIES

Many systems have been employed for the checking and care of portable equipment. Most materials need to be locked when not in use, and should be checked in and out by the instructor or an attendant. The checking method will determine where the checking will be done. Equipment and supplies may be controlled by the teacher near or in the play areas (as in a sturdy gymnasium locking cabinet or field cart). Some administrators have suggested that portable equipment either be fastened to tables or kept in locking-type cabinets.

SPECIAL SECURITY AND SAFETY MEASURES

Stairs should be well lighted. In some cases, the edges of stairs should be marked. Objects in the building which may need to be identified for safety or position may need to be color coded or marked. In basement passageways and around motors and equipment, it is important to mark corners, low pipes or beams, and safety-zone areas. On main floors, it is desirable to mark exits, fire alarms and extinguishers, some traffic lanes, first-aid boxes, and to indicate service and toilet areas with their appropriate service designations by door labeling or signs at door-top height. Color coding and designation of objects can be accomplished by painting the objects or zones according to a color code.

ADMINISTRATIVE PLAN FOR DIRECTION

The employment of both a night watchman and a day watchman is considered desirable for sizable operations. Since illumination is helpful in establishing security, it may be desirable to install an automatic control to turn lights on or off according to the degree of darkness or light. Some agencies employ custodians to complete the custodial work at night, with the idea that lights and people at work discourage intruders.

Proper marking and identifying of areas, and the reasonable directing and supervising of activities will increase safety and security.

Some security plans limit building access to one entrance, which is checked by an attendant. Appropriate identification may be called for, and the individuals leaving will be observed. This plan may provide greater safety for persons, and add security in the control of equipment and supplies.

Vending machines should be in clearly-lighted areas where they can be seen from several points, and the money collected in these machines should be removed frequently.

OTHER FACTORS

Provisions should be made for the installation of: electric scoreboards; a central sound system and public-address system; motion-picture projectors; radio; television; high-fidelity equipment (monaural and stereophonic); and cleaning machines. Wall outlets should be installed near cuppee eyebolts to permit special lighting as needed. Controls for gymnasium lighting should be conveniently located, recessed, and keyed.

Drinking fountains and cuspidors should be accessible without causing a traffic or safety problem. It may be desirable to provide a drained catch-basin, with grills flush with the floor, to care for splash and overflow. Drinking fountains may also be located adjacent to the entrance of the gymnasium or in the foyer.

Cuppee eyebolts should be installed in all walls at approximately a 15-foot height and at 10-foot intervals for decorating convenience. They may also be used for attaching nets and other equipment to walls at other predetermined heights. Bulletin and chalk boards should be provided in places where needed. If wall space is available, such boards may be provided for each teaching station in the gymnasium.

SELECTED REFERENCES

Brewster, Sam F., **Programing, Planning and Construction of College and University Buildings.** Provo, Utah: Brigham Young University Press, 1963.

Caudill, William W., **Toward Better School Design.** New York: F. W. Dodge Corp., 1954.

Environmental Engineering for Schools. Washington, D.C.: U. S. Government Printing Office, 1961.

Essex, Don L. (ed.)., **Heating and Ventilating Recommendations for New York State Schools.** Albany: The University of the State of New York Press, 1955.

Gabrielsen, M. Alexander, and Miles, Caswell M., **Sports and Recreation Facilities for School and Community.** Englewood Cliffs, N.J.: Prentice-Hall, Inc., 1958.

Guide for Planning School Plants. National Council on Schoolhouse Construction, 1953.

Herrick, John H., et al, **From School Program to School Plant.** New York: Henry Holt and Co., 1953.

Houston, Ruth Elliott, **Modern Trends in Physical Education Facilities for College Women.** New York: A. S. Barnes and Co., 1939.

MacConnell, James D., **Planning for School Buildings.** Englewood Cliffs, N.J.: Prentice-Hall, Inc., 1957.

Trends in School Planning. Palo Alto, Calif.: Stanford University Press, 1955.

Planning America's School Buildings. Washington, D.C.: American Association of School Administrators, 1960.

Ramsey, Charles G., and Sleeper, Harold R., **Architectural Graphic Standards.** New York: John Wiley & Sons, Inc., 1956.

Reid, Kenneth, **School Planning.** New York: F. W. Dodge Corp., 1951.

Schools in the U.S.A., Building Bulletin No. 18. Washington, D.C.: U.S. Government Printing Office, 1961.

Scott, Harry A., and Westkaemper, Richard B., **From Program to Facilities in Physical Education.** New York: Harper and Brothers, 1958.

Seagers, Paul W., **Visual Environment for Schoolrooms.** Bloomington, Indiana: Division of Research and Field Services, Indiana University.

Taylor, James L., **School Sites—Selection, Development, and Utilization.** Washington, D.C.: U.S. Government Printing Office, 1958.

Terry, Harry, **Mechanical-Electrical Equipment Handbook for School Buildings.** New York: John Wiley and Sons, Inc., 1960.

Williams, Floyd J., How to Design a School for Good Hearing, **The Nation's Schools,** May, 1961.

Part Four

Aquatic Areas and Facilities

Chapter 12

DESIGN and CONSTRUCTION of SWIMMING POOLS

THE INCREASING participation in aquatic activities by Americans since the end of World War II has been nothing short of phenomenal. The American public spends billions of dollars each year in the pursuit of one form or another of aquatic activities.

Aquatics recognition is culminated in the new $1,500,000 Swimming Hall of Fame complex, begun in 1965 in Ft. Lauderdale, Florida. This Hall of Fame, recognizing outstanding achievement in swimming, diving, water polo, and synchronized swimming, will include an outstanding aquatic-research library.

The cost of providing facilities for aquatics (pools, beaches, lakes, and marinas) represents a substantial investment by communities, schools, and private enterprise. Therefore, it is imperative that careful planning precede construction in order to obtain a safe, efficient, and economical facility which will serve the needs of people for many years.

The purpose of this section of the Guide is to bring to the attention of planners, architects, engineers, and others who might be involved in the development of aquatic facilities the best and most up-to-date information available. Space does not permit extensive, detailed coverage of all aspects of design and construction of aquatic facilities, nor the complete range of such facilities. Thus, the material herein deals essentially with the problems associated with the planning of swimming pools, beaches, and camp waterfronts. It should prove helpful to architects, engineers, and professional personnel responsible for the administration of schools and recreation agencies.

VALUE OF AQUATICS

People participate in aquatic activities because these activities are fun and exciting, they help develop strong supple bodies, they have great social value, and they are extremely challenging. Besides these motivating factors, the ability to swim may, under certain conditions, be essential to the preservation of life. Furthermore, the ability to swim "opens the door" to a number of other exciting aquatic activities.

NEED FOR SCHOOL POOLS

Residential pools, motel and resort-hotel pools, and public municipal swimming pools have led the pool-construction program in the country in the postwar period. It is estimated that there are only about 2,000 school swimming pools in the United States, half of which are indoor pools for year-round use.

If pools were located in every school system in the quantity necessary to assure instruction for all children, every child could be taught to swim at an early age and there would be a drastic reduction in the annual drowning rate in this country. A swimming pool, therefore, is an essential instructional facility and, as such, deserves the same consideration as other school facilities.

PLANNING CONSIDERATIONS

Before a decision is made regarding the construction of a swimming pool in a school or community, certain basic data should be accumulated by those responsible for planning, through the study of such factors as:

- awareness of existing swimming facilities in the area
- type of program to be conducted
- estimated number of people who will use the pool
- optimum size and type of pool to meet program needs
- availability of suitable sites
- estimated construction cost
- estimated annual operating cost and probable income
- procedures for planning, financing, and operating the pool.

Securing the services of a competent, experienced planner is desirable to assure a completely-satisfactory pool. Many of the problems encountered in planning and constructing a pool fall in the fields of architecture and engineering, requiring special consideration of such factors as heating and ventilation, electrical wiring, plumbing, acoustics, water purification, structures, and landscaping. Consequently, the advice of persons competent in these areas is essential. Consultation with experienced pool operators and aquatic specialists, who will be responsible for the program to be carried on in the pool, is equally important. Continuous inspection of all work as construction progresses is the only means of making certain that the pool is being built according to specifications.

DESIGN CHARACTERISTICS OF SWIMMING POOLS

ESTABLISHMENT OF THE DESIGN PROGRAM

An outline of basic uses—a design program—must be established by the individuals building the pool and those who will be responsible for its operation. A design program, carefully establishing fundamental application and service needs that are desired in the overall scheme, is the primary engineering consideration. Design factors that must be included should be determined jointly by professional consultants and pool owners and operators.

When experienced pool professionals help to fashion the design program, some of the more practical aspects can be reviewed with respect to importance and purpose. **Function versus cost** is the constant struggle.

The design program, when completed, should represent a very careful balance of such factors as pool size, competitive requirements, recreational activities, diving interest, planned water activities, subsoil conditions, filtration-plant economics, advantageous shell construction, imposed budgetary restrictions, future expansion possibilities, code regulations, possible operational program changes, and imposed site or technical limitations which will affect the final pool design. The pool professional—engineer or architect—is charged with preparing plans and obtaining bids for a project after the design program is formulated.

Figure 77
Astoria Pool, New York City

The cost that the committee is usually concerned with is the initial construction sum. When finalizing the design program, the committee can receive valuable pricing assistance from: (1) a local contractor who has established an outstanding business record; (2) an experienced pool contractor who enjoys a good reputation of continuing success; and (3) a professional expert—registered architect or consulting engineer—specializing mainly in swimming pool, bathing, and/or recreational facilities.

The true cost is much more than the initial sum. All cost studies used to establish the design program should be on a comparative basis of "capitalized" costs computed for equal amortization periods, interest rate, maintenance and operating costs, and other factors pertinent to any engineering cost study. Many program disagreements have been settled summarily when alternate design factors were compared on the basis of pool life, interest rate, annual maintenance-cost differential, and initial-cost difference.

FACTORS AFFECTING POOL DESIGN

SIZE OF POOLS

One of the major criteria is the need for at least one competitive course as a design requirement for new swimming pools. Private apartment-house pools, smaller semipublic facilities, and combination display-fountain swimming pools are the noted exceptions.

Pool lengths are determined by AAU and NCAA specifications. After length requirements are established for the design program, the water area can be studied with respect to other program requirements. A minimum area will automatically be derived from the number and width of lanes used (7-foot lane recommended). Sometimes the rectangular pool is all that can be permitted. Obviously, the other program activities must be "tailored" to such a basic, competitive pool.

When diving or recreational swimming and group water activities are programmed, distinct pool areas have to be designated and designed for these purposes. Code regulations and previous experience dictate use factors that minimize the safety hazard inherent in all aquatic programs.

Pool dimensions for multiple usage are usually determined by a combination of the several pool areas required, superimposed or joined, for the best architectural and engineering results. The "T" and "L" designs have been modified in endless procession. The "I" and "H" have evolved. "Fans", "boomerangs", and "trapezoids" have been designed.

In many situations, pool size is regulated by the occupancy limit. For years, an accepted factor for pool use has been 25 square feet of pool area per capita. More recently, 15 square feet per capita has been shown to be adequate and safe for shallow-water recreational swimming, while 175 square feet per capita for instructional diving, and 45 square feet per capita for swimming lessons, are minimum areas.

Recent studies have shown that the total complex area has to be considered in determining required pool size and safety limitations. Health and municipal agencies, recognizing the problem of area overcrowding, have established design criteria regulating maximum occupancy of combined deck-and-pool areas. Minimum recommended occupancy design factors are shown in Table 8. Minimum deck widths have also been established. The ratio of pool deck to pool area should exceed the minimum proportions recommended in Figure 78.

TABLE 8
MINIMUM RECOMMENDED OCCUPANCY DESIGN FACTORS

Activity	Indoor Pools	Outdoor Pools
Shallow-Water Area (under 5'-0")		
Recreational Swimming	14 sq. ft./capita	15 sq. ft./capita
Advanced Swimming Instruction	20 "	25 "
Beginning Swimming Instruction	40 "	45 "
Deep-Water Area (over 5'-0")		
Recreational Swimming	20 "	25 "
Advanced Swimming	25 "	30 "
Diving (based on area within 30 ft. of deep-end diving wall)	175 "	200 "
Minimum Walk Width*	6 ft.	12 ft.
Sum of walk dimensions*, on either side of the pool length or width, shall not be less than	18 ft.	30 ft.

* Walk dimensions shall be horizontal clear deck width, not including any portion of the coping or interior gutter sections.

Final determination of the "safe bathing load," using the recommendations in Table 8, can be established by considering the supervision available, the method of instruction, and the nature of the activity being conducted. For example, one instructor with no assistance should only supervise 20 to 25 non-swimmers in a class.

While the size and occupancy factors indicated above will facilitate optimum pool design, other considerations are important. There is a correlation between pool capacity and repeated, or shock, loading. A filter plant well designed for one or two peak loads per day will be unsuited for a new (peak) load of swimmers every half-hour. Either the peak load (occupancy factor) or the design basis of the filtration plant has to be changed to ensure the purity of the pool water. Experienced judgment should be carefully exercised in determining capacity and related design where heavy loadings or unusual factors are operative. In the case of pools which will experience heavy loadings, larger capacity-sized filtration plants are essential.

SHAPE OF POOLS

The rectangular pool is generally satisfactory for all-purpose instructional use and is most frequently designed for indoors, where available space and enclosure cost are limiting factors. Fan-shaped pools provide the services of the rectangular pool plus added areas of shallow water which meet the needs for instruction, and accommodate both swimmers and beginners.

L-shaped pools provide the standard rectangle, with an additional section at one end. The advantage of separation of activities is important.

T-shaped pools feature a bay projecting from one side, and are used as alternates to "L"s in larger pool sizes. The added section is always smaller than the main pool, and usually constitutes the deep-water area. Separating deep-water from shallow-water programs is a safety improvement.

Z-shaped pools permit a very-shallow-water section in addition to the deep-water appendage. Again, the separate-activity section features are apparent.

Pools in the form of an "H" or an "I" have varying proportions designated solely for specific activities and are, in effect, multiple pools—connected at their contiguous lifelines. Costs of these pools may be higher than for other forms because of their greater wall surfaces per unit of swimming area.

Pool shape is also influenced by program emphasis on non-competitive activities. Separate diving pools with elaborate

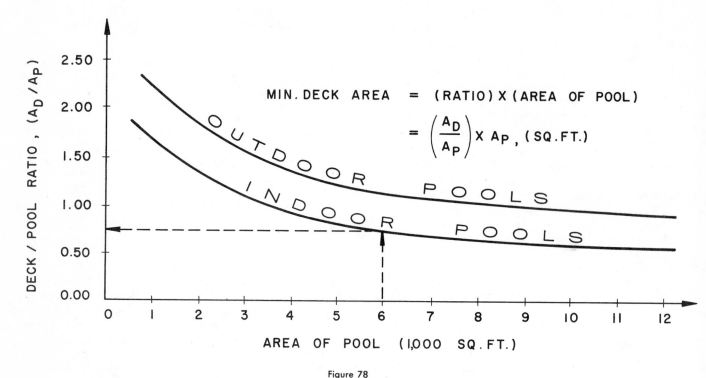

Figure 78
Minimum Recommended Area-Ratio Deck Area : Water Area

tower structures have increased in number in recent years. Lifesaving and water-safety instruction have imposed construction requirements previously overlooked. Water-polo interest and team contests necessitate the conformity of pool shape and depths to regulation sizes. Scuba-diving instruction has brought new emphasis on underwater sound systems, and easy pool egress. The popularity of synchronized swimming has led to the construction of new facilities and indicates new trends in area lighting and spectator accommodations.

WATER DEPTH

Water depths are determined by the various age groups using the pool. For educational purposes, a pool should be divided with lifelines, separating the water areas into deep (over 5'-0"), intermediate (3'-9" to 5'-0"), and shallow (2'-10" to 3'-9"). Familiarization pools, or so-called "wading" pools, are kept separate from the main pool. They are less than 24" in depth and are designed for separate activity and supervision.

The relationship of the bottom slope at water depths of 5'-0". or less, is of prime importance. A maximum pitch of 1:15 is recommended for all pools. Greater comfort and safety requires 1:20, and 1:25 for training and teaching. Sharper changes of slope, e.g., at the diving well, should be delineated with a red-stripe marker and lifeline. Minimum diving-well depths are exactly specified in standards of the FINA, AAU, and NCAA.

Pools are now being constructed with movable bulkhead walls to permit flexibility of area size and water depth. While initially high in cost, great flexibility of design program is possible with these facilities. Systems are also being perfected to vary the pool bottom. The program ramifications are apparent with a bottom capable of an infinite number of positions.

THE HYDRAULIC SYSTEM

All modern pools are designed for a recirculation and filtration system. Filters fall into two general classes: (1) granular

media (sand and gravel); and (2) diatomaceous earth or filter-aid. Granular-media filters for swimming pools are nearly always of the pressure-system type, while diatomaceous-earth units can be either pressure-system or vacuum-system. The flow in these systems can be reduced to the simple schematic diagram shown in Figure 80.

Each system includes: a pump for moving the water, piping to take the water from the pool and pass it through the filter and treatment units, and return piping back to the pool. Sterilizing and water-treatment additives are usually introduced in the return piping.

In the granular-media system, the water impurities are held on the top of the media bed (sand, anthrafilt, calcite, ground blast furnace slag, expanded shale, ground cinder, etc.). A coagulant (floc) acts to remove extremely small particles. The system is cleaned by reversing the flow and backwashing the bed.

Diatomaceous earth and/or filter-aid filters remove the water impurities as the flow passes through a thin layer of the diatomaceous earth or other filter-aid covering the filter elements. When the filter elements have become plugged with impurities and can no longer pass adequate water volume, the filter is cleaned by a backwash or by sluicing of the elements until they are entirely clean. A fresh layer (precoat) of diatomaceous earth is placed on the elements and the filter is returned to service. During the filter cycle, the element coating is kept porous and is prevented from early plugging, i.e., "short cycles", by the continuous addition of slight amounts of diatomaceous-earth slurry, also known as body coat.

POOL-SHELL CONSTRUCTION MATERIALS

Every pool shell is a foundation structure—**with the water on the inside**, and sometimes on the outside, too. In designing the pool shell, the particular soil mechanics must be thoroughly investigated. Borings—at least two at the shallow end and two at the deep end—provide vital reference information.

COMPETITION {INDOOR COURSE: 25 YDS. X 45' RECOMMENDED MINIMUM.
{OUTDOOR COURSE: 50 METERS X 60' RECOMMENDED MINIMUM.

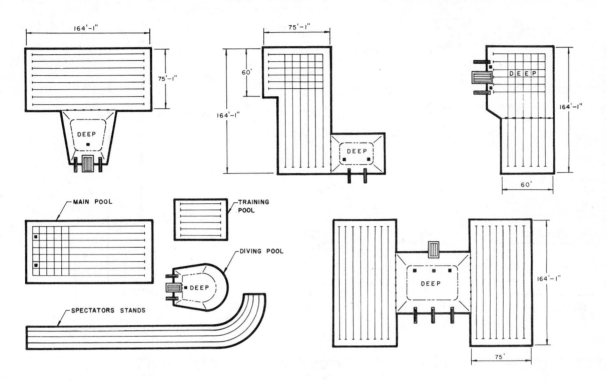

FREE-FORM (PRIVATE HOME, CLUB, MOTEL, ETC.)

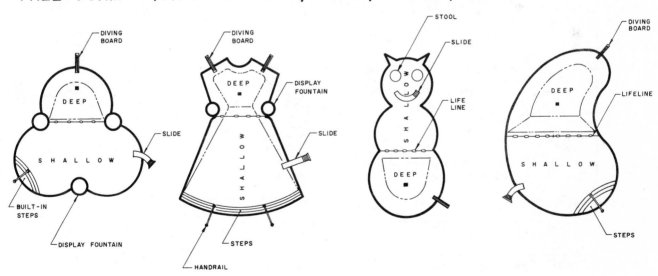

PREPARED BY

MILTON COSTELLO, CONSULTING ENGINEER

WANTAGH, NEW YORK 11794

Figure 79

Pool Shapes

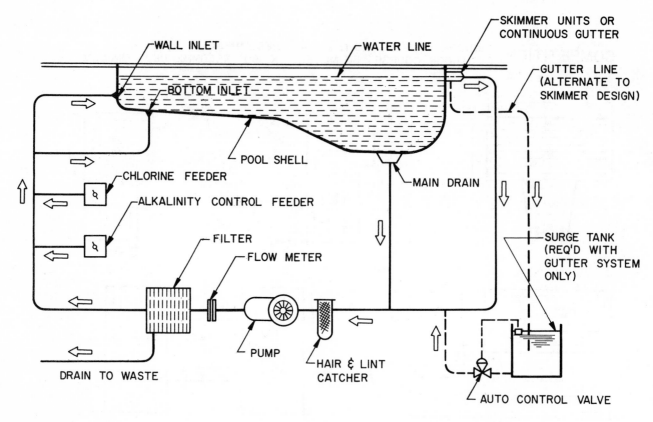

GRANULAR MEDIA AND PRESSURE DIATOMACEOUS EARTH FILTERS

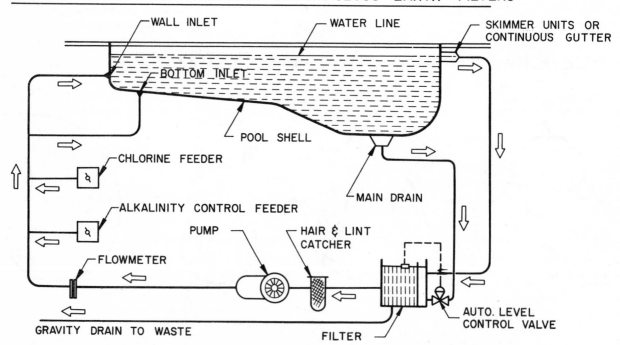

VACUUM TYPE DIATOMACEOUS EARTH FILTERS

NOTE: POOL OVERFLOW & VACUUM LINES HAVE BEEN OMITTED FROM ABOVE SCHEMATICS FOR CLARITY.

PREPARED BY

MILTON COSTELLO, CONSULTING ENGINEER

WANTAGH, NEW YORK 11794

Figure 80
Typical Pool Hydraulic Schematics

An experienced soils-investigation service should be engaged. Certified logs should show changes of stratum, spoon and casing blows at 5-foot intervals, the water table, the rock-core recovery, and all irregularities of the natural formations when present. Expert interpretation of boring logs should be obtained and then a shell construction used that will best satisfy the parameters.

For elevated (roof-top) pools, the building construction will usually indicate the optimum method. For concrete buildings, pools using concrete support beams and integral-formed pool bottoms are usually at an advantage. For an all-steel building, structural steel fabrication has advantages.

In-the-ground pools have been developed using many construction materials and techniques for the shell construction, including the following: poured reinforced concrete, painted; pneumatically-applied concrete, painted; carbon steel, painted; aluminum, painted; corrugated stainless-steel sidewall, painted concrete bottom; precast, prestressed concrete wall, poured concrete bottom; and brick or concrete-block wall, poured concrete bottom.

POOL-SHELL EQUIPMENT

Gutters and Skimmers

Most public pools have used gutter systems for removing the surface water. While design inertia has kept gutter pools prominent, automatic-surface-skimmer designs are increasing in favor with health officials and pool experts.

Gutters are decidedly more costly to install. The water lip must be installed dead level for maximum effectiveness. Roll-out-type gutters permit the most comfortable pool use, while recessed gutters are generally more difficult to negotiate. The efficaciousness of a gutter system at flooded peaks or at times of less than overflow level, are the most serious complaints. Generally, a gutter system, especially the recessed type, costs very much more than the equivalent skimmer, tile band, and coping system. Coaches object to skimmer pools for training and competition because of wave roughness.

Surface skimmers are relatively new to pool construction. They are container-type devices set in the top beam. A 6″ vertical opening, 18″ long, permits surface water to be constantly skimmed over a floating plastic weir in the skimmer unit. Vertical adjustment of the water level is compensated automatically. Surface skimmers are easy to install and eliminate the tedium of leveling a gutter, which accounts for their almost universal acceptance for private and semipublic pools.

Inlets

Pool water is returned at different locations through connections in the pool shell. Inlets can be either the wall type or floor type. Wall-type inlets are essentially perforated plates diffusing the water as it is returned. So-called "eyeball" inlets have a single large orifice which can be adjusted to direct the water stream in one direction. Floor inlets permit the pool water to be introduced at interior-pool-floor locations. Floor inlets also project a shallow cone 360° in extent.

Wall inlets are excellent for smaller pools and for configurations that would be difficult to reach with floor inlets. Floor inlets can be used to advantage in larger pools to obtain better pool hydraulics and a self-cleaning action.

Drains

Drains are devices located at the pool bottom for the collection of deep-end water, and emptying the pool. Many styles are available. Essentially, a removable grate in frame, set flush with the bottom of the pool is used. The grate should have a net free area at least 6, and preferably 10, times the area of the suction pipe below, and should be firmly secured in place so that it cannot be removed by swimmers.

Main drains are also used as pool-water returns, similar to an inlet, and styles to accommodate these systems are available. Perforated drains are desirable for safety, and should never be located below the diving trajectory.

Hydrostatic Relief Valves

Hydrostatic relief valves can be the most important shell equipment provided. Every pool, when empty, is essentially a boat hull. Water beneath the hull tends to cause the pool to float. It is suggested that pools not be left empty for any considerable length of time since serious structural failures can occur when an empty pool is subjected to external hydrostatic pressures.

Vertical poppet valves are used to admit water to, and prevent a build-up of, external shell pressures. Part and parcel of the relief valve should be a quality well screen. The perforated pipes commonly used are grossly inadequate. A proper design requires a sieve analysis of the surrounding soil, and specification of a graded, granular filter pack with correct well-screen size to prevent migration of soil fines that would cause malfunction of the valve seat.

Underwater Observation Windows

Improved designs and construction techniques now permit these important shell fixtures to be economically installed. Windows are important for coaching and study of dives, swimming techniques, synchronized swimming, and lifesaving methods. Laminated glass is the most acceptable form and it can now be placed without the heavy bolting, machined frames, and gasketing formerly associated with waterproof submarine bulkheads.

Interior Steps and Ladders

Pool egresses should include recessed and built-in ladders integral with the pool shell. There should be no projections in the water volume. Grab rails are used for convenience on the recessed ladder.

At the shallow water, large built-in steps set behind the main wall line are a requirement. Built-in steps should have a handrail every 4′ to 5′. The leading edge of treads should have a 3-inch nonskid, red safety stripe.

Competitive Starting Blocks

The starting blocks can be mounted permanently into the deck during the competitive-swimming season. During the noncompetitive season, they can be removed and the apertures can be capped, making the pool better adapted for teaching or recreational use.

Lifeline and Lane Anchors

Only recessed, cup-type anchors with replaceable eye hooks or bars should be used.

Alarm Systems

Alarm systems for indicating the presence of persons in the water when the pool is closed and unsupervised can perform important watchman service. Troubles with early models are being corrected and practical systems are now available. Shell requirements must be planned to allow future installations.

Underwater Sound-Amplification System

Improvements in underwater speakers now ensure excellent service. Audio characteristics vary with pool configuration and volume. Manufacturers can make specific recommendations for optimum use of their equipment. Underwater niches, conduits, and deck boxes should be provided during the shell construction.

Automatic-Timing Systems

European competitive pools are using precision-timing equipment incorporated in the structure. Low-voltage starting buttons trigger separate timing units in each lane when constestants' feet leave the starting block. Public clocks show the time while referee control buttons permit recall and time signals at all pool locations. With world records tumbling by tenths of a second, these improved timing facilities will soon be required on all new competitive pools.

INTERIOR FINISHES, COPINGS, AND DECORATIONS

Pool finishes can be classified as: (1) coatings; (2) tile; (3) plaster; and (4) natural.

Coatings

Protective coatings are the most diverse group of pool finishes. These materials are applied to the finished interior surface, and fully reproduce the texture of the shell construction. Of the paints, rubber-base is the cheapest practical covering. One season's service is all that should be expected. Water-resistant oil vehicle paints are available at greater cost, and yield greater service.

Two-part epoxy compounds (cold glazing) are tough and durable when properly applied. Care must be exercised in thoroughly cleaning the shell, especially concrete, which requires etching, phosphate cleaning, and thorough rinsing. Systems with minimum finished thicknesses of 15 mils have an indicated service life of better than 10 years. Inexpert preparation or application can cause localized failures. Shell imperfections can be covered slightly.

Elastomer coatings, using neoprene-rubber and hypalon, can be built up readily over most shell materials, regardless of surface or joint condition. Imperfections are readily masked by the rubber, which should not be confused with rubber-base paints. Finished coatings approach 50-mil thickness and can be renewed at the end of their expected life of 5 to 10 years.

Other chemical coatings use polyvinylchloride, polysulphide, polyisoprene, and constantly new organic compounds to effect desirable film qualities. Continued research and long-term field testing on all coating applications are required before comparative recommendations can be established.

Tile

Tile remains the classical permanent swimming-pool finish. The cost of setting tile has restricted its use on many pools to the waterline band, where serviceability is paramount. Custom installations, however, still command the majesty of detail, design, and color spectrum possible with a mosaic-tile installation. Its service-free permanence remains unchallenged. Watertight and weatherproof (frostproof) installation specifications are available from the trade associations.

Plaster

Plaster finishes are medium-cost applications capable of 4 to 8 years of service life. Plaster mixes are prepared from granular media and cement (usually white), plus coloring, waterproofing, and hardening additives. White sand can be used, although "marble dust," or limestone powder, has proved most popular.

A thin dash coat of 1/8″ to 1/4″ is best applied on clean, rough shell surfaces to establish bond and to "true" the interior shell geometry. A hard, thin finish coat is then placed as soon as possible. Plaster must be cured underwater immediately after placement. The best guarantee for long service is avoidance of strong acid solutions when cleaning.

Natural

Natural, or integral, finishes are important in obtaining low capitalized costs. Precast-stone terrazzo construction has been effected successfully. Thin-set (1/4-inch), epoxy terrazzo finishes promise unusual permanence when applied to carbon-steel or concrete pool shells. Concrete made with white sand, light-colored coarse aggregate, and white cement provides surfaces with lifetime character. Thin-gauge constructions, featuring stainless-steel sidewalls and fittings, offer permanently-prefinished water surfaces.

Copings

Copings can provide attractive architectural decor for the most elementary pool. The coping should be incorporated in the overflow-and-gutter system. Recessed gutters, roll-out, step-down, deck-level, elevated-curb, and modifications of these forms have evolved in many satisfactory styles. Local codes have influenced designs. A good coping must be of substantial permanent material, have continuous surfaces without crevices or corners, be nonslip when wet, be installed hydraulically true for the intended filtration service, serve as a handhold from pool side, and be firmly secured to the pool shell.

Precast-concrete sections are used to the greatest extent for pool copings. An infinite variety in color, surface texture, aggregate detail, and form is available. The heavy weight of the concrete has been a major drawback to the use of some of the better products at locations remote from the manufacturer.

New coping products have been developed using lightweight forms and materials. They include mosaic-tiled extrusions, preformed thin-section products having marble-epoxy formulations, etc. Natural and artificial lightweight aggregates are being used in cast concrete to overcome the weight problem and provide new textures. Semiprecious stones have been used for opulent coping applications.

Decorations

Decorative motifs and colorful ceramic figures are available for inclusion on the shell finish. Thematic emblems and abstract designs can be incorporated for unusual interest. The pool finish can be given fine decorative interest by judicious inclusion of these decorations.

Once the pool finish has been selected, the most important characteristic is color. For outdoor swimming pools, white should be used. Certain coatings tend to yellow after long exposure, and a bluish white may be preferable. For indoor pools, dead white, bluish white, or a mosaic random pattern of whites and light blues are excellent. Light-blue ceilings and walls on indoor pools, with proper lighting, can greatly improve the appearance of the filtered water. It is important to note that properly-filtered water is blue. The deeper the water, the deeper the blue. The white finish permits a greater degree of pool safety and maintenance of sanitary condition, and enhances the natural reflection that yields the highly-saturated blue color of the water in a good pool.

PIPING TECHNIQUES

Piping for the recirculation system should be carefully selected. The hydraulic system is subject to many deteriorating actions. Operating pressure is never a serious consideration. Most systems operate at 20 to 30 pounds-per-square-inch (psi) pressure, or less. Pressure diatomaceous-earth filters require the highest operating heads, usually in the range of 50 to 60 psi. Pumps for swimming-pool service generally have shut-off heads of less than 75 psi.

Recirculation piping should always be hydrostatically tested at a minimum of 75 psi. The test pressure should be maintained for at least two hours. It is possible to obtain a good piping system that meets these conditions, using iron, copper, cement-asbestos, aluminum, stainless steel, or plastic pipes.

Consideration should first be given to the pipe sizes. These can be readily computed during the initial planning. Suction velocities—5 feet per second (fps), or less—are always limited by the particular pump-suction conditions. Discharge velocities should be kept below 10 fps, but economic considerations dictate flows as high as 15 fps in the larger (over 4-inch) sizes. The National Swimming Pool Institute committee report on piping materials and corrosion calls attention to the corroding influence on nonferrous materials caused by higher flow rates. For the chemical services normal to swimming-pool operation, certain materials cannot be used where they would be subject to attack.

In many instances, the characteristics influencing piping design are external. Brackish, or acid, soils are prevalent at many pool sites. The external chemistry can be overriding and should be carefully investigated.

Subsoil support is also a major influence in the choice of piping material. The piping must be designed to compensate for soil settlement, expansion and contraction under operating conditions, and hydraulic reactions at changes of direction. Galvanic couples and stray electrolytic currents should be anticipated and corrected in the design.

Drainage and winter protection are important design considerations in northern climates. Accessible clean-outs and servicing connections should be provided initially.

In the pump room, the piping and all other equipment should be painted in accordance with an interesting and functional color code. Operating valves should be numbered and identified with brass tags. Lines should be neatly marked with flow arrows and identifying lettering. Valve schedules and operating instructions should be wall-mounted under glass.

ILLUMINATION SYSTEMS

Underwater lighting must be installed in accordance with the latest revision of Article 680, National Electrical Code, NBFU, or with the stricter requirements of local authorities. Consultation with the local inspection agency of the NBFU, or other governing agency, should be effected during the design-program planning to learn of local inspection requirements. If underwater lighting is used, it should be grounded to the cold-water system, and an authoritative electrical engineer should pass on the effectiveness of the installation.

Disagreement exists on recommended illumination levels. The practice developed by the industry is based on an index of watts per square foot. Values of 0.75 to 1.50 watts per square foot are common, but they are definitely low. Standards for general illumination have doubled every ten years since 1930. It appears that values of 2.5 to 3.0 watts per square foot (for incandescent-lamp fixtures) are required to develop the foot-candle intensity needed for the visual tasks of an active aquatic program. Water volume has a great influence on lighting levels throughout the pool shell.

More attention to the design spacing of underwater light units is sorely needed. The IES recommendation yields good results, although what appears to be needed is a volumetric basis of calculation similar to the "zonal cavity" computations being introduced to the profession. Current studies of underwater foot-candles should provide valuable new design data. At the publication date of this Guide, experiments are being conducted in the use of fluorescent light fixtures in continuous strips at the pool perimeter. Reduced source brilliance, decreased surface specularity and reflection, higher interior-illumination levels of the shell, and reduced operating costs are effected as compared with conventional underwater fixtures currently used.

White lighting is recommended for swimming pools used for night bathing. White lighting, containing a very light tinge of blue, has been used successfully. For pools that are lighted for nighttime use, amber lighting has proved most effective in minimizing insect attraction. Other colors reduce the transmission of light to a serious extent and cause the swimmers to appear garish.

Area lighting should be designed by a lighting specialist. Illumination levels greater than 125 F.C. are desirable for an active indoor program. Outdoor-pool programs require 60 to 100 F.C. on the deck surfaces as a minimum supplement to the underwater lighting.

Excessive source glare can only be obviated by a sufficient number of fixture locations. The fixture mounting height should be at least 30' for uniform comfort levels, and glare reduction.

Colored spotlights can be used effectively for architectural interest and for highlighting the diving tower, starting blocks, ladder locations, tile walls, and other areas. Ultraviolet-lamp (black light) bug traps can be used most effectively on outdoor pools, and especially in conjunction with amber lighting.

Infrared heating lamps and quartzline heating fixtures, in addition to providing light, can be used effectively for projecting radiant heat to ensure extra comfort at principal activity locations.

POOL MARKINGS

Pool markings should be very carefully specified on the detailed plans. All markings should be installed originally with some degree of permanency. Lines and targets should preferably be in tile. Game, synchronized-swimming, and teaching-station indicators should be distinct, but subordinate to competitive markings.

For pools with a coating finish, the outside edge of markings should be cut into the shell for permanent reference. Lines can be cut into concrete with a carborundum wheel, after which any contrasting color can be applied.

Tiled pools should have the lines and markers installed in the pattern. High-visibility contrast colors should be carefully selected for this work. Plastered pools should have lines cut similar to those recommended above for the coating finish, or tile strips and markers should be placed on the shell prior to plastering. Similar means can be employed to obtain distinct permanent markings on natural-finished pools.

From the design program, the pool engineer can specify and exactly delineate for the contractor the lines and markings for: safety lines, step edges, recessed ladders, competition lanes and turn-around targets, diving references, water polo and games, swimming and underwater instruction, synchronized swimming, teaching stations, and special program requirements of the operating staff.

DIVING STANDS

Diving stands afford opportunities for singular distinction. A tower structure can be placed and designed so as to be the center of attraction of a pool complex. Many "package" forms are available to fit any budget. Where more aesthetic expression is desired, stands and tower structures can be custom-designed. In many situations, a single custom-engineered structure costs less than multiple "package" towers.

High-diving platforms are becoming increasingly popular and their inclusion in the design program is strongly recommended. All platforms 3 meters high, or higher, should be constructed with a nonskid open-grate surface to permit the diver to view the water area below. An elevator was provided for divers using the 10-meter tower at the Olympic Swimming Stadium in Rome, Italy, during the 1960 Olympic Games.

For indoor diving, the ceiling height above the highest springboard or platform should be very carefully verified before construction. The clear height above the highest springboard should be at least 15'. A diving platform should have a minimum of 10' of clear space above.

DECK SPACE

Adequate deck space around the pool can materially contribute to its successful operation. Outdoor pools require a maximum of space, and their decks should be sized as shown in Figure 78. Deck ratios of 3:1 and 4:1 will afford even more convenient operation. Decks are preferably located so that sunbathers will be facing into the sun between noon and 4:00 p.m., while they are also looking toward the shallow pool water. This arrangement will readily accommodate the diving section so that the sun will be at the diver's back.

Large decks can be designed so as not to appear like overwhelming "seas of concrete". The use of different textures and colors, and the arrangement of accessory plantings, decorative walls, and fountains are vital planning functions. An excellent opportunity exists in the planning of the pool deck. Too many false economies have been effected through unimaginative and poorly-planned deck areas.

Decks for outdoor pools should be carefully engineered and controlled during placement. The preponderant majority of outdoor-deck installations fail in the area adjacent to the pool because of poorly-specified compaction practices. A competent soil consultant can best advise on particular soil conditions. Where possible, the contract should provide for construction scheduling that will allow a maximum self-consolidation period after the pipe trenches are filled, and before the decks closest to the pool perimeter are poured. In certain soils, a two-foot overburden placed for a short period will develop the necessary relative density to prevent future settlement problems. There is nothing more disheartening, at an otherwise excellent facility, than cracked and settled decks adjacent to the pool. The effort to obtain expert advice for a first-class job is, again, well worthwhile.

Impervious soils can also cause serious problems, especially in freezing climates. The same is true for decks on soils of high capillarity. In either case, freezing water soon destroys the best-designed decking. Engineering designs must provide base courses that will be drainable, and decks that can be caulked or sealed against run-off.

Indoor pools cannot be designed for such generous deck areas. The minimum area, however, should be at least equal to the recommendations shown in Figure 78. Walk widths should be a minimum of 6' indoors and 12' outdoors. The sum total of clear walk dimensions in any one direction should exceed the recommendations shown in Table 8.

Decks have to be textured to prevent slipping when wet. Within the 10-foot border around the pool, all areas must be carefully pitched at 1/4" per foot. Cricket lines, drainage flow, and finish elevations at the pool perimeter and adjacent deck area must be carefully denoted on the construction plans, and their placement strictly supervised.

SWIMMING-POOL ENCLOSURES

Pool enclosures have created considerable interest in recent years because of the increased utilization they provide. In very-cold locations, the permanent building is as important as the pool proper. Problems unique to all pool enclosures can be particularly vexing for a permanent building. The designer must definitely account for: tolerable sound levels, humidity and temperature control, condensation effects, ventilation, traffic pattern (spectators, locker entrance, instruction areas, etc.), and lighting design. These interrelated factors demand the coordinated technical direction of highly-skilled professionals.

Since World War II, the indoor-outdoor pool has been introduced. These combination pools usually feature a sectionalized building. Parts of the structure can be transported so as to provide an open exposure, preferably Southern. Rotating dome sections, telescoped buildings, and sliding glass walls and roofs have been used effectively. Serious consideration should be given to the construction of two separate pools when the question of the indoor-outdoor pool is an issue. The cost of constructing a two-pool complex is usually no more than that of the combination facility.

Removable covers offer wide latitude for pool-area utilization. These enclosures are primarily for the extension of the outdoor swimming-pool season. Originally, removable hothouse aluminum hoops covered with polyethylene film were used on small pools. More substantial aluminum-frame structures have been developed, including long-span structural trusses, permanently enclosed. The glass walls and roof are removable, and, for some installations, the frames may be removed in a day's time.

Air-supported structures are marketed that rely on a slight positive pressure to inflate and maintain the flexible-membrane covering. Problems with draftiness, acoustics, lighting, and condensation exist. The shelters can be erected or removed in a day's time. They are a practical investment where swimming instruction is the primary pool function and the cost of an improved partial or removable cover is prohibitive.

Membrane covers using ribs of compressed air have been patented. The ribs are sewn into the cover and function as structural hoops when inflated to full pressure. The cover is securely anchored to the deck when serving to extend the outdoor season.

Other practical removable covers and engineering compromises are possible.

Partial, permanent frames with open centers offer great promise. Permanent "skins" of formed transparent plastic provide a clear covering on unobtrusive lightweight frames. This open dome extends upward from the edge of the deck to the central opening, approximately 22' above the pool perimeter. The lower 8' can be partially permanent, or fully removable. Heating will be achieved by radiant pipes in the deck slab and exterior seat walls, supplemented by overhead infrared radiant-heating fixtures. Entering snow or rain (through central opening above pool) does not detract from the high utilization. The maintenance of **outdoor**-pool architectural and aesthetic values prevails while providing a year-round **indoor**-pool facility. Low maintenance and relative cost make the construction extremely attractive.

THE INDOOR SWIMMING POOL

When considering the building of a swimming pool, an important decision which must be made is whether to construct an indoor or outdoor pool. The outdoor pool can be larger, will usually cost less, and certainly will provide an excellent summer aquatic facility for the community. On the other hand, an indoor pool extends the aquatic opportunities throughout the entire year, which results in a 100 percent return on the community's investment.

Most educators firmly believe that, whenever possible, an indoor rather than an outdoor pool should be constructed. The indoor pool has far greater utility than the outdoor pool and its activities will not be limited by weather. An indoor pool enjoys efficiency of administration and maintenance not realized by its outdoor counterpart. If the pool is constructed without windows and has adequate lighting over the entire deck and water area, it can be supervised easily and safely, and will always be a clean, pleasant place for both swimmers and spectators.

In addition to the increasing number of school swimming pools, America has benefited from having many excellent indoor pools in YMCAs, YWCAs, Boys' Clubs, and other youth-serving agencies, which yearly conduct a large percentage of the teaching of swimming to the children of the community. To round out the network of indoor pools in America, there are thousands of private and hotel-type facilities which are largely used for leisure-time aquatics, and a few municipally-operated pools.

IMPORTANCE OF SCHOOL POOLS

It is important that the schools assume a more vigorous role in developing and promoting aquatic facilities and programs, because aquatics is not only an essential part of the physical education program, but also the most popular recreation activity among youth. The teaching of swimming can be accomplished easier and more effectively at the elementary-school age level. It is the hope of professional people that, as America's school system grows, small, shallow "training pools" will be constructed in elementary schools throughout the country.

Learn-to-swim classes should be provided for children and adults not involved in the school's physical education program. As soon as such a teaching program has been established, many related aquatic activities, such as lifesaving, synchronized swimming, skin and scuba diving, and competitive swimming (for the better swimmers), can be introduced. During the year, a general water-safety program should be offered to assist the student body in becoming acquainted with boating and other water-safety precautions.

RECOMMENDED SIZES FOR INDOOR POOLS

The most troublesome problem related to the acquisition of indoor swimming pools is the cost of the housing over the pool. Pool enclosures may range in cost from an amount equal to the cost of the construction of the pool basin and filter plant to a cost which is five to ten times this amount. One of the pressing needs is for low-cost pool enclosures which have a minimum life of 20 years.

THE ELEMENTARY-SCHOOL POOL

The elementary-school pool, or training pool, which is designed primarily for instructional purposes, is one. of the most desirable pools to be constructed in the community. It is not costly—since diving is excluded—thereby making it possible to use a low ceiling (regular classroom height of 8-1/2' to 10' is suitable). The water depth usually ranges from 2' in the shallow end to 4' or 4-1/2' in the deep end. The overall dimensions of the pool are as follows:
- minimum width: 16'
- desirable widths: 20', 25', or 30'
- minimum length: 36'
- desirable lengths: 50', 60', or 75'

The minimum dimensions of 16' x 26' should not be constructed except where it is impossible to build a larger size. In these small pools, the capacity for swimming instruction is only 15. When community use is to be made of the pool, the recommended minimum size is 60' x 25'.

Some school districts find they have vacant classrooms resulting from shifts in enrollment or population. A training-type pool may be easily inserted into an area usually occupied by the space of two classrooms. The filter plant and dressing room can be located in a third classroom, or constructed as an addition to the two classrooms if outdoor space is available adjacent to the two classrooms being used to house the swimming pool.

THE JUNIOR-HIGH-SCHOOL POOL

The junior-high pool should be larger than the elementary-school pool. The recommended dimensions are:
- minimum width: 25'
- desirable widths: 30', 36', or 42'
- minimum length: 60'
- desirable length: 75'

Diving is not essential for the junior-high-school pool, but a one-meter or deck-level board is desirable. If no diving is to be included, then the water depth should range from 3' at the shallow end to 5' at the deep end. The ceiling height in such a pool should be between 10' and 12'. When diving is to be included, the ceiling height should be 16', with a water depth of 9'.

THE HIGH-SCHOOL POOL

The high-school pool should be designed to serve the total aquatic needs of the high-school students, and, in some instances, the total community's needs. The typical aquatic program of the high school will include:
- instruction in swimming and diving
- water safety, lifesaving and survival swimming
- recreational swimming and diving
- special activities: skin and scuba diving, synchronized swimming, and bait casting
- basic boating and canoeing instruction
- competitive swimming
- swimming for the disabled

The high-school pool should be adequate in size to meet the needs listed above. The recommended dimensions are as follows:
- minimum width: 36'
- desirable width: 45'
- minimum and
    desirable length: 75'-1"

Figure 81
Mott Elementary School Pool, Flint, Michigan

Figure 82
Lincoln Junior High School Pool, Wyandotte, Michigan

Figure 83
Evanston Township High School Pool, Evanston, Illinois

The recommended water depths for high-school pools are:
- shallow end: 3'-6" (3' when pool is to be used by elementary schools)
- deep end (under diving board): 9' for one-meter diving board; 12' for three-meter springboard

For ceiling heights and deck space, see the section on "Design Characteristics of Swimming Pools."

THE COLLEGE OR UNIVERSITY POOL

The total enrollment of students in the institution will determine the size and number of swimming pools needed. In some situations, three or four pools might be necessary. The objectives of the program are basically the same as for the high school, except that in situations where a professional physical education curriculum exists, the needs of this curriculum should be included in the important program objectives.

The most desirable size of university swimming pools serving an enrollment of 10,000 students is 50 meters in length, with a minimum of six 7-foot lanes (eight lanes more desirable). This size pool should have incorporated into it, by use of a bulkhead or through the use of the L- or T-shape design, a regulation NCAA and AAU "short course", which measures 75' in length and a minimum of 45' in width (the width may be greater;

thus a rectangular pool 50 meters long and 75' wide would meet both requirements listed above).

A separate diving well and, in some instances, a shallow instruction pool are desirable features of the university swimming complex. A pool planned by a college or university which is smaller than the 50-meter pool recommended above should be a minimum of 75' long and 45' wide. It should have six 7-foot lanes for competitive swimming. A separate diving well should be considered.

OTHER INDOOR POOLS

Indoor pools located in voluntary youth-serving agencies (Boys' Clubs, Ys, etc.) or hotels, or those under the sponsorship of municipal-recreation departments or commercial agencies should conform to high-school or college standards. If young children are to be served, the depth at the shallow end should be reduced to 36" or 39".

The preceding discussion regarding the need for school swimming pools should not be construed as eliminating the responsibility of municipalities, particularly recreation departments, or voluntary youth-serving agencies, such as the Ys and Boys' Clubs, for providing indoor facilities for their constituents.

SPECIAL FEATURES OF THE INDOOR POOL

ACOUSTICS

The very latest acoustical treatment of walls and ceilings should be used in order to reduce the noise in the pool. The high swimming-pool noise level and the difficult nature of the facility itself make it essential to treat not only the ceiling, but also at least two of the walls of the natatorium with appropriate waterproof, fungus-resistant, acoustical material.

VENTILATION

The proper movement of air which will control humidity and condensation while at the same time not prove uncomfortable to the swimmers must be carefully studied. The chief factor is the proper location of air intakes. If located at deck level, they are liable to cause drafts which are uncomfortable to swimmers.

OVERHEAD LIGHTING

There should be a minimum lighting level of 50 footcandles at the deck and water levels. The lights should be directed over the water as well as over the deck.

UNDERWATER LIGHTS

The top of the lights should be at least 2′ below the water surface in the shallow end. The lights on the end walls should be so placed that they are located directly under the mountings for the racing-lane anchors. The sidewall lights should be at least 2′ below the surface in the shallow end and lower in the deep end. A suggested location in the deep end is a point halfway between the surface and the bottom. The lights should be so placed that they will not be opposite each other and will be angled 3° to 5° toward the bottom. This will increase the illuminated area.

The lights on the deep and shallow ends should be on separate switches so they may be turned off during swimming meets. The entire system must be grounded properly and meet the latest requirements of the National Electric Code (NBFU). For further details, see the section on "Design Characteristics of Swimming Pools."

DECKS

All decks and floors should be on nonslip tile or other nonslip material. The decks should be a minimum of 6′ wide up to a maximum of 20′.

Wide decks increase the opportunity to conduct good swimming instructional programs. If a narrow 6-foot-wide deck is used on one side, then the opposite deck should be at least 12′ wide. There should be at least 15′ of deck at the deep end and at least ten feet at the shallow end. The decks should slope toward the drains, which are located at the edge of the pool, not back away from the pool.

COLORING

The coloring in the natatorium should be light and cheerful. Pure-white tile should always be used on the inner shell of the tank. Once water is put into the pool, the white tile will provide a clean, sparkling impression to the water, which is not true in pools where a colored tile is used. A contrasting dark-brown or black tile is very appropriate for the bottom lines.

There are three other areas to be considered in selecting the color scheme: the deck, walls, and ceiling. White or light blue are suggested for the ceilings. Light colors, but never yellow—usually two complementary colors—give the desired effects for the deck. A darker deck (shades of brown) will give a clean appearance. Light-colored decks tend to show every sign of dirt.

OFFICE AND STORAGE SPACE

Office and storage space is needed. The instructor needs a desk and filing space to plan and record the aquatic activities. The office should be so located that it commands complete view of the swimming area. It is suggested that the swimming-pool side of the office be of glass.

MAINTENANCE ROOM

A pool-maintenance room, directly adjacent to the deck, for house-cleaning supplies and off-season equipment is necessary for proper health and sanitation. The minimum recommended size of the room is 100 square feet.

INSTRUCTIONAL-EQUIPMENT ROOM

An instructional-equipment room for the storage of kick boards, swim fins, inner tubes, diving rings, face masks, water-safety instructional equipment such as torpedo and ring buoys, and guard jackets should be provided. A minimum size of 100 square feet is recommended.

PUBLIC-ADDRESS SYSTEM

The public-address system has become an essential feature of the swimming pool. It should be permanently built into the natatorium at the time of construction. It is suggested that 12 to 24 low-level speakers be strategically located in the ceiling. This will greatly eliminate dead spots and echoes. Underwater public-address systems are being developed, and their use is most helpful in conducting synchronized swimming programs. There should be 2 to 4 wall jacks available for connecting microphones.

CEILING

The ceiling should be 15′ above the highest diving board.

DIVING AIR OUTLET

Installation of an air-bubbling outlet on the bottom of the pool under each diving board will disturb the water enough so that divers in competition will have clear visibility of the surface of the water. Portable air compressors with hose connections are suggested for older pools.

SPECTATOR SPACE

A balcony is an integral part of the swimming facility. Parents and friends will want to watch all phases of the swimming program. A balcony size of 600 to 1,200 square feet is suggested. It is desirable to have it raised and railed in so that spectators will find it impracticable to climb out and go on the deck.

Roll-away bleachers may be used where a balcony is impractical or too costly. When not in use and rolled back, such bleachers provide added deck teaching space.

Special ventilation for the balcony, so that the air temperature may be colder than at the deck level, provides for greater comfort of the spectators. Floor drains are also suggested in the balcony for proper maintenance of the area.

LOCKER ROOM

It is desirable for health and sanitation reasons to have special swimming-pool locker rooms. Skillful planning of the natatorium, however, will make it possible for swimmers to use the gymnasium locker rooms, and, conversely, the pool lockers can be used in special situations by students using the gymnasiums.

The design of the swimming-pool locker room must be analyzed to ensure good procedure patterns. Points for consideration are: (1) entrance to the locker room; (2) ticket collector; (3) suit distribution and the collecting of valuables; (4) clothing storage; (5) toilets; (6) shower rooms; (7) dressing area; and (8) entry to the pool.

The following points related to procedures for leaving the pool should be analyzed: (1) leaving so as not to conflict with the incoming class; (2) suit-disposal area; (3) towel-and-drying area; (4) towel disposal; and (5) dressing and leaving the locker room.

LOCKERS

Lockers should not be more than 5' high. Children should not have to climb up on benches to hang up their clothes. A locker of 12" x 12" x 5' is recommended, although where space is a problem, half-lockers (30" high) can be used.

WET TOILET

A "wet" toilet area, separate and different from other toilet areas, to comply with local and state requirements, should be provided for pool users in a location where it can be supervised.

GENERAL OPERATING PROCEDURES

The pool should be considered an essential part of the educational plant, and the program an integral part of the school curriculum. Therefore, the cost of heating and lighting the pool should be a part of the overall school operating expenses.

One maintenance man should be trained to maintain the entire swimming facility, just as other men are trained to maintain classrooms, auditoriums, and grounds. Filtration and backwashing, the testing of water, chemical treatment, the sanitizing of decks and floors, the care of air and water temperatures, and the handling of towels, suits, and other equipment are but a few of his duties.

The role of the instructor has changed greatly since the end of World War II. Prior to that time, the pool instructor's position might be held by a young man not holding a teaching certificate. This practice has changed drastically to the point where administrators are, for the most part, hiring men and women who have been trained in professional physical education programs.

When hiring a swimming pool director, the first point to consider is his maturity and his dedication to the job. As the years go on, his value to the community will be measured by how he meets the demands of his job. There are three basic criteria which may be used in the selection of the director:

- A man should only be placed in charge of a swimming pool when he has proved that he knows what to do in case of an emergency. He must have an emergency plan ready which will ensure the community that everything possible will be done in times of emergency. He must be a Red Cross Certified Instructor in Water Safety and should also hold a certificate in first aid.
- He should be very conscious of pool sanitation and health.
- He must be more than a coach. He must be interested and qualified in conducting and promoting all phases of the aquatic program so that both children and adults will enjoy using the swimming pool.

The preceding material has presented many of the desired practices and features essential to the operation of a successful indoor-swimming program. School and recreation administrators should be well informed about the requirements and specifications of the type of pool they desire, and be familiar with the program potentials.

OUTDOOR SWIMMING POOLS

In the development of any outdoor swimming pool and related facilities, there should first be a master plan of the area in which the swimming pool is to be located. A swimming pool by itself is never as successful as a pool planned in conjunction with other recreational facilities, such as baseball diamonds, tennis courts, volleyball courts, a craft center, and a community-center building. One activity complements another, and a pool thus related to other recreational facilities will be much more successful and will be easier to administer.

Residential pools and pools designed for hotels and motor courts are used almost exclusively for recreational swimming and sunbathing. On the other hand, pools at private clubs, city parks, and recreation areas are normally used for both recreational and competitive swimming. Competitive swimming is the impetus for wide usage of the pools by youths and young adults.

Publicly owned and operated pools probably constitute the largest market today for outdoor pools. An increasing number of public pools are being built each year. The private-swimming-club-pool idea is fast expanding. The club pool takes care of a great need and is an excellent idea, but it generally will not take care of the needs of a community. The vast majority of potential swimmers come from families which cannot afford a family membership in a public pool, or an individual membership, or pay the daily gate fee. Therefore, the building of swimming pools for the general public today is largely a governmental responsibility, whether it be municipal, county, state, or federal.

CLASSIFICATION OF OUTDOOR POOLS

PUBLIC POOLS

Public pools are ordinarily those owned and operated by municipalities, counties, schools, park districts, states (as in state parks), and the Federal Government (as in a national park).

PRIVATELY-OWNED POOLS

The second category of sponsorship is the privately-owned pool which serves the public. The YMCA, YWCA, Boys' Clubs, YMHA, and other organizations build outdoor pools, or indoor-outdoor pools, which serve both winter and summer needs.

At most country clubs today, an outdoor swimming pool is considered a necessity if the club is to be a family-type club rather than just a golf club. These pools must be attractively designed, well built, and expertly operated. The private swimming club is expanding and serves a real need, particularly in the suburban areas.

Most apartment houses are including a swimming pool in their complexes because they realize this is a necessity if the apartment units are to be rented at capacity. Roof-top pools are no longer unique.

Many public-housing projects are including swimming pools. These are, of course, publicly owned, but are considered private since the use of the pool is restricted to the occupants of the particular housing project.

Hotels are fast coming to realize that they must have a pool, and the outdoor pool is the usual thing. In many northern communities, the pool has been enclosed, either by a permanent or semipermanent structure.

Pools are included as a must at resorts and resort hotels and motels. Motels for transients must also include a pool, even though some of them seem to be satisfied with the smallest pool which will answer the purpose—in many instances, a pool only 20′ x 40′ is installed.

It is interesting to note that some motels have become aware of the nonuse of the pools by motel guests at the middle of the day, and the pools are being made available to community groups during this slack period. In several instances, the pools have been opened to underprivileged or low-income groups which have no other swimming facilities available.

COMMERCIAL POOLS

Commercial pools are classified as those operated for a profit by an individual owner or corporation. These pools are usually separate and independent of any other recreational facilities. Many such pools were built in the past 25 or 30 years, but experience has proved that a pool by itself is not as good a business proposition as a pool along with other recreational facilities. These additional facilities can include a par-3 golf course, golf driving range, miniature golf course, bowling lane, skating rink, group-picnicking area, and similar facilities.

TYPES OF POOLS BY DESIGN

The **rectangular swimming pool** was probably the original pool shape and a great many rectangular pools are still being built. Some of the first pools were 50′ x 100′, or even 100′ x 200′. Many indoor pools were 30′ x 60′, and, in some few cases, 35′ x 75′. The rectangular pool of 45′ x 75′ is quite acceptable today both indoors and outdoors, since it includes the 25-yard short course for competitive swimming. In some cases, a pool 60′ wide—or preferably 75′ (25-yard short course)—and 50 meters long (164′-1/2″) is also quite acceptable.

The rectangular pool has a comparatively-low construction cost and is easy to supervise. However, in small pools there is a low percentage of shallow water, and only one competitive activity can be operated at a time. The rectangular pool is a traditional-type pool, but it is not as dramatic or as interesting as some of the "free-form" pools which can easily include the proper competitive-swimming lengths, make possible larger deck areas, offer an interesting shape which fits into the landscape, and give variety and interest to the activities.

The **"T"-shaped pool** was probably one of the first pools to break away from the rectangular shape and it is, today, a very fine shape for a pool. The top of the "T" can be 45′ x 164′-1/2″, preferably 60′ x 164′-1/2″, and sometimes 75′ x 164′-1/2″, thereby providing both the short and long courses, and an entire area of so-called "shallow water" which is 3′-3″ to 5′-0″ in depth.

The lower part of the "T" should be reserved for the diving area and should be separated from the top of the "T" by a float line. This is probably one of the most popular pool designs, although the **"L"-shaped pool** includes the same features, except the deep area is placed at one end rather than in the middle.

The **"Z"-shaped pool** is also extremely functional, having the competitive-swimming lengths and general swimming area in the center of the "Z", the diving area offset from the main part on one side, and the extremely shallow area (extending to 2′) off the other side of the general swimming area. In this shape, the swimming area could be the 25-yard or 50-meter distance. In some cases, the "Z"-shaped pool can include both the 25-yard and 50-meter lengths, keeping in mind, of course, that recreational swimming is the prime objective, but the objectives of a good recreational area and competitive swimming lengths can be combined in such a pool. The most obvious advantages in the "T"-, "L"-, and "Z"-shaped pools are: the separation of divers and swimmers, tending to eliminate the danger of collisions; and the provision of more shallow-water area. These shapes do, however, present some supervision problems.

The **multiple-pool** idea is an extremely good one, especially in instances where funds are not available to build all the swimming facilities desired at one time. The program can be phased so that only one pool is built at a time.

In a country club where there is need to spread out the use of the pool area and have pools for different groups—adults and juniors—a competitive pool, a diving pool, and a play pool (for the small children) will be found most advantageous. The adult pool has been conceived to provide a special area for adults only, and this is particularly desirable in a country club setting where alcoholic beverages are served around a pool.

The **junior pool** is a pool ranging from 2′ to 3′ in depth, where swimming instruction can be conducted for young people —ages up to ten.

The **tots' play pool**, more commonly known as the wading pool, has a water depth of 0.0″ to 15″ or 18″. It is designed for the comfort and convenience of youngsters below the age of six. The more complete tots' play pool includes a 6′ to 10′ walk surrounding the pool, and the entire area is enclosed with a barrier, such as a 3-foot chain-link fence (knuckle-finish top and bottom) or a masonry sitting wall for the parents or others accompanying the small tots.

The separate **diving pool** has many advantages. Since there is usually a conflict between swimmers and divers, the safety feature is a good justification for the separation of the main pool from the diving pool.

There are advantages, certainly, to the separate pools, safety being the principal one. However, the separate pools cost more, require a greater number of lifeguards, require more extensive mechanical and water-treatment systems, and occupy more space.

Free-form pools are ordinarily restricted to resort pools and residential pools. This shape is not favored for the public or institutional-type pool.

The **spray pool** is popular in many communities. In some instances, the water goes to waste, and in other locations, the spray pool is combined with a wading area. Spray pools of 30′ to 40′ in diameter have been designed as multiple-use areas so that they can also serve as dance and roller-skating areas. In the majority of cases, the pool with a wading area has proved more popular than the spray pool.

RECOMMENDED SIZES FOR OUTDOOR POOLS

It has been customary for cities to construct large pools. A large pool may, in some cases, be desirable. Most authorities agree, however, that a pool 50 meters long (164′-1/2″) and 45′, 60′, or 75′ wide, with a diving area off to one side (as is possible in the "T" or "L"), is as large a pool as any community needs. If a pool of this size does not adequately serve the needs of the community, then it would probably be advantageous to have a second pool in another location. A pool is usually more popular and more successful if children and adults do not have to travel out of their own neighborhood.

In cities where a pool with 25-yard and 50-meter competitive-swimming lengths—including a large recreational swimming area—can be justified, it is quite possible that this is the most desirable method of providing swimming facilities. As this pool is outgrown, or as the need of additional swimming facilities is evident, it may be that the next pool or next group of pools should be what is ordinarily called the "neighborhood pool." This is a rectangular or fan-shaped pool of approximately 45' x 75'. An "L"-shaped pool with a swimming area of 45' x 75' and a diving area of 40' x 42' would be even better. The neighborhood pool has the advantage of making it possible for persons to put on their bathing suits at home. It also enables them to swim with their friends.

In designing a pool for a neighborhood or community, the size of the swimming pool should be in direct proportion to the number of people to be served. In cities of 30,000 population or less, the daily average attendance may be expected to be from 5 to 6 percent of the population, about one-third of whom will be at the pool at any one time during the day. On peak days, the pool may be used by as many as 10 percent of the population.

GENERAL PLANNING CONSIDERATIONS

Adequate area is needed around a pool, not only to dignify its setting and location, but to serve as a buffer from nearby streets and residences. Space must also be provided for parking and for other recreational areas and facilities.

A pool should not be located in a low spot. Water from the surrounding area will drain into the pool, and, unless precautions are taken for proper drainage around the edge of the pool, considerable water will penetrate the area under the deck and floor and be a source of constant annoyance and engineering problems.

A pool should not be located in a grove of trees. Leaves fall into the pool and keep it dirty, clog up filters and the hair and lint catcher, and in many ways keep a pool in an unsatisfactory condition. Trees also keep the sun away from the pool, and to be successful, the pool area must have sunshine. The pool should be so located that buildings and trees to the west of the pool are at such a distance that they will not shade the pool in the late afternoon.

Location in relation to streets is most important. A pool must be near main traffic arteries for good circulation and for accessibility, but the pool itself should not be too near a busy street. The dirt from the street will blow into the pool and give considerable trouble in the filtration system. If possible, the pool should be set back 200' to 300' or more from the street.

Recreation facilities supplementing a swimming pool can consist of: recreation buildings or community centers; softball and baseball diamonds; a football field; pitch-and-putt, par-3, or regulation golf courses; a multiple-use paved area; an area for playground equipment for both small children and older groups; and parking areas. Court games can also be included—tennis, croquet, shuffleboard, badminton, handball, horseshoes, paddle tennis, table tennis, deck tennis, roller skating, and volleyball.

Pools are often built in an area just large enough for the pool, no provision being made for other facilities. **A swimming pool should be a part of an over-all recreational-facilities development whenever possible.** If circumstances will permit, **the bathhouse should be designed as a section of a community recreation center.** This is especially true where the

building includes a gymnasium, the same dressing rooms serving the swimming pool during the summer and the gymnasium in the winter. It is quite possible that the dressing rooms will require a little more space, but this will certainly be more economical than designing multiple dressing areas. The bathhouse can be used the year-round, rather than just during the summer months. Relating the pool to the community center reduces the cost of administration and operation.

In those instances where the pool and a community recreation building are not related, a separate bathhouse is required. Of the many new ideas in bathhouse design, one of the most interesting is the bathhouse without a roof other than the roof covering the immediate dressing space around the wall and the toilet facilities. Showers are usually out in the middle in the sunshine, and, in some cases, flowers and grass areas have been incorporated in the interior of the bathhouse. The clothes checkroom is, of course, completely covered and can be secured. This type design is economical to build and, while it will probably require more space, it is the type of bathhouse that is ventilated. It is, however, subject to vandalism to a greater extent than the closed bathhouse.

When space is at a premium, a roof is essential for either a summer or year-round bathhouse. The best plan is a roof with sky domes to permit natural light. All windows can be omitted since adequate light will come in through the sky domes. Vent domes and exhaust fans can be used for circulating the air. This will provide a bathhouse that is vandalproof, economical to construct, and easily maintained. Rest rooms and dressing rooms should be kept to a minimum size and the construction should be simple so that the cost will be minimized.

The pool and deck area should be completely surrounded with a chain-link fence at least 7' high with knuckle-finish top and bottom. This fence is a safety feature for those using the pool, and also contributes to maintaining proper control of the facility. Plantings on both sides of the fence are desirable. The wading pool, or play pool, and space for the smaller children, usually located immediately adjacent to the swimming pool, should be separated from it by a fence and gate.

The matter of prevailing winds is an important feature. When the water is cool, the swimmer is not interested in having the wind dry him off too fast, thereby causing him to become chilled. Therefore, swimmers should be protected from prevailing winds by proper orientation of the pool and bathhouse so that the bathhouse is on the side of the prevailing wind. A canvas may be hung on the fence, a plastic or glass panel may be provided, or a masonry wall may be installed to shield bathers from the wind. In northern climates, the use of windbreaks is almost essential.

In order that a pool may receive full usage, **overhead and underwater lights should be provided for night use.** Overhead lighting should be a minimum of 1.2 to 3.0 watts per square foot of pool surface. Championship meets require a 30-footcandle level of illumination 3' above the water surface. Overhead lighting can be provided by overhead floodlights mounted on 30-foot-high steel poles.

The underwater lighting of a pool should be planned with great care. If possible, the lights should be placed on the sidewalls rather than end walls. If they are placed on the end walls, they should be on a separate electrical circuit so they can be turned off during swimming meets. Otherwise, the swimmers will be looking directly into the lights. Underwater lights placed on the end walls also present difficulties in that swimmers, in making flip turns at the ends of the swimming lanes, might kick and break the glass lenses. The lights should be placed near the bottom of the pool and should be located directly under the float lines and away from the centers of the swimming lanes so swimmers will not kick the lights in turning. Underwater lights are valuable for safety and for aesthetics. It is recommended that 2.0 to 2.5 watts per square foot of water area be provided.

CONSTRUCTION AND DESIGN FACTORS

WATER DEPTH

Pools used for both recreational and competitive swimming often have a water depth in the shallow end of only 3′ or 3-1/2′, but provisions are made for flooding the gutters so as to secure extra depth during swimming meets. The water depth at the shallow end of a pool, as recommended by AAU, should be 4′. This depth will enable swimmers to make turns. Between 75 and 85 percent of the water area of a pool should have a depth of less than 5′. This is important because more than 85 percent of the swimmers will use the shallow water—only a small percentage will be in the deep water at one time.

DIVING FACILITIES

Nothing adds more to the attractiveness of a swimming pool—from the standpoint of both the swimmers and the spectators—than good diving facilities. While the one and three-meter boards have long been in use, many pools are now installing diving towers with the 3, 5, 7-1/2, and 10-meter diving platforms.

For the ten-meter platform, which is 32′-10″ above the water surface, the minimum depth of the water must be 16′ at a point 7′ from the back wall of the pool. The hopper bottom should be at least 20 feet wide, and it should rise gradually to a water depth of 14′ at a point 42′ from the back wall of the pool. The overall diving area should extend a minimum length of 60′ to a water depth of 6′, and the minimum width of the diving area should be 45′.

The five-meter platform should be 16′-5″ above the water surface, with a minimum water depth of 12-1/2′, although a 14-foot depth is recommended. The three-meter board should be 10′ above the water surface and the minimum depth of the water should be 12′. The board is so installed that the end of the board is 5′ beyond the edge of the pool wall. The one-meter board is similarly installed, the board being 39.37″ above the water surface, and the water depth being nine feet.

The diving platforms will provide facilities for practice for various events and for official AAU and accredited Olympic try-outs and meets. The diving towers should preferably be constructed of reinforced concrete.

POOL FINISHES

It is the generally-accepted practice that outdoor pool walls and floor be painted with a good pool paint. A pool should be painted pure white and not an off-color white. One good reason for this is that dirt or silt in the pool is immediately evident and attracts the attention of those responsible for keeping the pool clean. More important, however, is the safety feature, since objects on the bottom of the pool are easily visible in a pure-white pool. Then, too, the appearance of the pool water is improved by using a pure-white background since this brings out the natural blue color of the clear water. A pool should never be painted with blue or green paint.

A very-fine pool finish is obtained by using white-marble-dust plaster, which should be applied during the construction period, or it may be applied to an old pool. This finish is more permanent than paint and will, if cared for properly, last eight years or more. This finish is preferred over painting, but to be successful, it must be applied by qualified technicians.

The finish of the floor and walls of a pool should neither be too rough nor too smooth. If the floor is too smooth (for instance, glazed tile), the swimmer will slide down. If it is too rough, the swimmer's feet will be scratched and hurt, and also the pool will be difficult to keep clean.

WATER TEMPERATURE

The water temperature is important in a swimming pool. If the water is too cold, as is often the case when the source of the water is a deep well or a spring, it is not comfortable for swimming. The most desirable temperature for outdoor-pool water will vary with the region of the country and the atmospheric temperature. The colder the air temperature, the warmer the water, and vice versa. In colder climates, water temperatures of 78° to 80° F should be maintained, and in air temperatures of 90° F or more, the pool water should be maintained at 72° to 74° F to be comfortable for the bathers.

DECK SPACE

It is important that the maximum amount of deck space be provided for the outdoor pool because the deck space greatly increases the capacity of a pool. Surveys have revealed that approximately one-third to one-half of the total number of swimmers in the pool area are in the water at one time. The cost per square foot of the walk or deck around a pool will usually be less than ten per cent of the square-foot cost of the water area. In addition to being used by the swimmers for sunbathing and lounging, the deck area, when it is of sufficient width, can be used for spectator seating during competitive-swimming meets and other water events. Temporary bleachers can be used, and the spectators should be separated from the swimmers by a rail or a nylon rope. In most cases, the spectators are seated outside the fence. The deck area should always exceed by 100 per cent, if possible, the square footage of the water area of a pool and should be raised 6″ to 9″ above the surface of the water.

To reduce the glare around a swimming pool, color introduced into the concrete walk or deck has been very popular and effective. One of the approved methods of introducing color is the application by hand of powdered color just before the concrete sets up, the powder being worked into the surface by the concrete finisher.

While red and green are sometimes used, black (which results in a grey concrete surface) is probably the most successful and is also the most economical. Even though colored concrete may absorb heat to a greater degree, it reduces the glare and makes for a more attractive pool.

It is of the utmost importance that the slope of the deck be not less than one-quarter inch per foot, and that there be no low spots in the deck. The deck should have a nonslip surface.

It is important to include deck drains, and to slope the deck toward the drains in order to remove standing water from the deck's surface.

LADDERS AND STEPS

Ladders or steps are essential to a pool, but they must be carefully located. They should not be located at the end of a pool where they will interfere with competitive-swimming events, and where congestion will be caused during recreational-swimming periods when as many as ten or more people

Figure 84
Ten-Meter Tower, Castel View Town and Country Club, Atlanta, Ga.

may be waiting a turn at the diving board or platform. If the ladders or steps are located on the sides of the pool, the divers will swim away from the boards or diving tower after resurfacing. It is recommended that all ladders or steps in a pool be recessed in the wall, or, where this is impossible, that they be of the removable type.

Steps leading into the pool—that is, steps set back into the wall, not projecting into the pool—are very popular and functional. They provide a place where people can sit in the water, and where mothers can sit and be near their children. They also provide an easy way to enter and leave the pool. The step treads should have a surface that will give traction to prevent slipping, and, as an added safety measure for those using the steps, handrails should be provided.

Steps have a functional value in teaching, since persons can place their hands on the steps and practice kicking as a part of a learn-to-swim program. However, steps should never be located where they will interfere with swimming lanes.

SPECTATORS

A point to consider in connection with the operation of a pool is its financial success. Although the major portion of the pool revenue will come from the swimmers themselves, a large part of the success of the pool will depend upon public interest. Adequate provision for spectators—who are usually the parents and friends of the swimmers, particularly of the younger age group—will go far toward insuring full utilization of the pool facilities.

Suitable seating and rest-room facilities should be provided for spectators, but should be so arranged that the spectators and bathers are completely separated. If at all possible, permanent seats should be built, of a type that will require no maintenance. The seats should be placed so the spectators will have their backs to the afternoon sun. The ideal arrangement is to have bleachers parallel to the competitive course and in a good position from which to view diving exhibitions.

AUXILIARY EQUIPMENT

There is need for facilities for making announcements, for calling people to the telephone, and for the playing of music. A public-address system, originating in the central clothes check-room or manager's office and making use of modern music-distribution systems and a microphone for making announcements or calling to the telephone, is recommended. The system should include multiple speakers properly located around the pool and in the bathhouse. Microphone plug-in outlets are also needed around the pool deck in locations where they will be available for the clerks and announcers for competitive swimming and diving meets. This eliminates the need for extending the cable for long distances, which may be dangerous and expensive. The same microphone outlets can be used for announcing water shows and similar events.

Underwater speakers are also recommended. These are especially helpful in calling swimmers back to the starting line when false starts are made, and in giving instruction to swimmers and divers, particularly synchronized-swimming groups, when their heads are below the water surface.

WADING, JUNIOR, AND SHALLOW-WATER INSTRUCTIONAL-TYPE POOLS

Wading pools for the small children vary from the very simple square or rectangular pool to a series of pools with sprays and water cascading from one to the other. Depth of the water varies from 8" to 24". The pool should be enclosed by a fence,

and should be separately controlled for the safety of the small children. The pool should also have a nonskid bottom to prevent slipping on the part of the children. It is not considered economical to wall off one section of a swimming pool to serve as a wading pool. The reason for this is that a wading pool costs only about 30 percent of the unit cost of a regular swimming pool. The separate wading pool or tots' play pool provides a separate and safer place for the young children.

In a typical design utilizing three small circular wading pools, water flows from the center pool into the two outer ones and is then pumped back into the upper pool. These pools can be elevated above the deck, and the pool coping or curb will serve as a seat for parents and others watching over the small children.

The tots' play pool or wading pool should be separated from the swimming-pool area by a three-foot chain-link fence or low sitting wall. This barrier will prevent the children from straying into the deeper-water area and also adds to the safety of the smaller children in that it keeps the older children from running through the wading pool.

A pool for the smaller children—not simply a wading pool or spray pool, but rather a play pool—can utilize a free form with some innovations to provide play opportunities, and will be more attractive (even to older children) than the conventional round or rectangular wading pool. One such play pool, designed as two squares lying parallel to each other, is joined together at a center point by a passageway approximately 5' wide.

Popular additions to these tots' play pools are sculptured concrete figures—usually a frog, seal, whale, turtle, baby elephant, or others with sprays—on which the children play and slide. These figures create an interesting environment for the youngsters and give play value to the pools.

BATHHOUSE AND SNACK BAR

There are two schools of thought regarding the checking of clothes: one supporting the locker system, and the other the plastic-bag or basket system. While the old-fashioned lockers—operated with keys which all too often are lost—are passe, some community pools are installing coin-operated lockers similar to those found in railroad stations, bus terminals, and airports. This system reduces administrative costs by eliminating the need for operating personnel. Another desirable aspect of the coin-operated locker is that it produces revenue.

The basket checking system has been quite popular, but many adults complain that their clothes are crushed, and more and more communities are turning to the plastic-bag-type checking system. The bags are made on a coat hanger, have pockets for shoes, and keep the clothes in good condition. They take up little space, being used on straight racks or turntable-type racks, and are easy to handle.

The bathhouse should not be oversized, but should have the capacity to accommodate the potential swimming load. The vast majority of people using neighborhood or community pools now dress at home, so the bathhouse can be smaller than would be required when the majority of the swimmers change clothes at the pool.

The floors should be of a nonslip-type material which can be easily cleaned. Wood should be omitted from the bathhouse. The walls should be of glazed tile. If this type of construction is used, the entire bathhouse can be hosed down without damage to the structure. Omission of all exterior windows is recommended since adequate light and ventilation can be better provided by sky domes, vent domes, and exhaust fans. Some of the toilet facilities should be properly sized for small children, rather

Figure 85
Pool with Spectator Seating

than having all facilities for adults. The dressing compartments should be equipped with hooks or a place to hang the plastic clothes-check bags and clothing while dressing or undressing. The circulation of traffic (swimmers) should be good and the control worked out so that a minimum of personnel will be required to operate the bathhouse.

The carrying of food and drink into a pool area should be strictly forbidden. When planning a pool, the need for providing places for swimmers to eat should be borne in mind. A snack bar should be provided which will open onto the pool area, but be located in a small restricted area separated from the swimming area, with proper screening from the wind. Food is in great demand around a pool and should always be available. This special eating area provides a place for the bathers to eat and socialize, it establishes another activity spot at the swimming pool, provides a colorful addition to the pool setting, and the revenue derived from the sale of the food can be used in the pool operation. Tables should be available and shade should be provided by a shelter or by gay umbrellas. Sunshine is needed around the pool, but bathers sometimes prefer shade for the snack-bar area.

The snack bar should be arranged so as to serve spectators and swimmers from the same bar, but in separate areas usually divided by a wall or fence.

COST ANALYSIS

The construction cost of pools and bathhouses is directly related to the region of the country in which the installations are being made, the labor-and-material cost index in that particular area, the number of projects being bid on or under construction at the time of bidding, and the time of the year at which bids are taken. Swimming pool builders—whether specializing in pool building or general contracting—ordinarily have more business in the late winter, spring, and early summer in the south, and early summer in the north. Naturally, their prices are higher at that time as compared with bid prices secured during the late summer and the fall when there is not as much pool business and builders are trying to hold together their staff and labor force.

With the above factors in mind, it is difficult to indicate an approximate cost per square foot for the construction of a swimming pool. A breakdown of the general cost of a pool is shown in Table 9. The square-foot cost is calculated by taking the total cost for column II and dividing it by the water-surface area. It should be remembered that this pool was built in the south. Prices will be proportionately higher in the north.

The cost will vary with the size of the pool—the smaller the pool, the higher the square-foot cost, and vice versa. The Murphey-Candler Pool in DeKalb County, Georgia, has 8,600 square feet of surface water and was constructed and put into use at the beginning of the 1964 swimming season. The cost operation for the 1964 season was $8,500, with a gross revenue of approximately $18,000.

TABLE 9

**Breakdown of Cost of Swimming Pool, Bathhouse, and
Services, Murphey-Candler Park, DeKalb County, Georgia
(Constructed in 1964)**

I Items	II Actual Cost	III Percent of Cost
Layout and finish grading	$ 500.00	.56
Grading and excavation	900.00	.99
Concrete	45,275.00	49.85
Coping (brick)	800.00	.88
Equipment—water treatment and deck	9,000.00	9.93
Electrical—pool	4,500.00	4.96
Mechanical—piping around pool	16,000.00	17.62
Pipe tunnel	2,800.00	3.09
Steel reinforcing	6,500.00	7.16
Painting—epoxy finish	3,000.00	3.31
Fencing	1,500.00	1.65
Total cost of Pool	$90,775.00	100.00

Cost of Bathhouse	$20,000.00
Electrical for bathhouse	2,000.00
	$22,000.00

Pool is modified "L" shape, 8,600 sq. ft. water area, of which 80% is shallow area (3' to 4-1/2'), six lanes for 25-yard short course (75 ft.) and six lanes for 50-meter long course (164'-1/2"). The pool will accommodate 350 persons in the water at one time.

Cost of swimming pool per square foot—$10.56.

Chapter 13

PURIFYING and EQUIPPING SWIMMING POOLS

WATER TREATMENT AND FILTRATION

THE "OLD swimming hole" provided recreation for a few in the murky water of a natural reservoir with few or no controls. Modern swimming pools, filled with potable water from the municipal distribution system, nearly always require additional treatment of the water before the safety regulations can be met. Furthermore, regulations are constantly being upgraded. The best possible quality of water must be provided to: (1) ensure maximum underwater visibility for effective lifeguarding and swimming instruction; (2) prevent the spread of communicable disease under ever increasing pool-load densities; and (3) provide maximum bather comfort with minimum eye, ear, and skin irritation.

It is the function of the water-conditioning plant of a swimming pool to provide the required equipment to accomplish these objectives. A properly-planned equipment room is the first step in this direction. The second, and probably equally-important step, is to train the pool operator in the proper practices of water-quality control. The plant itself cannot provide satisfactory results unless the operator understands the function of each piece of equipment, the goals he is attempting to achieve, and the effect of water chemistry and additive chemicals on this objective.

Four main factors must be provided: filtration, disinfection, pH control, and total alkalinity control. A pool where all four factors have been properly considered will have water with a sparkling clarity and a naturally-blue color against a white background, and the water will not irritate skin or membrane tissue.

pH CONTROL

Lack of attention to pH control is the main cause of irritation. pH is a term commonly used to indicate the relative condition of acidity and alkalinity in water. The pH measurement denotes the position in a scale of numbers from 0 to 14, where 7.0 represents neutrality, the point where neither a predominance of acid ions or alkaline ions exists. Below pH 7.0 and approaching pH 0.0, solutions become more acid. Above pH 7.0, solutions become more alkaline as pH 14.0 is approached.

Many arbitrary pH standards have been set for pool water, ranging from pH 7.0 to pH 8.5. It is generally agreed that a pH of 7.8 is the most desirable for pools using chlorine disinfectant. Proper operational attention can easily maintain a pH of 7.6 (minimum) to 8.0 (maximum), and these limits should be strictly enforced. Corrosion problems may develop below pH 7.2, which is also the recommended lower limit with the use of bromine compounds as a disinfectant (pH 7.2-7.4).

The pH will be automatically lowered by the continuous addition of gaseous chlorine, alum, body acids, or other acid-forming products. The pH will be automatically raised by the addition of the sodium or calcium chlorine compounds. The pH can be quickly and easily checked by using a standard test kit with proper sample tubes, a dechlorinating agent, and a calibrated measuring device with correct indicator solution and sufficient color standards to make accurate comparisons. The pH should be checked at least once each day and a record kept of the test result plus any corrective action taken.

To correct pool water where the pH is too low, carefully controlled quantities of soda ash should be added. The quantity of soda ash required to correct for the lowering effect of chlorine will be approximately the weight of chlorine that has been added. To correct water where the pH value is too high, measured amounts of muriatic acid must be added.

ALKALINITY

Whereas pH is a qualitative type of measurement, it only indicates the relative amount of hydrogen ions present in the water. It fails to indicate the amount of true alkalinity or "total alkalinity" (bicarbonates, carbonates, and hydroxide) present. The quantity of bicarbonate and carbonate alkalinity should therefore be determined independently.

Naturally-hard waters contain large quantities of carbonates and bicarbonates in solution combined with other elements. These waters have a greater tolerance to absorb acid-producing chemicals, such as chlorine, with little effect on pH values.

Naturally-soft water has very little alkalinity present, and the control of pH alone is insufficient. Alkalinity determinations should be performed by methods outlined in "Standard Methods for the Examination of Water and Sewage," published by the American Water Works Association. Total alkalinity of at least 50 ppm should be established and maintained. About 20 pounds of soda ash will add 10 ppm alkalinity to 100,000 U.S. gallons of water. If the alkalinity is very low (under 35 ppm), lime should be used to provide the required calcium along with soda ash to provide the carbonate group.

DISINFECTION

The purpose of adding disinfectants to pool water is to prevent the spread of communicable disease. It is economically and operationally impractical to render the water completely free of bacteria at all times. The objective, therefore, is to create a water environment wherein the unintentional introduction of bacteria, both pathogenic and nonpathogenic, will instantly encounter destructive forces to prevent their spread or reproduction.

Disinfectants are not only consumed by bacteria, but they also combine with other chemical elements in a multitude of chemical processes. Chlorine, for example, combines readily with the never-ending supply of ammonia in the water to form chloramine or "combined chlorine", which, although still a disinfectant, is far too slow-acting to be effective. Fortunately, an excess of chlorine over that required to combine with ammonia will render the chloramines unstable and the resulting breakdown of the chloramine will release gaseous nitrogen. It is essential that this practice be carried out to get rid of the ammonia being continuously added, and also to enable the creation of the desirable water environment where a "free" and rapid-acting form of chlorine can be maintained as a "residual".

There are many disinfectants on the market, the relative merits of which are discussed as frequently as pool people get together. There is something to be said in favor of each type. However, until specific scientific evidence conclusively commands a change in practice throughout the total industry, the chlorine compounds will continue to be the most widely used disinfectants.

Free residual chlorine can be identified with a simple test kit containing sample tubes, measuring droppers, a supply of indicator solution (orthotolodine), and color comparator standards ranging from 0.1 ppm to 2.0 ppm. Both free and combined (chloramine) residuals will react to produce color for comparison purposes. The distinguishing feature is that free chlorine residual reacts instantaneously, whereas chloramine residual reacts slowly, full color development taking place over approximately a five-minute interval. For best results, samples should be precooled to about 40° F. A true determination of free and combined chlorine residual can be determined by the orthotolodine-arsenite test. A reasonable indication can be obtained by cooling the sample, adding orthotolodine, and making an immediate comparison. The instantaneous color comparison should be recorded as free residual. After five minutes, a further comparison will provide the total residual. Subtraction of the "free" reading from the "total" reading will provide the chloramine residual present. Both should be recorded.

In the morning, before the bathing load of the day, all chlorine residual should be free and the amount should be a minimum of 0.8 ppm and can safely range as high as 1.5 ppm. During the day, chloramine will develop as ammonia load is added. It is desirable to provide a chlorine application rate sufficient to ensure that at least 50 percent of the total residual will be available as free chlorine residual so that the breakdown of ammonia will continue. At the end of the swimming day, the chlorinator should be set for night operation so that a complete recovery to 100 percent free chlorine will occur overnight, thus providing the proper residual to begin the next day. Experience in each pool will differ in the quantity of disinfection chemical required. The designer should provide a machine to dispense chlorine on a continuous basis, at a rate up to 10 ppm, based on the recirculation rate of flow. Hand application of chlorine is not recommended.

FILTRATION

Filtration of water is simply a mechanical method to screen out solids existing in suspension in the water in order to improve light penetration for better visibility. Many types of filters are manufactured and many different particle sizes of filter media can be obtained. It is obvious that the larger the filter-particle size, the larger will be the pore spaces through which solids can pass. Specifications for the proper gradation of

filter media are contained in Chapter 11 of the American Water Works Association text entitled "Water Quality and Treatment" (Second Edition), and many other reference texts.

Filtration is not effective in removing dissolved impurities such as iron, manganese, color, or live bacteria. These must be chemically altered to take a solid form so the filter can trap them. Oxidation is often the chemical reaction required, and chlorine is a strong oxidizing agent as well as disinfectant. It is also a bleach and aids in the removal of false or interfering colors in the water.

The complete recirculation system, which includes the filter, should be designed to provide a rate of flow which will ensure that all the water in the pool will be filtered at least once every six hours. The tremendous interest in swimming, both instructional and recreational, is placing an ever increasing bather load on the pool. Wherever possible, provision should be made so that the water turnover time can be reduced to less than six hours if the load increases, or if public-health regulations become more stringent.

TYPES OF FILTERS

Filters may be classified in two ways: by the filter media used, and by the location with respect to the pump (see Figure 80, Chapter 12).

FILTER MEDIA

Slow Sand Filters

Slow sand filters are seldom used today because of the size of filter bed required. Fine sand is used with gravity flow.

Rapid Sand Filters

Rapid sand filters are very common and use a specific gradation of sand supported by a graded gravel bed in which there is an under-drain and backwash system. The maximum rate of flow is usually defined not to exceed 3 gpm (U.S.), and the minimum backwash rate of flow should be 12 gpm (U.S.) per square foot of filter area.

Advantages—The advantages of rapid sand filters are as follows:
• Media are permanent—100% recovery on backwash.
• Low cost of operation—requires normal chlorination and chemicals—uses inexpensive alum.
• Minimum maintenance care annually.
• Longer filter runs.
• Fine filtrate characterstics when coagulant is used.

Disadvantages—The disadvantages of rapid sand filters are as follows:
• Installation requires more space.
• Initial purchase cost higher—freight is large factor in more remote areas.
• Interior condition of filter not readily inspected (long years of experience have established that inspection is not required if filter is properly operated).
• To facilitate backwashing, either a multi-unit installation will be required so that the circulation pump can deliver backwash water at a sufficient rate, or a second, high-capacity pump will be required in the installation.

Diatomaceous-Earth Filters or Filter-Aid

Although diatomaceous earth had been used successfully in other industries, notably brewing, malting, dry cleaning, and soft-drink preparation, the history of its introduction to the swimming pool industry has been stormy. In the potable-water-conditioning field for municipal water supply, the acceptance of diatomaceous earth as an equivalent to rapid sand filtration has been notably limited. This substance, an inert, light, granulated, siliceous compound, should be an ideal filter medium. Perhaps the lack of sufficient research into the particular swimming-pool requirements caused the deficiencies in some of the earlier filter designs and methods of operation. Too many early installations failed to meet performance claims. With accumulated experience and modern knowledge, however, there is no reason why a diatomaceous-earth filter should fail to deliver water of equivalent clarity to that of a rapid sand filter, and exhibit good service characteristics.

Advantages—Diatomaceous-earth filters have demonstrated the following advantages:

- Since the media can be made to adhere to vertical or inclined surfaces, the space required to provide surface area to satisfy any given recirculation rate is far less than sand, resulting in considerable savings in the initial cost of the installation, housing, and equipment.
- Since the media are completely wasted at each filter washing, no concealed or protected bacterial colonies can be generated within the filter media.
- Normal tank design, with viewing ports or open elements, provides good visibility of the filter elements so that the operator has no doubts about the effectiveness of the backwash.
- Much less backwash water is required when compared with sand filters, resulting in a lower water bill and less make-up water to be treated for the pool.

Disadvantages—The disadvantages of diatomaceous-earth filters are as follows:

- The main disadvantage of diatomaceous-earth is the higher cost of operation created by the complete disposal of media at the end of each cycle.
- There is a slight disadvantage in having to store and handle a considerable quantity of diatomaceous earth on the pool site, and in accurate measurement of quantities.
- Diatomaceous earth is abrasive and can cause rapid deterioration in pump glands, impellers, and pipes (good engineering design can minimize or eliminate this complaint and the resultant high maintenance costs).
- The power requirements are higher for pressure-diatomaceous-earth installations.
- Interruption in the recirculation flow causes the media to leave the elements, and a backwashing is required before the system can be put back into operation.
- Improper backwash operation can permit diatomaceous earth to enter the pool, creating cloudiness and poor visibility.

Anthrafilt Filters

Anthrafilt is another name for anthracite (hard) coal. For filters, it is washed and graded to approximately the same-size particles as filter sand. It can be furnished in any special sizes to meet specific requirements of consulting engineers. Anthrafilt is approximately one-half the weight of sand and has greater irregularity of particles. Anthrafilt filters are similar to sand filters.

High-Rate Sand Filters

The high-rate sand filter, a development of recent years, is a deep bed of sand, supported on a porous bedplate of fine well screen, and operated under high pressure. Turbidity is collected throughout the entire bed depth, using surface adhesion, the irregularities in the particle surface, and the intergranular spaces created by the particle sizes. Filter rates of 20 gpm per square foot of surface area are used. Backwash rates are also 20 gpm per square foot. Backwash times of five minutes conserve water.

The difficulty is to determine when the filter requires washing, since differential pressures or reductions of flow rate are not effective indicators. When the bed is saturated with dirt particles, the filter becomes ineffective. A turbidometer is required to determine this saturation point. This is an expensive instrument which offsets the space and cost advantage as compared to rapid sand filters.

FILTER LOCATION

Pressure

Both sand and diatomaceous-earth pressure filters operate on the discharge side of the pump, thus requiring closed pressure vessels. They are entirely satisfactory, and, if properly designed, manufactured, and operated, can turn out very satisfactory results.

Advantages—The advantages of pressure filters are as follows:

- Since operation is under pressure, head losses due to the media saturation with dirt particles can be allowed to reach larger differentials, thus extending the length of the filter cycle and reducing man-hour requirements for backwashing.
- Installations using only one pump can be made above the ground.

Disadvantages—The disadvantages of pressure filters are as follows:

- Filter shells are more costly to manufacture and heavier to transport and erect.
- The maintenance of filter elements is a more time-consuming job involving opening up the tank to get at them.

Suction

Suction types include gravity-sand and vacuum-diatomaceous-earth filters located ahead of the pump in the recirculation system.

Advantages—Suction filters have the following advantages:

- Filter tanks are open, permitting visual inspection of the bed at all times.
- Tanks can be of lightweight materials which are less costly to construct, transport, and erect. Tanks are frequently fabricated on the site, using reinforced concrete.
- Cleaning the filter elements in the open tank is simple.

Disadvantages—Suction filters have the following disadvantages:

- Unless proper consideration is given to design shapes and internal flow patterns, media are distributed less evenly, some settling to the bottom where they are wasted.
- Suction filters must be located in the hydraulic system below the level of water in the pool, thus requiring excavation and below-ground construction not otherwise necessary.

SWIMMING-POOL EQUIPMENT AND ACCESSORIES

Every swimming pool needs certain basic equipment for safe and efficient operation. This equipment should be purchased in advance of the completion of the pool. In recent years, many gadgets, swimming aids, training devices, and play items have been manufactured for use in and around water.

Many swimming instructors advocate the use of artificial devices, such as fins, masks, life vests, and kick boards, to teach a person to swim. Others believe these devices represent a "crutch" to the beginner and should not be used. Devices have proved helpful to nonswimmers in reducing initial fear of the water. They are also an aid in the development of the basic mechanics of swimming.

Naturally, a person should never be classified as a beginner or swimmer until he can swim the minimum prescribed distance without the use of any support. Furthermore, nonswimmers using support devices should be under direct supervision at all times.

SAFETY EQUIPMENT

LIST OF ESSENTIAL EQUIPMENT

- **Ring buoys**—Approved construction material is unicellular plastic (permanently buoyant). Recommended size is 15″ or 17″ equipped with 60′ of throw line. Minimum of two to a pool. An adequate rack or hook should be provided for displaying buoys prominently in the pool area.
- **Lifeguard chairs**—Must be placed in strategic locations, the number based on the size and type of pool.
- **Reaching rescue pole**—Must be lightweight and accessible to everyone on the deck. Recommended length is 12′ to 14′.
- **Torpedo rescue buoys**—Must be made of approved flotation material, complete with shoulder straps and sufficient line to tow victim.
- **Shepherd's crooks**—Aluminum or stainless steel. 1-1/4″ x 14′ with curved hook used to retrieve or assist a swimmer.
- **Safety lines**—To separate water areas.
- **Electronic sonar water device** (alarm).
- **Pool fencing**—For outdoor pools.
- **Pool cover**—A pool cover for the outdoor pool is considered to provide better safety than fencing since it puts a lid over the water, thereby actually sealing in the potential danger. A fence is too often a challenge to children to climb.
- **First-aid kit.**
- **"Mouth-to-mouth" resuscitation device.**
- **Light portable resuscitator.**
- **Telephone**—In pool office, located on separate line. A visible chart should be located near the telephone listing the phone numbers of the police, fire department, and doctor.
- **Chart**—Predominantly displaying general regulations and safety rules.
- **Diving boards**—If proper depth is available.
- **Vacuum cleaner**—For cleaning bottom of pool.
- **Gas mask**—Approved by U.S. Bureau of Mines. Should be readily accessible **outside** the chlorination room for emergency service.

LIST OF OPTIONAL EQUIPMENT

- **Canoe and boat**—For teaching basic elements of canoeing and boating.
- **Rescue surfboard.**
- **Lounging chairs.**
- **Automatic pool cover.**
- **Starting blocks.**

INSTRUCTIONAL AIDS

LIST OF RECOMMENDED EQUIPMENT

- **Kick boards**—Made of unicellular plastic. A basic popular teaching device for development of leg action, and also a

supporting device. A kick board should be permanently buoyant.
- **Inflatable tubes and rings**—Used for arm and leg training.
- **Swim fins**—Used widely in beginning instructional teaching.
- **Goggles**—To develop confidence.
- **Mask**—For underwater work.
- **Snorkel**—For skin and scuba diving.
- **Swim "bubbles" or trainer**—Buoyant teaching belts used for the support of beginning swimmers.
- **Teaching pole**—Can be attached to shepherd's crook pole.
- **Swim vest or life jackets**—For nonswimmers.
- **Portable compressed-air bottles**—For underwater familiarization, instruction, and scuba diving.

LIST OF OPTIONAL EQUIPMENT

- **Slides**—Made of Fiberglas or stainless steel with steel supports. The last two feet of the slide should extend over the water.
- **Pace clocks**—Used in training for competitive swimming. Two units are desirable. They should be moisture-resistant and be a minimum of 30″ in diameter.
- **Scoreboards**—Either electric or manually operated.
- **Chalkboards**—Fixed on the wall.
- **Electronic scoreboards**—For swimming meets.
- **Glass-enclosed bulletin boards**—Hung on wall mounts.
- **Electric clock**—Moisture-resistant, minimum of 24″ in diameter.
- **Equipment racks and hangers.**
- **Deck chairs and benches.**

DIVING BOARDS

Diving boards vary greatly in performance and life. The following types of boards are currently on the market:
- **Wood**—Laminated sections of marine wood with plastic coating and nonskid surface material.
- **Fiberglas**—Laminated sections of wood with Fiberglas wrapping to afford greater strength and durability. The Fiberglas is covered with a polyester (plastic) resin with nonskid surface material.
- **Stainless steel**—Aircraft-specification stainless-steel sheets with welded sections with nonskid surfacing.
- **Aluminum**—One-piece extrusions or several extrusions spot-welded, fused, or glued together. The extended one-piece aluminum board has received the widest acclaim.

STARTING BLOCKS

To conform to official specifications, a starting block should measure 30″ from the surface of the pool water to the top of the takeoff platform. The blocks must be equipped with a handgrip or bar for backstroke starts. It is preferable that they also be equipped with a quick-release mechanism so they may be easily removed when not in use. Starting blocks are made of wood, Fiberglas, aluminum, or galvanized pipe, or are built in as a part of the wall.

POOL-CLEANING EQUIPMENT

The most desirable way to clean the pool bottom is to use a pool vacuum cleaner, thus permitting the cleaning and removal of dirt and debris without emptying the pool. Portable vacuum-cleaner units are more popular with outdoor facilities.

Pumps with motors are mounted on steel bases equipped with pneumatic rubber tires, permitting easy handling. Suction hose of plastic or rubber, with a suitable vacuum-cleaner head and handle, provide a basic and necessary function in removing debris from the bottom of the pool. A discharge hose attached to the pump discharge fitting, allows the waste material or water to go directly to a waste outlet.

OTHER EQUIPMENT

Water polo is a growing water sport with many clubs and institutions. Water-polo goals are made of aluminum, with nylon netting and rope. Water basketball, for recreation purposes, has been adapted to the pool as a result of the introduction of portable backstops.

Chapter 14

WATERFRONTS and BEACHES

Waterfronts for the conduct of acquatic activities are found in children's camps, parks, resorts, marinas, clubs, hotels, residential developments, and other recreation areas. The waterfront, whether it is a beach, floating crib, dock, pond, lake shore, pool deck, or some other area where aquatic programs take place, must be properly located and constructed to insure the health and safety of the public using this facility. The post-World War II years have seen a tremendous development in children's camps in the United States, particularly day camps. Although many of the aspects of this chapter deal primarily with camps, most of the criteria may be applied to beach-front developments as well.

USE OF WATERFRONTS

The use of waterfronts varies with the program offered. The type of program will determine the nature of the waterfront, and yet the environmental situation, such as ocean, stream, or lake, may influence the type and design of the facility. The following categories of use identify the specific areas of the aquatic program:

- **Familiarization**—Familiarization involves programs acquainting the user with the water.
- **Instruction**—Instruction involves programs of teaching the user basic activities related to aquatics.

Figure 86
Callaway Gardens, Pine Mountain, Georgia

198

Figure 87
New York University Camp Waterfront

- **Recreation**—Recreation involves programs which are largely unstructured, for relaxing and refreshing the user, including participating in or watching special events such as synchronized swimming, water shows, and competitive swimming.
- **Competition**—Competition involves programs of training and competing in swimming and other aquatic activities.

The user of a waterfront should be able to participate in a variety of aquatic activities in order to attain the desired objectives. This is especially true in the camp setting, where the camper participates in the constructive fulfillment of inherent attitudes and aptitudes.

In planning the location and construction of natural and artificial waterfront facilities, definite criteria should be established. These criteria should reflect not only the camp program, but also the health and safety requirements.

PLANNING THE WATERFRONT LOCATION

CRITERIA FOR NATURAL WATERFRONTS

The natural-waterfront site should have certain characteristics to make it desirable for aquatic-program use. The recommended criteria for the selection of waterfront or beach sites are discussed below. Helpful check lists have also been provided.

Water Characteristics

The water content should be of a sanitary quality affording safe usage. The health conditions of a site are primarily judged by a careful examination of both its surrounding environs and its water content. The first is accomplished by a careful field analysis, the second by a laboratory analysis. Both examinations can indicate the bacterial quality and physical clarity of the water.

CHECK LIST:

- Surrounding water source
- Water quality (bacterial content)
- Water clarity (visibility test)

Water-Condition Characteristics

The circulation of the water through the potential waterfront site should be examined. Slow-moving water can produce swampy or built-up mud conditions, while fast-moving water can produce undercurrents and erosive conditions.

The ideal water temperature for swimming ranges from 72° to 78° F, depending upon the air temperature. The American Public Health Association indicates that less than 500 gallons of additional water per bather per day is too small a diluting volume unless there is sufficient application of disinfection.

CHECK LIST:

- Rate of water flow
- Rate of water turnover
- Water-level fluctuation
- Water constancy
- Availability of water
- Types of currents and undertow
- Outlet for water
- Eddies, floods, waves, or wash
- Weeds, fungi, mold, or slime
- Parasites, fish, animals
- Debris, broken glass, etc.
- Oil slick
- Odor, color, taste

Bottom Characteristics

The waterfront bottom should be unobstructed and clear of debris, rock, muck, mulch, peat, and mud. The waterfront should not be in an area where the channel shifts or silt builds up. The most desirable bottom is white sand with a gradual pitch sloping from the shallow to the deep end. The bottom should not be precipitous, too shallow, nor have holes, pots, channels, bars, or islands.

The bottom should be of gravel, sand, or stable hard ground to afford firm and secure footing. An investigation by taking soundings in a boat, and by making an actual underwater survey should be undertaken before a final decision is made on the location of the waterfront.

CHECK LIST:

- Bottom movement
- Amount of holes, debris
- Slope of subsurface
- Amount of area
- Condition of soil
- Porosity of bottom
- Average depth and various depths
- Bottom color

Climatic Characteristics

Continuous dry spells or numerous rainy seasons will cause the site to have water-retention problems. Dangerous storms, including tornadoes, lightning, hurricanes, and northeasters, create extremely dangerous waterfront conditions. The severity of the winter can also affect the waterfront. Ice and ice movement can cause damage to waterfront facilities and bottom. A south-southeast exposure is ideal so that maximum benefit is derived from the sun and there is least exposure to the wind.

CHECK LIST:

- Number of storms and type
- Prevailing winds
- Amount of ice
- Change of air temperature
- Amount of precipitation
- Fluctuation of temperature
- Sun exposure

Environmental Characteristics

The locale of the waterfront should be carefully examined for all influences on its construction and utilization. Zoning regulations, building codes, insurance restrictions, health ordinances, title covenants, and a multitude of other legal restrictions by the Coast Guard, Conservation Department, Water Resources Commission, public works agencies, and Fire Department should be studied. The arrangement of land uses and their compatibility to the project, transportation, utilities, community facilities, population, and area economics should also be considered.

CHECK LIST:

- Ownership and reparian rights
- Availability of water supply
- Zoning and deed restrictions
- Local, state, and federal regulations
- Adjacent ownerships
- Water patrol and a control agency

Program Characteristics

The waterfront should be so situated that it can be protected by a fence or other controlled access, particularly in a camp, marina, or other small area. It should also be internally segregated, i.e. bathing from boating, boating from fishing, and so on. The site should also have storage room for waterfront equipment, adequate spectator area for use during special events, a safety area near the lifeguard station or post, and ready access to a road.

CHECK LIST:

- Distance of waterfront from other areas
- Access road
- Separation of waterfront activities
- Area for unity of controls
- Space available for adjunct activities

Access Characteristics

The waterfront facility must be accessible by transportation available to the user. There should always be a means of vehicular access for emergency or maintenance use. The site around the waterfront and along its approach should be free of poison ivy, sumac, poison oak, burdock thistle, and other irritating plants.

CHECK LIST:

- Location for access road
- Poisonous plants
- Area accessible yet controllable

Area Characteristics

The waterfront bathing area should allow for at least 50 square feet for each user. There should be areas for instruction, recreation, and competition. The depth of the area to be used primarily for the instruction of nonswimmers should not exceed 3'. The area to be used for intermediate swimmers should not exceed 5-1/2' (primarily for competition). Smaller or larger swimming areas may be designed if users are divided differently.

The minimum recommended size for a camp swimming area is 60' by 30', and the desirable size is 75' by 45', providing a 25-yard short course.

CHECK LIST:

- Space for bathing
- Capacity of waterfront
- Water depths
- Division of bathing area into stations
- Size of boating area
- Size of fishing area

Shore Characteristics

The shoreline for the waterfront facility should be free of irregular rocks, stumps, debris, or obstruction. It should be a minimum of 100' long for bathing in a camp area and can be many miles long in a park beach.

There should be trees adjacent to waterfront areas to provide shade and wind protection. Large, high trees should be eliminated because they attract lightning, and moldy trees have many decayed overhanging branches. Too many trees of a deciduous nature create mucky shores and water bottoms because of their autumn leaves. There are fewer problems with coniferous trees.

CHECK LIST:
- Surrounding vegetation
- Slope of the shore
- Existing beach
- Extent of clearing
- Amount of debris

CRITERIA FOR ARTIFICIAL WATERFRONTS

In locating and considering an artificial waterfront, most of the same characteristics as described for natural areas should be examined. Additional criteria which should be considered are outlined below.

Environmental Characteristics

If all available bodies of water are being utilized, then artificial-waterfront facilities must be developed. In some cases, waterfront locations are unsatisfactory or unavailable for new camps or resorts. Thus, consideration must be given to utilizing undeveloped sites with sufficient watershed (runoff water), water table (underground water), and water bodies (surface water) for lakes, pools, or impoundments.

Water Characteristics

Before any site is selected, the perculation rate and, in particular, the permeability of the soil should be carefully checked in order to be sure that water will be retained. The stability and structure of the soil must also be determined (from test borings and/or test pits) because of the various types of dams, pump houses, dikes, pools, berms, spillways, and other structures which must be built.

Water-Content Characteristics

Unlike natural bodies of water, the content of artificial bodies can be controlled by chlorination and filtration. Runoff water obtained from storms, and contained in a pond or lake, should be collected by diversion ditches and fed to a reservoir and chlorination plant. This water can then be recirculated until potable water is obtained.

Underground water which is obtained from wells or springs can also be contained in a pond. This type of artificial water body usually would have a continuous flow and thus would need only a simple filtration system plus chlorination.

Surface water which is obtained from running streams is usually contained in a bypass pond or in a pond in the stream itself. Both methods require the construction of a dam. These artificial water bodies have continuous running water. However, gate valves and floodgates are required, especially during storms when there is a large flow of water to control. Unless there is a constant turnover or supply of clean water, these impoundments will require a filtration and chlorination system.

Climatic Characteristics

Climatic considerations are very important in developing artificial bodies of water and waterfronts. In most cases, natural bodies of water will fluctuate very little because of weather conditions. On the other hand, artificial bodies are solely dependent upon the climate because the water table, runoff, and stream flow depend on the amount and time of rainfall. All other climatic considerations mentioned for natural waterfronts generally apply to artificial waterfronts as well.

Drainage Characteristics

A low-lying area, regardless of its appeal, is not a good location for a pool or pond. Adequate drainage is essential so that surface and deck water will drain away from the water body, and so that the water body itself can be emptied without pumping. Ground water and frost action resulting from improper drainage can undermine a foundation by causing it to heave and settle.

WATERFRONT CONSTRUCTION

CRITERIA FOR NATURAL WATERFRONTS

The natural-waterfront facility should have features which make it both safe and usable. The following criteria are suggested as a basis for the construction of such a facility.

Bottom Characteristics

Most swimming facilities around natural bodies of water require the dragging and grading of the bottom subsurfaces to eliminate hazards. In many cases where definite improvement of the bottom is required, feed mat, mesh, or plastic sheets have to be laid down on top of muck and staked down. Once these sheets have been laid, sand must be spread over the mat surface. When the bottom is firm, sand can be spread 6" thick on top of ice in the crib area during winter. As the ice melts, the sand will fall fairly evenly over the bottom. This can only be accomplished, however, when the ice does not shift or break and float away.

Shore Characteristics

When a beach is constructed, a gentle slope of from 6' to 12' in 100' should be maintained. Where the waterfront requires a great deal of construction, a dock shoreline is recommended rather than trying to maintain an unstable beach. The ground above the water can then be developed with turf, terraces, decks, and boardwalks, depending upon the nature of the project. When the bottom drops off very quickly, the shore can be dug out to the grade desired underwater. This forms a crescent-shaped waterfront with an excellent beach.

Access Characteristics

Access roads and streets around waterfront areas should be acquired by the owner, if possible, to keep the area buffered from conflicting uses.

These roads should be made durable and be attractively maintained. Access roads should have clear horizontal and vertical vision so that pedestrian and vehicular conflict can be prevented.

Program Characteristics

The waterfront in small recreation areas, such as camps or resorts, should be completely enclosed by planting or fencing. There should be a central control for ingress and exit. Many facilities require the use of check in-out boards, tickets, and other similar devices for controlling the use of the area. The waterfront bathing, boating, and fishing facilities should be separated, each with its own control.

CRITERIA FOR ARTIFICIAL WATERFRONTS

Both artificial and natural waterfronts should have certain features which make them safe and usable. In improving and developing an artificial waterfront, most of the same considerations should be rendered as illustrated for the natural waterfront. The following criteria should be carefully considered in providing an artificial waterfront.

Bottom Characteristics

When constructing an artificial beach, the grade should be the same as that recommended for natural shores—6' to 12' in 100'. For reservoirs and ponds, there should be a minimum of 9" of large crushed stone, then 4" of well-graded smooth gravel to fill in the voids, and then 9" of washed medium sand. Where the sand beach terminates at a depth of approximately 7' of water, it is recommended that rip-rapping be established to resist the tendency of the beach sand to move down the slope. The area above the beach should also be ditched where the natural slope of the ground exceeds that of the beach. Thus, the slopes of the beach should be approximately 6 percent below the water and 10 percent above. For areas in tidal waters, a maximum slope of 1' for 15' can be established for the bottom below water line.

For pools, the bottoms are usually concrete, with the sides of concrete, welded steel, or aluminum plate. Such innovations as precast concrete slabs, plastic, and rubber are also being tried.

Shore Characteristics

In creating the shoreline for artificial bodies of water, there should be either a berm or dike if the water is to be confined. A steep slope to eliminate shallow areas is usually required to prevent weeds and other plant materials from growing in the water.

If the soil conditions will not allow a steep slope underwater—3' deep to retard water-plant growth—then bulkheads or docks will be required, or only a limited beach can be provided.

DESIGN AND CONSTRUCTION OF CAMP WATERFRONTS

The camp waterfront is usually composed of either permanent docks or floats to provide safe swimming and boating areas.

DOCKS AND FLOATS

Permanent structures are usually set on concrete, wood, or steel foundations, or piers or piles. The decks should be made in sections of 10' to 20' for ease in removing for repairs or winter storage. The dock should be constructed with at least a one-foot air space between deck and water. Underwater braces and other cross beams should be limited to prevent swimmers from becoming entangled in them. When water levels change, allowances should be made for the piers to be outside the deck limits so the deck can move up and down on sleeves or brackets. Walkways or decks should be a minimum of 6' wide, preferably 8' or 10'. They should be cross planked so swimmers will avoid splinters. The planking should not be less than 2" thick by 4" to 6" wide. Boards should be spaced a maximum of 1/4" apart to prevent toe-stubbing. The deck should be treated with a noncreosote-based preservative, since creosote will burn feet, plus a plastic, nonlead paint which is not heat-

absorbing. The paint should be white with a blue or green tint to reduce the glare and aid in reflection.

Flotation structures may be made of drums, balsa wood, cork, styrafoam, steel tanks, or other forms of flotation material. There are many innovations which have carried over from war days. Pontoon decks, for example, are sometimes made from surplus bridge parts, airplane fuel tanks, or fuel-oil tanks. All such materials should be treated with red lead after scraping, sanding, and repairing. A frame should be constructed of 2" x 8" boards to fit over and contain the supporting units. The frame should fit securely, yet be removable at the close of the season. Some flotation materials or devices are just placed in the framing under the floats without any type of anchorage to the frame. Galvanized steel or aluminum straps of 1/8" x 1-1/2" under the floating units will save time and effort to prevent sinking when these units acquire a leak and fill with water.

The various types of designs employed in waterfronts are shown in Figure 88. A typical well-laid-out camp waterfront is shown in Figure 89.

WATERFRONT EQUIPMENT

It is important to plan initially for all needed accessory equipment. The amount of equipment required will vary with the size of the waterfront. All necessary safety equipment must be located so as to afford immediate emergency use.

LIFEGUARD STATIONS

Lifeguard chairs should be placed at a point where the location of beach equipment and sunbathing limit lines do not interfere with the guards' vision of the water areas. Chairs should be a minimum of 6' to a maximum of 10' above grade. Usually lifeguard chairs are made of galvanized pipe or wood.

LADDERS

In all swimming cribs, there should be a ladder at least 2' in width placed at the sides in order not to interfere with persons swimming the length of the simulated pool.

LOG BOOMS

Logs fastened end to end can form a continuous lifeline around bathing limits in rustic settings and, at the same time, provide the safety to swimmers so necessary at a waterfront.

LEMMON LINES

Lemmon lines are small floats, attached by a nylon or plastic rope or cable, outlining and restricting swimming areas. They can be made of rounded wood, cork, or plastic.

MARKERS AND BUOYS

These are floats indicating the limits of areas or channels, or marking underwater obstructions, divers, moorings, and fishing nets. They are usually hollow cans or drums. They can also be flag buoys, a 6-inch-square wood block with attached flag, a wooden cross of 2" x 4" with can on top, or a metal ballast with flag.

RESCUE CRAFT

Boats should be of the round-bottom or dory type between 12' and 14' long. There should be lifesaving equipment in the boat at all times. The seats should be removable, and oarlocks should be of a permanent type. A catamaran, surfboards, and, in large beach waterfront facilities, helicopters supplement the lifeboat as a means of patrol.

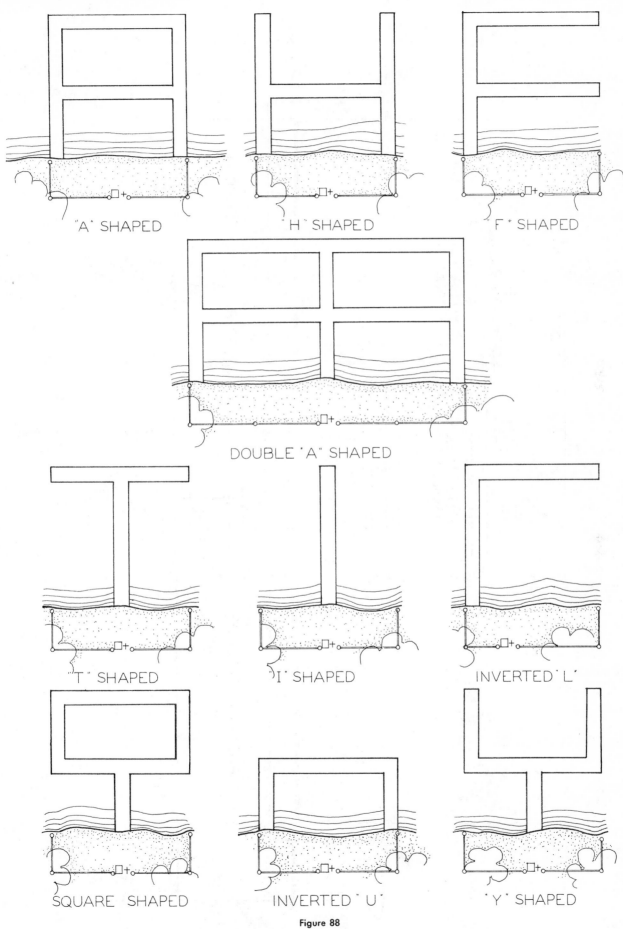

"A" SHAPED   "H" SHAPED   "F" SHAPED

DOUBLE "A" SHAPED

"T" SHAPED   "I" SHAPED   INVERTED "L"

SQUARE SHAPED   INVERTED "U"   "Y" SHAPED

Figure 88
Typical Waterfront Shapes

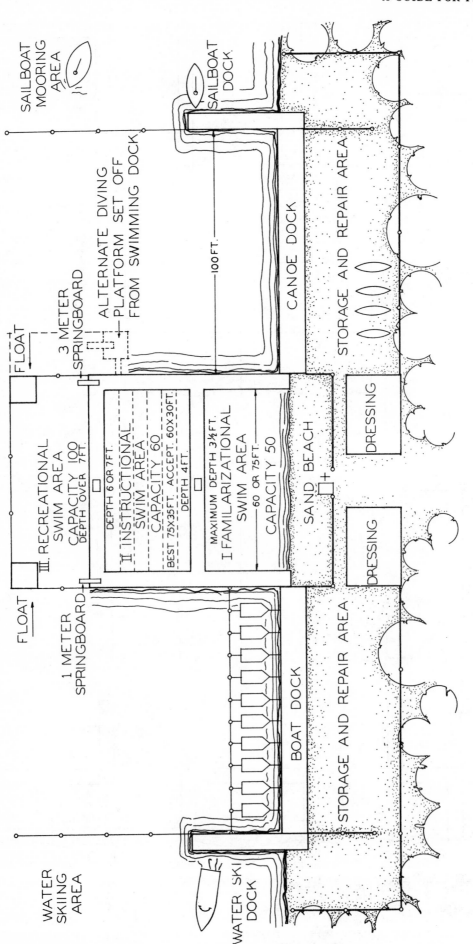

SAILBOAT MOORING AREA

SAILBOAT DOCK

ALTERNATE DIVING PLATFORM SET OFF FROM SWIMMING DOCK

100 FT.

CANOE DOCK

STORAGE AND REPAIR AREA

FLOAT

3 METER SPRINGBOARD

FLOAT

1 METER SPRINGBOARD

III. RECREATIONAL SWIM AREA
CAPACITY 100
DEPTH OVER 7FT.

DEPTH 6 OR 7FT.

II INSTRUCTIONAL SWIM AREA
CAPACITY 60
BEST 75x35FT. ACCEPT. 60x30FT.
DEPTH 4FT.

MAXIMUM DEPTH 3½FT.
I FAMILARIZATIONAL SWIM AREA
60 OR 75FT.
CAPACITY 50

SAND BEACH

DRESSING

DRESSING

WATER SKIING AREA

WATER SKI DOCK

BOAT DOCK

STORAGE AND REPAIR AREA

Figure 89

Typical Layout of Complete Waterfront

KICK RAILS

A rail for practicing and teaching swimming should be placed at water level. This can be made of galvanized pipe, wood rods, or rope.

TOWEL RACKS

Racks for drying towels and bathing suits should be installed at or near the waterfront.

MISCELLANEOUS EQUIPMENT

Life ring buoys should be spaced strategically around the waterfront on racks. These racks are usually in the form of a cross, with the ring suspended from the center and the rope wrapped around the ring from pegs protruding from each end of the cross. Torpedo buoys, bamboo poles, grappling irons, lifelines, shepherd's crooks, stretchers, blankets, microphones, and other such devices should be available to the lifeguards. Numbers indicating depths and the capacities of the crib and other swimming areas should be clearly visible. Kick boards should be available for practice as well as emergency use.

SELECTED REFERENCES

Council for National Cooperation in Aquatics, **The New Science of Skin and Scuba Diving.** New York: Association Press, 1962.

Gabrielsen, B. W., **Facts on Drowning Accidents.** Athens, Ga.: University of Georgia Press.

Gabrielsen, M., and Miles, C., **Sports and Recreation Facilities for School and Community.** Englewood Cliffs, N.J.: Prentice-Hall, Inc., 1958.

Gabrielsen, M.; Spears, Betty; and Gabrielsen, B. W.; **Aquatics Handbook.** Englewood Cliffs, N.J.: Prentice-Hall, Inc., 1960.

Means, Louis, and Gibson, Charles, **Planning School-Community Swimming Pools.** Sacramento: California State Department of Education, 1955.

Suggested Ordinance and Regulations Covering Public Swimming Pools. New York: American Public Health Association, 1790 Broadway, 1964.

Swimming Pool Age Magazine. Hoffman Publishers, Fort Lauderdale, Fla.

Swimming Pool Data and Reference Annual. Fort Lauderdale: Hoffman Publishers.

Swimming Pools for Schools. Stanford, Calif.: Stanford University Press, 1954.

Part Five

Health and Safety
Areas and Facilities

Chapter 15

HEALTH EDUCATION AREAS and FACILITIES

THE PURPOSES and objectives of the school health and safety program can be met only when facilities are provided to conduct the activities designed to accomplish these goals. This chapter attempts to define and point up facility needs related to the school health program in the light of the school's place in the community.

The American Association of School Administrators has said that intelligent self-direction of health behavior is the aim of health education. The very nature of the school dictates that education is the basic objective of any program conducted by the school. Education for health is a broad objective of the school program and the primary objective of all three interrelated parts of the school health program—healthful school living, health instruction, and health services.

It is important that school-health-program facilities be planned cooperatively by representatives of all groups concerned with their use. This means that representatives of medicine, dentistry, public health, nursing education, community groups, and community planners and builders should be involved. Planning must take into consideration the fact that the school health program is a part of the total community public-health program and, therefore, the school program should supplement, not duplicate, other community services and facilities. In planning new facilities, careful consideration should be given to existing facilities or those planned by other community agencies. Detailed plans and actual construction should be carried out with the advice of, and continued consultation with, those persons who will be responsible for the program for which the facility is provided. For example, the school nurse should assist in the planning of the nurse's facilities, and the health teacher should be consulted in planning the health instruction facilities.

While the guide lines suggested here are directed at the provision of facilities, it should be recognized that such provision does not assure wise use. Coordination resulting in effective utilization of facilities can be brought about only by a conscious effort. The school health coordinator serves to effectuate cooperative planning and use of these facilities. The school health committee, with special responsibilities for the program within a school, can do much to promote essential coordination of the program.

In suggesting guide lines for school-health-program facilities, it is recognized that no single set of standards can be universally adopted. Insofar as possible, the recommendations included herein will provide statements of principles which will underlie any set of standards. Varying community needs and philosophies will determine the details of specific requirements.

HEALTHFUL SCHOOL LIVING

The phrase "healthful school living" embraces all efforts to provide facilities and conditions at the school which are beneficial to the health and safety of pupils and school personnel. Providing an environment conducive to healthful school living is a legal and moral responsibility of the schools.

Those responsible for planning the physical plant as well as the education program should place great importance upon the environmental factors to which pupils are exposed. A pupil learns most from doing, and especially from those things which are a part of his conscious experience. Environmental factors make lasting impressions upon the individual. Careful attention to the problems of water supply, approved drinking fountains, sewage disposal, provision and maintenance of adequate toilet facilities, sufficient soap and towels, proper lighting and room color, heating, ventilating, air conditioning, safety, and construction that lends itself to good housekeeping procedures makes a twofold contribution to the well-being of the pupil. First, it has the immediate effect of protecting against disease and injury, and promoting and maintaining good health. Second, contact with a healthful school environment is an educational experience and preparation for future citizenship. In addition, the school may meet its obligation to the handicapped student, and/or the aging, by the avoidance or removal of architectural barriers.[1]

A healthful environment is important to the entire school and should be planned at the administrative level rather than be restricted specifically to any one program area. Decisions, supported by the advice of the program staff, must be made by administrators, architects, official agencies, and community planners in conformance with school-construction standards, codes, rules, and regulations.

School-building construction, heating, ventilation, lighting, plumbing, and decoration are specialties requiring specific training and experience. Those responsible to the citizens of a community for building an educational facility should exercise extreme care in determining the kinds and degree of expertness existing within an architectural firm before assigning it the responsibility for designing and planning a facility as important and complicated as a school building (see Chapter 11).

SCHOOL LUNCH FACILITIES

The school lunch facilities are a part of the healthful environment. The central administration of the school is responsible for the school lunch program. However, the health potential inherent and unique within the lunch program—prevention of dis-

[1] See Appendixes G and H.

ease, promotion and maintenance of good health, and opportunities for healthful educational experiences—makes it a part of healthful school living.

Eating places in schools should be attractive, colorful, pleasant, quiet, and ample in size and in seating capacity to permit the leisurely eating of a noon meal by all pupils and teachers who eat lunch in the room at any one time. The dining room should be adequately lighted, with walls, ceilings, and floors easy to clean and maintain. Table tops should be of smooth, impervious material that can be thoroughly cleaned. The dining room itself must be bulwarked by adequate kitchen facilities, including proper refrigeration, cooking, and dishwashing equipment, and space that permits the sanitary storage of foodstuff and utensils. Waste-disposal facilities must also be provided. Toilet and handwashing facilities must be adequate and convenient for school-lunchroom personnel. Additional toilet and handwashing facilities should be conveniently located for lunchroom patrons.

The type of food service used determines the nature of the facilities needed. Official health and educational agencies have experts in this area who can be called on for assistance. Also many of the larger colleges and universities have a staff skilled in institutional feeding, whose services may be secured in planning school lunchrooms.

Proper planning and provision for the school lunchroom are essential. Unless the food served is nutritious, clean, and wholesome, and the program educational in nature, the feeding of children cannot be justified as an appropriate function of the school. School-lunch facilities should meet the same health-department regulations as other eating places in the community.

ERRORS TO AVOID IN CONSTRUCTION

- Eating area and kitchen too small
- Inadequate lighting and poor ventilation
- Walls, floors, and ceilings of material difficult to clean and maintain
- Slippery floors
- Improper screening
- Inadequate refrigeration space
- Inadequate storage space
- Storage space that is not insect- and rodent-proof
- Inadequate toilet and handwashing facilities
- Cabinets poorly arranged and difficult to clean
- Multiple-use areas not compatible with food service
- Inadequate garbage and refuse disposal
- Inaccessible to and unusable by the disabled and aging

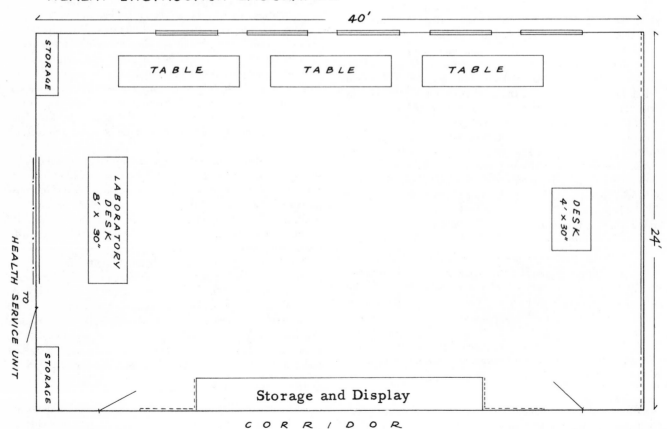

HEALTH INSTRUCTION LABORATORY

Figure 90

HEALTH INSTRUCTION

The purpose of health instruction is to provide health information and experiences which will lead to the establishment of attitudes and practices conducive to the conservation, protection, and promotion of individual, community, and world health.

This section of the Guide is concerned with the facilities essential to the conduct of health classes, including first-aid and safety instruction.

THE ELEMENTARY SCHOOL

For the elementary school, the general principle of the self-contained classroom is accepted. However, in order that there be maximum opportunity for health and safety instruction, it is important to have drinking fountains and handwashing and grooming facilities, and that there be ready access to toilets for the exclusive use of each room in the primary grades. In classrooms for intermediate grades, hand lavatories should be provided. In addition to the central storage space for equipment common to all rooms, each room should have storage space for health teaching aids especially suited to that class. A mobile laboratory table or a resource room equipped with facilities for demonstrations in health and science should be available.

THE SECONDARY SCHOOL

The basic space allotment for the health instruction facilities in the secondary school should be in harmony with generally-accepted standards for schoolroom size. However, due to the nature of activities involved in health and safety instructional programs, it is recommended that the space allowed for such instruction be increased approximately 35 percent above requirements for the regular classroom. This will result in a space allotment of 35 square feet per student, including storage space.

The space allotment should be sufficient to allow for such activities as vision and hearing screening, first-aid and safety instruction, and practical demonstrations, and for flexible teacher location. In addition to the conventional teacher's desk, provision should be made for laboratory demonstrations. This indicates the need for a laboratory-demonstration table which will provide space and facilities for demonstrations. Thus, provisions should be made for water, gas, and electricity, as well as storage space for heating devices, test tubes, flasks, beakers, and other equipment essential to such demonstrations. The diversity of teaching procedures requires that regular classroom arrangements be used at some times, but at other times floor space be available for practical instruction, such as practice in artificial respiration, splinting, and emergency transportation.

The suggested laboratory method of teaching will require adequate storage space as well as display areas for charts, mannequins, models, and equipment. First-aid equipment, such as blankets, bandages, splints, and stretchers will also be needed. For instruction in home nursing, such equipment as incubators, roll-away beds, pans, containers, and bedding will be required.

There should be a large amount of display space for the great variety of educational exhibits, literature, and pupil projects inherent in the health education program. This can be provided by allowing liberal space for tables and shelves, and by using all available wall space for bulletin boards and tackboards.

The health instruction laboratory should provide for the optimum use of such additional audiovisual devices as still pictures, slides, motion pictures, radio, and television. This will necessitate a liberal allowance of appropriately-located electrical outlets, shades, or curtains which will reduce the outside light, and a screen which may be mounted above the chalkboard behind the laboratory desk.

It may be desirable that there be convenient access between the health instruction laboratory and the health service suite in order that each may augment the total health program. For example, when home-nursing classes are meeting in the health instruction laboratory, there will be times when it is desirable to have free but supervised access to both facilities. Similarly, when there is occasion to have a large number of people using the health service suite, it may be desirable to have access to the health instruction laboratory for seating or other purposes. In some instances, it may be desirable to consider locating the health instruction laboratory near the science laboratories in order to facilitate joint use of equipment and supplies. In other instances, location in the area of the physical education facilities may be desirable.

The secondary-school health instruction laboratory should be an example of the ideal classroom environment, with special concern for color of walls, lighting, ventilation, temperature and humidity control, order, and cleanliness.

Figure 90 will serve to illustrate a suggested floor plan for the secondary-school health instruction laboratory intended to accommodate a maximum of 30 students.

Recognition should be given to the desirability of joint planning of school health facilities with public-health people and other community groups who might need access to such facilities, thus strengthening the total community health program. Such arrangements can serve to strengthen the program of all who are concerned with health by providing for dual use of such facilities without duplication and with a minimum of expense.

CHECK LIST FOR HEALTH INSTRUCTION FACILITIES

- Space for 35 square feet per pupil, maximum of 30 pupils
- Flexible teacher location
- Provision for various teaching methods, including laboratory demonstration
- Flexibility of seating
- Hot and cold running water and gas outlet
- Educational-exhibit space
- Storage space
- Provision for using audiovisual devices (electrical outlets, window shades, screens)
- Access to health service unit
- Exemplary environmental features
- Adequate handwashing facilities, drinking fountains, and toilets
- Air conditioning
- Accessible to and usable by the disabled
- Planned jointly for community use

HEALTH SERVICES

Health services contribute to the school program by: (1) facilitating learning; (2) encouraging pupils to obtain needed medical or dental treatment; (3) adapting school programs to individual-pupil needs; (4) maintaining a healthful school environment; and (5) increasing pupils' understanding of health and health problems. Following the principle that "program determines facilities," plans would include accommodations for:
- Appraising the health status of pupils and school personnel
- Counseling pupils, parents, and others concerning appraisal findings

- Encouraging the correction of remediable defects and the proper adjustment of those identified as not remediable
- Assisting in the identification and education of disabled pupils
- Helping to prevent and control disease
- Providing emergency service for injury or sudden illness
- Maintaining a cumulative combined health and accident file for each student

Health service personnel are not only charged with the responsibility for developing policies and procedures, but should also be consulted in planning programs and facilities. Policies and procedures are essential for the attainment of program objectives through the proper utilization of facilities and the protection of school populations under adverse or disaster conditions.

HEALTH SUITE

Whether in a small rural or a large urban school building, the health service suite will be used for a variety of activities. It may be the center for emergency care of injuries or sickness and health appraisals by nurses, physicians, dentists or dental hygienists, and psychiatrists or psychologists. Various types of systematized screening tests, such as tests of vision and hearing, may be conducted in this area.

The health suite is the logical place for conferences concerning a pupil's health problems involving the parent, teacher, doctor, nurse, and physical educator. A part of the suite should be used as a dressing room and another section should serve as a waiting room. Some space should be set aside for the isolation of a pupil when the situation warrants, and accommodations should be provided for pupils on a prescribed rest schedule. The suite will also need to provide space for the health service personnel, plus the necessary space for records and equipment.

The common concerns of school health service personnel and guidance personnel suggest the need for a close, cooperative working relationship. This would indicate the desirability of locating the units in close proximity to each other and the possibility of using a common waiting room.

The school health suite may, in some instances, also serve the community. Thus, the health suite and the adjacent health instruction area may be for well-child conferences and other preschool health activities. They may accommodate classes for expectant mothers, and other adult education activities. In those situations where the building and grounds are used for recreation purposes, the unit may serve as an emergency-care and first-aid station for those participating in the recreation program.

The fact that a health service suite is located within the school does not mean that programs for nonschool groups will be administered or manned by school personnel. Usually, these community health activities will be under the direct supervision of the official health agency. If community usage of the health service suite is expected, then those who will provide the service should be involved in the planning.

LOCATION

In locating a health service suite, consideration should be given to the variety of activities that will be carried on therein, and to conditions which will permit those functions to be carried on conveniently and efficiently. Some factors to be considered in the location of a health service suite are:

- It should be located along a corridor near a main entrance to the building so that it may be completely isolated from the remainder of the building, yet conveniently accessible from all parts of the building.

- It should be located on the first, or ground, floor.
- The location should be in close proximity to the administrative suite. In situations where full-time health service personnel are not contemplated, direct access should be provided between the area and the administrative office, the teacher's lounge, or an adjacent classroom. In the secondary school, advantages will accrue from locating the health classroom and the service suite so that there is convenient access between the two areas. This is especially true when school health facilities are utilized for community health services.
- The location and acoustical treatment should be such that corridor and outside noises are kept to a minimum.
- A maximum amount of natural light should be available.

ROOMS

All purposes for which the health service suite is designed may be carried out in one large unit, which may be subdivided into: (1) waiting room; (2) examining room; (3) resting rooms; (4) toilet rooms; (5) counseling room; (6) dental health room; (7) isolation room; (8) special screening areas (e.g., vision and hearing); and (9) office area for health service personnel and records. Depending upon the size of the school and its health policies, various combinations of the above spaces may be planned without affecting the efficiency of the services. For example, in smaller elementary schools, all services may be cared for in one room, provided proper screening is used and the administrative and health service suite are served by a common waiting room.

In larger schools, and especially in high schools, division of the unit into separate rooms is desirable. Thought should be given to the type of wall construction which provides for rearrangement of space allocation, since change in policies and school population will affect the nature and extent of health services. When remodeling old buildings, the same standards that apply to new structures should be maintained.

Guide lines based on accepted standards are recommended below.

Waiting Room

Schools with ten or more classrooms, or enrollments of 300 or more pupils should provide a waiting room, possibly in combination with guidance and/or administrative offices. It should be directly accessible to the corridor and the examining room. The waiting room should be separated from adjacent rooms by a full-height partition.

The decorations and furnishings should be designed to create a bright and cheerful atmosphere. The size is dependent upon enrollment and established health policies of the school (see Table 10).

Examining Room

Schools consisting of 6 or more classrooms, or an enrollment of 180 or more pupils, should include an examining room in the health suite. It should be directly connected with resting rooms and the waiting room, and should have access to toilets, the dental space, and any offices that are provided.

The location should provide for natural light and ventilation. The size and arrangement should be such that an uninterrupted distance of 20' is available for vision testing.

The room should be acoustically treated. If the examining room is to serve as a resting room (in small schools), screened cot areas should be provided. The space should be ample for proper arrangement or storage of the following equipment:

    desk, chair, typewriter

filing cabinets
platform scale with stadiometer
vision-testing equipment
movable spotlight
blankets and linens
folding screen
sterilizer and instrument table
cot or couch
cabinet for first-aid supplies

cup and towel dispensers
wastebasket and foot-operated disposal can
full-length mirror
audiometric testing devices

The size of the examining room will be determined by enrollment, the types of activities to be conducted, and the extent of use by medical and other health personnel (see Table 10).

TABLE 10
RECOMMENDED SIZES IN SQUARE FEET OF HEALTH-SERVICE FACILITIES FOR SCHOOLS OF VARIOUS SIZES

ENROLLMENT	200-300	301-500	501-700	701-900	901-1100	1101-1300
Waiting Room	80	80	100	100	100	120
* Examining Room	200	200	200	240	240	240
** Rest Room (total area for boys and girls)	100	180	220	260	300***	340***

Toilets.........48 square feet total area (provide one for girls and one for boys)

OPTIONAL AREAS

Dental Clinic	100 square feet for all schools
Office Space	80 square feet for each office provided
Eye Examination	120 square feet minimum for all schools

* Examining room areas include 6 square feet for clothes closet and 24 square feet for storage closets.
** For determining the number of cots, allow one cot per 100 pupils up to 400 pupils, and one cot per 200 pupils above 400. Round out fractions to nearest whole number. Allow 50 square feet of floor space for each of the first two cots and 40 square feet for each additional cot.
*** In schools enrolling 901 to 1,100, a three-cot rest room is suggested for boys and a four-cot rest room for girls, and in 1,101- to 1,300-pupil schools, a three-cot rest room is suggested for boys and a five-cot rest room for girls.
Note: For larger schools, add multiples of the above areas to obtain total needs.
State Department of Education, *School Planning Manual*, School Health Service Section, Vol. 37, November, 1954, Richmond, Va.

Resting Rooms

Resting rooms are essential in all schools. They should be directly connected with the examining room and toilets, or be accessible to them from a restricted hallway.

Separate resting rooms should be provided for each sex. A screened cot space may be a necessary arrangement in smaller schools.

The location should be such that natural light and ventilation, and quiet atmosphere are secured. If there are no full-time health service personnel available, the location should be such that supervision of the area may be conveniently provided from the administrative office or an adjacent classroom. Adequate space should be provided for cots (see Table 10), bedside stands, wastebaskets, and blanket and linen storage.

Toilet Rooms

A toilet room with stool and lavatory should be directly connected, or accessible by a restricted hallway, to the resting rooms in all schools with 10 or more classrooms, or with an enrollment of 300 or more pupils. In smaller schools, where the resting rooms are a part of the examining room or other space, provision should be made for convenient toilet facilities. A toilet room with a minimum of 48 square feet should be provided for each sex (see Table 10).

Storage Closets

Storage space, opening off each resting room, should be provided for linens, blankets, pillows, etc. In the smaller schools without separate resting rooms, such storage should be provided for in the examining room.

A ventilated cloak closet should be provided for school health personnel. If built-in storage facilities are not feasible, space should be allowed for movable storage cabinets.

Isolation Room

An isolation room as an integral part of the health service suite is desirable to insure privacy when required. It should be directly connected with the examining room, but apart from the resting rooms. A space for one cot and the necessary circulation area is sufficient in most instances.

Dental Health Service Area

This area should be considered an extension of the examining room, and school policies will determine whether or not specific space will be assigned for this service. Its relation to other areas should be the same as that of the examining room.

The same attention should be given to light and ventilation as is devoted to the remainder of the examining area. A floor area of approximately 100 square feet, if arranged properly, will provide adequate space for equipment necessary to carry on an acceptable school dental program.

Vision and Hearing Screening Areas

Such areas should be included as a part of the examining room. An uninterrupted distance of 20' should be provided for vision testing.

Audiometric testing will require an acoustically-treated room.

Offices

The provision of office space for health service personnel will depend upon the time they spend in the school. If this facility is provided, it should be connected with the waiting room, the examining room, and if possible, the corridor.

The minimum recommended space for two people is 80 square feet. Provision should be made for maintaining health and accident reports.

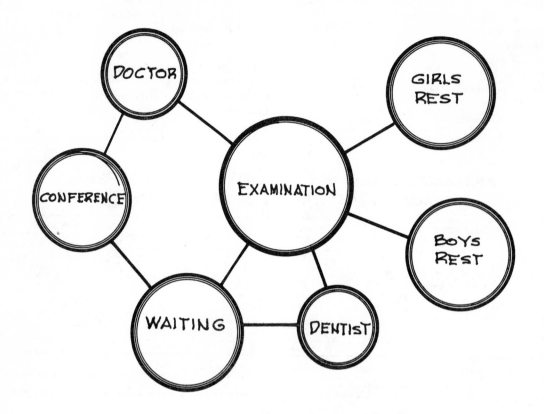

Figure 91
Space Relationship Diagram for a Health Suite

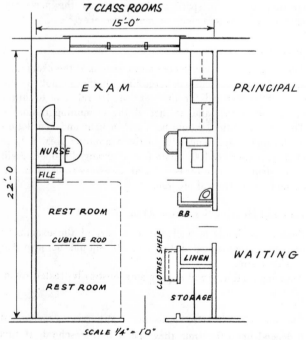

Figure 92

Source: State Department of Education, State Board of Health, *Recommendations for School Health Service Unit with Suggested Plans*, Columbia, South Carolina, 1953, p. 8.

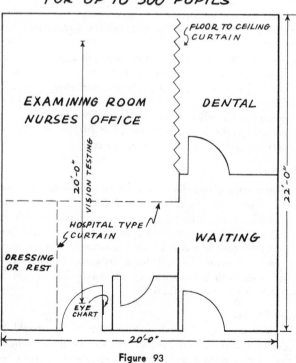

Figure 93

Source: The University of the State of New York, State Education Department, Division of School Buildings and Grounds, *Planning the School Health Suite*, Albany, New York, 1946.

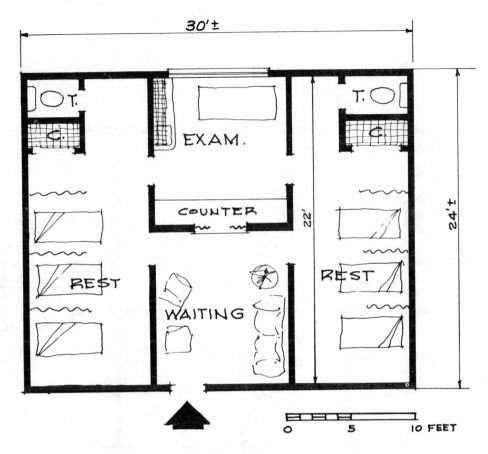

Figure 94

Suggested Health Suite for up to 700, Pupil School

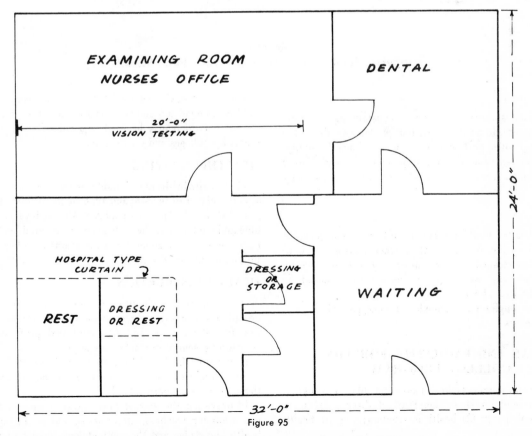

Figure 95

Suggested Health Suite for up to 800, Pupil School

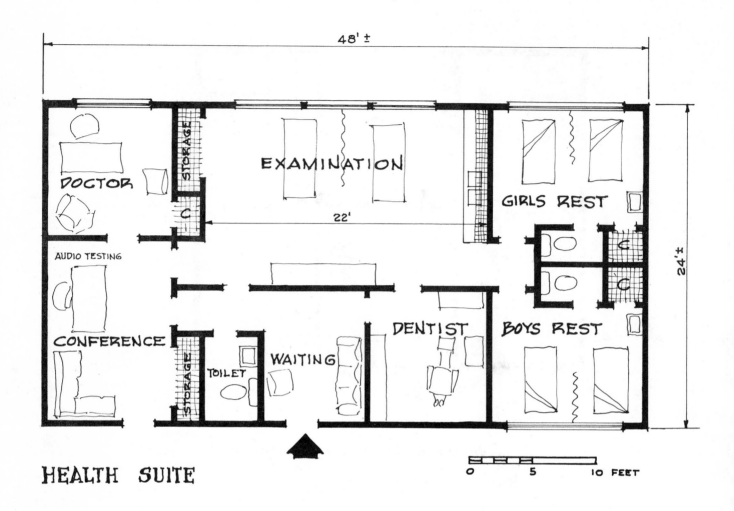

Figure 96
Suggested Health Suite for Over 1,100, Pupil School

Counseling Room

Although such space will not be in constant use, a room where the doctor, nurse, teacher, and parent can discuss a pupil's health is an important unit of the total health facility. Space large enough to accommodate a small table and 4 or 5 chairs is adequate. It may be used as office space for part-time health service personnel.

General Suggestions

The entire suite should present an informal and pleasant atmosphere. Flooring should be of a material which is non-absorbent, easily cleaned, and light in color. Lavatories used by personnel functioning within the examining room should be operable by the wrist, knee, or foot.

Figures 91 through 96 are examples of some possible health-suite arrangements.

AREAS AND FACILITIES FOR THE COLLEGE PROGRAM

The college and university health program, like the program at the other school levels, is comprised of three phases: (1) healthful school living; (2) health instruction; and (3) health services.

The American College Health Association has prepared a set of "Recommended Standards and Practices for a College Health Program", which may be used as a guide for developing programs for colleges and universities.

HEALTHFUL LIVING

The healthful-living considerations in the college are directly related to the size and type of institution, the services provided, and the facilities available. Although varying in magnitude and complexity, the college environmental-health program embodies the same general considerations as other institutions providing similar services.

HEALTH INSTRUCTION

Health instruction facilities in colleges and universities must be suited to meeting the responsibilities of: (1) health instruction for all students; and (2) additional professional health education essential in teacher preparation.

In meeting the health education needs of all students, the facilities required will be comparable in nature and scope to those in the secondary school.

In providing the special professional preparation in health education for teachers, attention should be given to special health knowledge and the methodology important to teachers.

This will dictate that teachers become acquainted with content, methods, equipment, and facilities, thus emphasizing the need to make the health education program for teachers an exemplary one.

HEALTH SERVICES

The college health service program will vary with the size and type of institution, ranging from small units with few demands, which can be met on a first-aid basis, to the large, comprehensive student health center providing services on a par, in both quantity and quality, with many hospitals. The diversity of facilities needed dictates that planning must be done in light of the immediate situation and that it must involve those who will use the facility, in cooperation with technical and professional planners.

SELECTED REFERENCES

American College Health Association, Recommended Standards and Practices for a College Health Program, Part II, **Journal of the American College Health Association,** Vol. 12, No. 1, October, 1963.

Joint Committee on Health Problems in Education of the National Education Association and the American Medical Association, **Health Education.** Washington, D.C.: National Education Association, 1961.

, **Healthful School Living.** Washington, D.C.: National Education Association, 1957.

, **School Health Services.** Washington, D.C.: National Education Association, 1964.

, **Suggested School Health Policies.** 4th ed. Washington, D.C.: National Education Association, 1964.

Planning the School Health Suite. Albany: The University of the State of New York, State Education Department, 1946.

School Planning Manual. Richmond, Va.: State Department of Education, Vol. 37, November, 1954.

State Department of Education and State Board of Health, **Recommendations for School Health Service Units.** Columbia, S.C.: State Department of Education, 1953.

Chapter 16

SAFETY EDUCATION AREAS and FACILITIES

ROLE OF SAFETY IN HEALTH, PHYSICAL EDUCATION, AND RECREATION

More than one-half of all school-jurisdiction accidents occur in physical education and athletic programs. This has been true for a long time, with little or no change reflected on a grade-by-grade, activity-by-activity, frequency, or rate basis. It is, therefore, incumbent upon the school's administration, generally, and staff involved in the health, physical education, recreation, and athletic programs, specifically, to maintain comprehensive accident records and to analyze accident occurrence with respect to the nature, type, place, frequency, and severity of the accident.

Safety education must, then, be structured into the program. A good safety education program does not restrict activities, nor does it protect at the expense of education. It does identify hazardous physical conditions and unsafe practices. The hazards should be corrected or eliminated. All activities and student participation should be studied to determine the nature and extent of safety education and supervision required to develop needed knowledge, skills, and attitudes.

Special facilities and equipment are not required to teach safe procedures and practices. It is important, however, that equipment for physical education and athletics be selected, purchased, and maintained from the point of view of accident prevention. The use of such equipment should incorporate a deliberate intent to provide instruction in safe practices.

DRIVER EDUCATION AREAS AND FACILITIES

The traffic-accident situation is a national disgrace which can be improved by drivers who are better informed, more skillful, and have an improved sense of moral responsibility. Such drivers can be developed through driver education.

The program of driver education is generally accepted as a responsibility of the school and, more specifically, as a function of health and safety and physical education departments. The guide lines outlined below are in keeping with approved standards and national recommendations.

INDOOR FACILITIES

For the indoor program, there should be a classroom, a psychophysical laboratory with testing devices, a simulator laboratory, and an office.

LOCATION

All indoor facilities should be on the first floor of the build-
ing, near the garage or parking space for the dual-control cars, and near the driving range if one is used.

CLASSROOM

Size

The recommended procedure is to combine the classroom with the laboratory for a combination room of 30' x 40'. Where separate rooms are used, the classroom should be of standard size.

Furniture and Equipment

In addition to the standard classroom facilities and equipment, such as chalkboard, bulletin board, desk, and chairs, the driver education classroom should provide facilities for the following special equipment:
- Motion-picture projector.
- Bookcases and storage cabinets for films, flip charts, testing equipment, models, etc.
- Demonstration table
- Demonstration equipment, including magnetic traffic board, working models, flannel boards, model signs, and signals

PSYCHOPHYSICAL LABORATORY

The psychophysical laboratory contains equipment needed to test the student's physical, mental, and emotional qualifications required for safe and skillful driving.

Size

When the combined room is not used, the laboratory should be at least 24' x 30'.

Furniture and Equipment

The needed furniture and equipment will include a demonstration table, chairs, worktables, and spaces to accommodate equipment for testing visual acuity, depth perception, color vision, field of vision, reaction time, steadiness, night vision, etc.

SIMULATOR LABORATORY

Driver education simulators are accepted as a means of providing the preliminary steps to behind-the-wheel instruction. Because of the nature of the simulator units, facilities for them should be considered as permanent installations, preferably in a separate classroom.

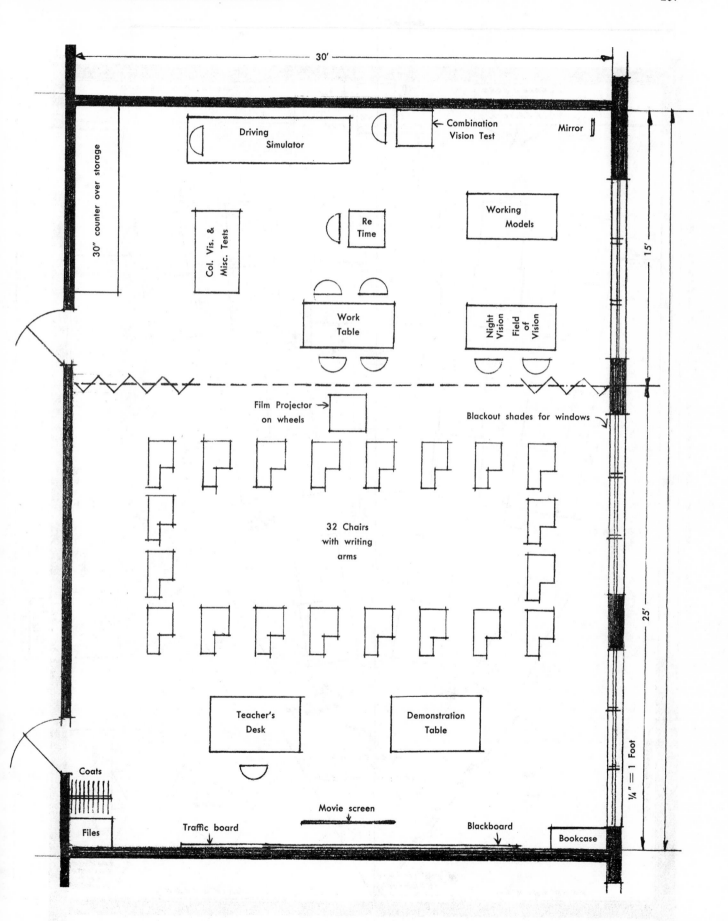

Figure 97
Driver Education Classroom and Laboratory

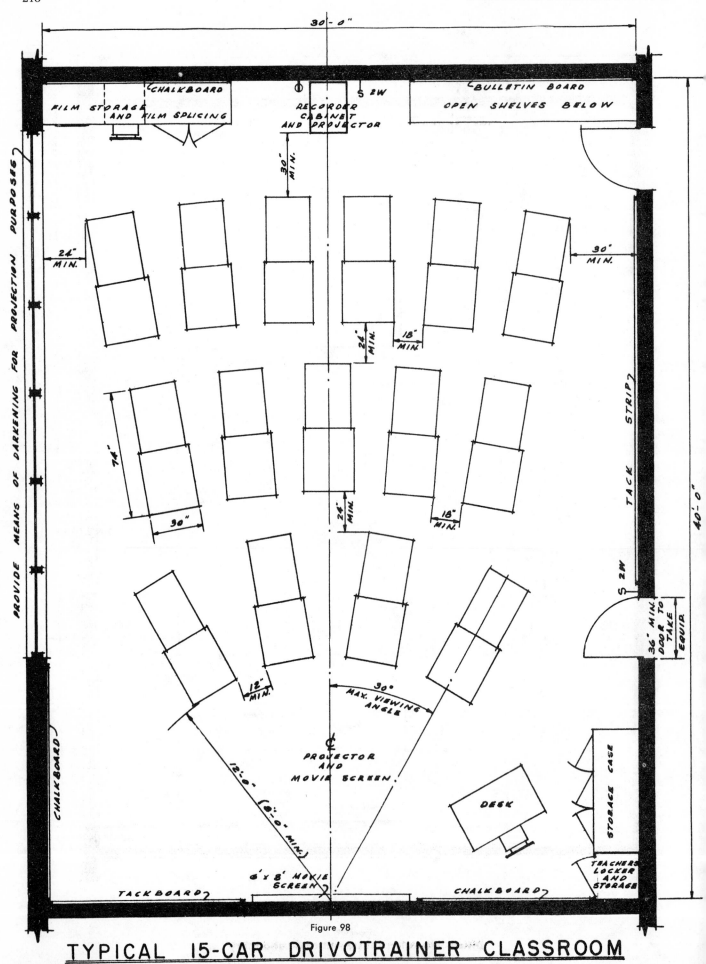

Figure 98

TYPICAL 15-CAR DRIVOTRAINER CLASSROOM

Size

The size of the simulator laboratory will depend on the number of simulator cars to be installed. A typical 8-car installation will accommodate 450 to 500 students per year, and a 16-car installation will accommodate 960 to 1,000. The room size for 8 cars should be 24' x 33'; for 16 cars, it should be 30' x 40'.

Furniture and Equipment

The room should be clear of obstructions that might interfere with the projector beam, and should be provided with the regular complement of chalkboard, bulletin board, tackboard, magnetic board, etc.

Layout

The cars are arranged in a semicircular fashion, with the first row a minimum of 8', preferably 10' to 12', from the screen, and with the outside cars not exceeding an angle of 30° from the screen. The first row should have the lesser number of cars.

A minimum of 24" should be allowed between the rows, with a 30-inch aisle down each side of the room. Aisle spaces must comply with state safety codes. The projector should be located in the center at the extreme rear of the room, and a 6' x 8' screen should be placed in the front of the room.

Manufacturers' specifications for electrical requirements should be followed. Ordinarily, the standard 120-volt, 60-cycle alternating current is required. It should be supplied through a double outlet located in the vicinity of the recording unit.

Lighting

Ample soft white fluorescent-light tubes recessed in the ceiling with semitranslucent shields to provide 100 footcandles of light at desk height should be installed.

Color

Pastel colors should be used. The woodwork and finishing should be compatible with color used on the walls. A reflection factor of 80 percent is needed for the ceiling, and 60 percent for the walls. The furniture should have a nonglare finish.

Heating and Ventilation

Heating and ventilation should be in conformance with standards required throughout the entire school system.

THE MOBILE LABORATORY UNIT

A mobile laboratory unit may be used when it is necessary to accommodate several locations, or to gain maximum use of the simulators by two or more schools.

Size

Since nearly all mobile classrooms are 12-place units, the size of the trailer should be not less than 52' nor more than 56' long inside. The inside height should be 8', with a width of 10'.

Furniture and Equipment

The rear of the trailer should contain 2 storage closets, a teacher's desk, a chair, built-in film-storage closets, and program racks. The mobile classroom should have good acoustics, waterproof materials inside and out, high-grade tiling on the floor, and windows at evenly-spaced intervals. For maximum safety, two 36" doors with safety latches should be located on the curb side. Like any other classroom, it should have good lighting, wiring, heating, and cooling systems.

Layout

The simulator cars should be arranged six on each side, one behind the other, with the step form of elevation for cars so all students can see the screen.

OUTDOOR AREAS AND FACILITIES

DRIVING AREA

Purpose

Behind-the-wheel instruction provides the skills necessary for safe and efficient driving.

Types

An on-street driving area is recommended for schools where traffic congestion is not a problem. First driving maneuvers should be conducted in locations such as school driveways where there is no traffic. As ability develops, students get experience driving in situations approximating normal driving conditions, and then, finally, in actual normal traffic situations.

Blocked-off streets are sometimes used when street traffic is too heavy and school driveways are not available to teach the first driving maneuvers. Arrangements should be made with the residents of the area and with police officials. Since advance driving skills are taught where other traffic is involved, streets should not be blocked off for an undue length of time.

An off-street driving range is recommended where land is available. Ranges should be laid out to simulate most physical situations associated with driving, such as: traffic signs, signals, and other control devices; parallel and angle parking; upgrade and downgrade situations; and simulated emergency situations. Space should allow for needed skill-test maneuvers. Different types of road surfaces should be provided. If night classes are conducted, the area should be lighted. The size of the driving range should be no smaller than 350' x 450'.

The multiple-car driving range has the advantage of accommodating several cars simultaneously under the supervision of one teacher, thus reducing the per-pupil cost. With this type of range, communication between the instructor and students is accomplished by means of radio or public-address system.

Recommended Equipment and Facilities

- Curbs for parking practice
- Intersections for various turn maneuvers
- Gravel area for driving and turn maneuvers
- Streets marked properly
- Streets that are both wide and narrow
- All signs—traffic-control signals, stop, warning, yield the right-of-way, regulatory, guide, and information
- Upgrade and downgrade roadways
- Simulated road surfaces—concrete, asphalt, and gravel
- Muddy surface for emergency situations
- Signboards found on normal roads
- Stanchions, guide-on, etc., for maneuvers

Points to Remember

- Determine the needs of the student and the objectives of the program.
- Provide as many realistic situations as possible.
- Design the driver-training area equal to the best facilities available.

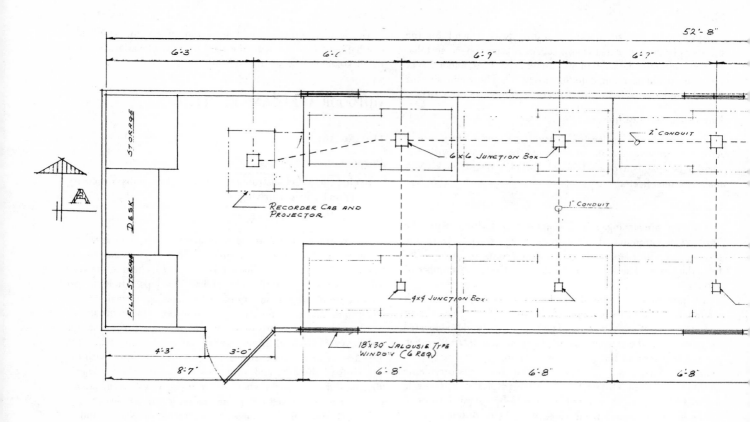

FLOOR PL

SCALE: 1/2" = 1'-0"

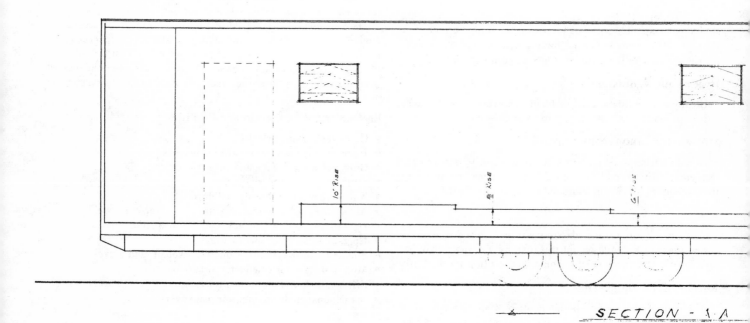

SECTION - A A

SCALE: 1/2" = 1'-0"

Figure 99
Mobile Laboratory Unit

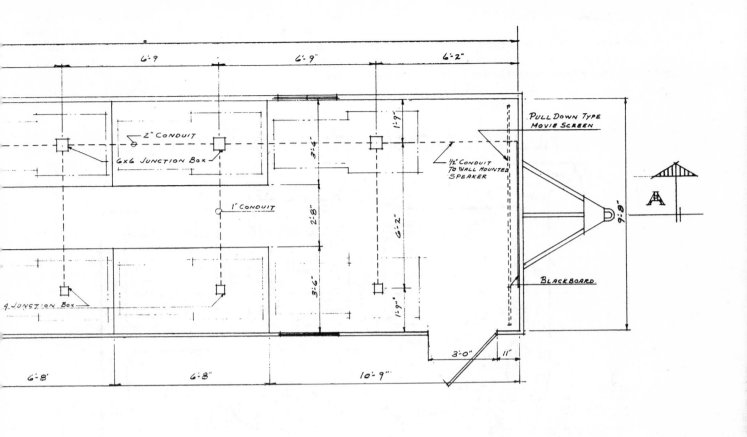

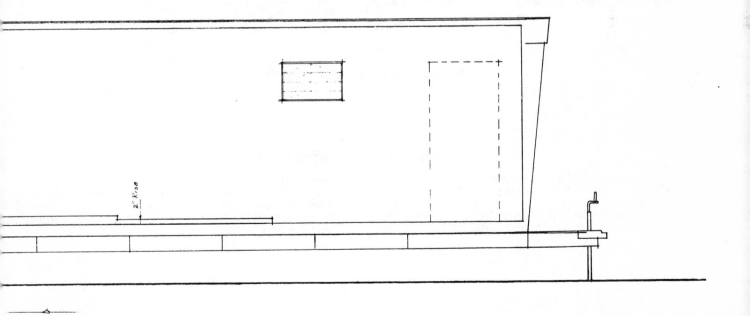

COLLEGE AREAS AND FACILITIES

The college driver education program is concerned with the preparation of teachers rather than the preparation of new drivers. Prospective teachers must be taught to use and evalu-ate all available facilities, equipment, and devices for driver education. Facilities, equipment, and devices for the college program must, therefore, be similar to those recommended for high schools, but with emphasis on a wide variety of makes and models.

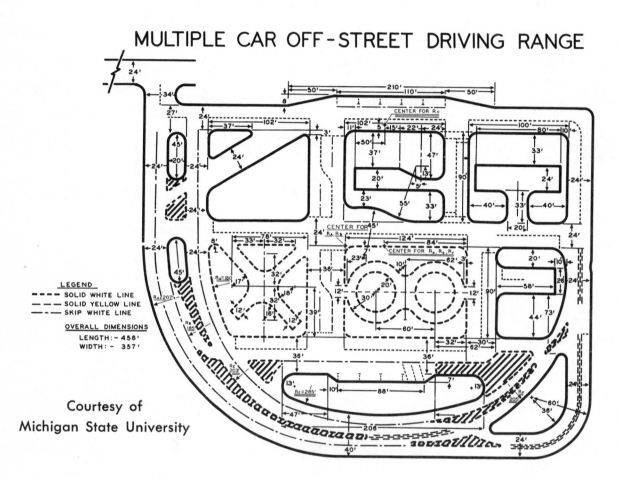

Figure 100
Multiple Car Off-Street Driving Range

SELECTED REFERENCES

Allgaier, Earl, **Classroom and Laboratory Facilities for a Driver Education Course.** Washington, D.C.: Traffic Engineering and Safety Department, May 18, 1964.

Brady, Leon, and Stack, Herbert J., **Highway Safety and Driver Educa-tion.** Englewood Cliffs, N.J.: Prentice-Hall, Inc., 1962.

National Commission on Safety Education (NEA), **Driver and Traffic Safety Education: Policies and Practices.** Washington, D.C.: The Commission, 1958.

Teacher's Manual for Driver Education. Springfield, Ill.: State De-partment of Public Instruction, 1958.

APPENDIX A

NATIONAL CONFERENCE ON AREAS AND FACILITIES FOR HEALTH, PHYSICAL EDUCATION, AND RECREATION

SPONSORING ORGANIZATIONS

American Association for Health,
Physical Education, and Recreation
Caswell M. Miles

American Association of School Administrators
Jordan L. Larson

American Camping Association
Reynold E. Carlson

American Institute of Park Executives
John P. Hewitt

American Recreation Society
Milo F. Christiansen

Association of College Unions — International
Loren V. Kottner

National Association of Recreational
Therapists
Phillip J. Walsh

National Association for Physical Education
of College Women
Leona Holbrook

National College Physical Education
Association for Men
Harold E. Kenney

National Conference on State Parks
Don Alexander

National Council on Schoolhouse
Construction
John L. Cameron

National Education Association
Jackson M. Anderson

National Federation of State High School
Athletic Associations
David C. Arnold

National Recreation Association
Joseph Prendergast

Society of State Directors of Health,
Physical Education, and Recreation
Harold K. Jack

School Facilities Council of Architecture,
Education, and Industry
Jordan L. Larson

The Athletic Institute
Theodore P. Bank

EXECUTIVE COMMITTEE

CHAIRMAN
Caswell M. Miles
State Department of Education
Albany, New York

VICE-CHAIRMAN
Milo F. Christiansen
Department of Recreation
Washington, D. C.

SECRETARY
Jackson M. Anderson
American Association for Health,
Physical Education, and Recreation
Washington, D. C.

TREASURER
Theodore P. Bank
The Athletic Institute
Chicago, Illinois

CONFERENCE DIRECTOR
Harold K. Jack
Temple University
Philadelphia, Pennsylvania

STEERING COMMITTEE

Jackson M. Anderson, American Association for Health, Physical Education, and Recreation, Washington, D. C.

Theodore P. Bank, The Athletic Institute, Chicago, Illinois

Karl W. Bookwalter, Indiana University, Bloomington, Indiana

George D. Butler, National Recreation Association, Sarasota, Florida

Frederick M. Chapman, University of Minnesota, Minneapolis, Minnesota

Milo F. Christiansen, District of Columbia Recreation Department, Washington, D. C.

George F. Cousins, Indiana University, Bloomington, Indiana

Robert W. Crawford, Department of Recreation, Philadelphia, Pennsylvania

Harold K. Jack, Temple University, Philadelphia, Pennsylvania

Caswell M. Miles, State Department of Education, Albany, New York

J. Keogh Rash, Indiana University, Bloomington, Indiana

Robert Yoho, State Board of Health, Indianapolis, Indiana

APPENDIX B

PARTICIPANTS IN THE
THIRD NATIONAL FACILITIES CONFERENCE
Biddle Continuing Education Center,
Indiana University, Bloomington
January 15-24, 1965

Aldrich, Anita—Chairman, Department of Physical Education for Women, School of Health, Physical Education, and Recreation, Indiana University, Bloomington, Indiana.

Anderson, Jackson M.—Assistant Executive Secretary, American Association for Health, Physical Education, and Recreation, Washington, D. C.

Arnold, David C.—Assistant Executive Secretary, National Federation of State High School Athletic Associations, Chicago, Illinois.

Bank, Theodore P.—President, The Athletic Institute, Chicago, Illinois.

Bartelma, David C.—Chairman, Department of Physical Education for Men, University of Colorado, Boulder, Colorado.

Beazely, A. E.—Consulting Engineer, Saskatoon, Saskatchewan, Canada.

Benedict, Paul H.—Superintendent of Schools, Vesta, New York.

Berke, Ira—Landscape Architect, Chicago Park District, Chicago, Illinois.

Bookwalter, Carolyn—Special Lecturer, School of Health, Physical Education, and Recreation, Indiana University, Bloomington, Indiana.

Bookwalter, Karl W.—Chairman, Graduate Division, School of Health, Physical Education, and Recreation, Indiana University, Bloomington, Indiana.

Bradley, Neil—Recreation Assistant, Unified School District, Long Beach, California.

Butler, George D.—National Recreation Association, Sarasota, Florida.

Cameron, John L.—U. S. Office of Education, Department of Health, Education and Welfare, Washington, D. C.

Carlson, Reynold E.—Chairman, Department of Recreation and Park Administration, School of Health, Physical Education, and Recreation, Indiana University, Bloomington, Indiana.

Chapman, Frederick M.—Associate Professor of Recreation, University of Minnesota, Minneapolis, Minnesota.

Costello, Milton—Consulting Engineer, Wantaugh, New York.

Counsilman, James E.—Associate Professor of Physical Education, and Swimming Coach, Indiana University, Bloomington, Indiana.

Cousins, George F.—Chairman, Department of Physical Education for Men, School of Health, Physical Education, and Recreation, Indiana University, Bloomington, Indiana.

Crawford, Robert W.—Commissioner, Department of Recreation, Philadelphia, Pennsylvania.

Daniels, Arthur S.—Dean, School of Health, Physical Education, and Recreation, Indiana University, Bloomington, Indiana.

Dhainin, Felix K.—Board of Park Commissioners, Minneapolis, Minnesota.

Gabrielsen, Milton A.—Professor of Education, New York University, New York, New York.

George, Jack F.—Director of Health, Physical Education, and Recreation, Roslyn Public Schools, Roslyn, New York.

Graves, Charles M.—Park and Recreation Specialist, The Charles M. Graves Organization, Atlanta, Georgia.

Hartvigsen, Milton—Dean, College of Health, Physical Education, and Recreation, Brigham Young University, Provo, Utah.

Haynes, Evan—Assistant Regional Director, Bureau of Outdoor Recreation, Lake Central Region, Ann Arbor, Michigan.

Hebel, Everett L.—Director, Office of Health, Safety, and Physical Education, State Department of Education, Trenton, New Jersey.

Hester, Oka T.—Director of Parks and Recreation, Greensboro, North Carolina.

Holbrook, Leona—Chairman, Department of Physical Education for Women, Brigham Young University, Provo, Utah.

Hughes, Wayne—Manager, School and College Department, National Safety Council, Chicago, Illinois.

Jack, Harold K.—Chairman, Department of Health, Physical Education, and Recreation, Temple University, Philadelphia, Pennsylvania.

Kaplan, Robert—Consultant in Health and Fitness, American Medical Association, Chicago, Illinois.

Kenney, Harold E.—Professor of Physical Education, and Manager of Facilities, University of Illinois, Urbana, Illinois.

Kottner, Loren V.—Director, Iowa Memorial Union, University of Iowa, Iowa City, Iowa.

Krueger, Charles E.—Chief, Division of Landscape Architecture, National Park Service, Western Office of Design and Construction, San Francisco, California.

Lengfeld, Fred—Associate Professor of Health, Recreation, and Physical Education, Wisconsin State University, LaCrosse, Wisconsin.

Loft, Bernard I.—Associate Professor of Health and Safety, School of Health, Physical Education, and Recreation, Indiana University, Bloomington, Indiana.

McCarthy, Robert E.—Principal, East Syracuse-Minoa Central High School, East Syracuse, New York.

McLelland, Malcolm J.—Consultant in Health and Physical Education, State Board of Health, Indianapolis, Indiana.

Miles, Caswell M.—Chief, Bureau of Physical Education and Recreation, State Education Department, Albany, New York.

Millman, David—Superintendent of Schools, Mechanicsville, New York.

Mittelstaedt, Arthur H., Jr.—Recreation Planning Consultant, Mineola, New York.

Nugent, Timothy—Director, Rehabilitation-Education Center, University of Illinois, Urbana, Illinois.

Perkins, James—Landscape Architect, Chicago Park District, Chicago, Illinois.

Perry, Russell—Director of Recreation, Wilmette, Illinois.

Porter, William—Landscape Architect, Chicago Park District, Chicago, Illinois.

Rash, J. Keogh—Chairman, Department of Health and Safety, School of Health, Physical Education, and Recreation, Indiana University, Bloomington, Indiana.

Robertson, David H.—Director of Swimming, New Trier High School, Winnetka, Illinois.

Seagers, Paul W.—Professor of Education, and School Building Consultant, Indiana University, Bloomington, Indiana.

Seidler, Armond H.—Chairman, Department of Health, Physical Education, and Recreation, University of New Mexico, Albuquerque, New Mexico.

Skea, Graham M.—Superintendent of Recreation, East Orange, New Jersey.

Smith, Julian W.—Director, AAHPER Outdoor Education Project, College of Education, Michigan State University, East Lansing, Michigan.

Spain, James M.—Director of Parks and Recreation, Florence, Alabama.

Stein, Thomas A.—Director, Architectural Barriers Project, National Society for Crippled Children and Adults, Chicago, Illinois.

Van Morgan, Harold—Chief, Planning Staff, Land Between the Lakes Project, Tennessee Valley Authority, Knoxville, Tennessee.

Ver Lee, Jay M.—Superintendent of Recreation, Oakland, California.

Vye, Lloyd—Camping Specialist, Department of Recreation, Philadelphia, Pennsylvania.

Wargo, Joseph B.—Director of Physical Education, Recreation, and Athletics, Flint Community Schools, Flint, Michigan.

Westkaemper, R. B.—Professor of Physical Education, Wisconsin State University, LaCrosse, Wisconsin.

Wilson, Ralph C.—Recreation Specialist, Soil Conservation Service, U. S. Department of Agriculture, Washington, D. C.

Yoho, Robert—Director, Division of Health and Physical Education, State Board of Health, Indianapolis, Indiana.

APPENDIX C

NON-PARTICIPANTS WHO CONTRIBUTED
TO ADVANCE PREPARATION OF MATERIALS
FOR THE THIRD NATIONAL FACILITIES CONFERENCE

Bale, J. R.—Chairman, Sports and Recreational Area Lighting Committee, Illuminating Engineering Society, Chicago, Illinois.

Bender, Jay—Southern Illinois University, Carbondale, Illinois.

Bland, Hester Beth—Indiana State Board of Health, Indianapolis, Indiana.

Brimhall, Pauline—Florida Extension Service, Tallahassee, Florida.

Christiansen, Holger—University of Minnesota, Minneapolis, Minnesota.

Conrad, Carson—State Department of Education, Sacramento, California.

Couch, Gertrude—University of Illinois, Urbana, Illinois.

Dittmar, James C.—Park and Recreation Department, Montgomery County, Pennsylvania.

Doell, Charles E.—Former Superintendent of Parks, Minneapolis, Minnesota.

Edmonds, Allen T.—National Park Service, Philadelphia, Pennsylvania.

Fleming, Prudence M.—Temple University, Philadelphia, Pennsylvania.

Geal, S. N.—American Camping Association, Bradford Woods, Martinsville, Indiana.

Hein, Fred V.—American Medical Association, Chicago, Illinois.

Hernlund, Vernon F.—Chicago Park District, Chicago, Illinois.

Hjelte, George—Former General Manager, Parks and Recreation Department, Los Angeles, California.

Hoffman, Robert—Publisher, Fort Lauderdale, Florida.

Holtzer, Charles—School of Education, New York University, New York, New York.

Jenny, John—Wilmington Public Schools, Wilmington, Delaware.

Johnson, Russell—Board of Park Commissioners, Minneapolis, Minnesota.

Keifer, Adolph—Equipment Manufacturer, Northfield, Illinois.

Kendall, Jerry—University of Minnesota, Minneapolis, Minnesota.

Kiphuth, Robert J.—Yale University, New Haven, Connecticut.

Knutson, Carl—Department of Education, St. Paul, Minnesota.

Larson, Jordan—Former President, School Facilities Council of Architecture, Education, and Industry, Mount Vernon, New York.

Leech, Robert—Indiana State Board of Health, Indianapolis, Indiana.

Lewis, Dan—University of Minnesota, Minneapolis, Minnesota.

Mackenzie, M. M.—Columbia University, New York, N. Y.

Mathewson, Faye S.—Former Superintendent, Union County Park Commission, Elizabeth, New Jersey.

Matthews, David—University of Illinois, Urbana, Illinois.

McCaffre, Charles—Michigan State University, East Lansing, Michigan.

Mitchell, Loren—National Rifle Association Counselor, Bloomington, Indiana.

Mood, Eric—Department of Public Health, New Haven, Connecticut.

Nicolette, Robert—University of Illinois, Urbana, Illinois.

Pond, Charles—University of Illinois, Urbana, Illinois.

Pound, Charles—Department of Parks and Recreation, West Chester, New York.

Romney, G. Ott—U. S. Department of Commerce, Washington, D. C.

Rugen, Mabel E.—University of Michigan, Ann Arbor, Michigan.

Schaller, Warren—Ball State Teachers College, Muncie, Indiana.

Shelton, Robert—University of Illinois, Urbana, Illinois.

Silva, Charles—Springfield College, Springfield, Massachusetts.

Smith, Jackson—Architect, New York, N. Y.

Smith, Sara Louise—Florida State University, Tallahassee, Florida.

Staley, Hanley—Pool Planner, Ithaca, New York.

Stelling, A. Carl—Planning Consultant, New York, New York.

Stump, William—Cocheysville, Maryland.

Taylor, James—Essex County Park Commission, Newark, New Jersey.

Terry, William L.—San Diego State College, San Diego, California.

Veenker, Harold—Purdue University, Lafayette, Indiana.

Wagner, Edward—Pool Builder, Darien, Connecticut.

Weber, Robert J.—State University of New York, Cortland, New York.

APPENDIX D

PARTICIPANTS IN PREVIOUS NATIONAL FACILITIES CONFERENCES

First National Facilities Conference Participants
Jackson's Mill, West Virginia, December 1-15, 1946

Abernathy, Ruth	Everly, Robert	Jones, Clayton	Romney, G. Ott
Andrews, Robert	Ferguson, Thomas C.	Jones, Grace	Roy, Walter
Ashcraft, J. Holley	Forsythe, Charles E.	Lensch, Dorothea M.	Schooler, Virgil
Ayars, George W.	Gable, Martha	Luehring, F. W.	Scott, Harry A.
Bank, Theodore P.	Gregg, Leah J.	Manley, Helen	Stafford, Frank S.
Barrett, Lewis R.	Hadden, Gavin	McClintock, Ralph	Streit, William K.
Beaghler, Amos L., M.D.	Hamon, Ray L.	McGowan, E. T.	Tarrant, Julian W.
Bookwalter, Carolyn	Hay, William H.	Miles, Caswell M.	Trent, W. W.
Bookwalter, Karl	Hernlund, Vernon F.	Miller, Ben W.	Van Horn, Paris J.
Butler, George D.	Hilton, Ernest	Nordly, Carl L.	Wilson, Charles C., M.D.
Camp, Marjorie	Hughes, William L.	Oppermann, Paul	
Christiansen, Milo F.	Hyatt, Chauncey A.	Petticord, B. R.	
Dane, C. Wesley	Jeffers, T. C.	Pritzlaff, August H.	

Second National Facilities Conference Participants
Kellogg Center, East Lansing, Michigan, May 4-12, 1956

Anderson, Jackson M.	Deach, Dorothy F.	Landis, Paul E.	Smith, Julian W.
Ashcraft, J. Holley	Dexter, Genevie	Lensch, Dorothea M.	Streit, William K.
Bachman, William E.	Doell, Charles E.	Leu, Donald J.	Svoboda, Robert L.
Bank, Theodore P.	Elmer, Arthur C.	Mathewson, F. S.	Taylor, J. L.
Barrett, Lewis R.	Forsythe, Charles E.	McGowan, E. T.	Terry, William L.
Bishop, Thelma D.	Gabrielsen, Milton A.	McNeely, Simon	Verhulst, Lucille H.
Champlin, Ellis H.	Graves, Charles M.	Miles, Caswell M.	Vernier, Elmon L.
Christiansen, Milo F.	Guillaume, Harold B.	Packard, Marion V.	Westkaemper, Richard B.
Coe, Merrell A.	Hernlund, Vernon F.	Pritzlaff, August H.	Whorlow, Merl I.
Coleman, Helen L.	Herrick, John H.	Rash, J. Keogh	Woolridge, James D.
Cooper, Shirley	Hughes, William L.	Rice, Edwin G.	Yoho, Robert
Daniels, Arthur S.	Jack, Harold K.	Scott, Harry A.	
Daubert, Russell B.	Jones, Thomas H.	Sharp, L. B.	

APPENDIX E

ATHLETIC FIELD AND COURT DIAGRAMS

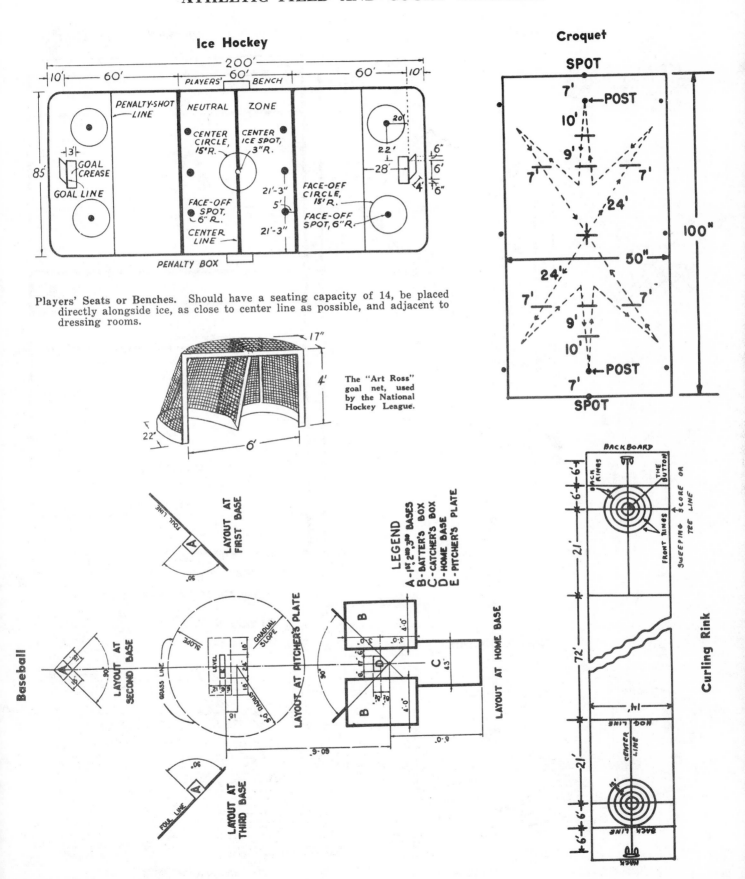

Ice Hockey

Players' Seats or Benches. Should have a seating capacity of 14, be placed directly alongside ice, as close to center line as possible, and adjacent to dressing rooms.

The "Art Ross" goal net, used by the National Hockey League.

Croquet

Baseball

Curling Rink

APPENDIX E

ATHLETIC FIELD AND COURT DIAGRAMS

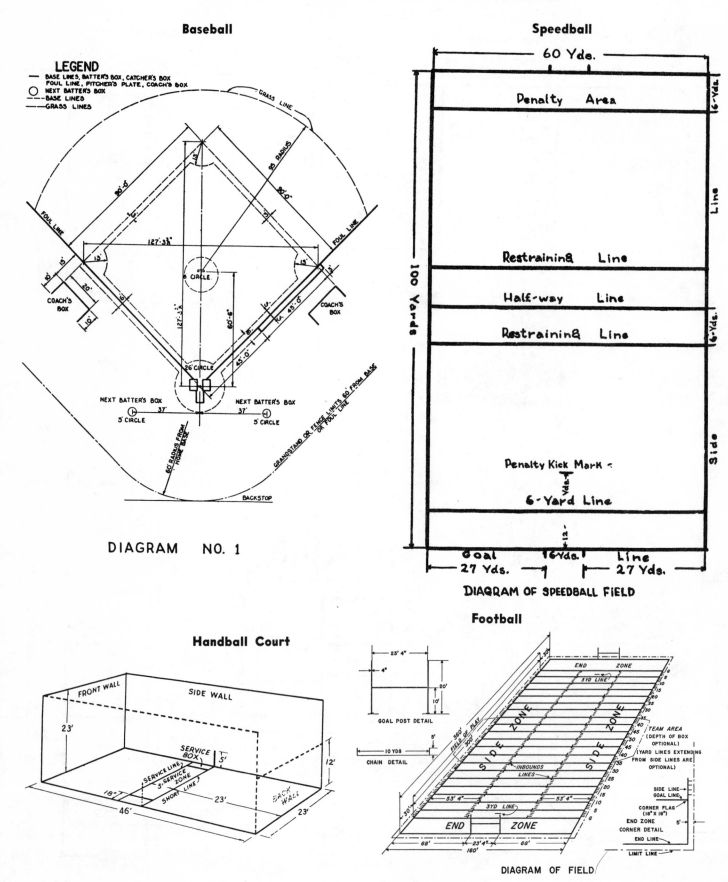

Baseball

DIAGRAM NO. 1

Speedball

DIAGRAM OF SPEEDBALL FIELD

Handball Court

Football

DIAGRAM OF FIELD

APPENDIX E
ATHLETIC FIELD AND COURT DIAGRAMS

Basketball

BASKETBALL COURT DIAGRAM

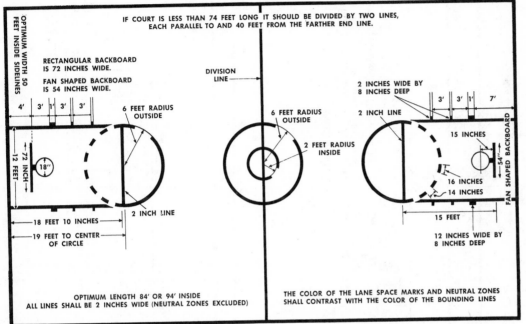

IF COURT IS LESS THAN 74 FEET LONG IT SHOULD BE DIVIDED BY TWO LINES, EACH PARALLEL TO AND 40 FEET FROM THE FARTHER END LINE.

OPTIMUM WIDTH 50 FEET INSIDE SIDELINES

RECTANGULAR BACKBOARD IS 72 INCHES WIDE.

FAN SHAPED BACKBOARD IS 54 INCHES WIDE.

DIVISION LINE

6 FEET RADIUS OUTSIDE

2 FEET RADIUS INSIDE

2 INCHES WIDE BY 8 INCHES DEEP

2 INCH LINE

15 INCHES

16 INCHES

14 INCHES

15 FEET

12 INCHES WIDE BY 8 INCHES DEEP

FAN SHAPED BACKBOARD

18 FEET 10 INCHES

19 FEET TO CENTER OF CIRCLE

2 INCH LINE

OPTIMUM LENGTH 84' OR 94' INSIDE
ALL LINES SHALL BE 2 INCHES WIDE (NEUTRAL ZONES EXCLUDED)

THE COLOR OF THE LANE SPACE MARKS AND NEUTRAL ZONES SHALL CONTRAST WITH THE COLOR OF THE BOUNDING LINES

Left End Shows Large Backboard for College Games.

MINIMUM of 3 FEET
Preferably 10 feet of unobstructed space outside. If impossible to provide 3 feet, a narrow broken 1" line should be marked inside the court parallel with and 3 feet inside the boundary.

SEMICIRCLE BROKEN LINES
For the broken line semicircle in the free throw lane, it is recommended there be 8 marks 16 inches long and 7 spaces 14 inches long.

Right End Shows Small Backboard for High School and Y.M.C.A. Games.

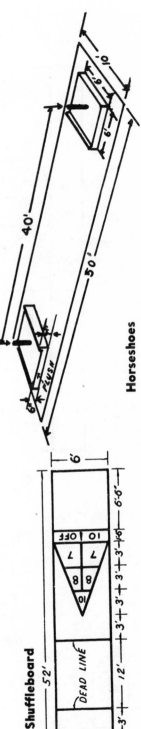

Horseshoes

Shuffleboard

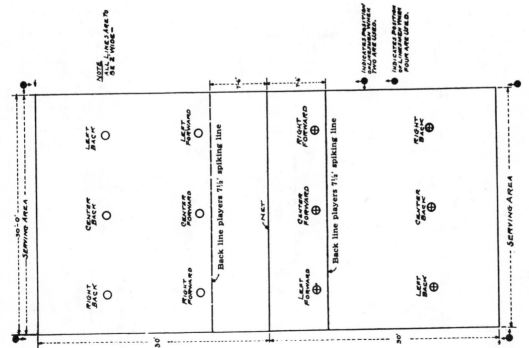

Volleyball Court
Showing Position Of Players At Start Of A Game

APPENDIX E

ATHLETIC FIELD AND COURT DIAGRAMS

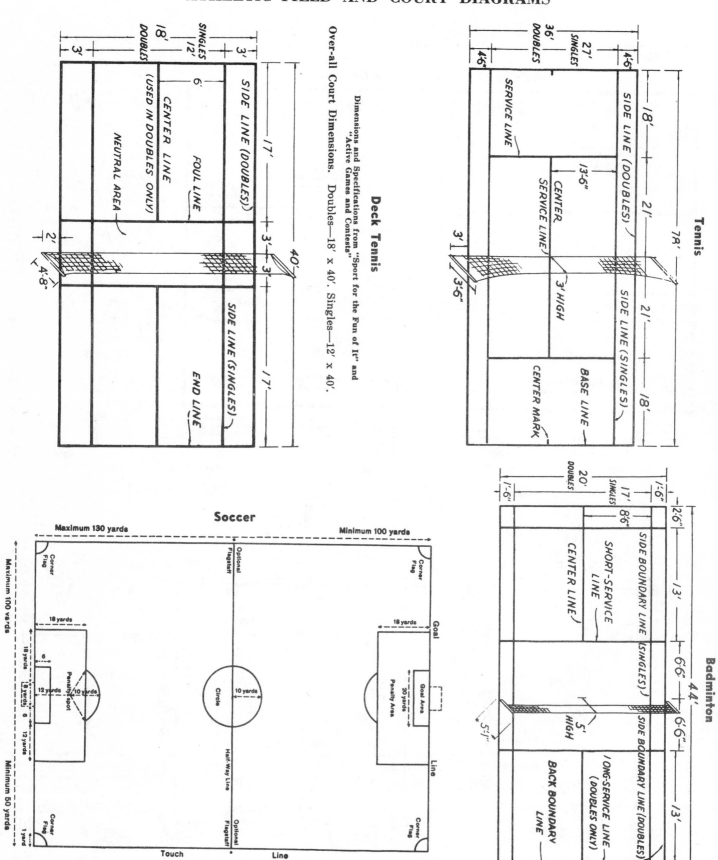

Deck Tennis

Dimensions and Specifications from "Sport for the Fun of It" and "Active Games and Contests".

Over-all Court Dimensions. Doubles—18' x 40'. Singles—12' x 40'.

Tennis

Soccer

Badminton

APPENDIX E

ATHLETIC FIELD AND COURT DIAGRAMS

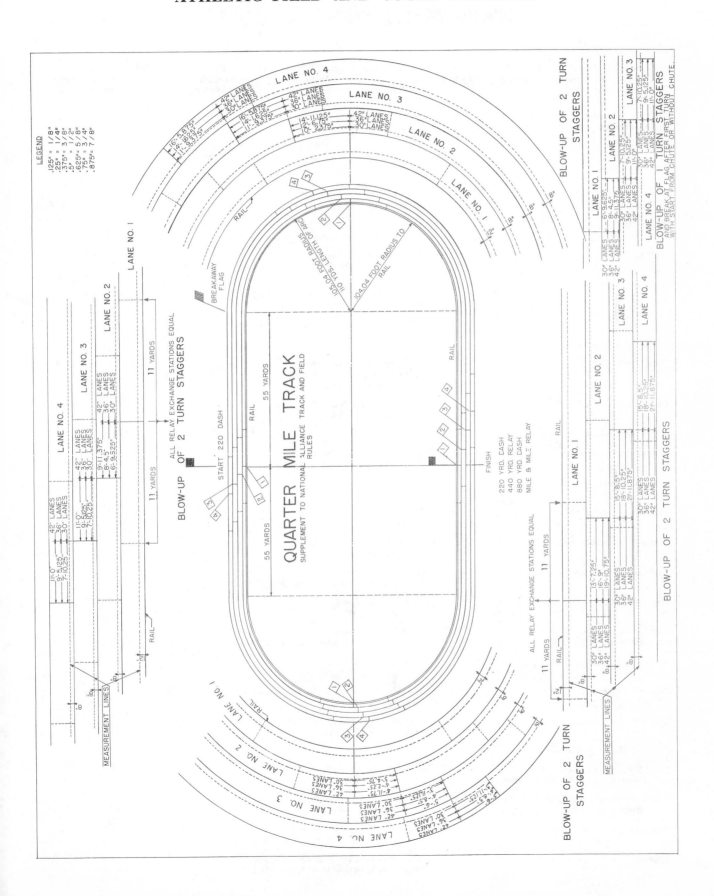

APPENDIX F

SOURCES OF OFFICIAL RULES

Many sporting goods stores carry rule books on a wide variety of sports. Check your local sporting goods store when in need of them. If you are unable to obtain the books you are seeking from local authorities, they may be obtained by writing to the following sources. To save time, it might be well to enclose payment with your order. (Note: Prices subject to change. Some prices include mailing charges.)

The following list is not all-inclusive. Therefore, The Athletic Institute would appreciate receiving information which will make this list more complete, or which will help correct such data as may become outdated.

THE ATHLETIC INSTITUTE
MERCHANDISE MART
ROOM 805
CHICAGO, ILL., 60654

ACTIVITY	SOURCE OF RULES	COST
Aerial Tennis	Sells Aerial Tennis Co. Box 42, Kansas City, Kan., 66103	(free)
Archery (Field)	National Field Archery Assn. Rte. 2, Box 514, Redlands, Calif., 92373	$2.00
Archery (Target)	National Archery Assn. 23 E. Jackson Blvd., Chicago, Ill., 60604	$1.25
Archery (Indoor)	American Archery Council 23 E. Jackson Blvd., Chicago, Ill., 60604	$ .75
Archery (See DGWS listing)		
Badminton	American Badminton Assn. Donald Richardson, 20 Wamesit Rd., Waban, Mass., 02168	$ .25
Badminton	Dayton Racquet Co., 302 S. Albright St., Arcanum, Ohio, 43504	(free)
Badminton (See DGWS listing)		
Banball (Rules included)	General Sportcraft Co., Ltd. 33 New Bridge Rd., Bergenfield, N. J.	$.25
Baseball (Non-professional) Guide Annual w/rules	National Baseball Congress Wichita, Kansas	$1.75
Baseball (Copyrighted Rules)	National Baseball Congress Wichita, Kansas	$ .25
Baseball (American Legion)	American Legion, Box 1055 Indianapolis, Ind., 46206	$ .25 or 5 for $1.00
Baseball, Babe Ruth League	Babe Ruth League, Inc. 524½ Hamilton Ave., Trenton, N. J., 08609	(free)
Baseball, Little League	Little League Baseball, Inc. P. O. Box 925, Williamsport, Pa., 17704	$ .15
Baseball, Little League (Umpire's Handbook)	Little League Baseball, Inc. P. O. Box 925, Williamsport, Pa., 17704	$ .25
Baseball, Bronco-Pony-Colt	Boys Baseball, Inc. P. O. Box 225, Washington, Pa., 15301	(free)
Baseball, "Knotty Problems of Baseball" (Professional Rules)	The Sporting News, 2018 Washington Ave., St. Louis, Mo., 63166	$2.00
Baseball (Professional Rules Only)	The Sporting News, 2018 Washington Ave., St. Louis, Mo., 63166	$ .50
Baseball (See NCAA listing)		
Baseball Umpire's Handbook (Does not include actual rules)	American Amateur Baseball Congress P. O. Box 44, Battle Creek, Mich., 49016	$1.00
Baseball Scorer's Handbook (Does not include actual rules)	American Amateur Baseball Congress P. O. Box 44, Battle Creek, Mich., 49016	$ .50
Baseball, Rules in Pictures	American Amateur Baseball Congress P. O. Box 44, Battle Creek, Mich., 49016	$1.00
Baseball, Tournament Manual	American Amateur Baseball Congress P. O. Box 44, Battle Creek, Mich., 49016	$1.00

APPENDIX F

ACTIVITY	SOURCE OF RULES	COST
Baseball, League Organization	American Amateur Baseball Congress P. O. Box 44, Battle Creek, Mich., 49016	$ .35
Baseball (See High School listing)		
Basketball (See AAU listing)		
Basketball (See High School listing)		
Basketball (See NCAA listing)		
Basketball (See DGWS listing)		
Basketball (Biddy)	Jay Archer, 701 Brooks Building, Scranton, Pa., 18501	$ .10
Basketball, Balanced (Height Equalization)	John L. McHale, 66 Dale Road Eastchester, N. Y.	$ .50
Bicycling	Bicycle Institute of America 122 E. 42nd St., New York, N. Y., 10017	(free)
Billiards (Rules & Records)	Billiard Congress of America 20 N. Wacker Dr., Chicago, Ill., 60606	$1.25
Bocce	General Sportcraft Co., Ltd 33 New Bridge Rd., Bergenfield, N. J.	$ .25
Bocce	Lignum-Vitae Products Corp. 96 Boyd Ave., Jersey City, N. J.	(free)
Bowling (Duck Pin)	National Duck Pin Bowling Congress 1420 New York Ave., N. W., Washington, D. C., 20005 Washington, D. C., 20005	(free)
Bowling (Ten Pin)	American Bowling Congress 1572 E. Capitol Dr., Milwaukee, Wisc., 53211	$ .25
Bowling (See DGWS listing)		
Bowling, Women (Ten Pin)	Women's International Bowling Congress, Inc. 1225 Dublin Rd., Columbus 12, Ohio	(free)
Boxing (See AAU listing)		
Casting (Official Rules for Fly and Bait Casting)	American Casting Education Foundation P. O. Box 51, Nashville, Tenn., 37202	
Corkball	Rawlings Sporting Goods Co. 2300 Delmar Blvd., St. Louis, Mo., 63166	(free)
Croquet	General Sportcraft Co., Ltd. 33 New Bridge Rd., Bergenfield, N. J.	$ .25
Dartball	Wisconsin State Dartball Comm. c/o E. Dorow, Pres. 9333 W. Lincoln Ave., West Allis 19, Wisc.	$ .40
Darts	General Sportcraft Co., Ltd. 33 New Bridge Rd., Bergenfield, N. J.	$ .25
Deck Tennis	General Sportcraft Co., Ltd. 33 New Bridge Rd., Bergenfield, N. J.	$ .25
Fencing	Amateur Fencer's League of America William Latzko, 33 - 62nd Street, West New York, N. J.	$3.00
Fencing (See DGWS listing)		
Field Hockey (See DGWS listing)		
Field Hockey	General Sportcraft Co., Ltd. 33 New Bridge Rd., Bergenfield, N. J.	$ .25
Floor Tennis	U. S. Floor Tennis Assn. 1580 Sherman Ave., Evanston, Ill.	(free)
Football (See NCAA listing)		
Football (Junior League)	Pop Warner Football 3664 Richmond St., Philadelphia, Pa., 19134	$ .25
Football (Six-Man) (See High School listing)		
Football (See High School listing)		

APPENDIX F

ACTIVITY	SOURCE OF RULES	COST
Golf	U. S. Golf Assn., 40 E. 38th St., New York, N. Y., 10016	$ .25
Gymnastics (See AAU listing)		
Gymnastics (See NCAA listing)		
Gymnastics (See DGWS listing)		
Handball (See AAU listing)		
Handball	U. S. Handball Assn. 4101 Dempster St., Skokie, Ill.	$1.00
Horseshoes	General Sportcraft Co., Ltd. 33 New Bridge Rd., Bergenfield, N. J.	$ .25
Horseshoes (Professional)	National Horseshoe Pitchers Assn. of America, % Elmer Beller, 9725 Palm St., Bellflower, Calif.	(free)
Ice Hockey (See NCAA listing)		
Ice Skating	Amateur Skating Union of the U. S., % Edward J. Schmitzer 4135 N. Troy St., Chicago, Ill., 60618	
Indoor Hockey	Cosom Corp., 6030 Wayzata Blvd. Minneapolis, Minn., 55416	$ .25
Lacrosse (See DGWS listing)		
Lawn Bowling	American Lawn Bowling Association, % John W. Deist, Secretary, 1525 Ridge Court, Wauwatosa, Wisc., 53213	(free)
Marbles Shooting	National Marbles Tournament Cleveland Press Bldg., Cleveland 14, Ohio	(free)
Outings (See DGWS listing)		
Paddle Tennis	General Sportcraft Co., Ltd. 33 New Bridge Rd., Bergenfield, N. J.	$ .25
Paddleball	Rodney J. Grambeau, Sports Bldg. University of Michigan, Ann Arbor, Mich.	(free)
Quoits	General Sportcraft Co., Ltd. 33 New Bridge Rd., Bergenfield, N. J.	$ .25
Riding (See DGWS listing)		
Roller Hockey	National Roller Hockey Assn. of the U.S. 97 Erie St., Dumont, N. J.	
Roque	American Roque League, Inc. 4205 Briar Creek Lane, Dallas, Tex., 75214	$ .30
Scoopball (Rules for 26 different games)	Cosom Industries, 6030 Wayzata Blvd., Minneapolis, Minn., 55416	$ .25
Shooting (See National Rifle Assn. listing)		
Shuffleboard (Deck)	General Sportcraft Co., Ltd. 33 New Bridge Rd., Bergenfield, N. J.	$ .25
Shuffleboard (Table)	American Shuffleboard Leagues, Inc. 533 Third St., Union City, N. J., 07087	(free)
Skating (Figure)	U. S. Figure Skating Assn. 575 Boylston St., Boston, Mass., 02116	$3.00
Skating (Roller)	U. S. Amateur Roller Skating Assn. 120 W. 42nd St., New York, N. Y., 10036	$1.50
Skating (Speed)	Amateur Skating Union of the U. S. % Edward J. Schmitzer 4135 N. Troy St., Chicago, Ill., 60618	$1.00
Skeet Shooting	National Skeet Shooting Assn. 3409 Oak Lawn Ave., Suite 219, Dallas, Tex., 75219	$ .25
Skiing (See NCAA listing)		
Skiing (Downhill, Slalom, Giant Slalom, Jumping & Cross-Country, FIS and USSA Rules)	U. S. Ski Assn., % Gloria C. Chadwick, Executive Secy., Broadmoor, Colorado Springs, Colo.	$2.00
Skin Diving, Competitive (See AAU listing)		

APPENDIX F

ACTIVITY	SOURCE OF RULES	COST
Smash	Smash, 1024 North Blvd., Oak Park, Ill.	(free)
Soccer (See NCAA listing)		
Soccer (See DGWS listing)		
Softball (12″—fast and slow pitch)	Amateur Softball Assn., Suite 1300, Skirvin Tower, Oklahoma City, Okla.	$ .75
Softball (16″)	Umpires Protective Assn. of Chicago % Edw. Weinstein, Chairman, Rules Committee Apt. 710, 3550 Lake Shore Dr., Chicago, Ill.	$ .60
Softball (See DGWS listing)		
Speed-A-Way	Marjorie S. Larsen, 1754 Middlefield, Stockton, Calif., 95204	$1.25
Speedball (See DGWS listing)		
Spiral Tennis	General Sportcraft Co., Ltd. 33 New Bridge Rd., Bergenfield, N. J.	$ .25
Squash	U. S. Squash Racquets Assn. 200 E. 66th St., New York, N. Y., 10021	$2.50
Swimming (See AAU listing)		
Swimming (See NCAA listing)		
Swimming (Synchronized - See AAU listing)		
Table Tennis	General Sportcraft Co., Ltd. 33 New Bridge Rd., Bergenfield, N. J.	$ .25
Table Tennis (Instructions)	U. S. Table Tennis Assn., 210 Saturn Dr., North Star, Newark, Del.	$ .10
Table Tennis (Rules)	U. S. Table Tennis Assn., 210 Saturn Dr., North Star, Newark, Del.	(free)
Table Tennis (Instructions & Rules)	Nissen-Sico, 930 - 27th Ave., S. W., Cedar Rapids, Iowa	(free)
Takraw Game	General Sportcraft Co., Ltd. 33 New Bridge Rd., Bergenfield, N. J.	$ .25
Tennis (Includes Guide)	U. S. Lawn Tennis Assn., 51 E. 42nd St., New York, N. Y., 10017	$2.00
Tennis (Rules Only)	U. S. Lawn Tennis Assn., 51 E. 42nd St., New York, N. Y., 10017	$ .25
Tennis (See DGWS listing)		
Tennis	Dayton Racquet Co., 302 S. Albright St. Arcanum, Ohio 45304	(free)
Tennis Umpire's Manual (Includes Rules)	U. S. Lawn Tennis Assn., 51 E. 42nd St. New York, N. Y., 10017	$ .50
Tetherball (Inflated Ball)	W. J. Voit Rubber Corp., 3801 S. Harbor Blvd. Santa Ana, Calif., 92704	(free)
Tetherball (Inflated Ball)	General Sportcraft Co., Ltd. 33 New Bridge Rd., Bergenfield, N. J.	$ .25
Tether Tennis	General Sportcraft Co., Ltd. 33 New Bridge Rd., Bergenfield, N. J.	$ .25
Touch Football	The Athletic Institute 805 Merchandise Mart, Chicago, Ill., 60654	$ .75
Track & Field (See AAU listing)		
Track & Field (See High School listing)		
Track & Field (See NCAA listing)		
Turf Bowling (Boccie)	Lignum - Vitae Products Corp., 96 Boyd Ave., Jersey City, N. J.	(free)
Volleyball (Includes Rules)	U. S. Volleyball Assn., USVBA Printer P. O. Box 109, Berne, Ind., 46711	$1.00
Volleyball (See DGWS listing)		

APPENDIX F

ACTIVITY	SOURCE OF RULES			COST

Water Polo (See AAU listing below)

Weight Lifting (See AAU listing below)

Winter Sports (See DGWS listing below)

Wrestling (See NCAA listing below)

NCAA RULEBOOKS AND GUIDES

National Collegiate Athletic Bureau
Box 757, Grand Central Station
New York, N. Y., 10017

Baseball	$1.00	Ice Hockey	$1.00
Basketball	$1.50	Skiing	$ .75
Football	$1.50	Soccer	$1.00
Football Rules Interpretations	$1.00	Swimming	$1.00
Gymnastics	$ .75	Track & Field	$1.00
		Wrestling	$1.00

DGWS OFFICIAL GUIDES FOR WOMEN'S SPORTS, INCLUDING RULES

Division for Girls' and Women's Sports
1201 Sixteenth St., N. W., Washington, D. C., 20036

Aquatics	$1.00	Soccer-Speedball	$1.00
Archery-Riding	$1.00	Softball	$1.00
Basketball	$1.00	Tennis-Badminton	$1.00
Bowling-Fencing-Golf	$1.00	Track & Field	$1.00
Field Hockey-Lacrosse	$1.00	Volleyball	$1.00
Gymnastics	$1.00	Winter Sports & Outing Activities	$1.00

HIGH SCHOOL ACTIVITIES

National Federation of State High School
Athletic Assns., 7 S. Dearborn,
Chicago, Ill., 60603

Basketball:		Football:	
Rules	$ .40	Rules	$ .40
Casebook	$ .75	Casebook	$ .75
Player Handbook	$ .30	Player Handbook	$ .30
Officials' Manual	$ .40	Officials' Manual	$ .40
Baseball:			
Rules	$ .40	Football, Touch Football	$ .40
Casebook	$ .75	Six-Man Football	$ .40
Umpires' Manual	$ .40	Track & Field, Rules & Records	$ .50

OFFICIAL AAU RULE BOOKS AND GUIDES

Amateur Athletic Union of the U. S.,
231 W. 58th St., New York, N. Y., 10019

AAU Handbook	$1.75	Swimming (Synchronized)	$1.50
Basketball	$2.00	Swimming, Water Polo, & Diving	$2.00
Boxing	$1.75	Track & Field	$2.25
Gymnastics	$2.00	Weight Lifting	$1.50
Handball	$1.25	Wrestling	$1.75
Judo	$1.75		

NRA AND INTERNATIONAL SHOOTING UNION RULE BOOKS

National Rifle Assn., 1600 Rhode Island Ave., N. W.,
Washington, D. C., 20036

NRA High-Power Rifle	$ .25	ISU Center-Fire Pistol	$ .20
NRA Pistol	$ .25	ISU Rapid-Fire Pistol	$ .20
NRA Smallbore Rifle	$ .25	ISU Running Deer	$ .20
NRA Shotgun	$ .25	ISU Running Roebuck & Boar	$ .20
ISU Constitution	$ .20	ISU Clay Pigeon	$ .20
ISU General Regulations	$ .20	ISU Skeet	$ .20
ISU SB Rifle & Free Pistol	$ .20	ISU Bound Vol. (all rules)	$2.50
ISU Free Rifle & Army Rifle	$ .20		

APPENDIX G

REQUIREMENTS OF THE AGING AND THE DISABLED

A BRIEF PHILOSOPHICAL BASIS

ALL INDIVIDUALS have the same basic socio-psychological and physical needs, regardless of age, ability or disability, nationality, race, or religion, although these might manifest themselves in different ways. All of us have been privileged to travel the avenues of self-exploration, self-identification, self-expression, self-administration, and self-discipline in order that we might identify ourselves as a part of, and apart from, the rest of the world. We have had the opportunity to try many things, some by trial and error, some with success, and others with failure. Via these routes, we have been privileged to develop a concept of self which is essential to success, to health, and to happiness.

From childhood through adulthood, those learned and enjoyable experiences which are integral parts of health, physical education, and recreation were instrumental in fulfilling our basic socio-psychological and physical needs, affording each of us a better concept of self. These are so fundamental that most of us take them very much for granted. Yet, if we look about us, we will see that these basic things, in part or whole, have been denied the majority of our disabled population, and are being denied increasing numbers of aging. These are "living experiences," not isolated, remote, or clinical services.

Everyone in our society should have the inherent right to normal education, growth experiences, and social and recreational pursuits. Society, in all its components, must play an increasingly important part in returning the disabled to their rightful places in society, and in maintaining the aging as participating members of society. Imposed isolation is degeneration —physically, mentally, emotionally, and socially.

The disabled must be prepared for the normal reciprocities of life. They must understand that if they are to have normal privileges and opportunities, they must be prepared for normal risks, hazards, and failures. We must educate and equip, not solicit or over-protect disabled individuals. The people, and the concern or the lack of concern of the people, who surround the disabled person are of major significance. It is important to note how much the public benefits from normal, objective association with the disabled.

A disability is specific. It must not necessarily be a handicap. People and things make a disability a handicap. We must regard an illness or disability as an experience in the life of a person, not a disaster. It is an intense and persistent experience which has considerable impact on one's life, but given the proper opportunities, those with an illness or a disability will relate effectively to each and every one of us the true significance, or insignificance, of this intense experience. Social interaction will result in better and more realistic understanding, rather than the presently devaluating stereotypes now most commonly being applied to the disabled and the aging.

If health, physical education, and recreation have a purpose in the life of anyone, his purposes and objectives increase in magnitude and significance when related to the aging and the disabled, who, because of society's apathy, more than by personal desire, have been prone to inactivity and have had an excess of leisure time. Because of society's lack of understanding and foresight they have been denied the opportunity to participate and, thereby, have been denied experiences in growth and development which are essential to a favorable end product. They have also been denied many opportunities in adulthood, and as senior citizens, which enrich our lives both personally and professionally.

Certainly, if physical fitness is important to anyone, it is proportionately more important to the person with a disability. This is particularly true of certain physical disabilities in which physical maintenance is a major problem and a major objective.

Stating it simply, we should begin with the "normal" and deviate as little as possible in programming for, and working with, the disabled.

The lack of accessibility and usability of facilities for health, physical education, and recreation by the aging and the disabled has been a great deterrent to their participation.

Many administrators and professionals have not yet recognized the necessity and the desirability for planning facilities and equipment so that they will be equally usable by the "able" and the "disabled". They are not fully aware of the large numbers involved, and that these numbers are steadily increasing. They have failed to recognize the significance of this in the lives of the disabled and the aging. They are unaware of the full potential for participation that exists among the disabled and the aging. Because of the facilities in which many have had to function, they have seldom considered the various causes and manifestations of disability in their regular program concepts.

On the other hand, the disabled and the aging, over the years, have been somewhat apprehensive concerning their own abilities to participate, or they have been made to believe they could not do many things that we now know they can do, particularly if facilities and equipment are appropriately planned. They have been equally apprehensive about projecting themselves into many normal, objective, competitive, social settings, largely because of inaccessibility.

THE PROBLEM

The most frustrating of all problems to disabled and aging individuals are buildings and facilities, supposedly created for the public, that are designed in such a manner that they prohibit their full participation. It is equally frustrating to professional people dedicated to rehabilitation to find that architectural barriers prohibit the disabled individual, however well rehabilitated, from pursuing his aspirations, developing his talents, and exercising his skills.

Many of the disabled are afraid to venture forth because of the architectural barriers they encounter. Others have convinced themselves it is better to stay back because they feel they are a burden to others when they attempt to project themselves into normal social settings.

Although there are other problems, the one that is heard most often and the one that is presently enemy number one is **inaccessibility**.

In spite of forward-moving programs of physical restoration and rehabilitation, professionals in the field of rehabilitation are finding it very difficult to project clients into normal situations of education, recreation, and employment because of architectural barriers. Therefore, the problems inherent to the design of buildings and facilities quickly take on the role of "villain" and might revert the social and economic gains now evident to constructive rehabilitation.

The solution of these problems is not within the realm of professional rehabilitation workers. It must be a challenge to all architects, builders, designers, educators, engineers, manufacturers, and in all probability, legislatures and municipal leaders, with encouragement and guidance from those professionally engaged in medicine and rehabilitation. If more facilities in communities were accessible to, and usable by, the disabled and the aging, treatment centers, hospitals, and other institutions could make prudent use of these facilities, helping bridge the gap between patient and community, and helping to resolve some of the acute problems which face the patient upon discharge.

STATISTICAL SIGNIFICANCE

Alarming as it may seem, approximately one out of every seven people in our nation has a permanent physical disability. Among these cases are many different causes and manifestations of physical disability, and each has its own particular associated problems.

Contrary to what most people think, recent advancements in science and medical technology tend to magnify this problem. Medical science now makes it possible to save many lives, decrease the mortality rate at birth, and increase longevity, all of which greatly increase the numbers of individuals with permanent physical disabilities. It is further evident that the situation will get much worse before it gets better.

Also contributing to the increasing incidence of permanent physical disabilities is the advancing machine age, the continued expansion of industry, and the rapidly-increasing numbers of motor vehicles, both in total numbers and the percentage of populace ownership. Authorities anticipate over 200,000 traumatic paraplegics (individuals with spinal-cord injury resulting in both motor and sensory paralysis and, in most instances, secondary loss of control of organs) from automobile accidents per year.

Increases in leisure time have also contributed to the instances of such disabilities as traumatic paraplegia. Swimming and boating, or other water activities, for example, create thousands of such disabilities each year.

SOCIO-ECONOMIC SIGNIFICANCE

The human resources (talents and skills) among the disabled are of considerable socio-economic significance. These human resources are still being overlooked and neglected while we bemoan our lack of qualified personnel in various areas and levels of endeavor.

A large portion of our disabled and aging have been unnecessarily institutionalized or are to be found in back rooms, protected and pampered by solicitous parents, relatives, and friends. Experiences and statistics in this regard are dynamically startling and truly sad. An unnecessarily large proportion of our disabled young people have had to be placed in hospital schools, orthopedic schools, or provided home-bound instruction. The cost per capita of such schooling is many times the cost when they are included in the regular school system. A multitude of

other benefits are also to be derived by these people when they are properly included in regular schools.

WITH WHAT AND WHOM ARE WE CONCERNED?

We are basically concerned with making it possible for the great talents and resources of millions of disabled and aging individuals to be put to use for the betterment of mankind by the elimination of architectural barriers. More specifically, it has been our purpose to develop standards and specifications for all buildings and facilities used by the public so that they will be accessible and functional to the disabled and the aging.

In setting out upon this mission, it was recognized that the majority of buildings which we will be using within the next decade or two are already built. Therefore, the first problem was to determine what might be done to make accessible and functional the existing buildings which are now nonaccessible. The second task, and the simpler of the two, was the development of the standards for proper design and construction of new buildings and facilities.

We are concerned with the disabilities as identified and defined in Appendix H, along with those manifestations of the mentally handicapped, relating to the design and construction of buildings used by the public.

SOLVING THE PROBLEM

In October 1961, the American Standards Association officially released "American Standard Specifications for Making Buildings and Facilities Accessible to, and Usable by, the Physically Handicapped." The cosponsors of this project were the President's Committee on the Employment of the Handicapped and The National Society for Crippled Children and Adults. Extensive research, experimentation, and development were carried on at the University of Illinois, in part under a grant made to the University by the National Society for Crippled Children and Adults. A Steering Committee was appointed and, subsequently, a Sectional Committee was selected, with representation from more than 50 professions, trades, governmental agencies (federal, state, and local), national societies, and national associations. The standards referred to above were carefully scrutinized by all members of the Steering and Sectional Committees. The standards were then carefully reviewed by several boards and committees of the American Standards Association. Therefore, these standards constitute a very sound basis for action on the part of all those who are, or should be, interested in this problem.

These standards are concerned with all causes and manifestations of disability. They are concerned with, and applicable to all buildings used by the public. Although the specifications are applicable to all buildings regardless of the function of the building, they do not yet include specifications for some facilities of specific and unique purpose. They are being supplemented to include these. It should also be emphasized that these standards can and will be amended from time to time to keep pace with changing social and technological advancements.

On November 14, 1963, interested and authoritative persons met at the Athletic Institute offices to make a pilot investigation into the problems confronting the physically disabled in the use of health, physical education, and recreation facilities.

Subsequently, on February 9, 10, and 11, 1964, a workshop on this problem was held at the University of Illinois. There was broad representation among the participating personnel, which included not only those who would be able to contribute to the matters under consideration, but also those who would be instrumental in implementing these considerations.

SUMMARY

A little coordinated planning can open up many new worlds to millions of people. We are wasting shameful amounts of money and human resources because we have overlooked some relatively simple things. We must make all buildings and facilities accessible to, and usable by, the disabled and the aging.

The disabled and the aging can be accommodated in all buildings and facilities used by the public:

- independently and without distinction
- without loss of space or function to the general public
- without significant extra cost.

All standards and specifications which are recommended to facilitate the disabled and the aging will be of benefit to everyone. The standards referred to herein can be incorporated in any type of building regardless of the basic architectural concept.

APPENDIX H

AMERICAN STANDARD SPECIFICATIONS FOR MAKING BUILDINGS AND FACILITIES ACCESSIBLE TO, AND USABLE BY, THE PHYSICALLY HANDICAPPED

FOREWORD

(This Foreword is not a part of American Standard Specifications for Making Buildings and Facilities Accessible to, and Usable by, the Physically Handicapped, A117.1-1961.)

This standard supplements other American Standards relating to various aspects of buildings and facilities. Its specifications, which are the result of extended and careful consideration of available knowledge and experience on this subject, are intended to present minimum requirements. They are recommended for use in the construction of all buildings and facilities and for adoption and enforcement by administrative authorities, so that those individuals with permanent physical disabilities might pursue their interests and aspirations, develop their talents, and exercise their skills.

The ASA Sectional Committee, A117, which developed this standard, had the following representation:

LEON CHATELAIN, JR., Chairman   T. J. NUGENT, Secretary

Organization Represented

AFL-CIO

American Foundation for the Blind

American Hospital Association

American Hotel Association

American Institute of Architects

American Municipal Association

American Occupational Therapy Association

American Physical Therapy Association

American Society of Landscape Architects

American Society of Mechanical Engineers

American Society of Safety Engineers

American Vocational Association

Associated General Contractors of America

Association of Casualty and Surety Companies

Construction Specifications Institute

Federal Housing Administration

General Services Administration

Industrial Home for the Blind

Industrial Medical Association

Indoor Sports Clubs, Inc.

Institute for the Crippled and Disabled

National Bureau of Standards

National Congress of Organizations for the Physically Handicapped

National Council of Churches

National Council on Schoolhouse Construction

National Elevator Manufacturing Industry

National Paraplegia Foundation

National Rehabilitation Association

Organization Represented

National Safety Council

National Society for Crippled Children and Adults (sponsor)

Paralyzed Veterans of America, Inc.

Paraplegics Manufacturing Company

Plumbing Fixture Manufacturers Association

President's Committee on Employment of the Handicapped (sponsor)

Society of Industrial Realtors

Telephone Group

United Cerebral Palsy Associations, Inc.

U. S. Conference of Mayors

U. S. Department of Health, Education and Welfare

    Bureau of State Services

    Children's Bureau

    Division of Accident Prevention

    Division of Hospital and Medical Facilities

    Office of Education

    Office of Vocational Rehabilitation

U. S. Department of Labor

    Bureau of Employment Security

    Bureau of Labor Standards

U. S. Veterans Administration

University of Illinois Rehabilitation Center

The steering committee

K. Vernon Banta	Philip A. Klieger
Leon Chatelain, Jr.	T. J. Nugent
Clinton H. Cowgill	Jayne Shover
H. Dwight York	

APPENDIX H

1. Scope and Purpose

1.1 Scope

1.1.1 This standard applies to all buildings and facilities used by the public. It applies to temporary or emergency conditions as well as permanent conditions. It does not apply to private residences.

1.1.2 This standard is concerned with non-ambulatory disabilities, semi-ambulatory disabilities, sight disabilities, hearing disabilities, disabilities of incoordination, and aging.[1]

1.2 Purpose. This standard is intended to make all buildings and facilities used by the public accessible to, and functional for, the physically handicapped, to, through, and within their doors, without loss of function, space, or facility where the general public is concerned. It supplements existing American Standards, and reflects great concern for safety of life and limb. In cases of practical difficulty, unnecessary hardship, or extreme differences, administrative authorities may grant exceptions from the literal requirements of this standard or permit the use of other methods or materials, but only when it is clearly evident that equivalent facilitation and protection are thereby secured.

2. Definitions

2.1 Non-ambulatory Disabilities. Impairments that, regardless of cause or manifestation, for all practical purposes, confine individuals to wheelchairs.

2.2 Semi-ambulatory Disabilities. Impairments that cause individuals to walk with difficulty or insecurity. Individuals using braces or crutches, amputees, arthritics, spastics, and those with pulmonary and cardiac ills may be semi-ambulatory.

2.3 Sight Disabilities. Total blindness or impairments affecting sight to the extent that the individual functioning in public areas is insecure or exposed to danger.

2.4 Hearing Disabilities. Deafness or hearing handicaps that might make an individual insecure in public areas because he is unable to communicate or hear warning signals.

2.5 Disabilities of Incoordination. Faulty coordination or palsy from brain, spinal, or peripheral nerve injury.

2.6 Aging. Those manifestations of the aging processes that significantly reduce mobility, flexibility, coordination, and perceptiveness but are not accounted for in the aforementioned categories.

2.7 Standard. When this term appears in small letters and is not preceded by the word "American," it is descriptive and does not refer to an American Standard approved by ASA; for example, a "standard" wheelchair is one characterized as standard by the manufacturers.

2.8 Fixed Turning Radius, Wheel to Wheel. The tracking of the caster wheels and large wheels of a wheelchair when pivoting on a spot.

2.9 Fixed Turning Radius, Front Structure to Rear Structure. The turning radius of a wheelchair, left front-foot platform to right rear wheel, or right front-foot platform to left rear wheel, when pivoting on a spot.

1 See definitions in Section 2.

2.10 Involved (Involvement). A portion or portions of the human anatomy or physiology, or both, that have a loss or impairment of normal function as a result of genesis, trauma, disease, inflammation, or degeneration.

2.11 Ramps, Ramps with Gradients. Because the term "ramp" has a multitude of meanings and uses, its use in this text is clearly defined as ramps with gradients (or ramps with slopes) that deviate from what would otherwise be considered the normal level. An exterior ramp, as distinguished from a "walk," would be considered an appendage to a building leading to a level above or below existing ground level. As such, a ramp shall meet certain requirements similar to those imposed upon stairs.

2.12 Walk, Walks. Because the terms "walk" and "walks" have a multitude of meanings and uses, their use in this text is clearly defined as a predetermined, prepared-surface, exterior pathway leading to or from a building or facility, or from one exterior area to another, placed on the existing ground level and not deviating from the level of the existing ground immediately adjacent.

2.13 Appropriate Number. As used in this text, appropriate number means the number of a specific item that would be necessary, in accord with the purpose and function of a building or facility, to accommodate individuals with specific disabilities in proportion to the anticipated number of individuals with disabilities who would use a particular building or facility.

EXAMPLE: Although these specifications shall apply to all buildings and facilities used by the public, the numerical need for a specific item would differ, for example, between a major transportation terminal, where many individuals with diverse disabilities would be continually coming and going, an office building or factory, where varying numbers of individuals with disabilities of varying manifestations (in many instances, very large numbers) might be employed or have reason for frequent visits, a school or church, where the number of individuals may be fixed and activities more definitive, and the many other buildings and facilities dedicated to specific functions and purposes.

NOTE: Disabilities are specific and where the individual has been properly evaluated and properly oriented and where architectural barriers have been eliminated, a specific disability does not constitute a handicap. It should be emphasized that more and more of those physically disabled are becoming **participants**, rather than spectators, in the fullest meaning of the word.

3. General Principles and Considerations

3.1 Wheelchair Specifications. The collapsible-model wheelchair of tubular metal construction with plastic upholstery for back and seat is most commonly used. The standard model of all manufacturers falls within the following limits, which were used as the basis of consideration:

(1) Length: 42 inches
(2) Width, when open: 25 inches
(3) Height of seat from floor: 19½ inches
(4) Height of armrest from floor: 29 inches
(5) Height of pusher handles (rear) from floor: 36 inches
(6) Width, when collapsed: 11 inches

3.2 The Functioning of a Wheelchair

3.2.1 The fixed turning radius of a standard wheelchair, wheel to wheel, is 18 inches. The fixed turning radius, front structure to rear structure, is 31.5 inches.

APPENDIX H

3.2.2 The average turning space required (180 and 360 degrees) is 60 x 60 inches.

NOTE: Actually, a turning space that is longer than it is wide, specifically, 63 x 56 inches, is more workable and desirable. In an area with two open ends, such as might be the case in a corridor, a minimum of 54 inches between two walls would permit a 360-degree turn.

3.2.3 A minimum width of 60 inches is required for two individuals in wheelchairs to pass each other.

3.3 The Adult Individual Functioning in a Wheelchair [2]

3.3.1 The average unilateral vertical reach is 60 inches and ranges from 54 inches to 78 inches.

3.3.2 The average horizontal working (table) reach is 30.8 inches and ranges from 28.5 inches to 33.2 inches.

3.3.3 The bilateral horizontal reach, both arms extended to each side, shoulder high, ranges from 54 inches to 71 inches and averages 64.5 inches.

3.3.4 An individual reaching diagonally, as would be required in using a wall-mounted dial telephone or towel dispenser, would make the average reach (on the wall) 48 inches from the floor.

3.4 The Individual Functioning on Crutches [3]

3.4.1 On the average, individuals 5 feet 6 inches tall require an average of 31 inches between crutch tips in the normally accepted gaits.[4]

3.4.2 On the average, individuals 6 feet 0 inches tall require an average of 32.5 inches between crutch tips in the normally accepted gaits.[4]

4. Site Development [5]

4.1 Grading. The grading of ground, even contrary to existing topography, so that it attains a level with a normal entrance will make a facility accessible to individuals with physical disabilities.

4.2 Walks

4.2.1 Public walks should be at least 48 inches wide and should have a gradient not greater than 5 percent.[6]

4.2.2 Such walks should be of a continuing common surface, not interrupted by steps or abrupt changes in level.

4.2.3 Wherever walks cross other walks, driveways, or parking lots they should blend to a common level.[7]

NOTE: 4.1 and 4.2, separately or collectively, are greatly aided by terracing, retaining walls, and winding walks allowing for more gradual incline, thereby making almost any building accessible to individuals with permanent physical disablities, while contributing to its esthetic qualities.

4.2.4 A walk shall have a level platform at the top which is at least 5 feet by 5 feet, if a door swings out onto the platform or toward the walk. This platform shall extend at least 1 foot beyond each side of the doorway.

4.2.5 A walk shall have a level platform at least 3 feet deep and 5 feet wide, if the door does not swing onto the platform or toward the walk. This platform shall extend at least 1 foot beyond each side of the doorway.

4.3 Parking Lots

4.3.1 Spaces that are accessible and approximate to the facility should be set aside and identified for use by individuals with physical disabilities.

4.3.2 A parking space open on one side, allowing room for individuals in wheelchairs or individuals on braces and crutches to get in and out of an automobile onto a level surface, suitable for wheeling and walking, is adequate.

4.3.3 Parking spaces for individuals with physical disabilities when placed between two conventional diagonal or head-on parking spaces should be 12 feet wide.

4.3.4 Care in planning should be exercised so that individuals in wheelchairs and individuals using braces and crutches are not compelled to wheel or walk behind parked cars.

4.3.5 Consideration should be given the distribution of spaces for use by the disabled in accordance with the frequency and persistency of parking needs.

4.3.6 Walks shall be in conformity with 4.2.

5. Buildings

5.1 Ramps with Gradients. Where ramps with gradients are necessary or desired, they shall conform to the following specifications:

5.1.1 A ramp shall not have a slope greater than 1 foot rise in 12 feet, or 8.33 percent, or 4 degrees 50 minutes.

---

[2] Extremely small, large, strong, or weak and involved individuals could fall outside the ranges in 3.3.1, 3.3.2, 3.3.3, and their reach could differ from the figure given in 3.3.4. However, these reaches were determined using a large number of individuals who were functionally trained, with a wide range in individual size and involvement.

[3] Most individuals ambulating on braces or crutches, or both, or on canes are able to manipulate within the specifications prescribed for wheelchairs, although doors present quite a problem at times. However, attention is called to the fact that a crutch tip extending laterally from an individual is not obvious to others in heavily trafficked areas, certainly not as obvious or protective as a wheelchair and is, therefore, a source of vulnerability.

[4] Some cerebral palsied individuals, and some severe arthritics, would be extreme exceptions to 3.4.1 and 3.4.2.

[5] Site development is the most effective means to resolve the problems created by topography, definitive architectural designs or concepts, water table, existing streets, and atypical problems, singularly or collectively, so that aggress, ingress, and egress to buildings by physically disabled can be facilitated while preserving the desired design and effect of the architecture.

[6] It is essential that the gradient of walks and driveways be less than that prescribed for ramps, since walks would be void of handrails and curbs and would be considerably longer and more vulnerable to the elements. Walks of near maximum grade and considerable length should have level areas at intervals for purposes of rest and safety. Walks or driveways should have a nonslip surface.

[7] This specification does not require the elimination of curbs, which, particularly if they occur at regular intersections, are a distinct safety feature for all of the handicapped, particularly the blind. The preferred method of meeting the specification is to have the walk incline to the level of the street. However, at principal intersections, it is vitally important that the curb run parallel to the street, up to the point where the walk is inclined, at which point the curb would turn in and gradually meet the level of the walk at its highest point. A less preferred method would be to gradually bring the surface of the driveway or street to the level of the walk. The disadvantage of this method is that a blind person would not know when he has left the protection of a walk and entered the hazards of a street or driveway.

APPENDIX H

5.1.2 A ramp shall have handrails on at least one side, and preferably two sides, that are 32 inches in height, measured from the surface of the ramp, that are smooth, that extend 1 foot beyond the top and bottom of the ramp, and that otherwise conform with American Standard Safety Code for Floor and Wall Openings, Railings, and Toe Boards, A12-1932.

NOTE 1: Where codes specify handrails to be of heights other than 32 inches, it is recommended that two sets of handrails be installed to serve all people. Where major traffic is predominantly children, particularly physically disabled children, extra care should be exercised in the placement of handrails, in accordance with the nature of the facility and the age group or groups being serviced.

NOTE 2: Care should be taken that the extension of the handrail is not in itself a hazard. The extension may be made on the side of a continuing wall.

5.1.3 A ramp shall have a surface that is non-slip.

5.1.4 A ramp shall have a level platform at the top which is at least 5 feet by 5 feet, if a door swings out onto the platform or toward the ramp. This platform shall extend at least 1 foot beyond each side of the doorway.

5.1.5 A ramp shall have a level platform at least 3 feet deep and 5 feet wide, if the door does not swing onto the platform or toward the ramp. This platform shall extend at least 1 foot beyond each side of the doorway.

5.1.6 Each ramp shall have at least 6 feet of straight clearance at the bottom.

5.1.7 Ramps shall have level platforms at 30-foot intervals for purposes of rest and safety and shall have level platforms wherever they turn.

5.2 Entrances

5.2.1 At least one primary entrance to each building shall be usable by individuals in wheelchairs.

NOTE: Because entrances also serve as exits, some being particularly important in case of an emergency, and because the proximity of such exits to all parts of buildings and facilities, in accordance with their design and function, is essential (see 112 and 2000 through 2031 of American Standard Building Exits Code, A9.1-1953) it is preferable that all or most entrances (exits) should be accessible to, and usable by, individuals in wheelchairs and individuals with other forms of physical disabilty herein applicable.

5.2.2 At least one entrance usable by individuals in wheelchairs shall be on a level that would make the elevators accessible.

5.3 Doors and Doorways

5.3.1 Doors shall have a clear opening of no less than 32 inches when open and shall be operable by a single effort.

NOTE 1: Two-leaf doors are not usable by those with disabilities defined in 2.1, 2.2, and 2.5 unless they operate by a single effort, or unless one of the two leaves meets the requirment of 5.3.1.

NOTE 2: It is recommended that all doors have kick plates extending from the bottom of the door to at least 16 inches from the floor, or be made of a material and finish that would safely withstand the abuse they might receive from canes, crutches, wheelchair foot-platforms, or wheelchair wheels.

5.3.2 The floor on the inside and outside of each doorway shall be level for a distance of 5 feet from the door in the direction the door swings and shall extend 1 foot beyond each side of the door.

5.3.3 Sharp inclines and abrupt changes in level shall be avoided at doorsills. As much as possible, thresholds shall be flush with the floor.

NOTE 1: Care should be taken in the selection, placement, and setting of door closers so that they do not prevent the use of doors by the physically disabled. Time-delay door closers are recommended.

NOTE 2: Automatic doors that otherwise conform to 5.3.1, 5.3.2, and 5.3.3 are very satisfactory.

NOTE 3: These specifications apply both to exterior and interior doors and doorways.

5.4 Stairs. Stairs shall conform to American Standard A9.1-1953, with the following additional considerations:

5.4.1 Steps in stairs that might require use by those with disabilities defined in 2.2 and 2.5 or by the aged shall not have abrupt (square) nosing. (See Fig. 1.)

NOTE: Individuals with restrictions in the knee, ankle, or hip, with artificial legs, long leg braces, or comparable conditions cannot, without great difficulty and hazard, use steps with nosing as illustrated in Fig. 1a, but can safely and with minimum difficulty use steps with nosing as illustrated in Fig. 1b.

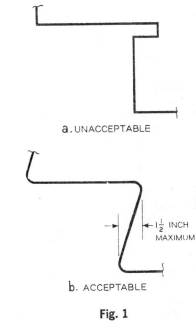

a. UNACCEPTABLE

$1\frac{1}{2}$ INCH MAXIMUM

b. ACCEPTABLE

Fig. 1

Steps

5.4.2 Stairs shall have handrails 32 inches high as measured from the tread at the face of the riser.

NOTE: Where codes specify handrails to be at heights other than 32 inches, it is recommended that two sets of handrails be installed to serve all people. Where traffic is predominantly children, particularly physically disabled children, extra care should be exercised in the placement of handrails in accordance with the nature of the facility and the age group or groups being serviced. Dual handrails may be necessary.

5.4.3 Stairs shall have at least one handrail that extends at least 18 inches beyond the top step and beyond the bottom step.

NOTE: Care should be taken that the extension of the handrails is not in itself a hazard. The extension may be made on the side of a continuing wall.

5.4.4 Steps should, wherever possible, and in conformation with existing step formulas, have risers that do not exceed 7 inches.

APPENDIX H

5.5 Floors

5.5.1 Floors shall have a surface that is nonslip.

5.5.2 Floors on a given story shall be of a common level throughout or be connected by a ramp in accord with 5.1.1 through 5.1.6, inclusive.

EXAMPLE 1: There shall not be a difference between the level of the floor of a corridor and the level of the floor of the toilet rooms.

EXAMPLE 2: There should not be a difference between the level of the floor of a corridor and the level of a meeting room, dining room, or any other room, unless proper ramps are provided.

5.6 Toilet Rooms.
It is essential that an appropriate number[8] of toilet rooms, in accordance with the nature and use of a specific building or facility, be made accessible to, and usable by, the physically handicapped.

5.6.1 Toilet rooms shall have space to allow traffic of individuals in wheelchairs, in accordance with 3.1, 3.2, and 3.3.

5.6.2 Toilet rooms shall have at least one toilet stall that—

(1) Is 3 feet wide
(2) Is at least 4 feet 8 inches, preferably 5 feet, deep
(3) Has a door (where doors are used) that is 32 inches wide and swings out
(4) Has handrails on each side, 33 inches high and parallel to the floor, 1½ inches in outside diameter, with 1½ inches clearance between rail and wall, and fastened securely at ends and center
(5) Has a water closet with the seat 20 inches from the floor

NOTE: The design and mounting of the water closet is of considerable importance. A wall-mounted water closet with a narrow understructure that recedes sharply is most desirable. If a floor-mounted water closet must be used, it should not have a front that is wide and perpendicular to the floor at the front of the seat. The bowl should be shallow at the front of the seat and turn backward more than downward to allow the individual in a wheelchair to get close to the water closet with the seat of the wheelchair.

5.6.3 Toilet rooms shall have lavatories with narrow aprons, which when mounted at standard height are usable by individuals in wheelchairs; or shall have lavatories mounted higher, when particular designs demand, so that they are usable by individuals in wheelchairs.

NOTE: It is important that drain pipes and hot-water pipes under a lavatory be covered or insulated so that a wheelchair individual without sensation will not burn himself.

5.6.4 Some mirrors and shelves shall be provided above lavatories at a height as low as possible and no higher than 40 inches above the floor, measured from the top of the shelf and the bottom of the mirror.

5.6.5 Toilet rooms for men shall have wall-mounted urinals with the opening of the basin 19 inches from the floor, or shall have floor-mounted urinals that are on level with the main floor of the toilet room.

5.6.6 Toilet rooms shall have an appropriate number[8] of towel racks, towel dispensers, and other dispensers and disposal units mounted no higher than 40 inches from the floor.

5.7 Water Fountains.
An appropriate number[8] of water fountains or other water-dispensing means shall be accessible to, and usable by, the physically disabled.

5.7.1 Water fountains or coolers shall have up-front spouts and controls.

5.7.2 Water fountains or coolers shall be hand-operated or hand- and foot-operated. (See also American Standard Specifications for Drinking Fountains, Z4.2-1942.)

NOTE 1: Conventional floor-mounted water coolers can be serviceable to individuals in wheelchairs if a small fountain is mounted on the side of the cooler 30 inches above the floor.

NOTE 2: Wall-mounted, hand-operated coolers of the latest design, manufactured by many companies, can serve the able-bodied and the physically disabled equally well when the cooler is mounted with the basin 36 inches from the floor.

NOTE 3: Fully recessed water fountains are not recommended.

NOTE 4: Water fountains should not be set into an alcove unless the alcove is wider than a wheelchair. (See 3.1.)

5.8 Public Telephones.
An appropriate number[8] of public telephones should be made accessible to, and usable by, the physically disabled.

NOTE: The conventional public telephone booth is not usable by most physically disabled individuals. There are many ways in which public telephones can be made accessible and usable. It is recommended that architects and builders confer with the telephone company in the planning of the building or facility.

5.8.1 Such telephones should be placed so that the dial and the handset can be reached by individuals in wheelchairs, in accordance with 3.3.

5.8.2 An appropriate number[8] of public telephones should be equipped for those with hearing disabilities and so identified with instructions for use.

NOTE: Such telepones can be used by everyone.

5.9 Elevators.
In a multiple-story building, elevators are essential to the successful functioning of physically disabled individuals. They shall conform to the following requirements:

5.9.1 Elevators shall be accessible to, and usable by, the physically disabled on the level that they use to enter the building, and at all levels normally used by the general public.

5.9.2 Elevators shall allow for traffic by wheelchairs, in accordance with 3.1, 3.2, 3.3 and 5.3.

5.10 Controls.
Switches and controls for light, heat, ventilation, windows, draperies, fire alarms, and all similar controls of frequent or essential use, shall be placed within the reach of individuals in wheelchairs. (See 3.3.)

5.11 Identification.
Appropriate identification of specific facilities within a building used by the public is particularly essential to the blind.

5.11.1 Raised letters or numbers shall be used to identify rooms or offices.

5.11.2 Such identification should be placed on the wall, to the right or left of the door, at a height between 4 feet 6 inches and 5 feet 6 inches, measured from the floor, and preferably at 5 feet.

[8] See 2.13.

APPENDIX H

5.11.3 Doors that are not intended for normal use, and that might prove dangerous if a blind person were to exit or enter by them, should be made quickly identifiable to the touch by knurling on the door handle or knob. (See Fig. 2.)

NOTE: Knurling can be imposed upon door handles or knobs by use of textured plastic.

EXAMPLE: Such doors might lead to loading platforms, boiler rooms, stages, fire escapes, etc.

5.12 Warning Signals

5.12.1 Audible warning signals shall be accompanied by simultaneous visual signals for the benefit of those with hearing disabilities.

5.12.2 Visual signals shall be accompanied by simultaneous audible signals for the benefit of the blind.

5.13 Hazards. Every effort shall be exercised to obviate hazards to individuals with physical disabilities.

5.13.1 Access panels or manholes in floors, walks, and walls can be extremely hazardous, particularly when in use, and should be avoided.

5.13.2 When manholes or access panels are open and in use, or when an open excavation exists on a site, particularly when it is approximate to normal pedestrian traffic, barricades shall be placed on all open sides, at least 8 feet from the hazard, and warning devices shall be installed in accord with 5.12.2.

5.13.3 Low-hanging door closers that remain within the opening of a doorway when the door is open, or that protrude hazardously into regular corridors or traffic ways when the door is closed, shall be avoided.

5.13.4 Low-hanging signs, ceiling lights, and similar objects or signs and fixtures that protrude into regular corridors or traffic ways shall be avoided. A minimum height of 7 feet, measured from the floor, is recommended.

5.13.5 Lighting on ramps shall be in accord with 1201, 1202, 1203, and 1204 of American Standard A9.1-1953.

5.13.6 Exit signs shall be in accord with 1205 of American Standard A9.1-1953, except as modified by 5.11 of this standard.

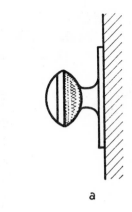

a

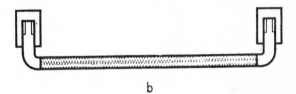

b

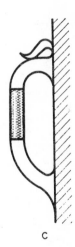

c

Fig. 2

Knurled Door Handles and Knobs

APPENDIX I
RECOMMENDED FACILITY ADAPTATIONS
FOR THE AGING AND THE DISABLED

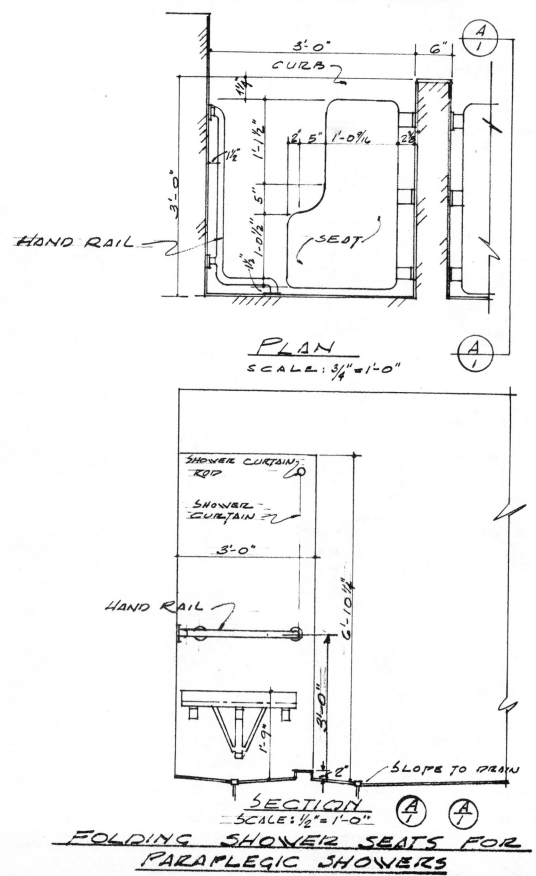

PLAN
SCALE: 3/4" = 1'-0"

SECTION
SCALE: 1/2" = 1'-0"

FOLDING SHOWER SEATS FOR
PARAPLEGIC SHOWERS

APPENDIX I

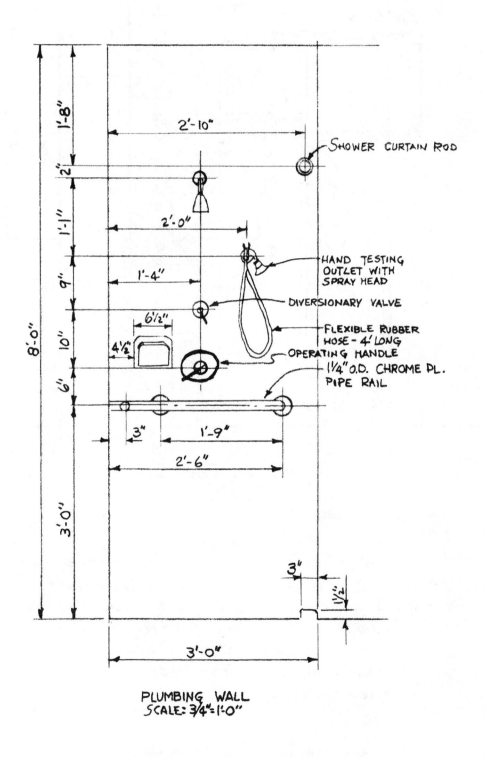

SHOWER FACILITIES

APPENDIX I

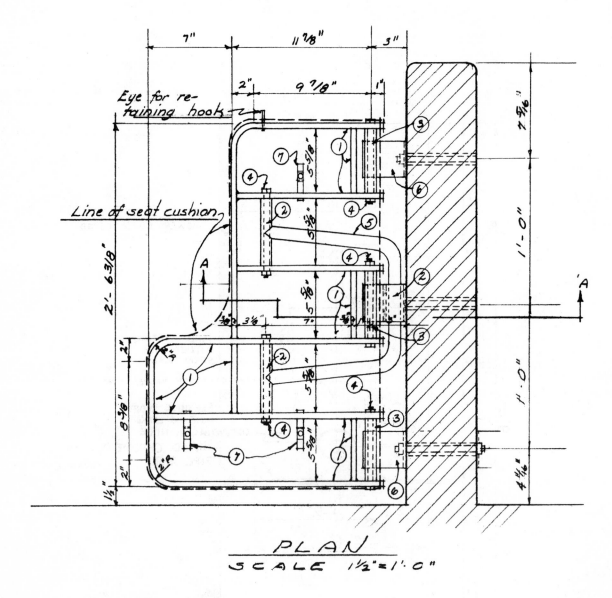

PLAN
SCALE 1½"=1'·0"

KEY

① - ⅜"×1¼" Flat bar aluminum alloy - shape shown
② - Seat bracket & guide - S.S. - See detail.
③ - 1" O.D. tubing - .203" thick - S.S. - Allow clearance. Weld to ⑥
④ - ½" φ Bolts - S.S. - 8" long - last 1⅛" threaded.
⑤ - 1" O.D. φ Bar - S.S. Shape shown.
⑥ - Seat brackets - 2 per seat S.S.
⑦ - Keeper - see Detail

FOLDING SHOWER SEATS
FOR PARAPLEGIC SHOWERS

APPENDIX I

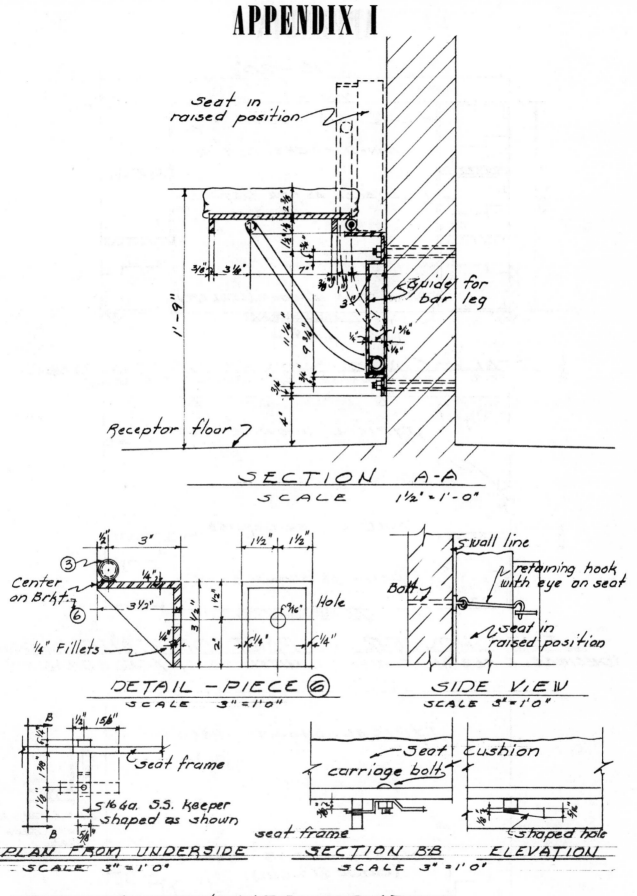

seat in raised position

Receptor floor

1'-9"

2 3/8"
1 1/2 1/4"
3/4"
3/16" 3 1/8"
7"
3/8"
3"
11 1/4"
9 3/4"
3/4"
3/4"
3"
4"
1 3/16"
1/4"

guide for bar leg

SECTION A-A
SCALE 1 1/2" = 1'-0"

Center on Brkt.
3
6
1/4" Fillets
1/2"
3"
1/4"
3 1/2"
1/4"
1 1/2" 1 1/2"
1 1/2"
3 1/2"
2"
1/4" 1/4"
9/16" Hole

DETAIL - PIECE 6
SCALE 3" = 1'0"

wall line
Bolt
retaining hook with eye on seat
seat in raised position

SIDE VIEW
SCALE 3" = 1'0"

B
B
1/2" 1 5/8"
1 1/2"
1 7/8"
1 1/8"
5/8"
seat frame
5164a. S.S. keeper shaped as shown

PLAN FROM UNDERSIDE
SCALE 3" = 1'0"

Seat Cushion
carriage bolt
seat frame

SECTION B-B
SCALE 3" = 1'0"

ELEVATION
shaped hole

FOLDING SHOWER SEATS
FOR PARAPLEGIC SHOWERS

APPENDIX I

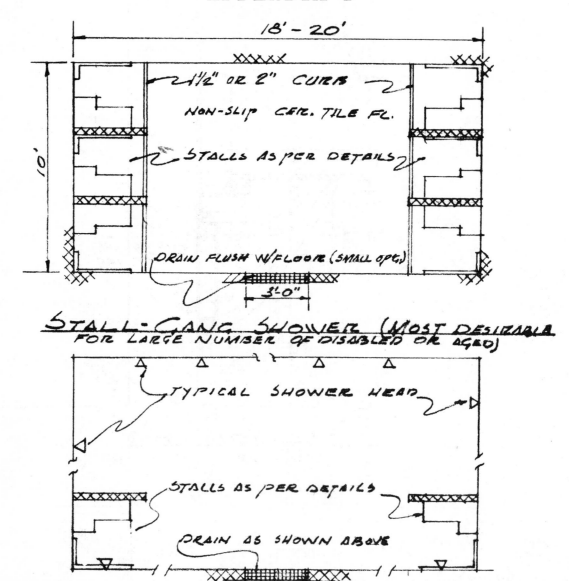

18' - 20'

10'

2½" OR 2" CURB
NON-SLIP CER. TILE FL.
STALLS AS PER DETAILS
DRAIN FLUSH W/FLOOR (SMALL OPT.)
3'-0"

STALL-GANG SHOWER (MOST DESIRABLE FOR LARGE NUMBER OF DISABLED OR AGED)

TYPICAL SHOWER HEAD
STALLS AS PER DETAILS
DRAIN AS SHOWN ABOVE

STALL SHOWER AS PART OF GANG SHOWER
(DESIRABLE FOR MULTI-USE; LIMITED NO. OF AGED & DISABLED)

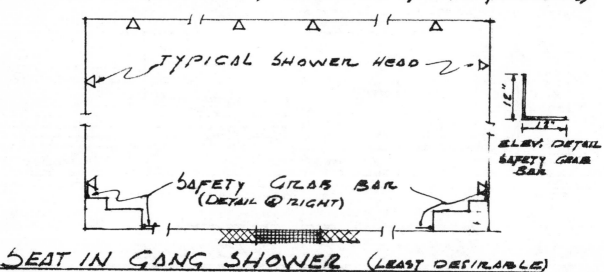

TYPICAL SHOWER HEAD
SAFETY GRAB BAR (DETAIL @ RIGHT)

3"
18"
ELEV. DETAIL SAFETY GRAB BAR

SEAT IN GANG SHOWER (LEAST DESIRABLE)

APPENDIX I

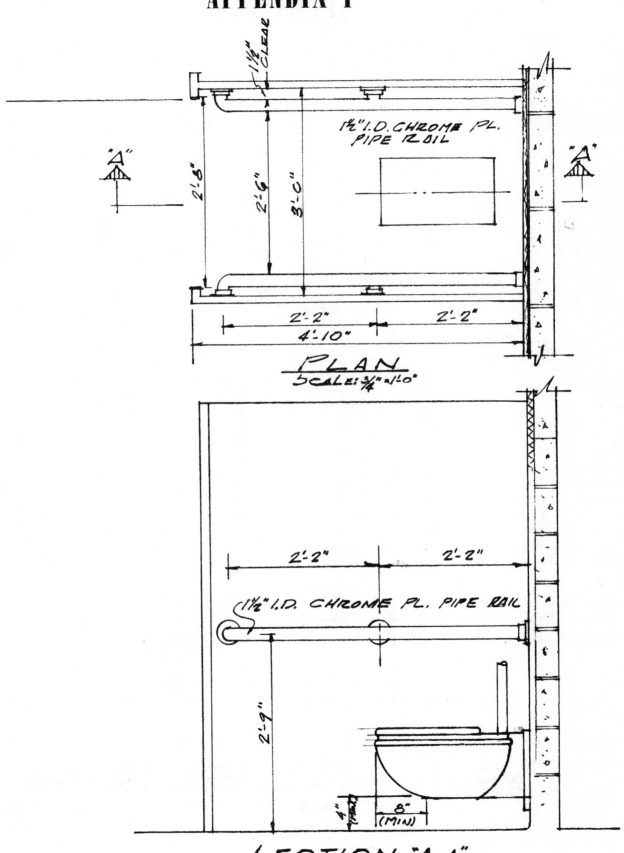

1½" CLEAR

1½" I.D. CHROME PL. PIPE RAIL

2'-8"

2'-9"

3'-0"

2'-2"   2'-2"

4'-10"

PLAN
SCALE: ¾"=1'-0"

2'-2"   2'-2"

1½" I.D. CHROME PL. PIPE RAIL

2'-9"

4"

8" (MIN)

SECTION "A-A"
SCALE: ¾"=1'-0"

STANDARD PARAPLEGIC TOILET STALL

APPENDIX I

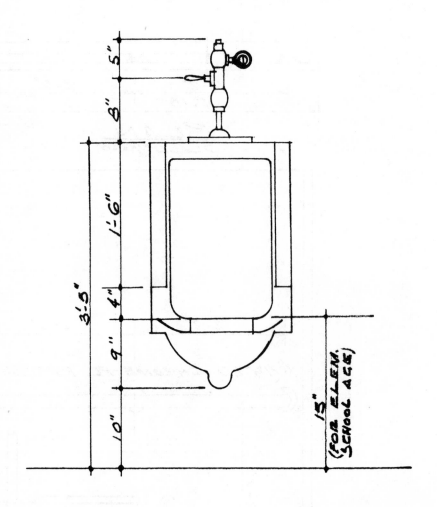

WALL MOUNTED URINAL
SCALE: 1"=1'-0"

APPENDIX I

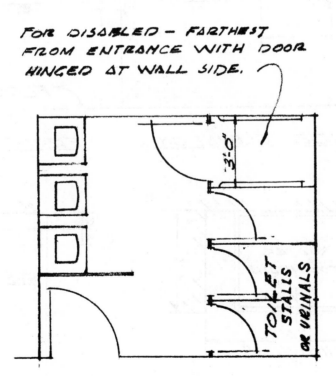

FOR DISABLED — FARTHEST FROM ENTRANCE WITH DOOR HINGED AT WALL SIDE.

3'-0"

TOILET STALLS OR URINALS

<u>SUGGESTED PLACEMENT OF WIDE STALL WITH OUTSWINGING DOOR IN TOILET ROOM</u>

<u>NOT TO SCALE</u>

APPENDIX I

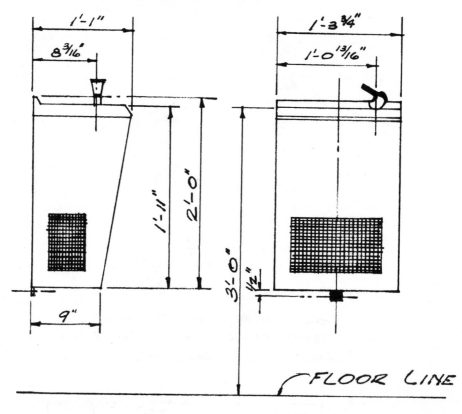

SIDE ELEVATION   FRONT ELEVATION

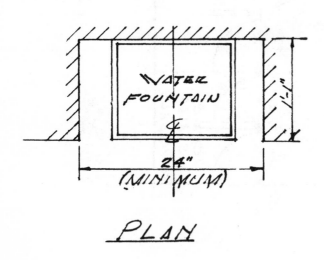

PLAN

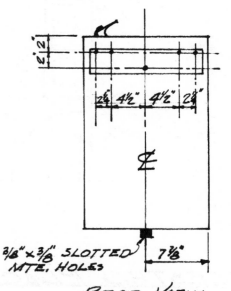

³⁄₈" × ³⁄₈" SLOTTED
MTE. HOLES

REAR VIEW
SHOWING MOUNTING

WATER FOUNTAIN - RECESSED IN WALL

SCALE: 1" = 1'-0"

APPENDIX I

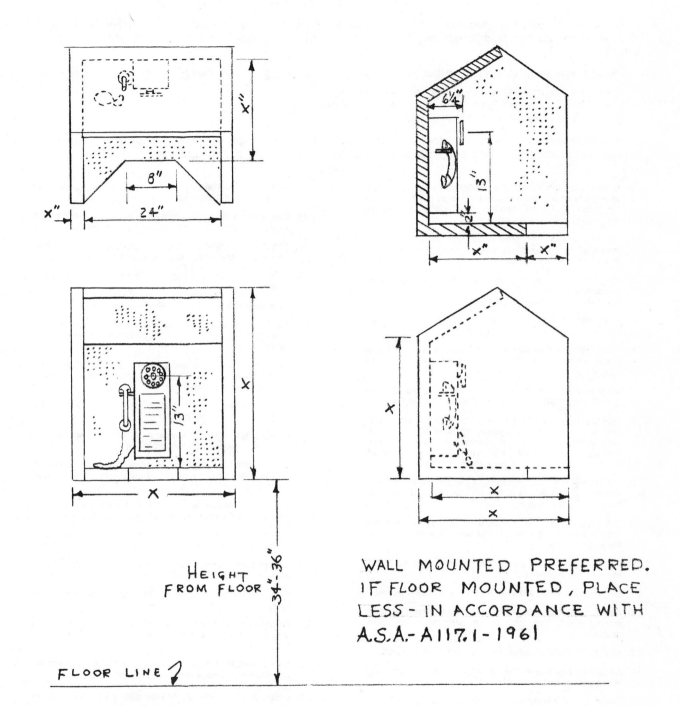

WALL MOUNTED PREFERRED.
IF FLOOR MOUNTED, PLACE
LESS - IN ACCORDANCE WITH
A.S.A.- A117.1 - 1961

PLAN of PLACEMENT of MODERN TELEPHONES
(SEVERAL DESIGNS AVAILABLE)
SCALE 3/4" = 1'-0"

TO BE EQUALLY USABLE BY ABLE &
DISABLED & SMALLER CHILDREN

256

APPENDIX J

CHECK LIST FOR FACILITY PLANNERS

As an aid to those responsible for planning facilities for physical education, health education, and recreation, a check list has been prepared. The application of this check list may prevent unfortunate and costly errors.

Place the appropriate letter in the space indicated in the right-hand margin after each statement:

A — The plans meet the requirements **completely.**
B — The plans meet the requirements **only partially.**
C — The plans **fail** to meet the requirements.

Soundly-conceived plans for areas and facilities are not achieved by chance or accident, but by initiative and action of knowledgeable people acting individually, in groups, and as agencies.

GENERAL

1. A clear-cut statement has been prepared on the nature and scope of the program, and the special requirements for space, equipment, fixtures, and facilities dictated by the activities to be conducted.

2. The facility has been planned to meet the total requirements of the program as well as the special needs of those who are to be served.

3. The plans and specifications have been checked by all governmental agencies (city, county, and state) whose approval is required by law.

4. Plans for areas and facilities conform to state and local regulations and to accepted standards and practices.

5. The areas and facilities planned make possible the programs which serve the interests and needs of all the people.

6. Every available source of property or funds has been explored, evaluated, and utilized whenever appropriate.

7. All interested persons and organizations concerned with the facility have had an opportunity to share in its planning (professional educators, users, consultants, administrators, engineers, architects, program specialists, building managers, and builder—a team approach).

8. The facility and its appurtenances will fulfill the maximum demands of the program. The program has not been curtailed to fit the facility.

9. The facility has been functionally planned to meet the present and anticipated needs of specific programs, situations, and publics.

10. Future additions are included in present plans to permit economy of construction.

11. Lecture classrooms are isolated from distracting noises.

12. Storage areas for indoor and outdoor equipment are adequately sized. They are located adjacent to the gymnasiums.

13. Shelves in storage rooms are slanted toward the wall.

14. All passageways are free of obstructions; fixtures are recessed.

15. Facilities for health services, health testing, health instruction, and the first-aid and emergency-isolation rooms are suitably interrelated.

16. Buildings, specific areas, and facilities are clearly identified.

17. Locker rooms are arranged for ease of supervision.

18. Offices, teaching stations, and service facilities are properly interrelated.

19. Special needs of the physically handicapped are met, including a ramp into the building at a major entrance.

20. All "dead space" is used.

21. The building is compatible in design and comparable in quality and accommodation to other campus structures.

22. Storage rooms are accessible to the play area.

23. Workrooms, conference rooms, and staff and administrative offices are interrelated.

24. Shower and dressing facilities are provided for professional staff members and are conveniently located.

25. Thought and attention have been given to making facilities and equipment as durable and vandalproof as possible.

26. Low-cost maintenance features have been adequately considered.

27. This facility is a part of a well-integrated master plan.

28. All areas, courts, facilities, equipment, climate control, security, etc., conform rigidly to detailed standards and specifications.

29. Shelves are recessed and mirrors are supplied in appropriate places in rest rooms and dressing rooms. Mirrors are not placed above lavatories.

30. Dressing space between locker rows is adjusted to the size and age level of students.

31. Drinking fountains are conveniently placed in locker-room areas or immediately adjacent thereto.

32. Special attention is given to provision for the locking of service windows and counters, supply bins, carts, shelves, and racks.

33. Provision is made for the repair, maintenance, replacement, and off-season storage of equipment and uniforms.

34. A well-defined program for laundering and cleaning of towels, uniforms, and equipment is included in the plan.

35. Noncorrosive metal is used in dressing, drying, and shower areas except for enameled lockers.

36. Antipanic hardware is used where required by fire regulations.

37. Properly-placed hose bibbs and drains are sufficient in size and quantity to permit flushing the entire area with a water hose.

38. A water-resistant, coved base is used under the locker base and floor mat, and where floor and wall join.

39. Chalkboards and/or tackboards with map tracks are located in appropriate places in dressing rooms, hallways, and classrooms.

40. Book shelves are provided in toilet areas.

41. Space and equipment are planned in accordance with the types and number of enrollees.

42. Basement rooms, being undesirable for dressing, drying, and showering, are not planned for those purposes.

43. Spectator seating (permanent) in areas which are basically instructional is kept at a minimum. Roll-away bleachers are used primarily. Balcony seating is considered as a possibility.

44. Well-lighted and effectively-displayed trophy cases enhance the interest and beauty of the lobby.

APPENDIX J

45. The space under the stairs is used for storage. _____

46. Department heads' offices are located near the central administrative office, which includes a well-planned conference room. _____

47. Workrooms are located near the central office and serve as a repository for departmental materials and records. _____

48. The conference area includes a cloak room, lavatory, and toilet. _____

49. In addition to regular secretarial offices established in the central and department-chairmen's offices, a special room to house a secretarial pool for staff members is provided. _____

50. Staff dressing facilities are provided. These facilities may also serve game officials. _____

51. The community and/or neighborhood has a "round table" —planning round table. _____

52. All those (persons and agencies) who should be a party to planning and development are invited and actively engaged in the planning process. _____

53. Space and area relationships are important. They have been carefully considered. _____

54. Both long-range plans and immediate plans have been made. _____

55. The body comfort of the child, a major factor in securing maximum learning, has been considered in the plans. _____

56. Plans for quiet areas have been made. _____

57. In the planning, consideration has been given to the need for adequate recreation areas and facilities, both near and distant from the homes of people. _____

58. Plans recognize the primary function of recreation as being enrichment of learning through creative self-expression, self-enhancement, and the achievement of self-potential. _____

59. Every effort has been exercised to eliminate hazards. _____

60. The installation of low-hanging door closers, light fixtures, signs, and other objects in traffic areas has been avoided. _____

61. Warning signals—both visible and audible—are included in the plans. _____

62. Ramps have a slope equal to or greater than a one-foot rise in 12'. _____

63. Minimum landings for ramps are 5' x 5', they extend at least one foot beyond the swinging arc of a door, have at least a 6-foot clearance at the bottom, and have level platforms at 30-foot intervals on every turn. _____

64. Adequate locker and dressing spaces are provided. _____

65. The design of dressing, drying, and shower areas reduces foot traffic to a minimum and establishes clean, dry aisles for bare feet. _____

66. Teaching stations are properly related to service facilities. _____

67. Toilet facilities are adequate in number. They are located to serve all groups for which provisions are made. _____

68. Mail services, outgoing and incoming, are included in the plans. _____

69. Hallways, ramps, doorways, and elevators are designed to permit equipment to be moved easily and quickly. _____

70. A keying design suited to administrative and instructional needs is planned. _____

71. Toilets used by large groups have circulating (in and out) entrances and exits. _____

CLIMATE CONTROL

1. Provision is made throughout the building for climate control—heating, ventilating, and refrigerated cooling. _____

2. Special ventilation is provided for locker, dressing, shower, drying, and toilet rooms. _____

3. Heating plans permit both area and individual-room control. _____

4. Research areas where small animals are kept and where chemicals are used have been provided with special ventilating equipment. _____

5. The heating and ventilating of the wrestling gymnasium have been given special attention. _____

ELECTRICAL

1. Shielded, vaporproof lights are used in moisture-prevalent areas. _____

2. Lights in strategic areas are key-controlled. _____

3. Lighting intensity conforms to approved standards. _____

4. An adequate number of electrical outlets are strategically placed. _____

5. Gymnasium and auditorium lights are controlled by dimmer units. _____

6. Locker-room lights are mounted above the space between lockers. _____

7. Natural light is controlled properly for purposes of visual aids and other avoidance of glare. _____

8. Electrical outlet plates are installed 3' above the floor unless special use dictates other locations. _____

9. Controls for light switches and projection equipment are suitably located and interrelated. _____

10. All lights are shielded. Special protection is provided in gymnasiums, court areas, and shower rooms. _____

11. Lights are placed to shine between rows of lockers. _____

WALLS

1. Movable and folding partitions are power-operated and controlled by keyed switches. _____

2. Wall plates are located where needed and are firmly attached. _____

3. Hooks and rings for nets are placed (and recessed in walls) according to court locations and net heights. _____

4. Materials that clean easily and are impervious to moisture are used where moisture is prevalent. _____

5. Shower heads are placed at different heights—4' (elementary) to 7' (university)—for each school level. _____

6. Protective matting is placed permanently on the walls in the wrestling room, at the ends of basketball courts, and in other areas where such protection is needed. _____

7. An adequate number of drinking fountains are provided. They are properly placed (recessed in wall). _____

8. One wall (at least) of the dance studio has full-length mirrors. _____

9. All corners in locker rooms are rounded. _____

CEILINGS

1. Overhead-supported apparatus is secured to beams engineered to withstand stress. _____

2. The ceiling height is adequate for the activities to be housed. _____

3. Acoustical materials impervious to moisture are used in moisture-prevalent areas. _____

4. Skylights, being impractical, are seldom used because of problems in waterproofing roofs and the controlling of sun rays (gyms). _____

APPENDIX J

5. All ceilings except those in storage areas are acoustically treated with sound-absorbent materials. _____

FLOORS

1. Floor plates are placed where needed and are flush-mounted. _____

2. Floor design and materials conform to recommended standards and specifications. _____

3. Lines and markings are painted on floors before sealing is completed (when synthetic tape is not used). _____

4. A coved base (around lockers and where wall and floor meet) of the same water-resistant material used on floors is found in all dressing and shower rooms. _____

5. Abrasive, nonskid, slip-resistant flooring that is impervious to moisture is provided on all areas where water is used —laundry, swimming pool, shower, dressing, and drying rooms. _____

6. Floor drains are properly located and the slope of the floor is adequate for rapid drainage. _____

GYMNASIUMS AND SPECIAL ROOMS

1. Gymnasiums are planned so as to provide for safety zones (between courts, end lines, and walls) and for best utilization of space. _____

2. One gymnasium wall is free of obstructions and is finished with a smooth, hard surface for ball-rebounding activities. _____

3. The elementary-school gymnasium has: one wall free of obstructions; a minimum ceiling height of 18'; a minimum of 4,000 square feet of teaching area; and a recessed area for housing a piano. _____

4. Secondary-school gymnasiums have: a minimum ceiling height of 22'; a scoreboard; electrical outlets placed to fit with bleacher installation; wall attachments for apparatus and nets; and a power-operated, sound-insulated, and movable partition with a small pass-through door at one end. _____

5. A small spectator alcove adjoins the wrestling room and contains a drinking fountain (recessed in the wall). _____

6. Cabinets, storage closets, supply windows, and service areas have locks. _____

7. Provisions have been made for the cleaning, storing, and issuing of physical education and athletic uniforms. _____

8. Shower heads are placed at varying heights in the shower rooms on each school level. _____

9. Equipment is provided for the use of the physically handicapped. _____

10. Special provision has been made for audio and visual aids, including intercommunication systems, radio, and television. _____

11. Team dressing rooms have provisions for:

    a. hosing down room _____

    b. floors pitched to drain easily _____

    c. hot- and cold-water hose bibbs _____

    d. windows located above locker heights _____

    e. chalk, tack, and bulletin boards, and movie projection _____

    f. lockers for each team member _____

    g. drying facility for uniforms _____

12. The indoor rifle range includes:

    a. targets located 54" apart and 50' from the firing line _____

    b. 3' to 8' of space behind targets _____

    c. 12' of space behind firing line _____

    d. ceilings 8' high _____

    e. width adjusted to number of firing lines needed (1 line for each 3 students) _____

    f. a pulley device for target placement and return _____

    g. storage and repair space _____

13. Dance facilities include:

    a. 100 square feet per student _____

    b. a minimum length of 60 linear feet for modern dance _____

    c. full-height viewing mirrors on one wall (at least) of 30'; also a 20' mirror on an additional wall if possible _____

    d. acoustical drapery to cover mirrors when not used and for protection if other activities are permitted _____

    e. dispersed microphone jacks and speaker installation for music and instruction _____

    f. built-in cabinets for record players, microphones, and amplifiers, with space for equipment carts _____

    g. electrical outlets and microphone connections around perimeter of room _____

    h. an exercise bar (34" to 42" above floor) on one wall _____

    i. drapes, surface colors, floors (maple preferred), and other room appointments to enhance the room's attractiveness _____

    j. location near dressing rooms and outside entrances _____

14. Training rooms include:

    a. rooms large enough to administer adequately proper health services _____

    b. sanitary storage cabinets for medical supplies _____

    c. installation of drains for whirlpool, tubs, etc. _____

    d. installation of electrical outlets with proper capacities and voltage _____

    e. high stools for use of equipment such as whirlpool, ice tubs, etc. _____

    f. water closet, hand lavatory, and shower _____

    g. extra hand lavatory in the trainers' room proper _____

    h. adjoining dressing rooms _____

    i. installation and use of hydrotherapy and diathermy equipment in separate areas _____

    j. space for the trainer, the physician, and for the various services of this function _____

    k. corrective-exercise laboratories located conveniently and adapted to the needs of the handicapped _____

15. Coaches' rooms should provide:

    a. a sufficient number of dressing lockers for coaching staff and officials _____

    b. a security closet or cabinet for athletic equipment such as timing devices _____

    c. a sufficient number of showers and toilet facilities _____

    d. drains and faucets for hosing down the rooms where this method of cleaning is desirable and possible _____

    e. a small chalkboard and tackboard _____

    f. a small movie screen and projection table for use of coaches to review films _____

APPENDIX J

HANDICAPPED, DISABLED, AND AGING

Have you included those considerations that would make the facility accessible to, and usable by, the disabled and the aging? These considerations include:

1. The knowledge that the disabled and the aging will be participants in almost all activities, not merely spectators, if the facility is properly planned. _____

2. Ground-level entrance(s) or stair-free entrance(s) using inclined walk(s) or inclined ramp(s). _____

3. Uninterrupted walk surface; no abrupt changes in levels leading to the facility. _____

4. Approach walks and connecting walks no less than 4' in width. _____

5. Walks with a gradient no greater than five percent. _____

6. A ramp, when used, with rise no greater than one foot in 12'. _____

7. Flat or level surface inside and outside of all exterior doors, extending 5' from the door in the direction that the door swings, and extending one foot to each side of the door. _____

8. Flush thresholds at all doors. _____

9. Appropriate door widths, heights, and mechanical features. _____

10. At least 6' between vestibule doors in series, i.e., inside and outside doors. _____

11. Access and proximity to parking areas. _____

12. No obstructions by curbs at crosswalks, parking areas, etc. _____

13. Proper precautions (handrails, etc.) at basement-window areaways, open stairways, porches, ledges, and platforms. _____

14. Handrails on all steps and ramps. _____

15. Precautions against the placement of manholes in principal or major sidewalks. _____

16. Corridors that are at least 60" wide and without abrupt pillars or protrusions. _____

17. Floors which are nonskid and have no abrupt changes or interruptions in level. _____

18. Proper design of steps. _____

19. Access to rest rooms, water coolers, telephones, food-service areas, lounges, dressing rooms, play areas, and all auxiliary services and areas. _____

20. Elevators in multiple-story buildings. _____

21. Appropriate placement of controls to permit and to prohibit use as desired. _____

22. Sound signals for the blind, and visual signals for the deaf as counterparts to regular sound and sight signals. _____

23. Proper placement, concealment, or insulation of radiators, heat pipes, hot-water pipes, drain pipes, etc. _____

24. Referral to Appendix H, ASA-A117.1-1961, "Making Buildings and Facilities Accessible to, and Usable by, the Physically Handicapped." _____

SWIMMING POOLS

1. Has a clear-cut statement been prepared on the nature and scope of the design program and the special requirements for space, equipment, and facilities dictated by the activities to be conducted? _____

2. Has the swimming pool been planned to meet the total requirements of the program to be conducted as well as any special needs of the clientele to be served? _____

3. Have all plans and specifications been checked and approved by the local Board of Health? _____

4. Is the pool the proper depth to accommodate the various age groups and types of activities it is intended to serve? _____

5. Does the design of the pool incorporate the most current knowledge and best experience available regarding swimming pools? _____

6. If a local architect or engineer who is inexperienced in pool construction is employed, has an experienced pool consultant, architect, or engineer been called in to advise on design and equipment? _____

7. Is there adequate deep water for diving (minimum of 9' for one-meter boards, 12' for 3-meter boards, and 15' for 10-meter towers)? _____

8. Have the requirements for competitive swimming been met (7-foot lanes; 12-inch black or brown lines on the bottom; pool 1 inch longer than official measurement; depth and distance markings)? _____

9. Is there adequate deck space around the pool? Has more space been provided than that indicated by the minimum recommended deck/pool ratio? _____

10. Does the swimming instructor's office face the pool? And is there a window through which the instructor may view all the pool area? Is there a toilet-shower-dressing area next to the office for instructors? _____

11. Are recessed steps or removable ladders located on the walls so as not to interfere with competitive swimming turns? _____

12. Does a properly-constructed overflow gutter extend around the pool perimeter? _____

13. Where skimmers are used, have they been properly located so that they are not on walls where competitive swimming is to be conducted? _____

14. Have separate storage spaces been allocated for maintenance and instructional equipment? _____

15. Has the area for spectators been properly separated from the pool area? _____

16. Have all diving standards and lifeguard chairs been properly anchored? _____

17. Does the pool layout provide the most efficient control of swimmers from showers and locker rooms to the pool? Are toilet facilities provided for wet swimmers separate from the dry area? _____

18. Is the recirculation pump located below the water level? _____

19. Is there easy vertical access to the filter room for both people and material (stairway if required)? _____

20. Has the proper pitch to drains been allowed in the pool, on the pool deck, in the overflow gutter, and on the floor of shower and dressing rooms? _____

21. Has adequate space been allowed between diving boards and between the diving boards and sidewalls? _____

22. Is there adequate provision for lifesaving equipment? Pool-cleaning equipment? _____

23. Are inlets and outlets adequate in number and located so as to insure effective circulation of water in the pool? _____

24. Has consideration been given to underwater lights, underwater observation windows, and underwater speakers? _____

25. Is there a coping around the edge of the pool? _____

26. Has a pool heater been considered in northern climates in order to raise the temperature of the water? _____

27. Have underwater lights in end racing walls been located deep enough and directly below surface lane anchors, and are they on a separate circuit? _____

28. Has the plan been considered from the standpoint of handicapped persons (e.g., is there a gate adjacent to the turnstiles)? _____

APPENDIX J

29. Is seating for swimmers provided on the deck? _____

30. Has the recirculation-filtration system been designed to meet the anticipated future bathing load? _____

31. Has the gas chlorinator (if used) been placed in a separate room accessible from and vented to the outside? _____

32. Has the gutter waste water been valved to return to the filters, and also for direct waste? _____

INDOOR POOLS

1. Is there proper mechanical ventilation? _____

2. Is there adequate acoustical treatment of walls and ceilings? _____

3. Is there adequate overhead clearance for diving (15' above low springboards, 15' for 3-meter boards, and 10' for 10-meter platforms)? _____

4. Is there adequate lighting (50 footcandles minimum)? _____

5. Has reflection of light from the outside been kept to the minimum by proper location of windows or skylights (windows on sidewalls are not desirable)? _____

6. Are all wall bases coved to facilitate cleaning? _____

7. Is there provision for proper temperature control in the pool room for both water and air? _____

8. Can the humidity of the pool room be controlled? _____

9. Is the wall and ceiling insulation adequate to prevent "sweating"? _____

10. Are all metal fittings of noncorrosive material? _____

11. Is there a tunnel around the outside of the pool, or a trench on the deck which permits ready access to pipes? _____

OUTDOOR POOLS

1. Is the site for the pool in the best possible location (away from railroad tracks, heavy industry, trees, and open fields which are dusty)? _____

2. Have sand and grass been kept the proper distance away from the pool to prevent them from being transmitted to the pool? _____

3. Has a fence been placed around the pool to assure safety when not in use? _____

4. Has proper subsurface drainage been provided? _____

5. Is there adequate deck space for sunbathing? _____

6. Are the outdoor lights placed far enough from the pool to prevent insects from dropping into the pool? _____

7. Is the deck of nonslip material? _____

8. Is there an area set aside for eating, separated from the pool deck? _____

9. Is the bathhouse properly located, with the entrance to the pool leading to the shallow end? _____

10. If the pool shell contains a concrete finish, has the length of the pool been increased by 3 inches over the "official" size in order to permit eventual tiling of the basin without making the pool "too short"? _____

11. Are there other recreational facilities nearby for the convenience and enjoyment of swimmers? _____

12. Do diving boards or platforms face north or east? _____

13. Are lifeguard stands provided and properly located? _____

14. Has adequate parking space been provided and properly located? _____

15. Is the pool oriented correctly in relation to the sun? _____

16. Have windshields been provided in situations where heavy winds prevail? _____

APPENDIX J

CONSTRUCTION PROGRESS CHECK LIST

	Jan	Feb	Mar	Apr	May	June	July	Aug	Sept	Oct	Nov	Dec
1. Excavation, Backfilling & Grading												
2. Conc Ftgs, Fdn, Slabs on Gr & Rebars												
3. Conc Cols, Beams, Pan Slabs & Rebar												
4. Conc Stairs, Rebar												
5. Conc Tapping												
6. Precast Roof Panels and Columns												
7. Masonry												
8. Cast Stone												
9. Structural Steel												
10. Steel Joists												
11. Miscellaneous Steel												
12. Steel Deck												
13. Chalk and Tack Boards												
14. Hardwood Flooring and Walls												
15. Mill work, Seating, and Telephone Booths												
16. Moisture Protection												
17. Roof Insulation and Roofing												
18. Sealants and Caulking												
19. Sheet Metal and Aluminum Extrusions												
20. Hollow Metal Doors and Frames												
21. Windows, Entrances, Glass, and Glazing												
22. Ceramic and Quarry Tile and Shower Stalls												
23. Terrazzo Work												
24. Rough Carpentry												
25. Resilient Floor Coverings												
26. Acoustical Tile and Insulation (Wires)												
27. Lathing & Plastering												
28. Painting												
29. Finish Hardware, Directories, Mailboxes												
30. Metal Lockers, Benches and Metal Casework												
31. Toilet Partitions and Toilet Accessories												
32. Misc. Specialties												
33. Swimming Pool Specialties												
34. Roll-up, Coiling, Accordian Drs (Track)												
35. Gymnasium Specialties (Anchors, etc.)												
36. Elevators & Dumbwaiter												
37. Mechanical												
38. Electrical												
39. Skylights												
40. Inspection, Punch List, and Cleanup												

APPENDIX J

PUNCH LIST FOR CONSTRUCTION JOBS

- [ ] Carpentry — rough, finish, cabinets, hardware

- [ ] Plumbing — water, sewer, gas, air, etc.

- [ ] Mechanical — heating, ventilation, structural

- [ ] Electrical — wiring, lighting, elect. capacity in circuit, clocks and belts, motor

- [ ] Insulation — thermal, sound

- [ ] Plastering

- [ ] Surface Materials:

- [ ]   1. Floors — seals, paint, tile, etc.

- [ ]   2. Walls — paint, plastic, tile, etc.

- [ ]   3. Ceilings — acoustical tile, paint

- [ ] Painting — paint, stairs, special finishes, e.g., carbonize

- [ ] Telephones

- [ ] Room-darkening drapes or shades

- [ ] Mailboxes

- [ ] Custodial room

- [ ] Door numbers

- [ ] Directory

- [ ] Directional signs

- [ ] Entrance shelter and mat

- [ ] Planning charges

- [ ] Keying of doors

- [ ] Moving charges

- [ ] Approvals

APPENDIX K

GLOSSARY

Accessibility: Facilities are conveniently available to those for whom they were designed to accommodate.

Accommodation: The process by which the eye changes from one distance to another.

Acoustics: The science of heard sound, including its production, transmission and effects; the qualities of a room that have to do with how clearly sounds can be heard or transmitted in it.

Adapted Activities: Those recreation events which have been adjusted to fit the needs, interests, and capabilities of the physically and/or mentally handicapped.

Adhesive: A substance that causes bodies to adhere to each other.

After Image: A visual response that occurs after the stimulus causing it has ceased.

Aggregate: Any hard material (usually sand and rock) for mixing in graduated fragments with a cementing material to form concrete, plaster, or the like.

Aging: Those manifestations of the aging processes that significantly reduce mobility to perform either physical or mental tasks, but are not accounted for in other categories.

Aims: Remote goals which guide one's thoughts and actions.

Ambulant: This implies walking or moving about. It describes the patient not confined to a bed and who can propel himself.

Angle of Reflection: The angle between the reflected ray and the normal or perpendicular to the point of reflection.

Angle of Refraction: The angle between the refracted ray and the normal or perpendicular drawn to the point of refraction.

Annunciator: An electrically-controlled signal board or station on which is indicated, usually by lights or a dropping shutter, which of the connecting lines is calling.

Apparatus: A collection or set of devices designed to contribute to physical development by providing opportunities for climbing, swinging, balancing, and performing gymnastic stunts.

Appraisal Survey: A method of evaluating the existing community recreation or school resources, program, and services in accordance with some established standards or criteria.

Aquatics: Water sports performed in or upon the water.

Arts and Crafts: Activities which serve as outlets for creative expression and provide opportunities to find satisfaction through making things with the hands, such as carving, modeling, weaving, painting, sewing, and photography.

Asbestos: A grayish mineral; a sylicate of calcium and magnesium which occurs in long, threadlike fibers; because it does not burn and is a nonconductor of electricity, it is used in fireproof curtains, roofing, and insulation.

Asphalt: A brown or black solid bituminous substance obtained largely as a residue from certain petroleums and which is insoluble in water. It is used for paving, roofing, in paints and varnishes, and in combination with other materials for floor tile.

Astigmatism: A condition where irregularity in the curvature of one or more of the refractive surfaces of the eye results in a blurred line image of a focused point.

Astragals: A small convex moulding of rounded surface, generally from half to three-quarters of a circle; a strip of moulding on the edge of folding doors.

Athletic Field: A specialized type of outdoor recreation area intended primarily for highly-organized games and sports, such as football, track, and baseball. Permanent seating facilities are usually provided and the area is often enclosed by a fence or wall. Athletic fields equipped with permanent seating facilities are referred to as stadiums.

Athletics: Sports activities based on organized competition, requiring a set of rules and a code of ethics, a high degree of skill, conditioning, and training. Examples of athletic contests are college football games, high-school basketball games, Amateur Athletic Union track-and-field meets, and intracommunity softball games.

Attractiveness: Aesthetically appealing; beautiful in terms of intended purpose.

Auxiliary: An additional, supplementary facility used to supplement the main facility.

Bathing Beach: A tract of land adjoining a lake, stream, or ocean. Facilities provided usually include a bathhouse, playground apparatus, picnic areas, courts for games, and space for parking.

Batten: A strip of wood put over a seam between boards as a fastening or covering.

Beam: Several nearly-parallel rays of light; a long, thick piece of wood, metal, or stone used on buildings.

Berm (or Dike): A narrow shelf, path, or ledge, as along the top of a scarp, or along a road.

Beveled: Sloping part of the surface; to slope at an angle.

Blinding Glare: Glare which is so intense that for an appreciable period of time no object can be seen.

Brightness: Luminous intensity created by direct emission of light from a source by transmission through a translucent medium or by reflection from a surface. The unit of brightness is the footlambert.

Brightness Balance: Specified limitations of brightness differences and brightness ratios within the visual fields which, if observed, will contribute toward visual comfort and good visual performance.

Brightness Contrast: The relationship between the brightness of an object and its immediate background.

Brightness Difference: The difference in brightness among the various reflecting surfaces and light sources within the total visual field as measured in footlamberts.

Brightness Ratio: The ratio of two brightnesses in the field of view.

British Thermal Unit: The quantity of heat (252 calories) required to raise the temperature of one pound of water one degree Fahrenheit at or near its point of maximum density (62° to 63°).

Bulkhead: An upright partition separating two parts in protection against fire or leakage, as a wall or embankment holding back earth, fire, or water.

Candlepower: The luminous intensity or illuminating capacity of a standard candle, as of a lamp measured in candles.

Casing: The act or process of encasing a frame, as of a window or a door.

Caulking: To fill in the seams or cracks with a filler.

Chair Rail: An encircling band on the walls around the room at chair height to protect walls from damage by chairs contacting them.

Chamfer: The surface formed by cutting away the angle formed by two faces of timber, stone, or metal; to furrow; to channel; to flute; to bevel.

Chlorinate: To combine chlorine with water for purification.

Circuit Breaker: A device that automatically interrupts the flow of an electric current.

Climate Control: A term used to include the control of heating, ventilating, and air conditioning.

Color: A property of light which depends upon its wave length or frequency; any one of the hues of the spectrum.

Color Discrimination: Color discrimination is the perception of differences between two or more colors.

Community: The community is a small city or a section of a larger city, primarily a residential area usually composing three to five neighborhoods, representing the service area of a secondary school and containing a business center. The people are held together by psychological, sociological, and economic bonds and may act together consciously or unconsciously in their chief concerns of life. The community creates, as a result of its common interests, certain institutions of legal, protective, educational, economic, recreation, and religious character. A community includes factors of interdependence and belonging and a sense of usefulness through contributing to the common good.

Community-Recreation-Center Building: A structure devoted exclusively or primarily to a diversified program of community recreation activities. Such features as a gymnasium, club rooms, social hall, craft rooms, game rooms, kitchen, auditorium, lobby, and service facilities are usually provided. The term "neighborhood center" is often used to describe a recreation-center building which serves a specific neighborhood.

Competition: Conscious or unconscious activity involving rivalry, in which one person or group tries to gain advantage over the other person or group; involvement of two or more opponents in a contest. This term can also mean rivalry with a previous record of an individual or group. Competition can occur without conflict, as in a friendly game of cards.

Complementary Colors: A pair of contrasting colors which, when mixed in proper proportion, give a neutral color or grey.

Comprehensive Survey: A study which provides an extensive, thorough investigation and analysis of the leisure and recreation pattern of a given locality. It includes an investigation of social, political, economic, and cultural causal relationships which have affected, are affecting, or seemingly will affect the future leisure and recreation services in a specific locality.

Concession: Authority, granted under contract with mutually-acceptable provisions by all parties concerned, given by recreation departments to operators permitting them to provide services and/or to sell commodities to patrons of recreation areas and facilities.

Condemnation: To pass an adverse judgment on; disapprove of strongly; censure; to prove guilty of wrong-doing; to declare unfit for service or use; to condemn private property for public use; the processes by which government exercises its rights of eminent domain.

APPENDIX K

Condenser: That which makes dense, concentrates, or compresses.

Convector: A medium of convection; the transmission of heat or electricity by the mass movement of the heated or electrified particles, such as air, gas, or liquid currents.

Co-recreation: Activities engaged in jointly by both sexes, such as dances, mixed choruses, and hiking.

Corrective Therapy: In physical medicine, a medically-supervised program of physical exercise and activities for the purpose of improving or maintaining the health of the patient through individual and group participation; specifically, techniques which have been designed to conserve and increase neuromuscular strength and skill, to re-establish and improve ambulation, to improve habits of personal health, and to promote relaxation by adjustment to physical and mental stresses.

Cove: A large hollow forming part of an arch in sections joining the walls and floor, or the walls and ceiling of a room.

Creative Recreation: Activities which provide opportunity for production, formation, origination, making new things, or remodeling old things; an outlet for man's creative urge. Arts and crafts, dance, drama, and music are examples of creative recreation.

Crowned Field: A curved field with the summit or highest point (crown) at the middle, running lengthwise. (A football field is crowned for the purpose of drainage.)

Dado: A term applied to the lower portion of walls when decorated separately.

Day Camping: A group experience in the natural environment under trained leadership requiring that the campers be absent from home only during daylight hours.

Decibel: The unit for measuring the relative loudness of sounds (as compared with the loudness of a sound that can just be heard by the ear).

Deck: A platform or floor, like a ship's deck or a swimming-pool deck.

Design: The architectural form, pattern, or scheme of construction of health, physical education, or recreation areas, facilities, and their units.

Diatomaceous: Containing or consisting of diatoms or their fossils (a number of related microscopic algae, one-celled or in colonies, whose walls consist of two parts or valves and contain silica).

Disabilities of Incoordination: Faulty coordination or palsy from brain, spinal, or peripheral nerve injury.

Discomfort Glare: Glare which produces discomfort; it does not necessarily interfere with visual performance or visibility.

District: The district is a large geographical planning unit of a large city, comprising a number of communities.

Drama Recreation: Activities which give form and order to theatrical impulses; such activities include the imaginative play of children, charades, pageants, and plays.

Driver and Traffic-Safety Education: Learning experiences provided by the school for the purpose of assisting students to become good traffic citizens and to operate motor vehicles efficiently and safely.

Driving Simulator: A teaching technique utilizing both films and electromechanical devices designed to simulate the driver's compartment of the automobile, to help students develop proper judgment, behavioral responses, and manipulative skills.

Dual-control Car: A car equipped with an extra foot brake (for instructor) for automatic transmissions, and an extra clutch and brake pedal for conventional transmissions.

Easement: A right or privilege that a person may have on another's land, as the right-of-way.

Eaves: The lower part of a roof projecting beyond the face of the wall.

Economy: Costs are kept at a minimum compatible with program needs, durability of materials, low maintenance, and attractiveness.

Elevation: A geometrical projection on a plane perpendicular to the horizon; an elevated place; the distance above or below the zero level or ground level.

Eminent Domain: The legal right of federal, state, and local governments to take any property required for public purpose. The right implies that the land must be taken by due process of law and that the owner from whom the land is taken receives reasonable compensation.

Environment: The aggregate of all the external conditions, surroundings, and influences affecting the place or individual.

Equipment: Movable furnishings as opposed to stationary property; relatively-permanent articles, furnishings, machinery, and devices used in administering, operating, and maintaining recreation programs and services.

Escutcheon: A shield or plate, as around a keyhole.

Experience: An actual and conscious living through an event, or events, as they occur; anything observed or lived through.

Extrude: To thrust out; to push out or force out; expel; to stick out; protrude; project.

Facade: The face or elevation of a building.

Facilities: Areas, structures, and fixtures essential to accommodate the program.

Familiarization: Involves programs acquainting the user, as with the water when teaching swimming.

Fascia: A wooden or stone band between moldings.

Fenestration: Windows and all other sources and means of control of natural light.

Field House: A facility providing enclosed and unobstructed space adaptable to various physical education and recreation activities, services, demonstrations, and meetings. It is often located on, or near, a playfield or athletic field. The term also refers to a service building used by people using the athletic field.

Fixed Turning Radius, Wheel to Wheel: The tracking of the caster wheels and large wheels of a wheelchair when pivoting on a spot.

Fixture: Something firmly attached, as a part or an appendage, such as a light fixture; equipment affixed to the surface of a building in such a manner that its removal would deface or mar the surface. (Legally, it is the property of the building.)

Flashing: Sheets of metal or other material used to waterproof joints and cages, especially of a roof.

Flexibility: Increase or decrease in kind and amount of use at reasonable cost and effort; a quality of elasticity of the muscles and the connecting tissues in the body.

Flush: Unbroken or even in surface; on a level with the adjacent surfaces; having no indentation.

Fluting: The vertical channeling on the shaft of a column.

Footcandle: The illumination at a point on a surface which is one foot from and perpendicular to a uniform point source of one candela (candle); a lighting term used to denote quantity.

Footlambert: A unit of brightness of a surface or of a light source. One footlambert equals one lumen per square foot. Candelas (candles) per square inch is an optional term for a unit of brightness of a light source. One candela (candle) per square inch equals 452 footlamberts.

Foot-pound: A unit of energy equal to the amount of energy required to raise a weight of one pound a distance of one foot.

Fulcrum: The support or point of support on which a lever rotates.

Fullers Earth: A clay-like, earthy substance used as a filter medium.

Furring: The leveling of a floor, wall, or ceiling, or the creating of air spaces with thin strips of wood or metal before adding boards or plaster; the act of trimming or lining.

Gable: The triangular portion of a wall, between the enclosing lines of a sloping roof.

Gallery: A communicating passage or wide corridor for pictures and statues; upper story for seats.

Glare: The sensation produced by brightnesses within the visual field that are sufficiently greater than the brightness to which the eyes are adapted to cause annoyance, discomfort, or loss in visual performance and visibility.

Glaze: Any impervious material—produced by fire—used to cover the body of a tile to prevent absorption of liquids and gases, to resist abrasion and impact, or to give a more pleasing appearance.

Glazed Tile: A hard, dense tile that has been glazed to prevent absorption, to increase its beauty, or to improve ease of cleaning.

Gradient: The grade or rate of ascent or descent; a rate of increase or decrease of a variable magnitude, or the curve that represents it.

Grid: A framework of parallel bars; a grating.

Gutter: A trough or channel along or under the eaves of a roof to carry off rainwater; also around the upper edge of a swimming pool.

Gymnasium: A building or part of a building devoted primarily to group activities such as basketball, gymnastics, volleyball, and dancing. It is equipped with gymnastic apparatus, a court area for playing athletic and game activities, dressing-room facilities, and seating arrangements for spectators.

Gymtorium: A combination facility designed to be used as a gymnasium or auditorium. Other combination facilities are cafetoriums (cafeteria and auditorium) and gymnateria (gymnasium and cafeteria).

Halfway House: A temporary home or club-like building for people who have been released from the hospital, but who are not ready to be totally returned to society. The house provides contact with other persons facing similar problems of readjustment to the community.

Handicapped: A person who has less than normal aptitude and/or ability for performing the ordinary tasks of life, or of a particular vocation or avocation. The usual reference is to a person physically handicapped, i.e., who has a specific anatomical or physiological deficiency (poor vision, hearing), but it may also apply to the mentally deficient, maladjusted, or retarded person.

Header: A wooden beam placed between two long beams with the ends of the short beams resting against it.

APPENDIX K

Health: A state of optimal physical, mental, and social well-being, and not merely the absence of disease or infirmity.

Health Coordinator: Staff member who devotes time and efforts to fostering and facilitating a cooperative working relationship among various staff members concerned with health education.

Health Education: The sum of experience which favorably influences knowledge, attitudes, and practices related to individual, community, and world health; bridging the gap between scientific knowledge and its application by people in their daily lives.

Healthful School Living: The utilization of a safe and wholesome environment; consideration of individual health, organizing the school day, and planning classroom procedures to favorably influence emotional, social, and physical health.

Health Instruction: The organized teaching procedures directed toward developing understandings, attitudes, and practices relating to health and factors affecting health.

Health-Instruction Laboratory: A combination conventional classroom and science laboratory with special provisions for demonstrations, displays, and exhibits related to health education.

Health Services: Those services which are designed for health appraisal, health protection, follow-up, and the promotion of optimal health for students and school personnel.

Health Suite: Room or combination of rooms providing facilities for emergency care, health appraisal, screening tests, isolation, and staff, and with additional toilets and waiting rooms.

Hearing Disabilities: Deafness or hearing handicaps that might make an individual insecure in public areas because he is unable to communicate or hear warning signals.

Hobby: An engrossing activity to which one frequently reverts and to which he gives his free time, such as stamp collecting, knitting, and gardening.

Hose Bibb: A faucet with the nozzle bent downward and threaded for hose connections.

Humidity: Moisture content of the air expressed in percent of maximum.

Ill and Handicapped: A collective term that includes all those classifications, by authorities, of persons suffering from disease or disability.

Impulsive: Acting briefly and as a result of impulse.

Indoor Center: A building, such as a school, church, or community center, which has the facilities needed to carry on recreation activities.

Instruction: The process of conveying facts or information, ideas, and concepts.

Integral: The result of integrating parts into a whole; necessary for completeness; essential; whole or complete.

Integration: Functional interrelationship; the process of making whole.

Interpretative: Explanatory; a conception of art, writing, program, structure, or concept; used to interpret.

Involved (Involvement): A portion or portions of the human anatomy or physiology, or both, that have a loss or impairment of normal function as a result of genesis, trauma, disease, inflammation, or degeneration.

Isolation: Placed and constructed to eliminate incompatible interferences.

Isolation Room: Area within the health suite providing for separation of one ill student from another to provide quiet and/or to protect others.

Jam: A side post of a doorway, window frame, fireplace, etc.

Joint: A place or part where two things or parts are joined together.

Lanai: Hawaiian veranda.

Leadership: The ability of one person, or a group of people, to influence others to recognize goals of common interest and to stimulate them to act cooperatively to achieve these goals.

Leisure: To be permitted; a bulk of time; a state of freedom; a minimum of obligation; a physiological and emotional necessity; identified by "when" rather than "how."

Liability: The responsibility of one who is bound in law and justice to do something which may be forced by action; a condition which gives rise to an obligation to do a particular thing to be enforced by court action; a responsibility between parties which the courts recognize and enforce; an unintentional breach of legal duty causing reasonably foreseeable damage.

License: A formal permission to do something; a document indicating certain permission; freedom to deviate from strict conduct, rule, or practice; generally may be permitted by common consent.

Light: Visible radiation—generally considered to be the electromagnetic radiations of wave lengths between 380 and 780 millimicrons, which are the violet and red ends of the visible spectrum, respectively.

Lintel: The horizontal timber or stone that spans an opening, as over doors or windows.

Louver: An aperture or frame with louver boards fitted in a slatted panel for ventilation.

Lumen: A unit of output of light source or of a luminaire.

Luminaire: Lighting unit, including lamps.

Maintenance: The keeping of recreation areas, facilities, equipment, and supplies in accordance with established standards and existing needs for effective operation.

Marina: A water dock or basin providing secure moorings for watercraft.

Master Plan for Recreation: A long-term guide for the systematic and orderly selection and development of recreation facilities and services over a given period of time. It might be composed of such elements as goals, organization structure, activity program, areas, facilities, personnel, and financial support.

Milieu: The total environment and surroundings within which an activity takes place. Milieu is frequently used as a synonym for environment.

Mobile Laboratory Unit: A driver-education classroom-laboratory on wheels to accommodate several locations.

Modality: A method of application, or the employment of any therapeutic agent: limited usually to physical agents.

Module: A standard or unit of measurement; the length of some part used to determine the proportions of a building.

Monitor: An instrument used for monitoring; a warning; a reminder; a test for intensity of quality.

Monolithic: Massively solid: single and uniform.

Motivation: The process of initiating conscious and purposeful action. It becomes objectified as an interest and usually leads to action in pursuit of that interest. A psychological interpretation is the application of incentives to an individual or group for whom activity is desired. This term is not to be confused with the psychological term "unconscious motivation."

Mullion: A slender, vertical dividing bar between the lights of windows, screens, etc.

Multiple-Car Driving Range: An area in an off-street location where a number of cars are used simultaneously for laboratory instruction under the supervision of one or more instructors.

Multiple-Use Areas and Facilities: Physical features designed and constructed to meet the space and facility requirements of several types of recreation activities. A gymnasium is an example of a multi-use facility—designed to serve more than one purpose.

Natatorium: An indoor aquatic facility.

Nearsightedness: A defect of vision caused by too long an eyeball or too convex a lens.

Negligence: Failing to act with reasonable care or prudent judgement under the circumstances involved.

Neighborhood: A segment of a community composed of a residential area in which the people may have common ethnic, social, and economic characteristics. They are generally served by the same elementary school and recreation center. The neighborhood may be bounded by barriers, such as thoroughfares, railroads, and waterways, and by commercial and industrial developments.

Neighborhood Park: A landscaped area with a more or less formal design intended to provide an attractive neighborhood setting and a place for recreation activities.

Neighborhood Playground: An outdoor play center designed to meet the recreation needs of a neighborhood, especially the children from 6 to 14 years old. Playgrounds are ideally located in the center of a neighborhood. An apparatus area, a playlot, a wading pool, and a shelter house are usually provided.

Nonambulatory Disabilities: Impairments that, regardless of cause or manifestation, for all practical purposes confine individuals to wheelchairs or beds.

Nonslip: Having the tread so constructed as to reduce skidding or slipping.

Nonslip Tile: Incorporates certain admixtures such as abrasive granules in the body or in the surface of the tile.

Nosing: The projecting edge of a step; that part of the tread which extends beyond the riser; a stair nosing.

Nuisance: An on-going and continuing condition which is injurious to health, is indecent or offensive to the senses, or is an obstruction to the free use of property so as essentially to interfere with the comfortable enjoyment of life and property.

Objectives: Short-range and realizable goals; goals which are more attainable than remote aims, but less attainable than immediate outcomes; attainable goals which guide one's thoughts and actions.

Observation Gallery: A platform or projecting upper floor attached to the back wall or sides of a room designed to permit seeing, watching, and observing.

APPENDIX K

Opaque: Does not transmit light; substances which will not allow light through.

Open Space: A relatively underdeveloped area provided within or near urban development to minimize feelings of congested living.

Organic: Of or pertaining to an organ or a system of organs.

Organism: An individual constituted to carry on the activities of life by means of organs separate in function but mutually dependent; any highly complex thing or structure with parts so integrated that their relation to one another is governed by their relation to the whole.

Orientation: The directional placement of a facility—establishing position.

Outdoor Center: An area designed to provide the space and facilities needed to carry on outdoor-recreation activities.

Outdoor Education: A process—taking place under leadership in natural surroundings—which is in or about the outdoors.

Outdoor Recreation: This term may refer to any type of recreation activity accomplished in the out-of-doors, such as outdoor band concerts, picnics, outdoor pageants, and outdoor dances. It usually refers to activities performed in the natural environment—canyons, mountains; nature and outing activities.

Outdoor Theater: A recreation facility designed to meet the needs for a suitable place to hold outdoor plays, pageants, concerts, and meetings. Outdoor theaters vary in size from those located on a playground to the large community type and are constructed in a natural setting, conforming to the characteristics of the area. Grassy slopes, sodded terraces, cement steps of terraces, or permanent or portable benches serve as seats for the spectators.

Outrigger: Any temporary support extending out from the main structure.

Park: An area permanently dedicated to recreation use and generally characterized by its natural, historic, and landscape features. It is used for both passive and active forms of recreation and may be designed to serve the residents of a neighborhood, community, state, region, or nation.

Park District: A subdivision of state government exercising within its jurisdiction the authority of a municipality. It may operate and maintain parks, recreation programs, police forces, airports, and other such facilities and programs as may be designated in the act establishing the district.

Park-School: The park-school is an area cooperatively planned by school and municipal authorities to provide programs of education and recreation for day-by-day use by the people of a neighborhood or community.

Parkway: Essentially an elongated park with a road running through it, the use of which is restricted to pleasure traffic. The parkway often serves to connect large units in a park system and is rarely found except in large cities.

Participant: This term is generally used in reference to a person not employed by the recreation agency who is taking part in a recreation activity or event promoted by the agency.

Peripheral Field: That portion of the visual field which falls outside the central visual field.

Peripheral Vision: Peripheral vision is vision outside the central visual field.

Permeable: That which can be permeated; open to passage or penetration, especially by fluids.

Persistence of Vision: Vision persisting after the exciting visual stimulus has been removed.

Physical Education: Physical education is the science of and skill of movement, using all types of sports and physical activities for the following specific purposes: to develop and maintain physical efficiency; to develop useful knowledge and physical skills; to teach students to act in socially useful ways; and to develop skills which may be used for physical recreation.

Pilaster: A rectangular feature in the shape of a pillar, but projecting only one-sixth of its breadth from a wall.

Planning: The development of an organized procedure, including the selection of goals and objectives and the tools of action necessary to carry out these goals. Planning involves taking into consideration the social and physical environment of an area as well as the role that recreation plays in area development.

Platform: A surface which is generally horizontal, flat, and raised, or a philosophical basis for a program of action.

Play: The willful and spontaneous natural expression of people which pervades many of the recreation activities of children and adults.

Playfield: A recreation area designed to serve the needs of a community or neighborhood having a population of 10,000 to 15,000 persons. Its essential features are a community recreation building, areas for sports and games, a playground for children, picnic areas, public parking, and, occasionally, a swimming area.

Playground: The playground is the basic recreation area in a residential neighborhood, providing a variety of recreation activities for people of all ages, primarily children of 6 to 14.

Playlot: A small area intended primarily for the play of preschool-age children and generally located in the corner of a neighborhood playground or near the center of one or more units of a multiple-family housing development. It is usually equipped with a sand box, slides, swings, and other playground apparatus. Totlots and playlots are synonymous.

Plaza: A small landscaped area rarely more than a block in size and often consisting of a triangle or circle at a street intersection.

Post Sleeves: Metal pipe, installed at ground level or slightly below, which receives posts to facilitate various activities.

Principle: A guiding rule for the planning, construction, use, or maintenance of a facility in accordance with its intended purpose; a rule of action or conduct; a fundamental rule; an intellectual concept; a guide to the requirements and obligations of right conduct.

Professional: Any practicing, trained, qualified person who makes his living administering, directing, leading, organizing, or planning activities; one who professes or declares openly his sentiments, beliefs, or skills, and offers instructional services therein. The work calls for special preparation, rigorous training, the application of scientific principles, and abiding by a code of ethics.

Proprietary Functions: Those services performed by a municipality, school, county, or other governmental unit for the specific benefit of the inhabitants of that unit in contrast to a benefit of the general public, or which may be conducted in competition with private enterprise.

Prudent: Carefulness, precaution, attentiveness, and good judgment as applied to action or conduct; capable of exercising sound judgment in practical matters; cautious; discreet in conduct; circumspect; sensible; not rash.

Psychophysical Equipment: Laboratory testing devices used to indicate a variety of abilities related to visual acuity, field of vision, distance judgment and depth perception, color vision, night vision, glare vision, glare recovery, reaction time, and steadiness of hand.

Public Relations: The creation of good will through information and education at every point of contact between the agency and its publics; some of the media used to promote good public relations are printed circulars and reports, program demonstrations, employee contacts, newspapers, radio, window displays, and public addresses; harmonious working relationships to inform, to correct misunderstandings, to change opinion, to gain support, to remove apathy, to modify attitude, to establish confidence, to develop awareness of importance of program, and to develop the partnership concept.

Rabbet: A groove or cut made in the edge of a board, etc., in such a way that another piece may be fitted in to form a point.

Ramps, Ramps with Gradients: Because the term "ramp" has a multitude of meanings and uses, its use in this text is clearly defined as ramps with gradients (or ramps with slopes) that deviate from what would otherwise be considered the normal level. An exterior ramp, as distinguished from a "walk," would be considered an appendage to a building leading to a level above or below existing ground level. As such, a ramp shall meet certain requirements similar to those imposed upon stairs.

Ray: A single line of light coming from a luminous point.

Recreation: To create anew, or to refresh from toil; what we do because we want to do it; re-creating the mind and body; wholesome and pleasurable behavior; action motivated by inner desire (no outer compulsion); spontaneity; not ordered, imposed, or forced; the individual has something to choose from and he is capable of making a choice; the motive is enjoyment and personal satisfaction, and the doing of it has its own appeal; the "when" is leisure, the "what" is recreation.

Recreation Areas: Land and water space set aside for recreation usage such as parks, playgrounds, lakes, and reservoirs.

Recreation, Commercial: Recreation services and activities, such as dance halls, bowling alleys, theaters, amusement parks, and carnivals organized primarily for profit and provided by business enterprises.

Recreation Facilities: Buildings and other physical features and provisions, such as swimming pools, community-recreation centers, stadiums, and outdoor theaters, designed and constructed for recreation use.

Recreation, Municipal (Public): A program of public recreation provided by the corporate body for persons residing in any one of the several types of governmental units having the power of local self-government. It is financed primarily by taxation and includes the establishment, operation, conduct, control, and maintenance of programs, services, areas, and facilities.

APPENDIX K

Recreation Museum: An area or facility for preserving and exhibiting recreation objects and artifacts.

Recreation, Private: A recreation program and/or services established under the auspices of an agency or organization which is supported by other than governmental funds. Private agencies usually serve a particular constituency and often limit their services to a given area of a city and to those invited by the agency. Recreation is often a technique rather than the primary purpose in private agencies.

Recreation, State: A recreation program or service offered by a state agency, such as the State Recreation Commission, Conservation Department, or Welfare Department, on a statewide basis. The services may include the operating of a public area and facility such as a state park, the carrying forth of statewide research, the planning and promotion of new recreation programs, and/or advising local groups on various problems relating to recreation.

Recreational Therapy: The medical application of an activity, voluntarily engaged in by the patient during the period of treatment or convalescence, that is enjoyable and personally satisfying to him, even though the patient's participation in it is structured to achieve a predicted result beyond the personal satisfaction.

Redevelopment: An additional developing process.

Reflectance (Reflection Factor): The percent of light falling on a surface which is reflected by that surface.

Reflected Glare: Glare resulting from specular reflections of high brightness in polished or glossy surfaces in the field of view. It usually is associated with reflections from within a visual task or areas in close proximity to the region being viewed.

Reflection Factor: The percentage of light reflected by a given surface.

Refrigerants: Any of the various liquids that vaporize at a low temperature, used in mechanical refrigeration.

Rehabilitation: The process of restoring a patient, through treatment and training, to satisfactory physical, mental, moral, vocational, or social status after injury or physical, mental, or social maladjustment.

Resident Camping: A sustained group-living experience in the natural environment under trained leadership in which the surroundings contribute through program to the emotional, physical, and social growth of the individual.

Resiliency: Ability to bounce back or spring back into shape or position after being pressed or stretched; elastic.

Resistance: Any opposing friction causing force; the reciprocal of conductance.

Riser: The vertical distance (and pieces) between the steps in a stairway.

Safety Education: Bridging the gap between scientific knowledge of safety and its application by people in daily living.

School Camping: An organized camping program conducted by a school as an integral part of the regular school program and emphasizing outdoor education.

Screening: Technique of observation and testing used to detect obvious deviations from the normal, or failure to meet minimum standards.

Scuba Diving: Diving with self-contained underwater breathing apparatus (air tank).

Seeing: Visual perception; the act of discerning or obtaining information by means of the eyes and brain, and requiring light upon the object to be discerned.

Semiambulatory Disabilities: Impairments that cause individuals to walk with difficulty or insecurity. Individuals using braces or crutches, amputees, arthritics, spastics, and those with pulmonary and cardiac ills may be semiambulatory.

Service Building: A structure affording the facilities necessary to accommodate the people using recreation facilities such as a golf course, swimming pool, or ice-skating rink. It may contain dressing rooms, lockers, toilets, shower rooms, check and storage rooms, a lobby or lounge, and a repair shop. Also, the term is used in reference to buildings which facilitate the operation and maintenance of the recreation system, such as greenhouses, storage buildings, and garages.

Shadow: The space from which light from a given source is excluded by an opaque object; the area of comparative darkness resulting from the interception of light by an opaque object.

Sheathing: The inner covering of boards or waterproof material on the roof or outside wall of a frame house.

Shelter House: A building, usually located on a playground or playfield, equipped with such features as an office for the director, space for storage, toilets, and a craft or play room.

Short-Term Residence Camp: A creative, cooperative experience in living in the out-of-doors in self-sufficient small groups for periods of five days or less.

Sight: The ability to see, which encompasses the object seen, the light reflected from it, the eyes which perceive it, and the sensory system which transmits this information to the brain.

Sight Disabilities: Total blindness or impairments affecting sight to the extent that the individual functioning in public areas is insecure or exposed to danger.

Sill: A heavy horizontal timber or line of masonry supporting a wall; a horizontal piece forming the bottom frame of a door or window.

Sleeper: A piece of timber, stone, or steel, on or near the ground to support some superstructure.

Social Recreation: Activities or experiences primarily engaged in to produce sociability, such as parties, banquets, club meetings, picnics, and dances. Social recreation uses as a medium the activities of sports, games, drama, music, dance, nature recreation, and arts and crafts. The motivating purpose is to bring people together.

Soffit: The ceiling or underside of any architectural member.

Special Recreation Areas and Facilities: Areas and facilities designed, constructed, and equipped to meet the requirements of a specific form of recreation activity, such as a golf course, swimming pool, and athletic field.

Specifications: Detailed description of the parts of a whole; statement of enumeration of particulars, as to size, quality, and performance; terms; something specified.

Sports Recreation: Activities which usually require a great deal of physical movement and the use of specific equipment and areas. Examples are golf, tennis, hunting, fishing, skiing, and corecreational softball. Athletics and sports are not synonymous; athletics is one of the many kinds of sporting activities frequently referred to as physical recreation.

Staggered: To arrange so that alternate intervals are used, as to space or time.

Stanchion: An upright bar, beam, or post used as a support; one of a pair of linked, upright bars.

Standards: Norms established by authority, research, custom, or general consent to be used as criteria and guides in establishing and evaluating programs, leadership, areas, facilities, and plans; as measures of quantity, quality, weight, extent, or value.

Stile: A vertical piece in a panel or frame, as a door or window; a set of steps used in climbing over a fence or wall.

Supervise: Oversee or manage a program, activity, or people, and arrange for economy of control and management.

Survey: A cooperative undertaking which applies scientific methods to the study and treatment of current recreation data, problems, and conditions. The limits of a survey are prescribed before execution, and its facts, findings, conclusions, and recommendations are made common knowledge and provide a base for intelligent, coordinated action.

Synthetic: Artificial; not real or genuine; a substance produced by chemical synthesis.

Tanbark: Any bark containing tannin (used to tan hides) and, after the tannin has been extracted, it is used to cover tracks, circus rings, and dirt floors in field houses.

Template: A short piece placed in a wall under a beam to distribute the pressure; also a beam spanning a doorway, or the like, and supporting joists.

Terra Cotta: Clayware having the surface coated with fine slip or glaze; used in the facing of large buildings for relief ornament or statues.

Terrazzo: A type of flooring made of small chips of marble set irregularly in cement and polished.

Thermostat: An apparatus for regulating temperature, especially one that automatically controls a heating unit.

Threshold: A piece of wood, stone, metal, etc., placed beneath a door; doorsill; the entrance or beginning point of something; the point at which a stimulus is just strong enough to be perceived or produce a response, as the threshold of pain.

Topography: The configuration of a surface, including its relief; graphic delineation of physical features of any place or region.

Tort: A legal wrong resulting from direct or indirect injury to an individual or to property. May result from "omission" or "commission."

Translucent: Transmitting light but scattering it so that details cannot be distinguished through the translucent medium.

Transparent: Allowing light to pass through so that objects behind can be seen distinctly.

Truss: To support or strengthen with a constructural truss; a bracket or modillion.

Underpinning: A supporting structure of the foundation, especially one placed beneath a wall.

Unglazed Tile: A hard, dense tile of homogenous composition deriving color and texture from the materials of which it is made.

Utility: The degree to which an area, facility, or instrument is designed to serve its purpose, and degree to which it is used; percent of usage during the workday adapted or available for general use or utility.

APPENDIX K

Validity: The degree to which an item or instrument actually does what it is intended to do.

Vestibule: A passage hall or chamber between the outer door and the interior of a building.

Vinyl Tile: Asphalt tile impregnated with vinyl.

Visual Task: Conventionally, designates those details and objects which must be seen for the performance of a given activity, and includes the immediate background of the details or objects.

Vitreous: Of, pertaining to, or derived from glass; like glass, as in color, brittleness, and luster.

Wainscot: A wood lining or paneling on the lower part of the walls of a room.

Walkway: Because the terms "walk" and "walks" have a multitude of meanings and uses, their use in this text is clearly defined as a pre-determined, prepared surface; exterior pathway leading to or from a building or facility, or from one exterior area to another, placed on the existing ground level and not deviating from the level of the existing ground immediately adjacent.

Weephole: To permit or let drops of water or other liquid exude from inner containers, from such sources as condensation or overflow.

Wilderness: A rather large, generally inaccessible area left in its natural state available for recreation experiences. It is void of development except for those trails, sites, and similar conditions made by previous wilderness users. (No mechanical transportation permitted).

Youth Center: A recreation building designed primarily to be used by adolescents. The center may be operated by a public or private agency or by a teen-age organization under adult guidance.

Zone Heating: To mark off or divide building areas for the purposes of area climate control.

INDEX

269

INDEX

INDEX

INDEX